The American Congress

Ninth Edition

Steven S. Smith
Washington University in St. Louis

Jason M. Roberts
University of North Carolina

Ryan J. Vander Wielen
Temple University

CAMBRIDGE
UNIVERSITY PRESS

CAMBRIDGE
UNIVERSITY PRESS

32 Avenue of the Americas, New York, NY 10013-2473, USA

Cambridge University Press is part of the University of Cambridge.

It furthers the University's mission by disseminating knowledge in the pursuit of education, learning, and research at the highest international levels of excellence.

www.cambridge.org
Information on this title: www.cambridge.org/9781107571785

© Steven S. Smith, Jason M. Roberts, and Ryan J. Vander Wielen
2005, 2007, 2009, 2011, 2013, 2015

Fourth edition published 2005
Fifth edition published 2007
Sixth edition published 2009
Seventh edition published 2011
Eighth edition published 2013
Ninth edition published 2015

Printed in the United States of America

A catalog record for this publication is available from the British Library.

ISBN 978-1-107-57178-5 Paperback

Cambridge University Press has no responsibility for the persistence or accuracy of URLs for external or third-party Internet Web sites referred to in this publication and does not guarantee that any content on such Web sites is, or will remain, accurate or appropriate.

CONTENTS

PREFACE

The American Congress has long been one of the most powerful legislative bodies in the world. Congress is now struggling with momentous issues such as health care, immigration, worldwide environmental problems, the stabilization of the world financial system, the rehabilitation of America's infrastructure, funding the U.S. system of retirement security, the war against terrorism, the place of the United States in the post–Cold War world, and the federal budget. These issues present serious challenges. They affect the interests of all Americans, they are highly controversial, and they involve complex public policies.

MAJOR FEATURES OF *THE AMERICAN CONGRESS*

UNDERSTANDING THE PLACE OF CONGRESS IN AMERICAN DEMOCRACY. Our primary goal in writing this edition is to instill in students and general readers an appreciation for the importance of a strong legislature in the American democracy. Such an appreciation requires an understanding of the constitutional setting in which Congress operates, the basic rules of the electoral and legislative processes, and the resources and strategies of members of Congress and other key players. Each chapter is designed to contribute to the reader's understanding by introducing key concepts, describing essential details of the process, and outlining general principles for understanding the subject.

THE CHANGING CONGRESS. In our efforts to introduce you to congressional politics, we emphasize the evolving nature of Congress. In writing a textbook, it is easy to describe current arrangements and create the impression that the rules and processes described have long been as described and are likely to stay that way for some time. We do not want to create that impression. Congress is organized by its members and is frequently changed by its members. Consequently, we emphasize the factors that influence legislators' thinking about their institution. Party conflict, competition with the executive branch, the drive for reelection, and other forces in congressional politics are discussed.

IMPORTANT IDEAS ABOUT CONGRESS. We also highlight important ideas in recent public commentary and political science research about Congress and its members. Although we do not organize our discussion around debates in the professional literature on Congress, we do not hesitate to observe differences of opinion among our colleagues in political science on critical subjects. Political scientists have offered competing and insightful perspectives on the sources of the incumbency advantage, the importance and motivations of legislative parties, the power of committees, and other subjects. We provide an accessible and balanced discussion of the deserving perspectives.

A STARTING POINT FOR YOUR RESEARCH ON CONGRESS. We provide a starting point for most undergraduate research projects on Congress by including suggested readings at the end of each chapter. We list both classic and recent works that will give you a quick pathway into the political science literature. Because we have provided a wide range of suggested readings, we have limited references to literature in the text.

We have not hidden our enthusiasm for congressional politics. To be sure, Congress is easy to dislike and often difficult to defend. The rough-and-tumble world of legislating is not orderly and civil, human frailties too often taint its membership, and legislative outcomes are often frustrating and ineffective. Still, we are not exaggerating when we say that Congress is essential to American democracy. We would not have survived as a nation without a Congress that represented the diverse interests of our society; conducted a public debate on the major issues; found compromises to resolve conflicts peacefully; and limited the power of our executive, military, and judicial institutions.

ORGANIZATION OF THE TEXT

Chapter 1 begins with an overview of the condition of the modern Congress. The chapter gives the reader a look at the general trends in American politics that are shaping the character of congressional policy making. It also reviews recent developments that have changed partisan control of Congress and altered the distribution of power within the institution.

Chapters 2 and 7 survey both constitutional and internal legislative rules to give an integrated perspective on the legislative game. The special character of American national legislative politics is the product of the Constitution, which created three institutions – the House of Representatives, the Senate, and the president – and set rules governing their interaction in the process of enacting public laws. In addition, the House and the Senate have developed different rules and practices that have a substantial effect on public policy.

Chapter 3 focuses on congressional elections. It covers the fundamental rules that govern these elections and details the advantages enjoyed by congressional incumbents in their efforts to stay in office. The chapter concludes by evaluating the importance of election outcomes for the policy choices made by Congress and the president.

Chapter 4 focuses on individual members. It begins by reviewing the variety of political goals that members pursue. It also considers the resources that members may mobilize to achieve their goals and the political actors who influence members' behavior. The chapter concludes by looking at the strategies that members pursue in voting and in policy leadership.

Chapters 5, 6, 7, and 8 concern the central components of the legislative process – parties, committees, and the chamber floors. Parties and committees are not mentioned in the Constitution, yet the interaction of parties and committees defines the decision-making process in the modern Congress. The emphasis is on both the development of congressional parties and committees and the recent changes that have altered the character of congressional decision making in important ways. While detailing the activity that takes place on the House and Senate floors, Chapter 8 concludes with an overall perspective on how parties, committees, and the floors relate to each other.

Chapters 9, 10, and 11 consider the major institutions and organizations with which Congress interacts – the president and executive branch, the courts, and interest groups. In each case, the emphasis is on the way in which the resources and strategies of the institution or organization affect its relations with Congress.

Budget politics and process are the concern of Chapter 12. Budget politics has become a nearly dominant feature of congressional politics, and many important procedural developments have occurred in recent years. This chapter emphasizes the importance of the evolving budget process for the distribution of power in Congress.

A SPECIAL APPENDIX

We have added an appendix on spatial theories of legislative politics. Spatial theory now plays a central role in the political science of legislative politics. Students at all levels benefit from understanding the basic ideas in spatial theory. We suggest that you read the relevant sections of the appendix along with the core chapters. We think it will enrich your understanding of the political strategies pursued by legislators and presidents and give you some basis for understanding the determinants of legislative outcomes.

ACKNOWLEDGMENTS

We are very pleased to be publishing this edition of *The American Congress* with Cambridge University Press. We are grateful for the skill, creativity, and enthusiasm of Robert Dreesen in managing this project. Brianda Reyes at Cambridge has also provided superb support for the project. Over the years, members of Congress and their staffs have been remarkably generous with their time. Thank you. We thank our many colleagues who write and teach about Congress. No authoritative textbook would be possible without their contributions and encouragement.

Steven S. Smith, Jason M. Roberts, and Ryan J. Vander Wielen

1 The Troubled Congress

President Barack Obama delivers his State of the Union address in the House chamber in the U.S. Capitol on Tuesday, January 20, 2015.

For most Americans today, Congress is our most frustrating political institution. National surveys put approval of Congress's performance well below approval for the president and the Supreme Court. In fact, during most of the 2010–2015 period, well below 25 percent of Americans approved of Congress's performance, and their approval dipped to 9 percent in late 2013. Stalemate on important issues, frequent delays in getting must-pass bills enacted, messy wheeling and dealing, and partisanship that many people viewed as excessive underlay the sour ratings.

STUDYING CONGRESS

Congress is not easy to understand. Its sheer size – 535 members and more than 25,000 employees – is bewildering. Its system of parties, committees, and procedures, built up over the course of two hundred years, can appear remarkably complex and serves as an obstacle to public understanding. Perhaps most frustrating is that Congress also is important and exciting. No other national legislature has greater power than does the Congress of the United States. Its daily actions affect the lives of all Americans and of many people around the world. It checks the exercise of power by the president, the courts, and the bureaucracy. If you want to understand the forces influencing your welfare, you must understand Congress.

Let us begin with three tips about Congress. First, you must realize that the legislators themselves determine most features of the policy-making process in Congress. The Constitution provides some essential details, but only a few. It establishes a House and a Senate, provides for presiding officers in both houses, provides that both houses must approve legislation, implies that legislation is approved by majority vote, and gives the president a veto that can be overridden by a two-thirds vote of both houses. But the Constitution does not provide rules that specify how legislation is to be prepared for votes and does not mention the organizational arrangement of committees, parties, leaders, and staff that we now take for granted. These parliamentary rules and organizational features are determined by the members of Congress.

Second, you must keep in mind that Congress is always changing. It changes because it is a remarkably permeable institution. New problems, whatever their source, invariably create new demands on Congress. Elections bring in new members, who often alter the balance of opinion in the House and Senate. Elections also frequently result in a change in majority party control of Congress, which leads to a transfer of agenda control from one party to the other both on the floor and in committees. In addition, each new president asks Congress for support for his policy program. Members of Congress often respond to these requests by passing new legislation. But as lawmakers pursue their personal political goals, compete with one another for control over policy, and react to pressure from presidents, their constituents, and lobbyists, they sometimes seek to gain an advantage or to remove impediments to action by altering the procedures and organization of Congress itself. The result is frequent change in the committees, parties, procedures, and informal practices that form the legislative process.

Third, you must keep your own partisanship in check. That is not easy. For many people, being sophisticated about politics is knowing who is right and who is wrong about the issues of the day. As social scientists, however, we want to understand *why* politicians behave as they do, including how they organize the political institutions that they run. As a rule, we find that members of Congress organize its parties and committees, and elect its leaders, with their own interests and the interests of those they represent in mind. In trying to understand human behavior in this unique context, it pays for us to remain somewhat dispassionate.

Explaining the ongoing changes in Congress is the central focus of this book. We begin in this chapter by highlighting several developments in American politics that have transformed congressional politics. These developments – including changes in the roles of parties and their leaders, changes in the way that the media covers Congress, an evolution in standards for public ethics, a rise in plebiscitary politics, a war on terrorism, new information technologies, new forms of organized efforts to influence Congress, and new kinds of issues– have altered the context of congressional policy making in basic ways.

A PARTISAN, CENTRALIZED CONGRESS

Developments of the past three decades have produced a Congress that behaves differently from the Congress of the middle decades of the twentieth century. Congress is now a far more partisan place, with the parties sharply divided on most important issues, and it is an institution whose agenda, committee work, and policy choices are made far more frequently under the supervision and guidance of the top party leaders. These two features of today's Congress – the polarization of the political parties and the centralization of policy making – are closely related. The relationship between partisan polarization and centralization is our central theme.

Polarized Parties

In the mid-twentieth century, both houses of Congress seemed to have evolved fairly stable decision-making processes that featured strong committees, weak parties, and weak central leaders, which gave the appearance of a decentralized way of legislating. It was labeled "decentralized" because much deference was given to the work of the committees, which wrote and reviewed the details of most legislation. The chairmen (few women were elected to Congress in those days) dominated their committees so that each house appeared to be run by a couple of dozen powerful committee leaders. Top party leaders – the Speaker of the House and the Senate majority leader – scheduled legislation for floor consideration, but they did not play a significant role in setting committee agendas or designing the content of legislation. Instead, they supported and facilitated the efforts of the committee chairmen and became involved whenever their assistance might prove useful.

During this era, the two parties in the House and Senate comprised quite heterogeneous memberships. By virtue of the party affiliation that they acquired in getting elected to Congress, nearly all representatives and senators were automatically members of either the Democratic or the Republican party conference in their chamber. Wide differences in the kinds of districts and states that elected them produced substantial differences among the elected members of each party in their ideological or policy views. Perhaps most notably, the Democrats were divided between those legislators, largely from outside the South, who advocated for stronger civil rights policies to combat discriminatory election laws, segregation, and other racist policies, and those southerners who still viewed their party as the party of the Civil War Confederacy. Republican legislators, too, were divided between those who favored using the federal government to address economic and social problems – a group largely from the urban Northeast and Midwest – and those who opposed a stronger federal role.

Over the last quarter of the twentieth century, Democrats and Republicans became more polarized. The process of polarization had many elements, which include these developments since the 1960s:

- Southern states changed from being one-party Democratic to being largely dominated by Republicans. Starting in the 1970s, mainly conservative Democrats were replaced by conservative Republicans, making the Democrats in Congress more uniformly liberal and the Republicans in Congress more conservative.
- Conservative and moderate Republicans in northeastern states, who once dominated that region, were replaced by liberal Democrats.
- Political elites, most notably congressional Republicans, took stronger, more ideological positions and provided more polarized cues to the electorate.
- Political activists, first on the Republican side, recruited candidates with stronger ideological commitments for office and mobilized support for them in primary and general election campaigns.
- The emergence of political narrowcasting – the creation of cable television, talk radio, and the Internet – provided new outlets for programs targeted to narrower and sometimes more extreme political audiences.

Stimulated and reinforced by these developments, the congressional parties became more polarized. This is illustrated in Figures 1.1 and 1.2, which show the average liberal-conservative score for Democrats and Republicans in the House and Senate. The scores are based on a statistical analysis of the roll call voting record that incorporates all members and votes cast in each two-year Congress from 1961 to 2014.

Trends in party polarization are similar in the two houses of Congress. In both the House and the Senate, Republicans moved further in the conservative direction than Democrats did in the liberal direction. That is, this polarization is

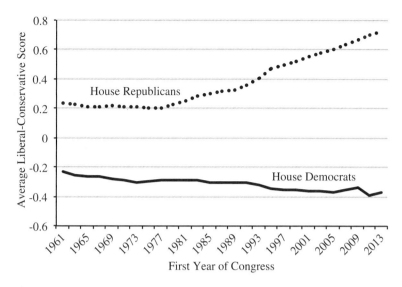

Figure 1.1 Polarization of House Parties, 1961–2014. Source: voteview.com. DW-NOMINATE means for each party.

due more to changes among congressional Republicans than to changes among congressional Democrats. The changes started a few years earlier in the House (the late 1970s) than they did in the Senate (the early 1980s); in recent years, the distance between the parties is large in both houses.

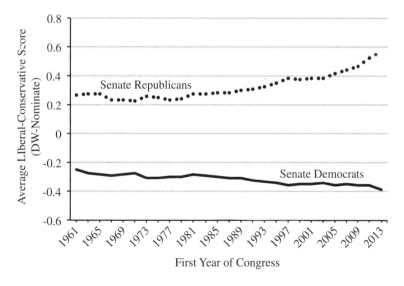

Figure 1.2 Polarization of Senate Parties, 1961–2014. Source: voteview.com. DW-NOMINATE means for each party.

Their polarization is more than a matter of the parties' having trouble finding common ground on issues of national importance. It involves very different perspectives on what those issues are. That is, the two parties differ in the issues to which each gives priority. Republicans are far more likely than Democrats to emphasize the burdens of taxes, regulation, and national security; Democrats are much more likely to emphasize poverty, education, the environment, and other problems that the government should address. As a result, the partisan battle that has been raging in Washington for the last quarter century now involves very different perspectives on the proper role of government, over ends as well as means.

Centralized Policy Making

In the mid-twentieth century, the heterogeneous congressional parties produced a legislative process that was *decentralized*. That is, the many standing committees and their chairmen were the dominant players in designing legislation. A bill would be written by the members of the House committee and the Senate committee that had jurisdiction over the issue, often with little participation by other legislators, including top party leaders. An occasional amendment to the bill might pass on the House or Senate floor, but most members were fairly deferential to the committee that recommended the bill. If the bill went to a conference committee to resolve the differences between the House and Senate versions of the bill, the conference committee would be made up of the senior members of the two committees. Another bill on another issue would similarly be written by members of another pair of House and Senate committees. Few key issues would be decided on the House or Senate floor. The process looked quite decentralized, with power centered in the multiple standing committees of the House and Senate.

One consequence of heterogeneous parties and a committee-oriented process was a limited role for party leaders. With the members of each party somewhat divided on important issues, a strong, aggressive party leader would likely have alienated many members of his party and intensified animosities among fellow members. The best leadership style was either to steer the party away from issues that would deeply divide it or to be a facilitator in finding consensus and compromise. Top leaders tended to leave the details of legislation for the committees to determine and simply make themselves available to assist the chairmen when asked. In the House, leaders tended to avoid calling meetings of the full conference or caucus, preferring instead to deal with committees, factions, and individuals as required.

In the late 1960s and early 1970s, a strong push by liberal Democrats in the House to revitalize their party organization led to more frequent meetings and important reforms. The reforms took two forms: (1) to democratize the internal workings of committees and reduce the power of committee chairs, and (2) to enhance to power of the Democratic Speaker by giving him more influence over committee assignments, the referral of legislation to committees, and the Rules Committee. The first set of reforms seemed to decentralize power further by giving more power to subcommittee chairs. This led observers to worry about the ability of the House to act quickly and coherently on complex policy problems.

By the 1980s, as liberals became more dominant among Democrats, the House Democratic party caucus showed signs of revitalization. Steps were taken to centralize the legislative process more in the hands of the Speaker of the House. The leaders of the House Democrats, Speakers Thomas P. "Tip" O'Neill and Jim Wright, were pressured by liberals to be more assertive. O'Neill became somewhat more aggressive in setting an agenda, but he did so reluctantly and selectively. Wright, however, took the reins of the legislative process gladly and aggressively. Wright expected committees to act on the party agenda and committee leaders to be loyal to the party. He also became a leader in trying to change U.S. policy toward Nicaragua. Wright resigned his speakership after the Republican Newt Gingrich, a future Speaker of the House, leveled charges against him. A House Ethics Committee report partially confirmed the charges that Wright had earned speaking fees in excess of those allowed by House rules and that his wife had been given a job to circumvent the limit on gifts. The Wright episode was viewed as a sign of rising partisanship, first by his assertiveness as Speaker and then in the Gingrich effort to undermine his speakership.

House Republican conservatives also were agitating for a stronger party in the 1980s. Gingrich led a conservative faction – the Conservative Opportunity Society – that demanded less cooperation with majority party Democrats, stronger conservative stances on important issues, and more loyalty from moderate Republicans who sometimes voted with the Democrats. Gingrich hoped to present a clear choice to Americans and, at the same time, force Democrats from conservative districts to choose between their party leaders and their more conservative electorates at home. Giving Democratic leaders few Republican votes would force some Democrats to vote with their party and put their own reelection at risk.

Gingrich was elected Speaker of the House in 1995, just after the Republican Party gained a House majority for the first time since 1954. He quickly moved to dominate every phase of the legislative process for the majority party. No significant committee chairmanship, committee assignment, or action on major legislation occurred without his direction or at least his approval. He set a schedule for committee action on legislation and demanded that it be followed. He carefully constructed conference committees to ensure that his perspective guided negotiations with the Senate. Gingrich served as Speaker only through 1998. His successors – Republican Dennis Hastert, Democrat Nancy Pelosi, and

Republican John Boehner – loosened the reins over committees to some degree, but the Speaker remained the central player in the House on nearly all important issues throughout the next two decades.

The new conservatives, particularly from the South, were central to the process of partisan polarization. Gingrich, for example, was elected from a district in the northern suburbs of Atlanta, Georgia, that had never elected a Republican to Congress before. Once in office, the new conservatives advocated stronger conservative positions and encouraged outside conservatives to organize, create media outlets, and field more conservatives for elective office. Among Democrats, liberals urged more effective legislative and public relations efforts to counter the conservatives. By the mid-1980s, House politics not only reflected changes in the electoral coalitions of the two parties, but members of the House, particularly Gingrich and his allies, were defining clearer and more ideological alternatives for the public to judge. By the 1990s, southern, conservative Republicans were rising to leadership positions and taking the lead in setting strategy for their party.

The Senate is a somewhat different but closely related story. The Senate lacks a presiding officer with the power of the House Speaker. The vice president of the United States presides over the Senate, and when the vice president is absent (most of the time), the president pro tempore, or a senator he designates, presides. Because the vice president may not be of the same party as the Senate's majority party, the Senate's presiding officer has not been granted much power. Moreover, the minority can sometimes block the majority by filibustering legislation – that is, refusing to allow a bill to be considered or to be voted upon. As a result, the Senate's majority leader does not have as much power as the House Speaker. Power cannot become as centralized in the Senate majority party's top leader as it can in the House Speaker.

Nevertheless, as the Senate parties became more polarized, senators looked to their top leaders to set party strategy, order the floor agenda, protect party interests in the design of legislation, and respond to the minority party. Senators who were former members of the House, particularly Republicans elected during the Gingrich era, contributed to the polarization of the Senate and were advocates for pursuing more aggressive party strategies. Recent leaders have been more deeply involved in determining the content of legislation and parliamentary strategies than were leaders in the 1960s and 1970s. While not as centralized as the House, the Senate, too, has shifted more responsibility to party leaders as the parties have become more polarized.

Associated with polarized parties has been sharpened partisan rhetoric. Open animus toward the other party has surfaced more frequently in the House and Senate. Leaders of the two parties, who in the past were often personal friends, today often have little personal relationship with each other and would be distrusted by many of their party colleagues if they did. Although most members observe the formal courtesies of congressional proceedings, impolite, insulting, and uncivil comments are now commonplace on the House and Senate floors, in press conferences, and in campaigns. For insiders and outsiders alike, congressional politics has become quite unpleasant and top leaders have become far less likable.

DIVIDED PARTY CONTROL AND POLITICAL STALEMATE

The combination of polarized parties and divided party control of the House, Senate, and presidency has produced frequent delays and sometimes gridlock in national policy making. Most legislation requires approval by the House, the Senate, and the president. If the president vetoes a bill, both houses of Congress must have a two-thirds majority to override the veto and force a bill into law. That seldom happens. When the two parties split control over the three institutions and that split is associated with deep differences about policy, as it has been in the last two decades, the costs of compromise are perceived to be great and long delays in acting on important legislation, even deadlock, can result.

Divided party control is a common condition in the federal government in recent decades. In Table 1.1, the majority party in each house of Congress and the party of the president are indicated. Divided party control of the three institutions is far more common than unified party control in the last half century. As the parties have become more polarized, this divided party control has created more tension between the institutions controlled by different parties and has increased the probability of stalemate over policy. Stalemate, in turn, leads to efforts to blame the other side and intensifies the partisan rhetoric that so many Americans dislike.

Recent Congresses, with divided party control and polarized parties, enacted very little legislation and managed to fund federal departments only after protracted negotiations. The 2010 elections brought a Republican majority to the House, while the Senate and the president remained Democratic. The minority Senate Republicans filibustered many of the Democrats' bills and blocked action on many of the president's nominees for executive branch positions and judgeships. The majority House Republicans blocked many serious amendments that Democrats wanted to offer to their legislation. And the House and Senate each passed many bills that the other house refused to consider and pass, even in a different version. The result was, at least as measured by the number of bills passed, very unproductive Congresses. As Figure 1.3 shows, a modern record-low number of bills were passed and pages of text enacted into law in the Congresses of 2011–2012 and 2013–2014.

TABLE 1.1. Party control of the Senate, House, and presidency, 1971–2015

Congress	First year of Congress	Senate majority party	House majority party	President	Divided/unified control
91	1969	Democrats	Democrats	Republican	Divided
92	1971	Democrats	Democrats	Republican	Divided
93	1973	Democrats	Democrats	Republican	Divided
94	1975	Democrats	Democrats	Republican	Divided
95	1977	Democrats	Democrats	Democrat	Unified
96	1979	Democrats	Democrats	Democrat	Unified
97	1981	Republicans	Democrats	Republican	Divided
98	1983	Republicans	Democrats	Republican	Divided
99	1985	Republicans	Democrats	Republican	Divided
100	1987	Democrats	Democrats	Republican	Divided
101	1989	Democrats	Democrats	Republican	Divided
102	1991	Democrats	Democrats	Republican	Divided
103	1993	Democrats	Democrats	Democrat	Unified
104	1995	Republicans	Republicans	Democrat	Divided
105	1997	Republicans	Republicans	Democrat	Divided
106	1999	Republicans	Republicans	Democrat	Divided
107	2001	Democrats	Republicans	Republican	Divided
108	2003	Republicans	Republicans	Republican	Unified
109	2005	Republicans	Republicans	Republican	Unified
110	2007	Democrats	Democrats	Republican	Divided
111	2009	Democrats	Democrats	Democrat	Unified
112	2011	Democrats	Republicans	Democrat	Divided
113	2013	Democrats	Republicans	Democrat	Divided
114	2015	Republicans	Republicans	Democrat	Divided

The Acquired Procedural Tendencies Taken to New Extremes

Chapters 7 and 8 describe the elements of the policy-making processes of the House and Senate and emphasize an important theme: House procedures allow a cohesive majority party to pass the legislation it wants, whereas Senate procedures allow a sizable and determined minority to block a majority's efforts to pass legislation. The sharp divide between the parties in the last two decades has encouraged the parties to more fully exploit parliamentary procedures. The acquired procedural tendencies of the two houses – majority party dominance in

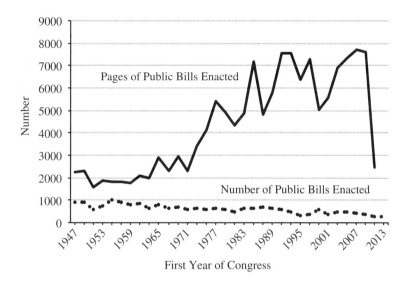

Figure 1.3 Number of Public Laws Enacted (*dashed*) and Pages Enacted (*solid*), 1947–2014.
Source: www.gpoaccess.gov/statutes/browse.html.

the House and minority party obstructionism in the Senate – have been pushed to new extremes.

In the House, the majority party leadership can use resolutions from the Committee on Rules, which is controlled by the Speaker, to limit opportunities to amend bills on the floor. The percentage of such resolutions – called special rules – that restrict amendments has climbed steadily upward over the past three decades (Figure 1.4), whereas the number that allowed all amendments eligible under the standing rules plummeted. The result is that the minority party has lost many opportunities to offer amendments to majority party legislation.

The heightened partisanship of recent decades is evident in the use of the Senate filibuster (Figure 1.5), a parliamentary tactic that is not available in the House. Because the Senate lacks a general rule limiting debate, senators can refuse to stop talking in order to allow the Senate to vote on a pending motion or measure – a tactic called a filibuster. A filibuster obstructs Senate action and can be overcome only with a three-fifths majority of senators voting on most matters – a procedure called cloture. In the highly partisan Senate of recent Congresses, the minority party has more frequently attempted to block majority party legislation and the majority party has responded with more cloture motions. This parliamentary arms race has contributed to sharper partisan rhetoric about which party is to blame for legislative outcomes.

After years of frustration with minority party obstructionism, Senate Democrats moved to limit the ability of a minority to block action on nominations. Through a parliamentary ruling (see Chapter 7), they reduced the number of

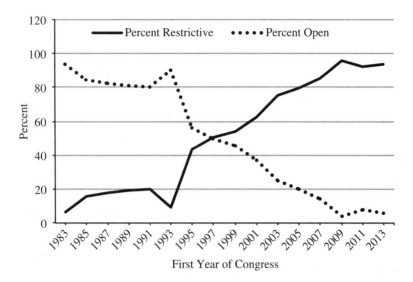

Figure 1.4 Percentage of Open and Restrictive Special Rules in the House, 1983–2014.
Source: House Committee on Rules, activity reports for selected Congresses.

votes required to close debate on an executive or judicial branch nomination (except Supreme Court nominations) to a simple majority, down from the three-fifths majority that is specified in the Senate's standing rules. Once that was accomplished, the Democrats used the cloture motion to close debate on dozens of nominations that Republicans had refused to allow to come to a vote, greatly increasing the use of cloture in 2014.

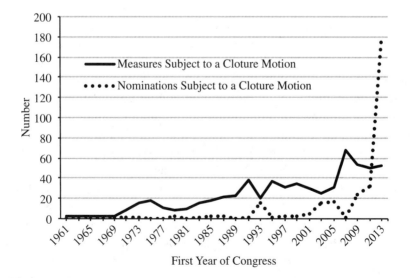

Figure 1.5 Percentage of Legislation and Nominations Subject to Cloture Votes in the Senate, 1961–2014. Source: senate.gov; calculations by the authors.

Will Polarized Parties, Centralized Decision Making, and Procedural Warfare Last Forever?

A Congress with a record of passing so little legislation and seemingly plagued with so much gamesmanship has stimulated strong and diverse commentary. Thomas Mann and Norman Ornstein, two political scientists who have been on the scene in Washington since the early 1970s, have coauthored two books, *The Broken Branch* and *It's Even Worse Than It Looks*, that reflect their view of where divided party control, polarization, and, particularly, Republican strategies have taken Congress. An op-ed they penned captured their theme: "Let's Just Say It: The Republicans Are the Problem." Republicans, it almost goes without saying, argued that a "do-nothing" Congress, or at least a Congress that stands in the way of approving the recommendations of President Barack Obama's administration, is just fine. Passing numerous, lengthy bills that are bad for America is a bad way to evaluate Congress.

Will polarized parties and centralized power in Congress last forever? They will not, but we do not have a good idea about when they will moderate. In the past, the rise of powerful factions, particularly factions that involve members of both parties, have undercut both polarization and centralized power. This can happen in association with new issues to which the established parties are slow to adjust. Just after the turn of the twentieth century, the progressives and some populists played this role. International crises can alter our politics in important ways as well, but they tend to be short in duration and without lasting effects on the way political forces are aligned on domestic issues.

Reforms have been proposed to address some of the sources of polarized parties. One experiment is underway in California. All candidates in a congressional district run in one primary election, and the two top vote getters face each other in the general election. This means that two Democrats (or two Republicans) could contest the general election. In that case, we might expect the Republican who appeals most to Democrats to win the general election, which creates an incentive for moderation. Other reforms include campaign finance reform to reduce reliance on big money from extreme groups, procedural reform in Congress to insure fairness and encourage compromise, and stimulating higher turnout in elections to balance the effects of more motivated extremist voters.

A frequent response to reform proposals that are offered to reduce partisan polarization is that we do not need new rules – we just need more responsible politicians and more effective leadership. It is not so simple. The problem is necessarily rooted in who is recruited to run for office, backed with money and organization, and then elected to Congress. The views of party activists, the attitudes of primary electorates, and the nature of the parties' electoral coalitions shape who the candidates are and their approach to policy making. For the most part, in our experience, we get the behavior in office that is advocated by candidates in campaigns.

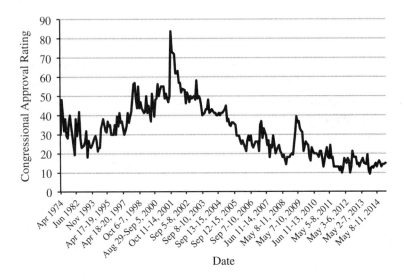

Figure 1.6 Percentage Approving the Way That Congress Is Handling Its Job, 1974–2014.
Source: Gallup Poll.

AN UNPOPULAR CONGRESS

The stalemated Congresses of the last few years have not been popular with the general public. In Figure 1.6, Congress's approval rating since the mid-1970s is shown. On a somewhat irregular basis, the Gallup organization has asked individuals in a sample of adult Americans whether they "approve or disapprove of the way Congress is handling its job." The percentage who approve is reported in the figure. The "approval rating," as it is informally called, seldom exceeds 50 percent. In the data shown, the average is 32 percent. The approval rating hovered around 50 percent late in the Clinton administration when a Republican Congress and a Democratic president stopped years of battling with each other, the economy was doing well, and budget agreements were relatively easy to negotiate. It also went to very high levels as President George W. Bush and Congress responded to the terrorist attacks on September 11, 2001. Far more common is for Congress to receive the approval of only about a third of Americans.

Congress versus the President

Typically, Congress runs in parallel with, but lower than, the president in approval ratings, as Figure 1.7 shows for the 2001–2014 period for the Bush (2011–2008) and Obama (2009–2014) administrations. New presidents typically start

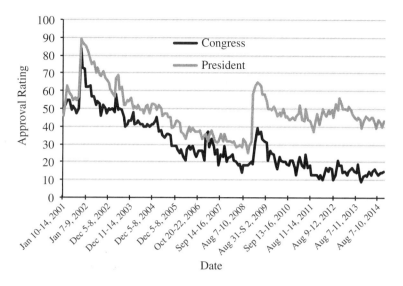

Figure 1.7 Percentage Approving the Way that Congress and the President Are Handling Their Jobs, 2001–2014. Source: Gallup Poll.

with approval ratings exceeding 60 percent and then experience a decline, and the recent two presidents are no exception. Congress's approval rating usually falls substantially below the president's rating – in this series, Congress's rating is an average of 18 percent lower than the president's rating. Congress simply is seldom as popular as the president.

There are exceptions to the rule that Congress is less popular than the president. The cooperative response of Congress and the president to the terrorist attacks in late 2001 that produced very high ratings for both institutions was one obvious example. The other exception was in early 2007, just after a new Democratic majority took over the House and Senate, when Congress experienced a small improvement in its ratings whereas President Bush continued to show the same low ratings that he had had for some time. Otherwise, Congress consistently receives weak approval ratings.

A reasonable hunch about Congress's low approval rating is that the legislative process does not look appealing to many Americans. Congress speaks with many competing voices, its outcomes involve compromises that frustrate parts of the public, and its scandals featuring individual legislators are common. Moreover, when party control of Congress is unified, supporters of the other party are unlikely to approve of Congress's performance. When party control is divided and Congress is deadlocked on important issues, supporters of neither party are likely to approve of the institution's performance. Divided party control, polarized parties, a deadlocked Congress, and the public relations problems common to Congress are a recipe for very low approval ratings.

Congressional Scandals

Scandals, even when they involve a single member, add to the public's frustration with Congress and have contributed to the institution's low ratings in opinion polls. Some of the highlights are provided in the box "Highlights of Recent Congressional Ethics Scandals." A consequence is that Congress has become a never-ending source of comic relief, like the joke about the senator who dozed off during a roll-call vote, was jerked awake when his name was called, and reflexively yelled out, "Not guilty." There also is the joke about the member who kept referring to the presiding officer as "Your Honor."[1] But seriously . . . it seems fair to say that a large majority of today's members behave ethically. It is even reasonable to argue that today's cohort of members is at least as ethical as any past cohort. No doubt the ethical standards applied by the public, the media, and Congress itself are higher today than at any other time. Yet, there is no denying that the seemingly regular flow of scandals harms Congress's standing with the American people.

Highlights of Recent Congressional Ethics Scandals

- In 1989, House Speaker James Wright (D-Texas) resigned after Republicans charged him with ethics violations for receiving extraordinarily large royalties on a book he wrote.
- In 1989, questions about the propriety of campaign contributions were raised in the "Keating Five" affair, which concerned the relationship between five senators and a prominent savings-and-loan owner seeking to block an investigation of his financial dealings.
- In 1991, Senator David Durenburger (R-Minnesota) was condemned in a unanimously approved Senate resolution for a book deal and for seeking reimbursement for expenses for staying in a condo that he owned.
- In 1995, a long investigation of sexual harassment charges against Senator Robert Packwood (R-Oregon) led to his forced resignation from office.
- In 1995, Representative Dan Rostenkowski (D-Illinois), former chairman of the House Ways and Means Committee, was found guilty of illegally receiving cash for personal use from the House post office. He later served a prison term.
- In 1997, Speaker Newt Gingrich (R-Georgia) agreed to pay $300,000 in fines based on charges that he had used nonprofit organizations for political purposes and had misled the House Committee on Standards of Official Conduct.
- In 1998, Representative Jay Kim (R-California) pleaded guilty to charges involving more than $250,000 in illegal campaign contributions.
- In 2002, Representative James A. Traficant, Jr. (D-Ohio), was convicted of receiving bribes in exchange for helping businesses get government contracts and of engaging in a pattern of racketeering since taking office in 1985.
- In 2004, House Majority Leader Tom DeLay (R-Texas) was issued letters of admonition by the House Ethics Committee for improperly promising to endorse the son of Representative Nick Smith (R-Michigan) in exchange for Smith's vote on

1 Paul Boller, *Congressional Anecdotes* (New York: Oxford University Press, 1991), 18.

a bill and for attending a fund-raising event with lobbyists for a company that was lobbying him on pending legislation.

- In 2005, Representative Duke Cunningham (R-California) resigned and pleaded guilty to taking more than $2.4 million in bribes and related tax evasion and fraud, the largest financial sum involving an individual member.
- In 2006, Representative Tom DeLay (R-Texas) resigned after being indicted in Texas for laundering money through a national party committee in his effort to redistrict Texas congressional districts. He was convicted in 2010.
- In 2006, Representative William Jefferson (D-Louisiana) won reelection to the House but was denied a Ways and Means Committee assignment after FBI agents videotaped him appearing to solicit a bribe and later found $90,000 of the marked cash in his freezer – making this the "cold cash" scandal. Jefferson was defeated for reelection in 2008 and given a thirteen-year prison sentence in 2009.
- In 2006, Representative Mark Foley (R-Florida) resigned after it was disclosed that he sent sexually explicit e-mail messages to underage House pages.
- In 2006, Representative Bob Ney (R-Ohio) pleaded guilty to making false statements and participating in a conspiracy in receiving thousands of dollars in gifts from lobbyist Jack Abramoff. A Ney aide pleaded guilty to receiving gifts. Separately, Abramoff pleaded guilty to charges of conspiracy, fraud, and tax evasion.
- In 2008, Senator Ted Stevens (R-Alaska) was convicted of seven counts of failing to disclose gifts related to the renovation of his Alaska home on his Senate financial disclosure forms. His conviction was later overturned because of prosecutorial misconduct.
- In 2008, Representative Tim Mahoney (D-Florida) confessed that he had had an extramarital affair with a staff member. Shortly after, news reports indicated that Mahoney had attempted to buy the staff member's silence; Mahoney's wife filed for divorce, and he was defeated for reelection.
- In 2010, Representative Charles Rangle (D-New York) was censured for violating House rules in using his office to raise money for a college building named after him and for failing to disclose financial assets, as well as for violating New York City rules by housing his campaign committees in rent-controlled apartments.
- In 2011, Senator John Ensign (R-Nevada) resigned his seat before the completion of a Senate investigation into his activities following an extramarital affair with a staff member. The activities included payments to the staff member's family and arranging for the employment of the staff member's father as a lobbyist. The Ethics Committee referred the matter to the Justice Department.
- In 2011, Representative Anthony Weiner (D-New York) resigned after it was disclosed that he had sent lewd photos of himself to women via Twitter.
- In 2012, Representative Laura Richardson (D-California) was fined by the House for breaking federal law and House rules in pressuring her staff to campaign for her and destroying evidence. After her reprimand by the House, she was defeated for reelection by a fellow Democrat.
- In 2014, Representative Tray Radel (R-Florida) resigned a few months after being arrested for buying cocaine in the District of Columbia.
- In 2015, Representative Michael Grimm (R-New York) resigned his seat after pleading guilty to federal tax evasion charges for failing to disclose wages and receipts in a restaurant business in which he had invested after retiring from the FBI.

While a few individuals in Congress manage to keep a steady flow of scandal-ous news coming from Capitol Hill, the modern media have a voracious appetite for it. Norman Ornstein notes that changes in electronic and print media have led to a greater emphasis on the negative and sensational side of Congress. He refers to this as the "tabloidization" of media coverage:

> The drive to emulate the National Enquirer and the Star has spread to the most respect-able newspapers and magazines, while network news divisions have begun to com-pete with tabloids like "Inside Edition" and "Hard Copy" with their own tabloid shows like "Prime Time Live" and "Dateline: NBC," and with changed coverage on the nightly news.

Stories or rumors of scandal – both individual and institutional – have domi-nated news coverage of politics and politicians in recent decades more than at any time in modern history, and not just in terms of column inches or broadcast minutes, but in emphasis as well:

> The expansion of radio and cable television talk shows also seems to have increased the speed with which bad news about Congress is disseminated and the frequency with which bad news is repeated. On many of these programs, there is a premium on a quick wit and a good one-liner and little time for sober, balanced commentary.[2]

Groups supporting term limits for Congress and other reforms probably have influenced public opinion, too. Term-limit advocates argue that congressional incumbents are a privileged class. Incumbents, in this view, have created a system in which various benefits of office – including biased districting, free use of official resources, fund-raising leverage, and cozy relations with lobby-ists – give them an unfair advantage that can be overcome only through radical reform. The more extreme versions of this argument suggest that incumbents have been corrupted by their experience in Washington. Incumbents are said to have developed an "inside-the-beltway" mentality (the Beltway is the free-way that encircles the District of Columbia and its inner suburbs) or to suffer from "Potomac fever" (presumably a condition brought on by proximity to the famous river).

Politicians, of course, quickly latch on to themes that resonate with the public. As a result, running for Congress by running *against* Congress, an old art form in American politics, has gained an even more prominent place in recent cam-paigns. Indeed, many recent arrivals on Capitol Hill promised to end "business as usual" in Washington and to push through reforms to "fix" Congress – to end the system of congressional perks, to stop the influence of special interests, and so on. The repetition of anti-Congress themes undoubtedly contributes to the low ratings for Congress and its members in public opinion polls.

---

2 Norman J. Ornstein, "Congress Inside Out: Here's Why Life on the Hill Is Meaner Than Ever," *Roll Call* (September 20, 1993): 27.

Hate Congress, but Love Your Member of Congress

While Congress languishes with low approval ratings, individual members of Congress continue to do quite well. Members of Congress are among the most severe critics of the institution, but they keep running for reelection and winning. In 2014, 390 incumbents sought to fill the 435 seats of the House of Representatives and more than 96 percent of those incumbents were successful. Senators seeking reelection in 2014 were successful in 23 of 28 races.

How do incumbent members of Congress manage to be so successful with their institution being so unpopular? Most incumbents fit their districts and states reasonably well. Typically, Gallup finds that about 70 percent of the public approves of the way its own U.S. representative is handling his or her job – even when overall approval of Congress's performance dips below 20 percent. Moreover, many, if not most, members run *for* Congress by running *against* Congress. The incumbent's argument that he or she should be reelected to continue the fight against the bad guys in Washington seems to work well. Senator Jeff Flake (R-Arizona) once tweeted that "earthquakes hit Washington, next week hurricanes, after that frogs and locusts, then the worst plague – Congress returns." We return to incumbents' reelection success in Chapter 3.

Other Trends in Congressional Politics

The polarization of congressional parties and the centralization of power and frequent stalemate that comes with it have been the most conspicuous changes in Congress over the last few decades, but they are not the only important ones. Several long-term trends in American society and politics, along with changes in the behavior of legislators and their institution, have transformed congressional politics from a somewhat insular, D.C.-centered process to a much more competitive, open, and partisan process. We introduce these subjects here; most are discussed at greater length in later chapters.

Changing Membership: Regional Shifts

In recent decades, demographic and social changes in American society have altered the composition of Congress in important ways. One such change has been in the allocation of House seats to the states. The 435 seats of the House are reapportioned every ten years to reflect changes in the distribution of the nation's population across the states. A formula established by law guides the Census Bureau, which calculates the number of districts for each state every ten years after the decennial census. Population shifts have allowed certain states in the South and West to gain seats in the House of Representatives at the expense of several eastern and midwestern states. The regional shifts

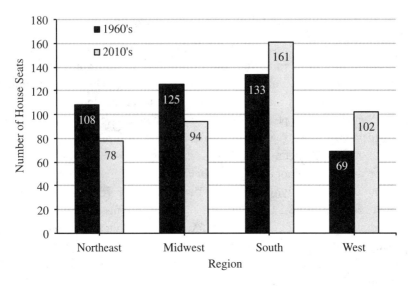

Figure 1.8 Number of House Seats by Region, 1960s (*black*) and 2010s (*gray*). Source: Census Bureau.

are visible in Figure 1.8. The South and West gained even more seats after the national census in the year 2000 – again at the expense of the industrial Northeast and Midwest.

The redistribution of seats away from the northern industrial states reduced the political clout of those states at a time when they could use it. The need for infrastructure repairs, worker retraining, low-income housing, and other government services is severe in the old industrial states, but the declining influence of these states diminishes their ability to acquire financial assistance from the federal government. Indeed, the shift of power to the more conservative regions of the country has undercut congressional support for a major federal role in the rehabilitation of the industrial cities of the northern-tier states.

The population growth in the South and West is the result of that region's economic growth, an influx of workers from the older industrial states and other countries, and the expansion of the region's middle class. The most obvious consequence of these developments is that the South is no longer a one-party region, as it was just three decades ago. Republicans are now competitive in Senate races throughout the South and hold most House seats as well. As recently as 1960, Republicans held no Senate seats and only 6 of 104 House seats in the states of the old Confederacy. After the 1992 elections, Republicans held 13 of the 22 Senate seats and 48 of the 125 House seats in the region, with the largest numbers in Florida and Texas. The southern Senate seats were critical to Republicans between 1981 and 1986, when the party controlled the Senate, and again after 1994. The 2010 reapportionment continued the shift of House seats away from the East and Midwest to the South and West and from the more Democratic to the more Republican regions.

Changing Membership: Women and Minorities

Beyond the changes in regional representation and partisan composition in Congress, Capitol Hill has also acquired a sizable contingent of women and minorities. The growing strength of women's and minority groups, the acquisition of political experience by women and minority politicians in state and local government, and new voting laws have all contributed to the recent improvement in these groups' representation in Congress. In 1993, the Senate gained its first Native American, Ben Nighthorse Campbell (D-Colorado), who later switched parties, and its first black woman, Carol Moseley-Braun (D-Illinois). Figure 1.9 shows the gains that women, African Americans, and Hispanics have made in Congress in recent years, and even more – many more – women and minorities have been running for Congress.

As the Center for American Women and Politics reports, new records for the number of women who filed for candidacy for Congress were set in 2012 – 299 in the House and 36 in the Senate. For the general election, the number of women on the ballot was 166 for the House and 18 for the Senate. The numbers were down a little in 2014 – 31 women filed for Senate races and 15 were on the general election ballot, and 250 women filed for House races and 159 were

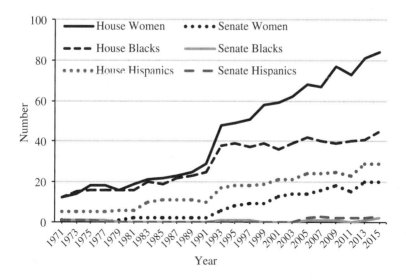

Figure 1.9 Number of Women and Minorities in the House and Senate, 1971–2015. Source: *Vital Statistics on American Politics* (Washington, DC: Congressional Quarterly Press, 2000), p. 201; http://innovation.cq.com/newmember/2010elexnguide.pdf; some entries for the 114th Congress collected by the authors. Numbers reflect membership at the start of the Congress.

on the general election ballot. Overall, about 104 women served in Congress in 2015, still less than 20 percent of the membership, up from 82 ten years earlier.

Women and minorities are still underrepresented in Congress relative to their proportions in the population, but few doubt that women and minority law-makers have already had a substantial impact. Most obviously, the Congressional Caucus for Women's Issues, the Congressional Black Caucus, and, to a lesser extent, the Congressional Hispanic Caucus have become important factions within the House Democratic Party. For the first time, women and minority representatives made up a majority of the House Democratic Caucus in 2013. At this writing, only two African Americans serve in the Senate. Republican Tim Scott represents South Carolina, and Democrat Mo Cowan serves in the Senate as an interim senator for Massachusetts. They are only the seventh and eighth African Americans to be seated there. Two legislators, Representative Tom Cole (R-Oklahoma), a member of the Chickasaw Nation, and Ben Lujan (D-New Mexico), usually are listed as the only Native Americans in Congress in 2013. Cole was elected chair of the National Republican Congressional Committee, his party's campaign committee, in late 2006, a post he gave up after the 2008 elections.

The presence of more women and minorities has changed the mix of voices heard in congressional debates. Social and economic problems seem to be more frequently discussed in the first person today – that is, more members refer to their personal experience when addressing their colleagues and constituents. In addition, more legislation reflecting the issues emphasized by women and minorities has been introduced. Generally, issues important to these groups have been given higher priority by party leaders, particularly Democratic leaders.

Only one woman, Representative Nancy Pelosi (D-California), has been the top leader of a congressional party. Pelosi was elected Speaker in 2007 after the Democrats won a majority of House seats in the 2006 elections. She had been elected the Democrats' minority leader in late 2002 after serving in the number two position, Democratic whip, for two years, and she returned to minority leader following the 2010 elections. Other women have held lower party leadership positions. Many women have gained sufficient seniority to chair important committees and subcommittees.

Only two African Americans have served in one of the top three leadership positions in a congressional party. J. C. Watts of Oklahoma served as House Republican Conference chair in 1998–2002. James Clyburn of South Carolina was elected the House Democratic caucus vice chairman in 2002 and chairman in 2004, and then, in 2006, was elected Democratic whip, a position that he still holds. When Representative Robert Menendez of New Jersey became the House Democratic Caucus chair in 2002, he became the highest-ranking Hispanic legislator in the history of Congress. He gave up the post when he was appointed to fill a Senate vacancy in late 2005.

Recent Firsts

Recent Congresses have seen a variety of "firsts" in its membership. Representative Keith Ellison (D-Minnesota) became the first Muslim member of Congress in 2011. In 2013, Tulsi Gabbard (D-Hawaii) became the first Hindu member of either house and Mazie Hirono (D-Hawaii) became the first Buddhist senator. That same year, Tammy Baldwin (D-Wisconsin) became the first openly gay senator and Kyrsten Sinema (D-Arizona) became the first openly bisexual member of Congress. And with the election of Mia Love (R-Utah) in 2014, Congress has its first Republican African American woman in its membership.

Changing Membership: Previous Occupations

Notable changes have occurred in members' occupational profiles. Congress is still dominated by lawyers and businesspeople, with more than 200 lawyers and about 200 members with business backgrounds in the House and Senate in 2011. The number of farmers has declined – down from about 75 in the 1950s to a little more than two dozen in recent Congresses. Educators have become more numerous – more than 80 in 2011. Overall, the occupational backgrounds of members are now somewhat more diverse than they were three or four decades ago.

These trends in the membership of Congress – the shift to the Sunbelt, the increasing numbers of women and minority members, and the greater diversity in members' previous experience – are likely to continue. The professions of law and business still dominate, but a wider range of experiences are reflected now in the membership of Congress than a generation ago.

Girl Scouts and Congress

Mother Jones has observed that along with a record number of women in the Senate, the 113th Congress (2013–2014) had a record number of former Girl Scouts. According to the *Mother Jones* count, fourteen of the twenty female senators were Girl Scouts, compared to 8 percent of American women overall. Including the House, 60 percent of women in Congress were reported to have been Scouts.

Source: http://www.motherjones.com/mojo/2012/11/thats-senator-girl-scout-you.

GOVERNING AS CAMPAIGNING

In a representative democracy, we hope that there is a strong linkage between governing and campaigning. Elected officials' desire for reelection underpins our ability to hold officials accountable. Broadly speaking, campaign promises are (and should be) related to governing, and election outcomes are (and should be) shaped by performance in office. Inevitably, then, the line between governing and campaigning becomes blurred.

In recent decades, campaigning has become more fully integrated with governing. No longer is governing done in Washington and campaigning done at home. The daily routines of members and top leaders are now geared to the demands of campaigning. For most legislators, few days go by without there being some time and effort devoted to winning the next election.

The cost of modern campaigns drives much of the regular attention to campaigning. In recent years, the average victor in a Senate race spent more than $10 million, and the average House victor spent more than $1.5 million. For an incumbent seeking reelection, that is an average of more than $32,000 for each week served during a six-year Senate term and almost $15,000 for each week served during a two-year House term. Many races are far more expensive. And these sums do not include additional hundreds of millions of dollars spent by parties and independent groups on congressional campaigns. Competitive pressures, between incumbents and challengers and between the two parties, have produced a never-ending search for cash.

Governing-as-campaigning is facilitated by new technologies. Advances in transportation allow most members of Congress to be back home in their districts or states most weekends. Public opinion polls, which allow the public's views to be registered with legislators, have become more affordable because of advancements in digital technology. Leaders and parties sponsor focus groups to learn about nuances and shadings in public attitudes. Radio and television call-in shows enable nearly every constituent to talk directly to a member of Congress from time to time. Satellite technology lets members communicate easily and inexpensively from Washington with groups in their home state or district. All members of Congress maintain websites with press releases and other publications, most have some form of streaming media on their sites, and some maintain blogs.

Social networking media puts members' daily routines and thoughts on display with instant public reactions. In late 2014, nearly 90 percent of members of Congress were on Facebook or Twitter, and most had both. Many legislators were using Flickr, Instagram, and YouTube for posting photos and videos. A few had Pinterest, Tumblr, and Google Plus accounts, too. Staffs for the parties and individual legislators often tweet and blog on behalf of their principals.

Members of Congress, and certainly candidates for Congress, find the new information technologies irresistible. Members love to demonstrate their commitment to keeping in touch with their constituents by being among the first to use a new innovation in communications. To be sure, members face real problems reaching constituents in districts and states with ever-growing populations. The average House district has nearly 740,000 people, up from about 300,000 in 1940 and 400,000 in 1960. Still, the political value of appearing to be connected to constituents drives elected officials to exploit new technologies.

It is almost a cliché to call members of today's Congress political entrepreneurs. The term is used to indicate members' relative independence from local and national parties. Candidates for congressional office now develop their own campaign organizations, raise their own money, and set their own campaign strategies. This independence from the political parties in getting elected tends to carry over when the winners take office. Once in office, members use official resources and exploit their relationships with interest groups and political action committees for political advantage. Knowing that they are on their own when it comes to getting reelected, members take full advantage of taxpayer-supported travel opportunities and communications technologies to maintain a high profile at home. These topics are addressed in Chapters 3 and 4.

Congressional leaders have changed their ways, too. To assist their party colleagues, most party leaders spend many evenings and weekends at fund-raising events. Most leaders have developed their own political action committees (leadership PACs, they have been called) to raise and distribute money. Leaders have formed public relations task forces within their parties, and the campaign committees of the congressional parties have greatly expanded their activities. Perhaps most important, congressional leaders now often use technology developed for campaigning in legislative battles. Professional consultants and pollsters help fashion legislative priorities and design public relations strategies. The parties' congressional campaign committees conduct opposition research – digging up dirt on your election opponent – against congressional incumbents of the opposite party. Media campaigns are now planned for major legislative proposals with the assistance of television advertising specialists. Money, media, and partisanship feed on each other.

Political scientist Robert Dahl gives a useful label to governing-as-campaigning – plebiscitary politics. Dahl is referring to the trend toward more direct communication between the public and elected officials and the demise of intermediaries – such as parties and membership organizations – that once served to represent or express public opinion to elected officials. Directly observed, rather than mediated, public views are more important than ever – which could not be further from Madison's aspirations for the national legislature.[3]

On its face, plebiscitary politics might seem to be a good thing: It seems better to have public opinion influencing members' decisions than to have highly paid lobbyists representing organized interests swaying their votes. But as Dahl notes, the effects of direct communication between the people and their representatives on Capitol Hill may not be so desirable. For one thing, elected officials and special interests might manipulate direct communication to their advantage.

---

3 Robert A. Dahl, "Americans Struggle to Cope with a New Political Order that Works in Opaque and Mysterious Ways," *Public Affairs Report* (Institute of Governmental Studies, University of California, Berkeley, September 1993): 1, 4–6.

If the communication is mostly one-way from elected official to voter and if politicians are the ones who choose the time and place for direct communication, then the process may create nothing more than a deceiving appearance of responsiveness.

More important, plebiscitary politics may undermine both representation and deliberation in legislative policy making. With respect to representation, the "public" that is likely to communicate directly to members may not be representative of members' larger constituencies. They will be people who are intensely interested in politics generally or in a single issue, and who can afford and know how to use new information technologies. If so, then members' impressions of public opinion may be distorted by such communication. With respect to deliberation, direct communication with more constituents could lead members to make premature public commitments on more issues, absorb more of the legislators' time, and reduce members' flexibility in negotiating compromises in the legislative arena. The possible result is that demagoguery and grandstanding would take precedence over resolving conflicts and solving problems.

A Changing Policy Environment

Their prominent place in the American political system gives members of Congress an opportunity to raise issues, encourage media attention, stimulate public discourse, and build public support on a variety of national and international problems. This is particularly true of senators, whose visibility and longer terms of office create more opportunities for drawing attention to causes they advocate. However, in the highly charged partisan environment of the last decade, with so much media coverage devoted to partisan conflict over a few issues on which top party leaders get most of the attention, individual legislators appear to have become less important as policy innovators and champions of new causes.

While Congress is shaping public discourse for the nation, issues usually arise quite independently of Congress that create demands for action from the public and generate new challenges for the institution and its members. In the last decade, the Great Recession, the fiscal policy questions of spending, taxes, and deficits, and many other issues – health care costs and accessibility, illegal immigration, climate change, and income inequality, among others – arose outside the halls of Congress, stimulating demands for new policy and motivating legislators to action. In most cases, they also generated deep divisions between the parties because they pricked already sensitive ideological dispositions about the proper role of government.

Such issues create challenges for the institution beyond the problem of deadlock between the parties. New issues often require the application of new expertise and the coordination of government agencies in new ways. Traditionally, the

House and Senate relied on standing committees to be a place where members could develop specialized knowledge of the matters under their jurisdiction and hire staff with technical expertise in law, economics, science, or other fields to assist the members in evaluating and writing policy proposals. In the early 1970s, Congress strengthened the expertise available to it by creating the Congressional Research Service (out of the old Legislative Reference Service) and the Congressional Budget Office, and by expanding the Government Accountability Office. In 1972, Congress also created the Office of Technology Assessment to assist it in evaluating scientific and technological issues, but a Republican-controlled Congress closed the agency in 1995 and it has not been replaced.

Legislators face serious challenges when legislating on technical subjects. When only a few members understand the technical details of issues and legislation, most members must look to staff, lobbyists, and others for advice on how to interpret alternative proposals. That places a great deal of power in the hands of people who are not elected policy makers. In many cases, legislating on scientific or technological subjects entails setting broad policy goals and delegating the power to make the necessary technical decisions to experts in the executive branch.[4] Although legislators are able to respond to demands for action in this way, they do so at the cost of enhancing the executive branch's power over the details of public policy.

In the last decade, Congress has struggled to manage large federal budget deficits – an imbalance of spending and revenues. In the late 1990s, it appeared that the federal budget would be in balance for the foreseeable future and that the politics of blame might be supplanted by a politics of claiming credit. At the start of 1998, the Congressional Budget Office projected measurable surpluses to the year 2008 and no deficits. Predictably, new policy initiatives were proposed by the Democratic president Bill Clinton, but few stood a chance of passage with the Republican majority in Congress. After George W. Bush was elected president in 2000, Republicans enacted a tax cut bill, passed in 2001, that seemed quite affordable to many observers. But a recession that settled in the economy and the terrorist acts of September 11, 2001, motivated large spending initiatives for New York City, the war against terrorism, and the war in Iraq. Suddenly, the president and Congress were facing long-term deficits once again.

After the Republicans regained a majority of House seats in the 2010 elections, intense conflict between the parties over the budget and fiscal policy dominated congressional politics. With President Obama, a Democrat, in the White House and a Democratic majority in the Senate through 2014, sharp differences over spending and tax policy produced prolonged battles over the budget. Negotiated

---

4 See Theodore J. Lowi, "Toward a Legislature of the First Kind," in *Knowledge, Power, and the Congress*, ed. William H. Robinson and Clay H. Wellborn (Washington, DC: Congressional Quarterly Press, 1991), 9–36.

budget deals produced budget constraints that greatly limited the policy options of the president and Congress in future years.

The federal budget deficit was a dominant force in legislative politics in the last decade. Other than in national security, few new federal programs were initiated, and much, if not most, of the period's important legislation consisted of large budget bills, particularly budget reconciliation bills. These bills, which are discussed in Chapter 12, were the handiwork of many congressional committees and affected the full range of federal programs over multiple years. This emphasis on large, all-encompassing budget bills that placed constraints on spending further reduced the ability of committees and individual members to pursue policy initiatives.

NEW FORMS OF ORGANIZED INFLUENCE

The number of interest groups in Washington and in the rest of the country multiplied many times in the last half century. By one count, the number of groups increased from about 1,000 in the late 1940s to well more than 7,000 in the early 1980s.[5] Because of lobbying registration requirements that were enacted in 1995, we know that the number of registered lobbyists has increased to more than 12,000 in recent years and, according to the Center for Responsive Politics, lobbyists spend about $3 billion per year on their activities. Registration is required for anyone who spends more than 20 percent of his or her time influencing legislation or has more than one contact with a covered government official. It excludes tens of thousands of people in the District of Columbia who are engaged in grassroots and advertising initiatives and are running large membership organizations in support of lobbying efforts. As the scope of the federal government's activity has expanded, federal programs, tax policies, and regulation have affected more people, which has stimulated the growth of organized groups establishing headquarters and lobbying in Washington. Technological developments in transportation, information management, and communications have enabled scattered people, corporations, and even state and local governments to easily organize, raise money, and set up offices and staff in Washington. Organized interests breed new organized interests as new groups form to counter the influence of other groups. The result has been a tremendous increase in the demands placed on members of Congress by lobbyists from organized groups.

5 Robert H. Salisbury, "The Paradox of Interest Groups in Washington – More Groups, Less Clout," in *The New American Political System*, 2nd ed., ed. Anthony King (Washington, DC: American Enterprise Institute, 1990), 203–209. For an analysis of the effects of these developments on Congress, see Barbara Sinclair, *The Transformation of the U.S. Senate* (Baltimore: Johns Hopkins University Press, 1989), 57–64.

Congressionally Speaking . . .

Each Congress has a two-year life span. Federal law sets the date for federal elections, but the Constitution specifies the starting date for each Congress. Before 1935, congressional elections in November of an even-numbered year preceded the convening of a new Congress the following March. Since 1935, after the ratification of the Twentieth Amendment to the Constitution, a new Congress convenes on January 3 unless Congress otherwise provides by law, as it often does to avoid weekends. Each two-year Congress is given a number – the 114th Congress convened in January 2015 – and is divided into two one-year sessions. Congressional documents are often numbered 114–1 or 114–2 to combine the Congress and session numbers.

Not only have interest groups proliferated, but they have also become more diverse. Economic interests – corporations, trade associations, and labor groups – greatly outnumber other sectors among lobbyists. In addition, many groups represent new industries, and "citizens" groups sprouted in the 1960s and 1970s and continue to grow in number. These groups are often outgrowths of national movements – such as those for civil rights, women's rights, children's rights, the elimination of hunger, consumers' rights, welfare rights, gay rights, environmental protection, and housing for the homeless. Many of these groups now enjoy memberships numbering in the hundreds of thousands.

Along with their increasing number and diversity, groups have become more skilled in camouflaging their true identity. For most major legislative battles, coalitions of interests form and take all-American names, pool their resources to fund mass media campaigns, and often dissolve as fast as they were created. Many of the coalitions are the handiwork of entrepreneurs in law firms, consulting outfits, and public relations shops who are paid to coordinate the activity of the coalitions they spearhead.

The roots have been taken out of grassroots lobbying. New technologies and consumer and membership databases give lobbyists the capacity to make highly targeted, efficient appeals to stimulate constituency demands on Washington. By the late 1980s, computerized telephone messages allowed groups to communicate with many thousands of people within a few hours. Technology now allows a group to telephone its own members, a targeted group (such as one House member's constituency), or the general public; briefly interview the respondents about their views on a subject; and, for respondents who favor the group's position, provide a few more facts to reinforce their views, solicit them to write letters to members of Congress, and quickly transfer the calls to the appropriate Capitol Hill offices before the respondents hang up. Several groups have developed television programs – some shown on the many cable television channels that are available in most communities – as a way of reaching specific audiences. Lobbyists exploit e-mail and interactive video technologies to motivate citizens to flood Congress with messages. As a result, for a group with money, the absence of a large membership is not much of an obstacle to generating public pressure on members of Congress.

Congressionally Speaking . . .

Every ten years, the Census Bureau counts the number of people living in the United States. On the basis of that count, the Census Bureau allocates seats in the U.S. House of Representatives to each of the states according to a formula set in law. This allocation is called *apportionment*. States then draw the boundaries of districts for the House of Representatives, a process known as *districting*. Districting is controversial because it may advantage one of the parties or certain incumbent legislators. In most states, congressional district lines are determined by state legislatures and governors. Republicans' success in the 2010 elections gave them control of both houses in twenty-five state legislatures (sixteen for Democrats) and of both the legislature and governorship in twenty states (eleven for Democrats). This allowed Republicans to have a significant advantage in drawing district lines that will remain in place until after the 2020 census.

NATIONAL SECURITY AND DECLINING CONGRESSIONAL POWER

Perhaps the most serious challenge to Congress's role in the American constitutional system is secret government necessitated by national security. The war against terrorism has revived fears that secrecy in the national security agencies of government will threaten Americans' civil liberties and undermine Congress's ability to influence the direction of policy, to oversee the expenditure of public funds, and to hold executive officials accountable. Executive branch officials are hesitant to reveal certain information to members of Congress because they do not trust legislators to keep the information secret. For their part, legislators cannot know what information is being withheld from Congress, so secret government tends to breed distrust on Capitol Hill.

In the 1970s, in the aftermath of the Vietnam War and disclosures of intelligence agencies' misdeeds, Congress enacted laws to require notifying Congress of, and sometimes to grant to Congress the power to approve or disapprove, the commitment of armed forces abroad, arms sales, and covert operations. Congress also created intelligence committees and established other mechanisms for handling classified information. Presidents from both parties have not liked to be constrained by these laws, at times arguing that the laws unconstitutionally infringe on the president's powers. Many members of Congress, on the other hand, are happy to duck responsibility and accept the president's interpretation of events and of his powers, even at the expense of their own institution's standing in the constitutional system. The result: Congressional participation in national security policy making varies from case to case, driven by political calculations as well as by legal and national security considerations.

The fight against terrorism poses special challenges for members of Congress. More classified activity, more covert action, and a bewildering array of technologies are involved. Increased domestic police activity is conducted under the umbrella of national security. The need for quick, coordinated, multiagency action is intensified. Congress is not capable of effectively checking such executive action. Congress is open and slow, its division of labor among committees is not well matched to the executive agencies involved, and its members are hesitant to challenge the executive branch on high-risk policies and in areas where the public is likely to defer to the president.

Congressional participation in policy making related to the war against terrorism tends to be limited to a few members. The president consults with top party leaders, and agency officials brief members of the intelligence and defense committees. Average members are not regularly informed about developments in the war. They are asked to support funding for the war without having access to all relevant information.

More aggressive oversight of the national security agencies tends to occur when the party opposite the president controls one or both houses of Congress. With Republican majorities during most of the six years following the 9/11 attack, Congress did not actively pursue oversight hearings and investigations of the Republican administration's conduct of the war against terrorists or the war in Iraq. Democrats, after winning majorities in both houses in the 2006 elections, were more active in holding hearings on the Bush administration, as were the House Republicans in investigating the Obama administration after winning a majority in the 2010 elections.

In late 2014, the Senate Committee on Intelligence published a 525-page summary of its investigation of the Central Intelligence Agency's retention and interrogation program. The report, which took five years to prepare under supervision of the Democratic chair of the committee, focused on activities, including torture, that took place during the Republican Bush administration. By the time the report was released, Republicans already had won a majority of Senate seats in the next Congress and it was obvious that there would be no congressional action in response to the findings. The Democratic Obama administration expressed concern about the activities detailed in the report but promised no new action. The full report, comprising 6,000 pages, remains classified.

THE CHANGING CONGRESS

The manner in which representation and lawmaking are pursued in Congress have evolved in important ways in recent decades. As this chapter has implied, not all of these developments have improved representation or lawmaking. In the chapters that follow, many of these developments are given a closer look. However serious we may judge the problems of today's Congress to be, we should remember that Congress is a remarkably resilient institution. Its place in the political process is not threatened. It is rich in resources; critics even charge that it is too strong. Despite the attacks on Congress from many quarters, the legitimacy of its decisions is not seriously questioned by the chief executive, the courts, the states, or the American people.

We have emphasized the partisan polarization and centralized power in today's Congress. With the frequent overlay of divided party control of the House, Senate, and presidency in the last three decades, deepening divisions between the parties has made legislating more difficult. The result has been the more complete exploitation of procedural weapons, delays in acting on necessary legislation, and deadlock on issues that most Americans think require new policy. With no issues or political factions emerging to upset this pattern, it is likely to continue until one party gains effective control of all three institutions.

Even with deeply entrenched partisan divisions, trends in American society have been reflected, perhaps quite slowly, in the demographic composition and life experiences of the members of Congress. Changes in how political campaigns are run influence the everyday behavior of members who seek reelection. Legislators have adopted Internet-based technologies, including social media, to advertise themselves. Past policy decisions have created budget constraints on Congress that have greatly affected congressional politics. The ease of communication and travel, along with the flow of large sums of money, has altered the community of organized interest groups and lobbying efforts that surrounds Congress.

Perhaps the most significant concern is the state of congressional power in the American system. Congressional gridlock has encouraged presidents to more frequently assert constitutional and statutory authority to act unilaterally to address issues. And Congress acts less effectively as a check on presidential power in both international and national affairs when partisan considerations trump institutional interests in driving members' responses to presidential proposals and actions.

SUGGESTED READINGS

A. The following books address the dysfunction, low public esteem, and institutional challenges of Congress in recent years.

Fisher, Louis. *On Appreciating Congress: The People's Branch.* Boulder, CO: Paradigm Publishers, 2010.

Hibbing, John R., and Elizabeth Theiss-Morse. *Congress as Public Enemy*. Cambridge: Cambridge University Press, 1995.

Mann, Thomas E., and Norman J. Ornstein, *It's Even Worse Than It Looks: How the American Constitutional System Collided with the New Politics of Extremism*. New York: Basic Books, 2012.

B.   The following books discuss the importance of electing women and minorities to Congress and other public offices.

Carroll, Susan J. *The Impact of Women in Public Office*. Bloomington: Indiana University Press, 2001.

Dodson, Debra L. *The Impact of Women in Congress*. Oxford: Oxford University Press, 2006.

Lawless, Jennifer L., and Richard L. Fox. *It Still Takes a Candidate: Why Women Don't Run for Office*, Cambridge: Cambridge University Press, 2010.

Swain, Carol. *Black Faces, Black Interests: The Representation of African Americans in Congress*. Cambridge, MA: Harvard University Press, 1993.

Whitby, Kenny J. *The Color of Representation: Congressional Behavior and Black Interests*. Ann Arbor: University of Michigan Press, 1998.

DISCUSSION QUESTIONS

1   Why is Congress so unpopular? Why do individual members of Congress receive higher approval ratings than does Congress as a whole?

2   What are the important trends in the way that congressional policy making is conducted? What are the consequences of those trends for the role of individual legislators? What are the consequences of those trends for the role of parties and their leaders?

3   What effects are the demographic trends in the composition of Congress likely to have on policy making?

2 Representation and Lawmaking in Congress

The Constitutional and Historical Contexts

The caning of Charles Sumner (R-Massachusetts) by Preston Brooks (D–South Carolina). Brooks was upset by Sumner's speech against slavery.

Cartoonist rendition of the first brawl on the House floor between Matthew Lyon (Democratic-Republican-Vermont) and Roger Griswold (Federalist-Connecticut). Lyon allegedly spit in Griswold's face after a heated debate, and Griswold responded by attacking Lyon with a cane. Mayhem ensued as Lyon fought back with a fireplace poker as other House members looked on.

In representation and lawmaking, rules matter. The Constitution creates both a system of representation and a process for making law through two chambers of Congress and a president. One constitutional rule determines the official constituencies of representatives and senators; another determines how members of Congress are elected and how long they serve. Other constitutional rules outline the elements of the legislative process – generally the House, Senate, and president must agree on legislation before it can become law, unless a two-thirds majority of each chamber override a presidential veto. More detailed rules about the electoral and legislative processes are left for federal statutes, state laws, and internal rules of the House and Senate.

Although the constitutional rules governing representation and lawmaking have changed in only a few ways since Congress first convened in 1789, other features of congressional politics have changed in many ways. The Constitution says nothing about congressional parties and committees, yet most legislation in the modern Congress is written in committees. Committees are appointed through the parties, and party leaders schedule legislation for consideration on the floor. In this chapter, we describe the basic elements of the representation and lawmaking processes and provide an overview of the development of the key components of the modern legislative process.

REPRESENTATION AND LAWMAKING

Congress serves two, not always compatible, purposes – representation and lawmaking. Members of the House and Senate represent individual districts or states, yet they are entrusted to act collectively to make laws for the nation as a whole. Collective action on divisive issues entails bargaining and compromise – among the members of each chamber, between the House and the Senate, and between Congress and the president. For compromise to be possible, members sometimes must retreat from their commitments to their individual states and districts. Determining who must compromise – and how to get them to do so – is the essence of legislative politics. The process can be messy, even distasteful, but, if it is to serve the nation, it is unavoidable.

Congress can be properly evaluated only by understanding our own conflicting expectations about the institution and about the politicians who work within it. To sort out the issues, we begin with a brief introduction explaining how representation and lawmaking occur in practice on Capitol Hill. As we will see, achieving both perfect representation and perfect lawmaking, in the ways we desire each of them, is impossible.

Representation

REPRESENTATION BY INDIVIDUAL LAWMAKERS. Members of the House and Senate are expected to be *representatives* of their constituents back home. That is not a very precise job description. We might think that a representative's job is to faithfully present the views of his or her district or state in Congress – that is, to serve as a *delegate* for his or her constituents. A delegate-legislator, however, would not have an easy job because constituents often have conflicting or ambiguous views (or none at all) about the issues before Congress. Alternatively, a member of Congress might be considered a *trustee* – representing his or her constituents by exercising independent judgment about the interests of district, state, or nation. It is impossible to be a both a faithful delegate and a true trustee.

A third possibility is to see the representative as a *politico* – someone who behaves as a delegate on issues that are important to his or her constituents but on other issues has leeway in setting personal policy priorities and casting votes. Unfortunately, for many members of Congress, constituents are not likely to agree either about which issues are important or about when legislators should act as delegates and when they should exercise their own discretion. The challenge for the politician is to balance these legitimate, but often competing, expectations.

TABLE 2.1. Two forms of aggregating policy preferences in the public and in Congress

District	District's policy position on a 5-point scale	Legislator's policy position on a 5-point scale	Difference between district and legislator
A	5	1	4
B	4	2	2
C	3	3	0
D	2	4	−2
E	1	5	−4
–	–	–	–
	3.0	3.0	0.0

Source: Adapted from Robert S. Weissberg, "Collective vs. Dyadic Representation in Congress," *American Political Science Review* 72 (1978): 535–537.

REPRESENTATION BY CONGRESS. Even if individual legislators can be considered good representatives for their own constituents, we might still wonder whether Congress can adequately represent the nation as a whole. Congress could be considered a delegate or trustee of the nation. As a delegate institution, Congress would be expected to enact policies reflecting nationwide public opinion, but public opinion is often conflicted, ambiguous, or undeveloped. As a trustee institution, Congress would be expected to formulate policy in a manner consistent with its members' collective judgment about the nation's interests, whatever the state of public opinion. Members regularly invoke public opinion (a delegate perspective) or claim that Congress must do what is right (a trustee perspective) in their arguments for or against specific legislation.

COLLECTIVE VERSUS DYADIC REPRESENTATION. In practice, the correspondence between the quality of representation at the district or state level and that at the national level might be quite weak. To see this, imagine an issue on which five legislators from different districts take varying positions. As Table 2.1 illustrates, even if the legislators are not well matched to their districts, they can collectively represent the nation well. That is, *collective* representation can be good even when *dyadic* representation is not. Congruence between policy and public opinion may be poor at the state or district level but perfect at the national level. As a general rule, a legislative body will be at least as good a delegate for the nation as are individual members for their district or state.[1]

The logic of Table 2.1 does not guarantee that the House, the Senate, and the president will be able to agree on legislation. In fact, James Madison, the chief architect of the Constitution, hoped not. Madison argued that policy should not necessarily reflect the majority's views. He justified the creation of

1 Robert S. Weissberg, "Collective vs. Dyadic Representation in Congress," *American Political Science Review* 72 (1978): 535–547.

an independent executive branch (the presidency) and a bicameral legislature (the two chambers of Congress) on the grounds that policy should not simply reflect majority public opinion. He gave the president and the members of the two chambers terms of different lengths, specified different means of selecting them, and gave the president the power to sign or veto legislation. Madison expected the two chambers and the president to reflect different interests, which would reduce the likelihood that a majority could capture all three institutions and impose its will on a minority.

PARTY AND GROUP REPRESENTATION. We often think of political parties and other groups as representing parts of the nation. Nearly all members of Congress are recognized as either Democrats or Republicans and often are identified with other groups based on their gender, race, occupation, age, and other personal characteristics. Legislators, presidents, and the public usually see Congress in terms of its party composition. We speak of a "Republican Congress" or a "Democratic Congress," reflecting the importance of party control of the institution. Although voters choose between congressional candidates only in a single district or state, and no one votes directly for a Republican or Democratic majority in Congress as a whole, the party of the candidates and voters' views about which party should control Congress influence many voters and election outcomes. In turn, legislators tend to join with others of their own party to enact or block legislation, to develop and maintain a good reputation with the public, and to seek or retain majority control. Plainly, a great deal of representation occurs through the party mechanisms.

Although we do not often speak of a white-male, lawyer-dominated Congress, many people are conscious of the composition of Congress beyond its partisan or ideological makeup. A farming background is important for candidates in many areas of the country, whereas a union background is important in other areas. Organized caucuses of women, blacks, Hispanics, and other groups have formed among members of Congress, and groups outside Congress have developed to aid the election of more members from one group or another. It is said that increasing the number of women and minorities in Congress is essential because legislators' personal experiences can help shape their policy agendas. Moreover, the presence of role models in Congress may help motivate other members of these groups to seek public office.

THE TRADE-OFFS OF REPRESENTATION. We cannot hope for perfect representation in Congress. Our multiple expectations for representation can all be met only if Americans hold uniform views on questions of public policy. They do not. Trade-offs and compromise between the different forms and levels of representation are unavoidable. Neither the individual legislators nor the institution as a whole can simultaneously be a perfect delegate and a perfect trustee. In practice, we muddle through with mixed and changing forms of representation.

The Statue of Freedom stands on a pedestal at the top of the dome of the United States Capitol. It is bronze and stands 19.5 feet in height and weighs approximately 15,000 pounds.

Lawmaking

For Madison, representative government – also known as republican government – served two purposes. One was to make the law broadly responsive to the people. The other was to allow representatives, not the people themselves, to make law. This second purpose was, and still is, controversial. James Madison explained in *Federalist No. 10* that he hoped representatives would rise above the inevitable influence of public *opinion* to make policy in the public *interest*.

THE UNITARY DEMOCRACY MODEL. Madison's argument assumes that the common or public interest can be discovered by an elected representative through deliberation. In this view, the purpose of legislative debate is to discover those common interests through a process in which legislators share information, offer policy alternatives, and move toward a consensus on action to be taken. Building a consensus, rather than resolving conflicts by force of majority vote, is the object of this process. The emphasis on a common interest has led scholars to label this decision-making model *unitary democracy*.[2]

THE ADVERSARIAL DEMOCRACY MODEL. Madison's view may not be reasonable. Inherently conflicting interests may lead legislators to articulate those interests and decide controversies by the power of a larger number of votes. From this perspective, deliberation is viewed as needless delay to a majority that has no interest in compromise and has the votes to impose policies of its choosing. The majority naturally emphasizes the importance of efficiency and majority rule. The presence of conflicting interests leads us to call this decision-making process *adversarial democracy*.

THE TRADE-OFFS OF LAWMAKING. Congress cannot easily harmonize the ideals of both adversarial and unitary democracy. Deliberation and consensus building may seem to be the preferred model of decision making, but time and the compromise required will frustrate a majority eager to act. In practice, as for representation, Congress will make trade-offs among the ideal forms of lawmaking. Congress sometimes looks quite deliberative but will be pushed by majorities to be more efficient and will look, at least to outsiders, as quite adversarial and partisan. Moreover, the two chambers of Congress need not make the same trade-offs. As we see in later chapters, the smaller Senate continues to look more deliberative than the larger House, in large part because of significant differences in the rules that the two chambers have adopted over the decades to govern themselves.

The struggle to balance alternative models of representation and lawmaking never ends. Contending forces in American politics usually favor different models as they seek to define democratic processes that give them an advantage. An implication of our discussion is that most sides can find theoretical justification for their positions – to better represent Americans in Washington (usually meaning to increase the influence of one group or another) or to reform lawmaking processes (also usually meaning to increase the influence of one group or another). This is not to say that common interests do not sometimes exist or that the nation as a whole cannot at times be better represented. It is to argue that the history of Congress is not one of smooth progress toward "better" representation

2 Jane J. Mansbridge, *Beyond Adversarial Democracy* (Chicago: University of Chicago Press, 1983).

and lawmaking processes. Instead, it is a history of political conflict as parties and ambitious politicians sought to appeal for votes and determine policy choices.

THE PREDECESSORS OF CONGRESS

The First Congress convened on March 4, 1789, under the Constitution drafted in Philadelphia in the summer of 1787. Despite the newness of their institution, the members of the First Congress were not new to legislative politics. The American Congress shares the same roots as Great Britain's Parliament. The colonists brought with them British parliamentary practices and quickly established legislatures that governed in conjunction with governors appointed by the British crown. Beginning with Virginia's House of Burgesses in 1619, the colonial legislatures became both elected representative bodies and important lawmaking institutions almost immediately. Most of the legislatures followed procedures similar to those used in Parliament. Representation and lawmaking were well accepted features of self-governance long before the Constitutional Convention of 1787. Eventually, the usurpation of the powers of the colonial legislatures by British governors became a critical motivation for the Revolutionary War.

Besides their experience from the colonial era, the members of the First Congress had more recent legislative experience from participating in the Continental Congress and in their state legislatures in the years after independence. The first Continental Congress met in 1774, at the time of the Boston Tea Party and British assertion of military and political control over Massachusetts, as a step toward jointly working out differences between the colonies and the British government. The Continental Congress was not intended to be a permanent body but a temporary convention of delegates from the colonies. The crisis with Britain extended its life into the Revolutionary War, and its role in the new nation was formalized in 1781 with the ratification of the Articles of Confederation.

The Continental Congress was severely handicapped by its own rules. Very open floor procedures and a weak presiding officer undermined efforts to coordinate the diverse interests of the states and encouraged factionalism. The Articles of Confederation did nothing to change that. Although they legitimated the national government that the Continental Congress constituted, the articles gave the Congress few formal powers. The Continental Congress could not regulate commerce or raise taxes; and without executive and judicial institutions to implement and enforce the laws it passed, it was wholly dependent on the willingness of state governments to carry out its policies.

In contrast to the weak Continental Congress, most state legislatures were very powerful. The state constitutions adopted after independence gave the legislatures the power to appoint the state governors, guaranteeing that these officers would serve at the pleasure of the egalitarian, popularly elected branch. The new governors were not granted the power to veto legislation, and most were denied the power to make executive branch appointments, which were left to the legislature. Governors, it was hoped, would be mere administrators.

Soon legislative tyranny came to be viewed as a major problem. In the 1780s, an economic depression led debtors to demand relief from their creditors, and because debtors greatly outnumbered creditors, the legislatures obliged them. This undermined financial institutions, creating instability. Thomas Jefferson referred to the situation in Virginia as "elective despotism." Majority rule itself came to be questioned, and people began to wonder whether republican government was viable.

The practice of having a bicameral, or two-house, legislature was well established in the states by the time the Constitution was written in 1787. Britain had evolved a bicameral parliament based on its social class system, with the different classes represented in the House of Commons and the House of Lords. All of the American colonies except for Pennsylvania and Georgia had bicameral legislatures in 1776. Even after the Revolutionary War, when the British model was called into question, most states continued with a bicameral legislature. Debate over the proper relationship between the two chambers was frequent, and the states experimented with different means for electing their senates. Representing

A child sleds on Capitol Hill in March 2015. The Capitol Police Board continues to enforce a ban on sledding on the grounds despite pleas from members of Congress to allow sledding.

different classes in different institutions had lost its appeal, but the idea of preventing one house from becoming too powerful was widely discussed. By 1787, most political observers were keenly aware of the strengths and weaknesses of bicameral systems.

Congressionally Speaking . . .

The terms *unicameral* and *bicameral* come from the Latin word *camera*, which means "chamber." Under the Articles of Confederation, the national Congress was unicameral – one chamber – but many state legislatures were bicameral. The Constitution, of course, provided for a bicameral Congress. Among today's American state legislatures, only Nebraska's legislature is unicameral. Nebraska adopted the unicameral form in 1934 after using the bicameral form until then.

THE CONSTITUTION'S RULES OF THE GAME

Against the backdrop of an ineffectual Continental Congress and often tyrannical state legislatures, the framers of the national Constitution sought a new balance in 1787. They constructed a stronger national government with a powerful Congress whose actions could be checked by the president and the Supreme Court.

For the making of public law, the Constitution establishes a specific process, involving three institutions of government, with a limited number of basic rules. The House of Representatives, the Senate, and the president must all agree to enact a new law, with the House and Senate expressing their agreement by simple majority vote. If the president vetoes the measure, two-thirds of the members of the House and of the Senate must agree to override the veto. If any of the three players withholds consent or if a presidential veto is upheld, the legislation dies.

The Constitution also provides for the election of members of Congress and of the president, prohibits legislation of certain kinds, specifies the size of the majority required in Congress for specific actions, and identifies the player who must make the first or last moves in certain circumstances. In addition, the Constitution allows the Supreme Court to determine whether Congress and the president have abided by its rules.

The framers of the Constitution gave Congress tremendous political power. Article I, Section 8 of the Constitution grants to Congress broad discretion to "provide for the common defense and general welfare of the United States." It also specifies the basic powers of the national government and grants to Congress the authority to make laws to implement those powers. This general grant of power is supplemented by more specific provisions. Congress is given the power to tax, to regulate the economy, to create courts under the Supreme

Court, to create and regulate military forces, and to declare war. Section 9 grants Congress control over government spending: "No money shall be drawn from the treasury, but in consequence of appropriations made by law."

The Constitution entrusts the Senate with the authority to ratify treaties and confirm presidential nominations to executive and judicial offices. Congress can regulate congressional and presidential elections and must approve agreements between individual states and between states and foreign governments. The breadth of Congress's powers is reinforced in the "elastic clause," which provides that Congress can "make all laws which shall be necessary and proper for carrying into execution" the powers enumerated in the Constitution.

To protect members of Congress from personal intimidation by executive, judicial, or local officials, the framers of the Constitution devised several important clauses. First, beyond the age and citizenship requirements, the Constitution leaves to each house of Congress the authority to judge the qualifications of its members, to rule on contested election outcomes, and to punish or expel members for inappropriate behavior. Second, the Constitution protects members from arrest during and en route to and from sessions of Congress. Third, no member may be questioned by prosecutors, a court, or others about any congressional speech or debate. Members may be arrested and tried for treason, felonies, and breach of the peace, but they cannot be held personally liable by other government officials for their official actions as members of Congress.

Legislative Procedures

With respect to the details of the legislative process, the Constitution offers little guidance, with a few important exceptions. First, the framers of the Constitution were careful to provide that each chamber keep a journal recording its actions (Article 1, Section 5). Additionally, they required that the votes of individual members on any matter be recorded in the journal at the request of one-fifth of the members, known as "ordering the yeas and nays." In the Senate, the yeas and nays are taken by having a clerk call out each member's name and recording the response by hand. In the House, the yeas and nays have been recorded by an electronic system since 1973.

Second, the framers provided that tax bills originate in the House. Because the Senate was originally to be selected by state legislatures, with only the House directly elected by the people, it was thought that the initiative for imposing taxes should lie with the House. The Constitution provides that "all bills for raising revenue shall originate in the House of Representatives; but the Senate may propose or concur with amendments as on other bills." The Senate has used a variety of gimmicks to circumvent this restriction, but the House generally has jealously guarded its constitutional prerogatives and spurned Senate efforts to initiate tax bills.

Third, the Constitution requires that "a majority of each [house] shall constitute a quorum to do business" (Article I, Section 5). In principle, a majority of the members of a chamber must be present at all times, but like many other rules, this one is not enforced unless a member raises a point of order – that is, unless a member asks the chair for a ruling that a quorum is not present. This is sometimes used as a dilatory tactic. In the Senate, quorum calls have become a routine way to take a time-out – while the clerk calls the roll of senators' names, senators can confer in private or wait for colleagues to arrive. The most important implication of this constitutional provision is that a majority of members must be present and vote on a measure for the vote to count. To prevent absence from being used as an obstructionist ploy, the Constitution further provides that each house "may be authorized to compel the attendance of absent members."

The Legacy of 9/11 for the Constitution, Statutes, and House Rules

The terrorist attacks of September 11, 2001, led members of Congress and other congressional observers to worry about how the institution would function if an attack on the Capitol complex killed a large number of legislators. In 2002, the resolution providing for the adjournment of the 107th Congress provided that representatives and senators designated by the Speaker and Senate majority leader be allowed to call Congress into session in the event that those two leaders were killed or incapacitated. Without the provision, only the president could have called the Congress into special session, as the Constitution provides, but legislators believed that Congress should be prepared to act as an independent branch of government. In 2003, the House adopted three rules to address such a possibility. One rule requires the Speaker to establish a list of members who, in order, could serve as Speaker Pro Tem if the Speaker died or was incapacitated. This provision would allow the House to convene to elect a new Speaker. A second rule allows the Speaker to recess the House if there is an imminent threat to members' safety. Previously, the Speaker was not allowed to recess the House if business was pending. A third rule allows the Speaker to lower the number of members counted for the purposes of a quorum when a member dies, resigns, or is expelled. Without the change, a majority of the 435 possible members would have to be present for the House to conduct business. The new rule allows the total possible to be reduced to the number of seats that are currently filled.

In the view of some observers, the measures taken to date are inadequate. Enacted legislation to require special House elections of substitute legislators within forty-five days of a deadly attack is considered ineffective – no states have altered their laws to conform to the requirement. In 2005, the House adopted a rule that allows the House to act temporarily without a full quorum by empowering the Speaker (or his or her designee) to reduce the number required for a quorum after a series of lengthy quorum calls. Many observers doubt that this rule is constitutional because it appears to violate Article I, Section 5 of the Constitution, which provides that "a majority of each shall constitute a quorum to do business." A private study group recommended an amendment to the Constitution that would provide for quick and temporary appointment of replacements by state governors in the event of the death or incapacity of the incumbent, or by declaration of a national emergency by the House. The proposed amendment received only sixty-three votes in the House in 2004 and has not been voted on in the Senate.

The Senate is less of a problem. In nearly all states, governors are authorized by law to appoint replacement senators after the death of the incumbent. However, senators have expressed concern that the inability to gain a quorum in a national emergency would incapacitate the Senate. Legislation has been introduced to provide for temporary appointments if the majority and minority leaders jointly determine that the absence of a quorum to conduct business was caused by the inability of senators to discharge the duties of their office. States would determine how the temporary appointments would be made. No action has been taken on the proposal, which its sponsors recognized would have to be preceded by a constitutional amendment authorizing the process.

Counting a Quorum

Article I, Section 5 of the Constitution requires that a quorum be present for either the House or Senate to conduct business, but it is silent as to how one actually counts the quorum. Traditionally, a quorum was counted via a roll call vote, with members in attendance answering "present." In the late nineteenth century, House minority party members would often refuse to answer a quorum call in order to obstruct or delay House business. These "disappearing quorums" were effective because it was rare to have all elected House members present in the Capitol at the same time. As a result, House majorities struggled to enact legislation without first gaining consent of large segments of the minority party.

Frustration with the disappearing quorum boiled over at the outset of the 51st Congress (when minority party Democrats refused to vote on the seating of a Republican House member). House Speaker Thomas B. Reed (R-Maine) took the unprecedented step of ordering the clerk to count members who were present but not voting for the purposes of establishing a quorum. Contemporary accounts report that "pandemonium" reigned in the House as some Democrats sought to appeal and denounce the ruling; others tried to flee the chamber, and Reed ordered the doors locked to prevent this. After three days of heated debate, House Republicans supported Reed's assertion of his power to count a physical quorum and the disappearing quorum ceased to be an effective minority strategy in the House.

Finally, the framers outlined the process of presidential approval or disapproval of legislation (Article I, Section 7). After each chamber has passed a bill, it must be presented to the president, whose options depend on whether Congress has adjourned in the meantime. Congress has an opportunity to override a president's veto only if Congress remains in session (see box, "Constitutional Procedures for Presidential Approval or Disapproval of Legislation"). If Congress adjourns, the president can kill a bill by either vetoing it or taking no action on it (which is known as a pocket veto). Congress may pass a new bill if the president successfully kills a bill.

Constraints on Congressional Power

Although the framers of the Constitution intended Congress to be a powerful policy-making body, they also feared the exercise of that power. This concern produced: (1) explicit restrictions on the use of legislative power; (2) a system of three separate institutions (House, Senate, and president) that share legislative powers; (3) a system of direct and indirect representation of the people, in Congress and by the president; and (4) a Supreme Court that judges the constitutionality of legislation and interprets ambiguities in legislative outcomes. The result is a legislative process that cannot address certain subjects, is motivated by political considerations, is likely to involve bargaining, and is biased against enacting new legislation.

Constitutional Procedures for Presidential Approval or Disapproval of Legislation

If Congress remains in session, the president may sign a bill into law, veto the bill and send it with a statement of his objections back to the house in which the bill originated, or do nothing. If the president vetoes the bill, two-thirds of both houses must vote to approve the bill (and thus override the veto) for it to become law. If the president does nothing by the end of ten days (excluding Sundays), the bill becomes law.

If Congress adjourns before ten days, the president may sign the bill into law, veto it, or do nothing. Because Congress has adjourned, it cannot consider overriding a veto, so a vetoed bill will die. Likewise, if the president takes no action by the end of ten days (excluding Sundays), the bill will die. Killing a bill by failing to take action on it before Congress adjourns has come to be known as making a pocket veto.

There have been disputes between Congress and recent presidents about the meaning of a temporary congressional recess. Presidents have argued that they may pocket veto a measure or make a recess appointment while Congress is in recess for a holiday or another purpose, even though Congress has not adjourned *sine die* (formally adjourned at the end of a two-year Congress). Many members of Congress disagree. The Supreme Court sided with Congress in the case of *National Labor Relations Board v. Canning* (2014) and invalidated three recess appointments that had been made by President Obama.

EXPLICIT RESTRICTIONS. A list of powers explicitly denied Congress is provided in Article I, Section 9 of the Constitution. For example, Congress may not tax state exports, pass bills of attainder (pronouncing guilt and sentencing someone without a trial), or adopt ex post facto laws (altering the legal standing of a past action). The list of explicit limitations was extended by the 1791 ratification of the first ten amendments to the Constitution – the Bill of Rights. Among other things, the Bill of Rights prohibits laws that abridge freedom of speech, freedom of the press, and the freedom to peaceably assemble (Amendment 1) and preserves the right to a jury trial in certain cases (Amendments 6 and 7). The

Bill of Rights reserves to the states, or to the people, powers not delegated to the national government by the Constitution (Amendment 10).

In practice, the boundary between allowed and disallowed legislative acts is often fuzzy. Efforts by Congress to exercise its powers have often conflicted with individual rights or with powers asserted by the president and the states.

The Supreme Court has resolved many ambiguities about where the lines should be drawn around the powers of Congress, but many remain for future court consideration. In some cases, particularly in the foreign policy realm, the Supreme Court has left the ambiguities to be worked out between Congress and the president.

SEPARATE INSTITUTIONS SHARING POWER. Rather than creating a single legislature that represents the people and determines laws, the framers of the Constitution created three institutions – the House, the Senate, and the presidency – that share legislative powers. Formally, legislation may originate in either the House or the Senate, with the exception of bills raising revenue. The president may call Congress into special session and is required to recommend measures to Congress from time to time. The president's recommendations carry great weight, but the president cannot formally introduce legislation or compel Congress to act on the recommendations. Legislative measures are formally initiated in Congress, and once passed by both chambers, they must be sent to the president for approval or veto.

A special arrangement was established for treaties with foreign governments, which also have the force of law. The Constitution (Article II, Section 2) provides that the president "shall have power, by and with the advice and consent of the Senate to make treaties, provided two-thirds of the senators present concur." Therefore, the president formally initiates legislative action on a treaty by submitting it to the Senate, and a two-thirds majority of the Senate must approve it for the treaty to be ratified. The House is excluded from formal participation. Nevertheless, the House participates in foreign policy making by sharing with the Senate the power to restrict the uses of the federal treasury, to declare war, and to regulate foreign commerce. The House also participates in foreign policy decisions that require congressional appropriations or changes in American domestic law, such as trade agreements.

Just as the president is an integral part of legislating, the Congress is central to implementing laws. The Constitution obligates the president to "take care that the laws be faithfully executed" and grants to the president the authority to appoint "officers" of the United States. The Constitution, however, requires that the president's appointees be confirmed by the Senate, allows Congress to establish executive departments by law and the means for appointing "inferior" officers of the executive branch, and grants Congress the authority to remove the president or other officers for "treason, bribery, or other high crimes and misdemeanors." Perhaps most importantly, the Constitution requires that Congress approve funding for all government activities, a power that gives the institution the ability to limit the activities to which public funds may be dedicated.

Therefore, interdependence, not exclusivity, characterizes the powers of the House, the Senate, and the president.

DIRECT AND INDIRECT REPRESENTATION. The framers of the Constitution wanted the government to be responsive to popular opinion, but they also wanted to limit the possibility that some faction could gain simultaneous control of the House, Senate, and presidency and then legislate to violate the rights of others. Only members of the House of Representatives were to be directly elected by the people. Senators were to be chosen by state legislatures, and the president was to be chosen by an electoral college composed of individuals chosen by the states. Furthermore, House, Senate, and presidential elections were put on different timetables. The entire House is elected every two years, senators serve six-year terms (with one-third of the seats up for election every two years), and presidents stand for election every four years.

The result is a mix of constraints and opportunities for the legislative players. By providing for direct election for the House and indirect election for the Senate and president, the framers of the Constitution expected that electoral considerations would play an important part in shaping legislative outcomes. The framers, however, hoped that their indirect election, along with their longer terms of office, would desensitize senators and presidents to narrow interests and rapid shifts in public opinion. This safeguard was considered particularly important in the case of treaties and major appointments to the executive agencies and the judiciary, which are left to the president and the Senate.

Concern about the responsiveness of senators to special interests rather than to the public will led to the adoption in 1913 of the Seventeenth Amendment to the Constitution, which provided for direct election of senators. Direct election of senators reduced the difference between the House and the Senate with respect to their link to the electorate. Nevertheless, because senators represent whole states and representatives are selected from small districts regulated by size, along with the difference in their terms of office, it remains likely that the House and Senate will have somewhat different preferences about public policy and can frequently be controlled by different parties. The requirement that both chambers approve legislation creates a bias against the enactment of legislation and increases the probability that successful legislation will represent a compromise among competing views.

JUDICIAL REVIEW AND STATUTORY INTERPRETATION. Since 1803, when the Supreme Court issued its opinion in *Marbury v. Madison*, the federal courts have assumed the power to review the acts of Congress and the president and determine their constitutionality. This power of judicial review gives the courts, and ultimately the Supreme Court, the final authority to judge and interpret the meaning of the Constitution. The courts' interpretations of the Constitution often limit the policy options that can be considered by Congress and the president.

In addition, the federal courts interpret the meaning of laws passed by Congress – statutory interpretation. Individuals, organizations, and governments that are disadvantaged by executive branch interpretations of laws often file suit in federal courts. The courts are asked to resolve ambiguities or conflicting provisions in statutes. For guidance about congressional intentions, the courts rely on previous cases, congressional committee reports, the records of floor debate, and other sources on the legislative history of a statute. Court interpretations are often anticipated by legislative players and subsequently shape the legislative language employed by these players. Legislators, in turn, often take court rulings into account when drafting legislation.

Judicial review and statutory interpretation are exercised by federal judges who themselves are partially dependent on the legislative players. The Constitution provides that Congress may establish federal courts below the Supreme Court and that the president nominates judges to the federal courts with the consent of the Senate. Congress also has required that lower court judges be nominated by the president and confirmed by the Senate. To protect federal judges from the influence of presidents and members of Congress, however, the Constitution insulates them from potential sources of presidential and congressional manipulation by granting them life terms (although they may be removed by Congress for treason, bribery, or other high crimes and misdemeanors) and preventing Congress and the president from reducing their salaries. The effects of these provisions are discussed in Chapter 10.

CONGRESSIONAL DEVELOPMENT

Since the ratification of the Constitution, the United States has been transformed from a small, agrarian nation with little significance in international affairs to the world's largest industrial power and sole military and political superpower. Rapid changes occurred during the Industrial Revolution of the late nineteenth century, when industry was transformed by new technologies, many new states were added to the union, modern political parties took form, and federal policies gained greater significance. These conditions changed public demands on members of Congress, who in turn changed their expectations of their institution. By the early twentieth century, many features of the modern Congress had taken form. In the late twentieth century, the Cold War ended but was replaced by threats of world terrorism, economic and environmental challenges, and other developments that tested Congress's decision-making processes and increased the power of the president.

The Constitution provided only limited guidance to the House and Senate about how they should organize themselves. The House, according to the

Constitution, elects a Speaker to preside, whereas the vice president serves as the Senate's president. The Senate is also authorized to elect a president *pro tempore* (or "pro tem") to preside in the absence of the vice president. The Constitution implies that the House and Senate pass legislation by majority vote.

Congressionally Speaking . . .

In the context of the legislative process, *rules* can be a confusing term. Although the Constitution outlines the basic features of the legislative process, each house of Congress has lengthy rules governing its internal affairs. In addition, Congress has placed rules governing its proceedings in many statutes, such as the Budget Act, which sets a timetable and special procedures for considering budget measures. Standing committees have their own rules, such as rules establishing subcommittees and providing procedures for committee meetings and hearings. Each of the four congressional party organizations (House Democrats and Republicans, Senate Democrats and Republicans) has its own rules to govern the election of party leaders, create party committees, and govern meetings. Chamber, committee, and party rules have been elaborated in many ways in recent decades as reformers have sought to reduce arbitrary rule by committee and party leaders.

The Constitution says nothing about how legislation is to be prepared for a vote. Instead, it grants each chamber the authority to establish its own rules. Since their origin in 1789, the two houses of Congress have each accumulated rules, procedural precedents, and informally accepted practices that form their legislative processes. The two chambers have developed similar legislative organizations, but their parliamentary rules differ in important ways, which are detailed in Chapter 7.

The modern houses of Congress have parties and committees that organize nearly all of their activities. Nearly all legislation passes through one or more committees in each house. Members of those committees take a leading role in writing the details of bills, dominating floor debate on those measures, and representing their house in conference committee negotiations with the other house. Parties appoint members to committees, give order to floor debate, and are given proportional representation on conference committees. The majority party in each chamber takes the lead in setting the agenda. These can both be considered endogenous institutions because both were created by the members to meet their collective political needs.

Parties

We now assume that the presiding officer of the House, the Speaker, will be the leader of the majority party and will be responsible for setting the legislative agenda of the House. Similarly, we assume that the Senate's majority leader will

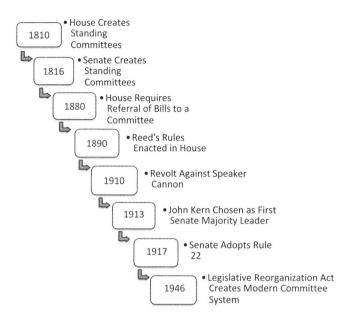

Figure 2.1 Timeline of Major Events in Congressional Development.

set the agenda for that chamber. In the early Congresses, however, no formally recognized party leaders existed. In fact, it took nearly a century for the House to develop something like its modern party-based leadership structure, and the Senate took even longer. The Constitution, of course, is silent on the role of parties in Congress. Congressional parties developed only gradually, as parties outside Congress formed to compete in elections. Politicians and others seeking to get elected or to elect others have always taken the lead in creating political parties. Congressional party organizations have formed among newly elected members of the same party or, as has happened a few times, when sitting members create new parties to compete for reelection. They have varied in strength and influence as the degree of consensus about policy goals and political strategies has varied among their members. See Figure 2.1 for a timeline of key events in congressional development.

EARLY FOUNDATIONS. Groups of legislators have collaborated to influence policy outcomes from the beginning. By the time of the Third Congress (1793–1795), shifting coalitions within the legislature had settled into partisan groups, which began making organized efforts to get like-minded individuals elected. In the administration of George Washington, these groups were led by opposing cabinet officers (Jefferson and Madison vs. Hamilton). For a generation, the parties remained groups of elites, largely members of Congress and executive branch officials who shared party labels – at first, Republicans and Federalists. The congressional and presidential elections of 1800 initiated a period of Republican dominance that lasted until 1824. During that period, when the Federalist

Party faded away, members had clear party affiliations and gradually developed party caucuses to coordinate party activities. There were still no formal party leadership posts in the House or Senate.

Until late in the nineteenth century, Speakers of the House were not their parties' top party leader. The one exception was Speaker Henry Clay of Kentucky, who, largely by force of personality, became the leading Whig late in his six nonconsecutive terms (the first starting in 1811). Generally, party factionalism, and sometimes assertive presidents, kept Speakers relatively weak. In fact, small shifts in the balance of power among factions within a party often led to the election of a new Speaker. Clay's successors in the speakership enjoyed the power to make committee assignments, but this ability was insufficient to provide a foundation for party leadership. In fact, the most coveted committee assignments were usually promised in advance during the multicandidate contests for the speakership itself. Meaningful party leadership came from informally identified leaders whose skills and factions made them suited to guiding party activities.

During the nineteenth century, the Senate did not have party leadership positions at all, except for caucus chairmen, whose duties and powers usually amounted to little more than presiding over caucus meetings. Strong regional leaders, like John C. Calhoun (D-South Carolina), Clay, and Daniel Webster (Whig-Massachusetts), tended to dominate Senate parties without holding formal leadership positions. The first steps toward more party-based control of the chamber were taken in the middle of the nineteenth century. Conflict over control of standing committees led the parties in 1845 to rely on caucus meetings to prepare committee lists, and in 1847 the Democrats created a "committee on committees" to coordinate the task of making committee assignments for the party. In late 1859, the new Republican Party formed its own committee on committees.

PARTY GOVERNMENT. The Civil War was an important turning point in the organization of the parties in Congress. Republicans were the dominant party during the war and began to use task forces and steering committees to coordinate the work of the House and Senate. After the war, the two major parties – now the Republicans and the Democrats – settled into broad regional divisions, with the Republicans powerful in the Northeast and the Midwest and the Democrats dominating the South. House Speakers during the 1860s and 1870s were not particularly strong, but they were the recognized leaders of their parties.

In the early 1890s, under Speaker Thomas Brackett Reed (R-Maine), rulings of the Speaker and new House rules gave the Speaker more power to prevent obstructionism and allow House majorities to act (see box "Counting a Quorum"). These changes, stimulated in part by intensifying partisanship on major issues, firmly established party-based governance in the House. For the next two decades, House decision making was highly centralized and under the control of the majority party's leader, the Speaker. Speakers Reed and "Uncle Joe" Cannon (R-Illinois) so firmly controlled the flow of legislative business that they were known as "czars." By the end of the first decade of the twentieth century, the press referred to Cannon's heavy-handed style as "Cannonism."

In the Senate, the presiding officer – the vice president – might not share the same party affiliation as the Senate majority and so was never trusted with powers similar to those of the House Speaker. During most of the 1800s, the parties had caucus chairmen but they did not acquire genuine leadership duties until very late in the century. Arthur Pue Gorman (D-Maryland), the Democratic Caucus chair, emerged as his party's floor leader in the 1890s, but Republicans did not follow his example. Instead, by the late 1890s and into the new century, a group of four Republican senators, led by Finance Committee chairman Nelson Aldrich (R-Rhode Island), dominated the party.

"Aldrichism" was sometimes paired with Cannonism in the press, but the absence of rules limiting debate or amendments in the Senate prevented the majority party from changing rules to bolster the authority of its leaders. As a result, minority party obstructionism was not overcome, as it was in the House. Any change in the rules that disadvantaged the minority party could be filibustered – that is, the minority could prevent a vote on a proposal to change the rules by refusing to conclude debate. Efforts by Aldrich and others to limit filibusters were themselves filibustered. Consequently, the ability of even the strongest majority party leaders to bring legislation to a vote was severely constrained by the possibility of a filibuster (see Chapter 7).

THE TWENTIETH-CENTURY PATTERN. In the first decade of the twentieth century, a fragmenting Republican Party altered congressional party politics for decades to come. Republican reformers in and out of Congress challenged Cannonism and Aldrichism. In 1910, a coalition of insurgent Republicans and minority party Democrats forced changes in House rules that substantially reduced the power of the Speaker. The Speaker was stripped of the chairmanship of and power to make appointments to the Rules Committee, which controlled resolutions that put important bills in order on the floor. In the next Congress, with a new Democratic majority, the Speaker's power to make committee assignments was turned over to a party committee.

In the Senate, with few formal chamber or party rules relating to leadership, the fading of Aldrichism was more gradual than was the revolt against Cannon in the House. By the time the Democrats had gained a majority in 1913, no leader dominated either party, although Gorman and his successors as caucus chairs were known as the top party leaders. At a time when his party and the new president, Woodrow Wilson, wanted firmer Senate leadership, John Kern of Indiana was elected Democratic Caucus chairman and, in that capacity, also was known as the majority leader, the first recognized majority leader in the Senate. Soon afterward, the Republicans created the position of minority leader, and both parties appointed "whips" to assist the top leaders in managing their parties' business on the floor.

For decades, neither House Speakers nor Senate majority leaders enjoyed the level of influence that Speaker Cannon and Senator Aldrich had possessed at the turn of the century. With a few exceptions, top party leaders fell into a pattern of supporting and serving the needs of committees more than trying to lead them. This pattern was maintained until the 1970s. Developments since that time are discussed in Chapter 5.

Committees

Members of the first Congresses were influenced by their experiences in the Continental Congress and in their colonial and state legislatures. They devised mechanisms to allow congressional majorities to express their will, while maintaining the equality of all legislators. They preferred that each chamber, as a whole, determine general policy through discussion before entrusting a subgroup of the membership with the responsibility of devising detailed legislation. Because legislators feared that committees with substantial policy discretion and permanence might distort the will of the majority, House committees in the first eight or nine Congresses usually took the form of special or select committees that dissolved when their tasks were completed.

EARLY FOUNDATIONS. The House took the lead in developing the foundations of a standing committee system. By 1810, the House had created ten standing committees for routine policy areas and for several complex policy areas requiring regular investigation. The practice of referring legislation to a select committee gradually declined thereafter.

In its formative years, the Senate used select committees exclusively on legislative matters; it created only four standing committees to address internal housekeeping matters. A smaller membership, more flexible floor procedures, and a much lighter workload – with the Senate always waiting for the House to act first on legislation – permitted the Senate to use select committees in a wider variety of ways than did the House and still maintain full control over legislation. Beginning in 1806, however, the Senate adopted the practice of referring to the same committee all matters relating to the subject for which the committee had originally been formed, creating implicit jurisdictions for select committees.

In the decades before the Civil War, the standing committee systems of both chambers became institutional fixtures. Both houses of Congress began to rely on standing committees for the preliminary consideration of legislation and regularly increased the number of committees. In the House, the number of standing committees increased from ten to twenty-eight between 1810 and 1825 and to thirty-nine by the beginning of the Civil War. The Senate established its first major standing committees in 1816 when it created twelve. It had added ten more by the Civil War.

The expansion of the standing committee systems had roots in both chamber and party needs. A growing workload and regular congressional interaction with an increasing number of executive departments combined to induce committee growth. The House then began to outgrow a floor-centered decision-making process. The House grew from 64 members in 1789 to 241 in 1833, which made open-ended floor debate quite chaotic.

In the House, partisan considerations also were important. Henry Clay transformed the speakership into a position of policy leadership and increased the partisan significance of committee activity. Rather than allowing the full House to conduct a preliminary debate, Clay preferred to have a reliable group of friendly committee members write legislation. The Speaker's control of committee appointments made this possible. During Clay's era, two procedural changes transformed committees' places in the sequence of the House bill process and further enhanced the committees' value to the Speaker. First, the practice of allowing standing committees to report legislation to the full House at their own discretion was codified for a few committees into the rules of the House in 1822. Second, Clay made referral of legislation to a committee before floor debate the norm. By the late 1830s, after Clay had left the House, all House committees could introduce new legislation and report it to the floor at will. Preliminary debate by the House came to be viewed as a useless procedure. In fact, in 1880 the House adopted a formal rule that required newly introduced legislation to be referred to committee, which meant that the participation of the full membership was reserved for review of committee recommendations.

Changes to the Senate's committee system came at a slower pace. The Senate tended to wait for the House to act first on a bill before it took up a matter so its workload was not as heavy as the House workload. Additionally, the Senate did not grow as quickly as the House. In 1835, the Senate had only forty-eight members, fewer members than the House had during the First Congress; and, in sharp contrast to the House, factionalism led senators and their weak party leaders to distrust committees and avoid referral to unfriendly committees. As a result, the Senate's standing committees, with one or two important exceptions, played a relatively insignificant role in the legislative process before the Civil War. The Senate retained a more floor-centered process.

PARTY CONTROL. In the half-century after the Civil War, the role of committees was strongly influenced by new issues associated with industrialization and the dramatic population growth, further development of American political parties, and the increasing careerism of members. Both houses had a strong tendency to respond to new issues by creating committees rather than enlarging or reorganizing existing committee jurisdictions. Party leaders often liked the opportunity to appoint friendly members to the new committee put in charge of a new issue. In addition, committee chairs resisted efforts to eliminate committees. By 1918, the House had acquired nearly sixty committees and the Senate had seventy-four. Nearly half of the committees had no legislative or investigative business, but their existence allowed their chairmen to be assigned an office and hire a clerk.

The rapid growth in the number of committees in the late nineteenth century did not lead to a more decentralized Congress. Because of the stabilization of the two-party system and the cohesiveness of the majority-party Republicans in the late 1800s, majority party leaders of both houses used the established committee systems as tools for asserting control over policy choices. In the House, the period between the Civil War and 1910 brought a series of activist Speakers who aggressively used committee appointments to stack important committees with friendly members, sought and received new bill referral powers, and gave the Rules Committee, which the Speaker chaired, the authority to report resolutions that set the floor agenda. With these powers, the Speaker gained the ability to grant a right-of-way to certain legislation and to block other legislation.

Senate organization in the years after the Civil War was dictated by Republicans, who controlled that chamber for all but two Congresses between 1860 and 1913. The Republicans emerged from the war with no party leader or faction capable of controlling the Senate. Relatively independent committees and committee chairs became the dominant force in Senate deliberations. By the late 1890s, however, elections had made the Senate Republicans a smaller but more homogeneous group, with a coterie of like-minded members ascending to leadership positions. This group controlled the chamber's Committee on Committees, which made committee assignments, and the Steering Committee, which controlled floor scheduling. These developments made Senate committees agents of a small set of party leaders.

Party dominance did not last. After the revolt against Speaker Cannon in 1910, party cohesiveness and party leaders' ability to direct the legislative process declined substantially. With less central coordination and weaker party leaders, the bloated, fragmented committee systems became intolerable. Additionally, the more independent members began to acquire small personal staffs in the 1920s and no longer needed the clerical assistance that came with a committee chair. As a result, both chambers eliminated a large number of committees, most of which had been inactive for some time. Some formal links between party leaders and committees were broken as well. Because of reforms within the House Republican Party organization and similar policies adopted by the Democrats, the majority leader no longer chaired a major committee, chairs of major committees could not serve on the party's Steering Committee, and no committee chair could sit on the Rules Committee.

THE MODERN SYSTEM. The broad outline of the modern committee system was determined by the Legislative Reorganization Act of 1946. By 1945, most members shared concerns about the increasing size and expanding power of the executive branch that had come with the New Deal programs of the 1930s and then World War II. Critics noted that the large number of committees and their overlapping jurisdictions resulted in unequal distributions of work and participation among members, caused difficulties in coordination between the House and the Senate, and made oversight of executive agencies difficult. Committees also lacked adequate staff assistance to conduct studies of policy problems and executive branch activities.

The 1946 act reduced the number of standing committees to nineteen in the House and fifteen in the Senate by consolidating the jurisdictions of several groups of committees. The standing committees in each chamber were made nearly equal in size, and the number of committee assignments was reduced to one for most House members and two for most senators. Provisions dealing with regular committee meetings, proxy voting, and committee reports constrained chairs in some ways. The clear winners, however, were the chairs of the standing committees, who benefited from expanded committee jurisdictions and the addition of more committee staff, which they would direct. Chairs also continued to control their committees' agendas, subcommittee appointments, the referral of legislation to subcommittees, the management of committee legislation on the floor, and conference delegations.

Committees appeared to be quite autonomous in both chambers for the next decade and a half. Committee chairs exhibited great longevity. More than 60 percent of committee chairs serving between 1947 and 1964 held their position for more than five years, including approximately two dozen who served for more than a decade. In addition, by virtue of southern Democrats' seniority, chairs were disproportionately conservative. Southern Democrats, along with most Republicans, constituted a conservative coalition that used committees to block legislation favored by congressional and administration liberals.

A set of strong, informal norms seemed to govern individual behavior in the 1940s and 1950s. Two norms directly affected committees. First, members were expected to specialize in matters that came before their committees. Second, new members were expected to serve an apprenticeship period, during which they would listen and learn from senior members and refrain from actively participating in committee or floor deliberations. These norms emphasized the development of expertise in the affairs of one's own committee and deference to the assumed expertise of other committees. The collective justification for these norms was that the development of, and deference to, expertise would promote quality legislation. By the mid-1960s, new cohorts of members, particularly liberals, proved unwilling to serve apprenticeships and to defer to conservative committee chairs. Many members began to demand major reforms in congressional operations.

A five-year effort yielded the Legislative Reorganization Act of 1970. It required committees to make public all recorded votes, limited proxy votes, allowed a majority of members to call meetings, and encouraged committees to hold open hearings and meetings. House floor procedures were also affected – primarily by permitting recorded teller votes during the amending process and by authorizing (rather than requiring) the use of electronic voting. These changes made it more difficult for House and Senate committee chairs to camouflage their power in legislative jargon and hide their domination behind closed doors. As we will see, however, the reform movement did not end with the 1970 act. In fact, the act only set the stage for two decades of change in the role of committees in congressional policy making. The developments since the early 1970s are discussed in Chapter 6.

CONCLUSION

Congress's place in the constitutional scheme of representation and lawmaking was shaped by the experience with the Continental Congress and the state governments in the years following the Revolutionary War. The Constitution made Congress more powerful than the Continental Congress had been, but it also limited its power by dividing the policy-making process among the two chambers and the presidency and by imposing explicit constraints on the kinds of law that can be made. The Constitution provided only the most rudimentary instructions on how the two houses of Congress were to organize themselves to make law. Gradually, as members struggled to control policy choices and to meet changing demands, legislators created the key features of the modern Congress:

- legislative parties, which gather legislators with common political interests;
- committees, which write the details of most legislation;
- leadership positions in both parties and committees, which are held by elected and appointed legislators who organize most legislative business; and
- rules, which are now very complex and govern the activities of individual legislators, parties, committees, and the parent chambers.

By the 1920s, Congress had taken its modern form, with a full complement of party leaders and standing committees.

SUGGESTED READINGS

A. The following books discuss the historical development of congressional institutions.

Cooper, Joseph. *Congress and Its Committees: A Historical Approach to the Role of Committees in the Legislative Process.* New York: Garland Publishing, 1988.

Jenkins, Jeffery A., and Charles Stewart III. *Fighting for the Speakership: The House and the Rise of Party Government.* Princeton, NJ: Princeton University Press, 2012.

Remini, Robert V., and the Library of Congress. *The House: The History of the House of Representatives.* New York: Harper Collins, 2006.

Wirls, Daniel, and Stephen Wirls. *The Invention of the United States Senate.* Baltimore: Johns Hopkins University Press, 2004.

B.   The following books focus on the causes and consequences of institutional change.

Haynes, George H. *The Election of Senators.* New York: Henry Holt, 1906.

Polsby, Nelson W. *How Congress Evolves: Social Bases of Institutional Change.* Oxford: Oxford University Press, 2004.

Schiller, Wendy J., and Charles Stewart III. 2014. *Electing the Senate: Indirect Democracy before the Seventeenth Amendment.* Princeton, NJ: Princeton University Press.

Zelizer, Julian E. 2006. *On Capitol Hill: The Struggle to Reform Congress and Its Consequences, 1948–2000.* 1st pbk. ed. Cambridge: Cambridge University Press.

C.   The following books focus on representation in Congress.

Bishin, Benjamin. *Tyranny of the Minority: The Subconstituency Politics Theory of Representation.* Philadelphia: Temple University Press, 2009.

Schiller, Wendy. *Partners and Rivals: Representation in U.S. Senate Delegations.* Princeton, NJ: Princeton University Press, 2000.

DISCUSSION QUESTIONS

1 Why did committees and parties develop more slowly in the Senate than in the House?

2 Compare and contrast the delegate and trustee roles as they relate to representation.

3 How does the bicameral nature of Congress affect lawmaking and representation?

4 How does the standing committee system increase legislative efficiency?

3 Congressional Elections

Senate Majority Leader Mitch McConnell (R-Kentucky), his wife Elaine Chao, and Vice President Joe Biden participate in the reenactment swearing-in ceremony on Tuesday, January 6, 2015. McConnell won reelection in November 2014 and became majority leader of the Senate in January 2015.

The year 2014 marked a bad election year for congressional Democrats. They lost a net of thirteen seats in the House and nine seats in the Senate. This further solidified the Republican House majority and gave the Republicans majority control of the Senate for the first time since 2006. Midterm elections that occur during a president's second term in office are historically bad for candidates who share a party affiliation with the president. In the 2006 midterm elections, which occurred during President George W. Bush's second term in office, Republicans lost large numbers of House and Senate seats, which caused them to lose control of both chambers for the first time since 1995. In 2008, Democrats, led by a strong presidential candidate in Barack Obama, added to their House and Senate majorities, even briefly enjoying a so-called filibuster-proof or sixty-seat majority in the Senate. In 2010, the tables were turned as Republicans gained sixty-five House seats and majority control of the chamber, and narrowed the Democratic Party's margin in the Senate. In 2012, Democrats gained seats in both the House and Senate elections, but failed to win enough House seats to recapture the majority.

Recent election cycles stand out among elections in the past few decades in that national-level issues dominated the discussion in many states and districts. In 2006 and 2008, Republicans were weighed down by the declining popularity of President George W. Bush, based in large part on the public's declining view of the war in Iraq in 2006, and the nation's economic collapse in 2008. In 2010, the public's ire over high unemployment rates and slow economic growth dragged down President Barack Obama's approval ratings and disproportionately affected many Democratic congressional candidates. In 2012 and 2014, elections were more congruent than ever. In fact, the correlation between the House vote and the presidential vote reached an all-time high in 2012.[1]

Even when national issues play a major role in congressional campaigns, the strategic decisions to run or retire made by current and prospective candidates have the largest effect in determining the partisan makeup of each chamber. In 2006 and 2008, Democrats saw very few incumbent members choose to retire, but Republicans saw a number of incumbents retire rather than seek reelection. In these elections, Democrats had a seemingly unlimited supply of good challengers willing to target vulnerable Republicans, but Republicans struggled to convince strong candidates to challenge Democratic incumbents. As the 2006 and 2008 fall campaigns shaped up, Republicans were forced to play defense in vulnerable states and districts, while leaving potentially vulnerable Democrats without seriously funded challengers. The 2010 and 2014 elections were a mirror image of 2006 and 2008. Very few incumbent Republicans retired, and a number of Democrats chose not to seek reelection. At the same time, many newly elected Democrats saw strong, well-funded Republican challengers emerge, and Democrats struggled ineffectively to hold on to many of the seats they had gained in the preceding elections.

We place our discussion of elections early in the book because the general policy preferences of the key players – the House, the Senate, and the president – are a product of elections. Elections are selection devices. They are intended to be competitive processes in which some candidates win and others lose. The winners arrive in Washington with certain personal policy views and an idea of what their supporters expect of them. Collectively, the winners give shape to the

1 Data reported by Gary C. Jacobson at the 2012 Postelection Conference at the University of Georgia.

balance of policy preferences within the House and Senate and determine the broad contours of agreement and disagreement among the House, the Senate, and the president. Policy alignments change to some degree with each congressional and presidential election.

The Changing Congress: Republicans Solve Their Primary Problem in 2014

The 2010 and 2012 election cycles both began with Republicans optimistic about their chances to retake majority control of the Senate. Both election cycles ended in disappointment for the party as they lost a number of potentially winnable races because of the weaknesses of their general election candidates. In 2012, potentially winnable seats in Missouri and Indiana were lost when the Republicans nominated candidates – Todd Akin in Missouri and Richard Mourdock in Indiana – who made controversial comments about rape. In 2010, Democratic Majority Leader Harry Reid survived his reelection battle in Nevada, mostly because of the poor quality of the Republican challenger. Similarly, in Delaware, Christine O'Donnell garnered enough Tea Party support to defeat longtime Delaware Congressman and moderate Republican Mike Castle in the Republican primary, only to lose by 17 percent in the general election amid a series of gaffes and embarrassing campaign moments, including one ad that saw her look into the camera and state, "I am not a witch."

In 2014, establishment Republicans worked to insure that high quality, electable candidates won key primaries. Republican Minority Leader Mitch McConnell said that his strategy was to "crush" groups trying to oust Senate incumbents, and the U.S. Chamber of Commerce spent large sums of money in support of its preferred candidates in states such as North Carolina, Georgia, and Kentucky. For the first time in two election cycles Republicans did not see a sitting senator lose a primary and their preferred candidates won primaries in all states that were thought to be competitive. This new strategy ruffled the feathers of many in the Tea Party wing of the Republican Party, but the results on election night 2014 showed that the strategy had helped secure a Republican majority in the Senate.

The connection between elections and policy is far from perfect. For one thing, election outcomes are influenced by factors other than the policy views of voters and candidates – such as personalities and scandals. For another, forces beyond constituency opinion and members' personal views are at work on most issues before Congress. Organized interest groups, expert and editorial opinion, and vote trading can influence policy choices. Moreover, most of the specific policy questions faced by Congress and the president do not arise in election campaigns, yet elections determine whether the same party controls the House, the Senate, and the White House; whether they lean in a liberal or conservative direction; and whether they are likely to agree on major policy questions. It is also the case that most voters are poorly informed about most issues facing Congress and the country, making it difficult for citizens to issue a mandate to the elected. In addition, the timing of elections muddy any "mandates" received by voters. At the outset of the 114th Congress (2015–2016), congressional Republicans and

From left: GOP Senators-elect David Perdue (R-Georgia), Cory Gardner (R-Colorado), Ben Sasse (R-Nebraska), Mike Rounds (R-South Dakota), Joni Ernst (R-Iowa), Minority Leader Mitch McConnell (R-Kentucky), Shelley Moore Capito (R-West Virginia), James Lankford (R-Oklahoma), Tom Cotton (R-Arkansas), Thom Tillis, (R-North Caarolina), and Steve Daines (R-Montana) pose for news photographers before their meeting in Leader Mitch McConnell's office in the Capitol on Wednesday, November 12, 2014.

Senator Thad Cochran (R-Mississippi) greets Jeanette Hardy at Windy City Grille during a tour of downtown Hernando, Mississippi, May 30, 2014. Cochran survived a tough primary battle to win reelection.

President Obama can each claim that the voters sent them to Washington to enact their – often-competing – policy proposals.

Elections influence the legislative game beyond the party affiliations and policy positions of members of Congress and presidents. Most members seek reelection, and they seek legislative opportunities and resources that will further that goal. As we see in later chapters, the structure and function of virtually every major feature of Congress – committees, parties, rules, personal offices, and staffs – reflect the influence of electoral considerations. As the political scientist David Mayhew wrote in 1974, and it is surely more true today: "[I]f a group of planners sat down and tried to design a pair of American national assemblies with the goal of serving members' reelection needs year in and year out, they would be hard pressed to improve on what exists."

Modern candidates for Congress face an electoral system that is decentralized and often focused on the candidate. The system is governed as much by state law as by federal law. Political parties can endorse candidates for Congress and try to see that their favored candidates win nominations, but they do not formally control the selection of candidates to run in the general election (see box "The Changing Congress: Republicans Solve Their Primary Problem in 2014"). Instead, any person who meets basic eligibility requirements may run in a primary election to gain a place on the general election ballot under a party's name. Most candidates build their own campaign organizations, raise their own campaign money, and set their own campaign strategies. They do so in 435 separate districts and 50 states, each with a unique blend of economic, social, and political conditions. The winning candidates often emerge from their campaigns with strong individualistic tendencies, which they bring with them to the halls of Congress.

In this chapter we describe the formal rules and informal practices that shape congressional election outcomes. We then look at different types of candidates and at the advantages of incumbency. Next, we consider national patterns in congressional elections, including the forces underlying divided party control of Congress and the presidency.

THE RULES GOVERNING CONGRESSIONAL ELECTIONS

More than two thousand candidates run in congressional primary and general elections in any single election cycle. Their candidacies are governed by a web of rules provided by the Constitution, federal and state law, and, for incumbents, the House and Senate. The rules have become increasingly complex as Congress and state legislatures, as well as the federal courts, have sought to prevent election fraud, to keep elections fair, and (on occasion) to tilt the rules in favor of one type of candidate or another. The rules concern eligibility for office, filing requirements, campaign finance restrictions, use of congressional staff, and many other matters. By shaping the strategies of candidates seeking election or reelection to Congress, these rules influence election outcomes and the political composition of the House and Senate.

The Constitution: Eligibility, Voting Rights, and Chamber Size

ELIGIBILITY. The Constitution requires that members of both chambers of Congress be citizens of the state from which they are elected, although this rule does not always prevent individuals from running to represent a state that is not their primary residence. For example, former Republican senator Elizabeth Dole had not lived in North Carolina in decades before winning a Senate seat there in 2002; similarly, many accused former Democratic first lady Hillary Clinton of moving to New York so that she could seek a Senate seat there. Members of the House must be twenty-five years old and must have been a citizen of the United States for seven years, and members of the Senate must be thirty years old and must have been a U.S. citizen for nine years. Candidates may be younger than the age requirements at the time they run for office, although they must have reached the required age before being sworn into office. Current vice president Joe Biden was only twenty-nine when he first ran for the U.S. Senate, but he was able to be seated after he turned thirty. House members must reside in the state but not necessarily in the district they represent, although most do. Representatives serve two-year terms. Senators serve staggered, six-year terms, with one-third of the seats up for election in each election year. Representatives' and senators' terms begin at noon on January 3 following each election or as soon thereafter as the House and Senate may determine by law.

VOTING RIGHTS. The Constitution leaves the "times, places, and manner of holding elections for senators and representatives" to the states, although Congress may enact (and has) certain federal regulations concerning elections. In 1845, for example, Congress fixed the date for congressional and presidential elections as the Tuesday following the first Monday in November, but this change was not fully implemented until 1880. Constitutional amendments have added several rules limiting the ability of states to regulate the right to vote in federal elections. The Fourteenth Amendment (ratified in 1868) bars restrictions based on race, color, or previous condition of servitude (slavery); the Nineteenth Amendment (ratified in 1920) bars restrictions based on gender; and the Twenty-Fourth Amendment (ratified in 1964) prohibits poll taxes (a tax that must be paid before a person can vote). Most recently, the Twenty-Sixth Amendment (ratified in 1971) guarantees the right to vote to persons eighteen years of age or older.

CHAMBER SIZE. By implication, the Constitution sets the size of the Senate – each state has two senators. Since the late 1950s, when Alaska and Hawaii joined the union, the Senate has had 100 members. The Constitution guarantees at least one representative for each state, but the specific size of the House is not dictated by the Constitution and instead is set by law. For more than a century, the House grew as the country's population grew and states were added to the union. Since 1911, federal law has left the House at 435 voting members. With the House's size fixed, a growing population has produced districts of increasing size – most districts now contain more than 700,000 citizens – a far cry from the 30,000 originally provided by the Constitution.

Filling Vacant Senate Seats: Variations in State Law

The Seventeenth Amendment gives state legislatures the option of having a special election or allowing the governor to appoint a replacement if a Senate seat becomes vacant. The amendment reads in part: "When vacancies happen in the representation of any State in the Senate, the executive authority of each State shall issue writs of election to fill such vacancies: *Provided,* That the legislature of any State may empower the executive thereof to make temporary appointments until the people fill the vacancies by election as the legislature may direct." As we describe here, controversy can arise with these appointments.

In Alaska, Senator Frank Murkowski (R) resigned from the Senate after winning the governorship of Alaska in 2002. He subsequently appointed his daughter, Lisa Murkowski, to fill the remaining two years of his term. Charges of nepotism surrounded Ms. Murkowski throughout the remainder of her father's term and during her own campaign for the seat in 2004, but she was able to secure a full term for herself by narrowly defeating her Democratic opponent. Alaska law was subsequently changed to provide for a special election in lieu of a gubernatorial appointment.

In Illinois, Senator Barack Obama (D) resigned from the Senate after winning the presidential election in 2008. By law, Illinois governor Rod Blagojevich (D) was permitted to name a replacement. Controversy erupted, however, when federal prosecutors arrested Blagojevich and charged him with numerous counts of corruption, including trying to trade the Senate seat for campaign contributions or a job for himself or his wife. Federal prosecutors released recordings from telephone wiretaps that included Blagojevich stating in relation to the Senate seat, "I've got this thing and it's [expletive] golden, and, uh, uh, I'm just not giving it up for [expletive] nothing." As Illinois legislators began to consider impeachment proceedings against Blagojevich, he appointed Roland Burris, a longtime Chicago politician, to the seat. Senate Democrats initially indicated that they would refuse to seat Burris given the controversy surrounding the appointment, but he was eventually allowed to join the Senate.

A House vacancy because of death or any other cause must be filled by a special election, which is called by the state's governor. A Senate vacancy, according to the Seventeenth Amendment, may be filled by election or appointment by the state's governor, as determined by state law (see box "Filling Vacant Senate Seats: Variations in State Law"). Generally, state laws provide for a temporary appointment followed by an election at the time of the next regularly scheduled federal election to fill the remainder of the term. A bill to give the District of Columbia a House seat has been debated in recent years. The Senate passed a bill in early 2009 that would have expanded the House to 437 voting members, with the District of Columbia receiving one seat and Utah the other, but the bill failed because of questions about its constitutionality and its political consequences.

Federal Law: Apportionment and Campaign Finance

APPORTIONMENT. After each decennial census, changes in the distribution of population among the states must be reflected in the allocation of House seats. Fifty seats are allocated automatically because of the requirement that each state have at least one representative. However, the constitutional requirement that seats "be apportioned among the several states according to their respective numbers" leaves ambiguous how to handle fractions when allocating all other seats. Congress, by law, establishes the formula for apportioning the seats. Population shifts over the past half-century have resulted in a redistribution of power from the industrial Midwest and Northeast to the South and the Southwest (see Chapter 1). In addition, since 1967, federal law has required that states with more than one House seat must create districts from which only one representative is elected (single-member districts).

CAMPAIGN FINANCE. The past three decades have witnessed a number of attempts to regulate campaign finance in an effort to produce more disclosure of donations, establish limits on donations and campaign expenditures, and limit the influence of individuals and groups that possess disproportionate financial resources. These efforts have not proved to be particularly effective. Interested political actors have found myriad "loopholes" in all pieces of legislation, and, as a result, the growth of campaign spending has continued unabated (see Figure 3.4). In addition, narrow majorities on the U.S. Supreme Court have consistently overturned and restricted the applicability of laws enacted to limit the role of money in election outcomes.

The Federal Election Campaign Act (FECA) of 1971, and important amendments to it in 1974 and 1976, created the Federal Election Commission (FEC) and established limits and disclosure requirements for contributions to congressional campaigns. The regulations were in some respects a response to scandals involving secret contributions to presidential candidates of large sums of money from wealthy individuals and corporations, some of which was used for underhanded activity. FECA restricted the size of contributions that individuals, parties, and political action committees (PACs) could make to candidates for Congress. FECA created no restrictions on how much congressional candidates may spend, and the Supreme Court has barred limits on how much a candidate or family members may contribute to their own cause. The law required groups and candidates to report contributions and expenditures to the FEC.

Under the law, membership organizations, corporations, and labor unions may create PACs to collect money from organization employees or members to pad resources for campaign contributions. Because PACs may contribute more than individuals, there is a strong incentive to create PACs, which grew in number from 608 in late 1974 to more than 4,000 in the mid-1980s and to more than 4,500 in 2010. The largest growth was in PACs tied to corporations, which numbered 1,552 in mid-2003, but growth has occurred in all categories – labor union PACs, trade association PACs, PACs formed by cooperatives, and PACs not connected to any organization.

The FECA-based limits on contributions reflected a judgment that contributions from the wealthy and corporations may be harmful to the system and that party participation is more desirable. The basic rules on contributions provide that

- individuals may contribute larger sums to candidates and parties than to PACs;
- parties may contribute larger sums directly to candidates than may PACs; and
- parties may coordinate a certain amount of spending with candidates, whereas PACs cannot.

The law emphasizes public disclosure of contributions to and expenditures by candidates, parties, and PACs. Full disclosure of all contributions must be made in reports to the FEC, all contributions of more than $50 must be individually recorded, and the identity of donors of $100 or more must be provided. Detailed reports on expenditures are required as well.

However, FECA has loopholes. Contributions may be bundled, for example, by gathering many individual or PAC contributions and offering them as a package to a candidate. Lobbyists and other interest group leaders can use bundling, without violating the limits on the size of individual contributions, to make very conspicuous contributions to candidates who might not pay much attention to much smaller, separate contributions. The Honest Leadership and Open Government Act of 2007 required disclosure of the identity of bundlers and the amount bundled.

Furthermore, the law did not initially regulate "soft money" contributions, which by the late 1990s had taken on increasing importance in congressional and presidential campaigns. Soft money was contributed by wealthy individuals and corporations to political parties to be used for television ads for the party (not specific candidates), party staff and office expenses, voter registration and get-out-the-vote (GOTV) efforts, and other purposes that are not directed by, but obviously benefit, the party's candidates. This loophole allowed individuals and PACs that had reached their limit in direct contributions to a candidate's campaign to contribute money to a party organization that can work on the candidate's behalf.

TABLE 3.1. Congressional campaign contribution limits under the Bipartisan Campaign Reform Act of 2002, for the 2013–2014 cycle

Type of contributor	Limits	Other provisions
Individuals	$2,600 per candidate for primaries $2,600 per candidate for runoff elections $2,600 per candidate for general election $10,000 to state, district, and local party committee per year (combined limit) $5,000 to other political committees per year Unlimited independent spending	The Supreme Court ruling in *McClutcheon v. FEC* eliminated aggregate limits on how much individuals can give to candidates, parties, and PACs. Independent spending is spending by an individual or political action committee for or against candidates without coordinating with a candidate.
Political parties	National party committees have no limits on donations to state and local party committees National party committees may give $45,400 per Senate candidate $5,000 per candidate or candidate committee per election	
Political action committees	$5,000 per candidate for primaries $5,000 per candidate for general election $15,000 per calendar year to a political party Unlimited independent spending	Independent spending is spending spending by an individual or political action committee for or against a candidate

Source: Federal Election Commission, www.fec.gov.

By the late 1990s, many had come to believe that the soft money loophole was allowing candidates, parties, and donors to circumvent the rules established by FECA. After almost a decade of bitter debate, proponents of campaign finance reform, including Senator John McCain (R-Arizona) and former senator Russ Feingold (D-Wisconsin), succeeded in convincing Congress to ban most uses of soft money with the Bipartisan Campaign Reform Act of 2002 (BCRA) – sometimes known as "McCain-Feingold." In addition to the ban on soft money, the BCRA increased the amount of hard money that individuals could contribute to campaigns, created exceptions to the hard money limits for candidates facing self-financed candidates, and restricted "issue advocacy" by independent groups in the sixty days prior to an election (see Table 3.1).

A separate loophole was generated by a 1996 Supreme Court ruling that eliminated limits on how much parties could spend on congressional campaigns as long as the spending was not coordinated with the individual candidates' campaigns. The ruling paved the way for a sharp increase in fund-raising and

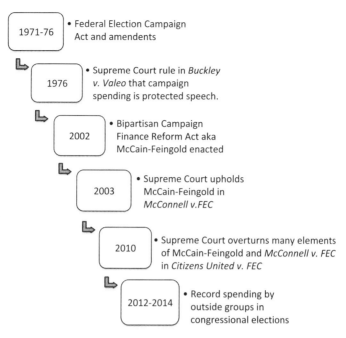

Figure 3.1 Major Developments in Campaign Finance Law.

spending by the congressional campaign committees. The Senate Republicans immediately set up a special unit to raise funds for these "independent" expenditures. Total expenditures by the parties' congressional and senatorial campaign committees exceeded $900 million for the 2006 election cycle, but fell to less than $600 million in 2010 because of increases in expenditures by other outside groups (see discussion of outside spending later in this section).

Both FECA and BCRA have faced many legal obstacles that have limited their effectiveness. Figure 3.1 summarizes the major developments in campaign finance over the past three decades. The Supreme Court ruled in *Buckley v. Valeo* (1976) that the free speech clause of the First Amendment to the Constitution applies to campaign spending. The argument is that individuals and groups must be free to spend money to express themselves. Many observers initially thought that this interpretation of the First Amendment meant that the Court would not let stand the BCRA restrictions on when groups can spend money to advocate issues. However, the Court initially did just that in *McConnell v. FEC* (2003) on the grounds that the restriction of free speech was minimal and justified by the government's interest in curbing corrupt practices. The Court, however, reversed itself in two landmark cases. First, in *FEC v. Wisconsin Right to Life* (2007), a bitterly divided 5–4 Court held that the restriction of so-called issue ads in the weeks prior to an election amounted to unconstitutional censorship. The Court held that if an ad could be reasonably interpreted as being about an issue and not expressly advocating the election or defeat of a particular candidate, it was permissible. Second, in *Citizens United v. FEC* (2010), a similarly constituted, conservative, five-justice majority further weakened the BCRA by overturning a provision that banned corporate funding of so-called electioneering communications. In addition, the ruling in *Citizens United* overturned the Court's own ruling in *Austin v. Michigan Chamber of Commerce* (1990), which held that corporations did not possess First Amendment rights to spend unlimited funds on political campaigns.

Many liberal individuals and groups are outraged by these two decisions because they fear that the decisions will allow major corporations to effectively "buy" elections and presumably elect conservative, pro-business candidates. Defenders of the ruling argue that the Court, by expanding the number of players who can attempt to influence elections, has created a more competitive political environment. The *Citizens United* ruling drew the attention of President Obama, who in a rare and dramatic move, directly criticized the Court's decision in a State of the Union Address, stating: "Last week, the Supreme Court reversed a century of law to open the floodgates for special interests – including foreign corporations – to spend without limit in our elections. Well, I don't think American elections should be bankrolled by America's most powerful interests, or worse, by foreign entities." A number of Supreme Court justices were in attendance for the address, and Associate Justice Sam Alito was seen shaking his head in disapproval and mouthing "not true" as President Obama spoke.

It is still too early to fully gauge the political effects of these two decisions, but the sheer amount of money spent in the wake of these rulings has been staggering. During the 2006 midterm election cycle, nonparty groups spent approximately $69 million, but in 2010 this number ballooned to more than $300 million – much of it concentrated in competitive races. In 2014, outside spending topped $550 million dollars. To put this in perspective, the four party campaign committees (DCCC, DSCC, NRCC, NRSC) combined to spend more than $650 million in 2014. At the current pace of increase, we may see outside spending exceed party spending by 2016.

State Law: Redistricting and Primaries

State laws continue to regulate many aspects of congressional elections. They exhibit a bewildering array of provisions. Two sets of state laws – those governing the drawing of district lines and those governing the process of gaining a place on the ballot – are particularly important.

REDISTRICTING. Among the most sensitive issues governed by state laws is the drawing of district lines for House seats. Because the composition of House districts can make the difference between winning and losing, the two major parties and individual politicians, particularly incumbents, often fight fierce battles

in state legislatures over the alignment of districts. These b
least every ten years, after the decennial census.

Following the 2010 census, the seven least populous sta
Montana, North Dakota, South Dakota, Vermont, and Wyo
allocated a single at-large House district, so redistricting was no
the other states, nine relied on commissions to draw their district line
number of other states having some role for commissions. The remainder o
states used the normal legislative process to draw lines. Incumbent members of
Congress often seek to influence state redistricting decisions, but their influence
varies. Redistricting is likely to be most controversial when a state loses one or
more seats and must pit incumbent members against one another in consolidated districts, or when the state legislature has seen a recent shift in partisan
control.

States face two significant constraints when drawing district lines. First, they
have to be as equal in population as is possible. Second, the Supreme Court has
moved to set standards to limit certain kinds of gerrymandering – the manipulation of district lines for political purposes – as well as some unintentional districting outcomes. In addition, the Court indicated in 1986 that districting plans
designed to advantage one political group (such as a party) over another may be
unconstitutional. However, just what constitutes impermissible "political gerrymandering" remains unclear as of the Court's latest decision on the topic, *Vieth
v. Jubelirer* (2004), in which the Court did not intervene in the case because it
recognized that it could not offer a workable solution.

Racial gerrymandering is another matter. Following the 1990 census, the federal courts at first let stand very oddly shaped congressional districts created
to give racial minorities a voting majority. These new districts were critical to
the election of more African Americans and Hispanics to the House of Representatives in 1992. Between 1993 and 2001, however, the Court made a series of
confusing rulings concerning the constitutionality of districts drawn with racial
motives. The decisions have forced federal courts to determine whether other
factors justified the redrawing of those districts' lines. By 2001, following the
new Supreme Court rulings, courts had ordered "majority-minority" districts to
be redrawn in Florida, Georgia, Louisiana, New York, North Carolina, Texas, and
Virginia. In early 2009, a narrowly divided Court ruled in *Barrett v. Strickland*
that the Voting Rights Act only required protection against minority vote dilu-
tion in districts in which racial minorities make up a majority of the population.
These controversies continued into the current round of redistricting, with states
such as Texas seeing numerous challenges to their redistricting plans.

Political and legal complications abound in redistricting. Failure to adopt a
timely redistricting plan or to meet legal standards often leads a federal district
court to design and impose a plan. After the 2010 census, federal courts became involved in redistricting in at least seven states, and state courts became

ved in several others. These cases often forced the postponement of candi-
filing deadlines and primaries.

PRIMARIES. State laws that govern the placement of candidates on the
November general election ballot are remarkably varied. All states provide for
primary elections as the means for choosing candidates for the November ballot
from the two major parties. In 2014, the earliest standard primary elections for
House and Senate seats were in Texas on March 4. The last standard primary was
in several northeastern states on September 9. Ten states require that a candidate
receive a specified percentage of the primary vote (more than 50 percent in most
cases) before being placed on the November ballot; if no candidate wins the
specified percentage, a runoff primary election is held soon thereafter.

The Changing Congress: It's a Jungle Out There

Three states – California, Washington, and Louisiana – have some form of the so-called
jungle primary that puts candidates for multiple political parties on the same primary
ballot. In California and Washington, the top two candidates from this primary move on
to the general election, even if they are in the same party. In 2012, eight of the fifty-three
California districts had two candidates from the same party on the general election ballot.
Louisiana holds its form of the jungle primary election on the day of the general election
because of its rule declaring a candidate the winner of the seat if he or she gets more than
50 percent of the vote. If no candidate obtains a majority, the top two move on to a runoff
election in December of an election year.

States vary in the way that they regulate voting in primary elections. Most
states have some form of closed primary: voters must register either in advance
or on Election Day as either a Republican or a Democrat and may vote only in
that party's primary. Open primaries, however, allow voters to choose to vote in
either party's primary at the polling place on Election Day. A few states have
hybrid systems or the primary rules vary by party.

Nearly all states have a system of plurality voting in the general election. That
is, the candidate with the most votes wins, even if that candidate receives less
than a majority of the total vote. Consequently, if more than two candidates
are on the ballot (usually a candidate from each major party plus minor party
candidates), the winner may receive far less than half of the votes.

ELECTION PRACTICE REFORM. In the wake of the 2000 presidential election
controversy, Congress sought to expand the federal role in national elections by
making it "easier to vote and harder to cheat." Congress enacted legislation in
2002, the Help America Vote Act (HAVA), which authorized almost $4 billion
to aid states in improving the mechanics of the election process. Close to $1 bil-
lion of this authorization was to assist states in replacing the infamous "punch
card" voting machines that were the source of controversy in Florida in 2000, as

well as to replace other outdated voting technology. The law also required that states must allow voters to cast "provisional ballots" in federal elections if their registration status is unclear. After demonstrating that the voter is properly registered, these provisional ballots are then to be counted as actual votes. The law seeks to reduce voter fraud by requiring identification for first-time voters, and a state-issued identification is now required to register to vote.

HOUSE AND SENATE RULES: OFFICE ACCOUNTS, STAFF, AND THE FRANK

The House and Senate have established rules to limit incumbents' use of their official offices, accounts, staffs, and other privileges for campaign purposes. Generally, incumbents may not use their offices or staffs for campaign purposes. For example, they may not accept campaign contributions in their official offices. Staff members are required to take leave without pay to work on their bosses' campaigns.

Dating back to the first Congress, members have been permitted free use of the mail by using their signatures in place of stamps. The use of their signature, called the "frank," is now regulated by a 1973 law that prohibits employing the frank for purposes "unrelated to the official business, activities, and duties of members" and for "mail matter which specifically solicits political support . . . or a vote or financial assistance for any candidate for any political office." In 1989, the House limited the number of district-wide "postal-patron" mailings that could be sent. The rules forbid explicit partisan and campaign references and allow only a limited number of references to the member per page.

The rules also bar mass mailings within sixty days of a primary or general election in the Senate and within ninety days in the House. Many members still use the frank within the sixty-day period for multiple batches of mailings of fewer than 500 pieces each to target certain groups within their districts or states, and members still use the frank more in election years than in nonelection years. However, the 1989 rule change combined with a further tightening of member allowances in 1995 have reduced the amount of money spent on franked mail from more than $100 million in 1988 to less than $8 million in 2013, although in 2012 (an election year) total expenditures on mail were approximately $25 million.

Until 1992, House members could send mass mailings at taxpayer expense to individuals living outside their district. Responding to a court ruling of that year, the House banned all mailings to more than five hundred persons outside a member's district. The restriction is a problem for members whose districts are redrawn in an election year and who seek to quickly communicate with their new constituents. The restriction also constrains members who are contemplating running for a statewide office, such as a Senate seat or governorship, who want to reach a larger electorate.

THE CANDIDATES

Personal ambition, more than any other factor, seems to drive people to run for Congress in the modern era. In recent years, party organizations have become more active in recruiting candidates. Interest groups, ranging from environmental groups to women's groups to manufacturing associations, seek candidates who reflect their viewpoint to run for Congress as well. Nevertheless, the initiative for the vast majority of candidacies rests with the candidates themselves. They are self-starters – independent political entrepreneurs who personally assess the costs and benefits before they assume the risks of running for Congress.

Conventional wisdom suggests that Congress is an ossified institution filled with well-entrenched incumbents. As usual, conventional wisdom is half right and half wrong. Incumbents are advantaged and usually win reelection when they seek it. However, it does not take very many voluntary retirements and electoral defeats in each election for substantial change in Congress's membership to occur over just a few elections. Despite the fact that 90 percent or more of incumbents seek reelection, it takes only a few years for substantial turnover in the membership to occur. In 2013, for example, more than half of House members had served less than ten years. In the Senate, only forty-six senators in the 113th Congress (2013–2014) had served more than two full terms.

Three types of congressional candidates should be distinguished: incumbents seeking reelection, challengers to incumbents, and candidates running in districts or states with an open seat (i.e., where the incumbent chose not to run or was defeated in the primary). As Figure 3.2 illustrates, several clear patterns have emerged in recent decades:

- most incumbents run for reelection and win;
- House incumbents are more successful than Senate incumbents in the typical election; and
- in the House, the percentage of incumbents who successfully seek reelection has reached new highs in recent elections.

Clearly, the odds are stacked against challengers, although challengers for Senate seats are more successful as a group than are challengers for House seats. The high rate of success for incumbents seeking reelection has led observers to note an incumbency advantage – something intrinsic to incumbent officeholders,

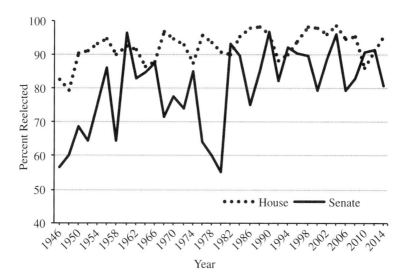

Figure 3.2 House and Senate Reelection Rates, 1946–2014. Sources: Norman Ornstein, Thomas Mann, and Michael Malbin., *Vital Statistics on Congress, 2001–2002* (Washington, DC: AEI Press, 2002); Paul Abramson, John Aldrich, and David Rohde, *Change and Continuity in the 2000 and 2002 Elections* (Washington, DC: CQ Press, 2003). Years 2004–2014 calculated by the authors. *Note*: The percentage includes only those seeking reelection.

their office and campaign resources, or the electorate that gives incumbents a built-in advantage over challengers.

One indicator of the strength of incumbents' advantage is the quality of the candidates who decide to run against them. Political scientists usually define a "quality" congressional challenger as someone who has held previous elective office. These individuals have typically served as state legislators, mayors, or in other visible offices. Quality candidates often have more fund-raising potential than nonquality candidates do, have represented a state legislative district that overlaps with the congressional district they live in, and have demonstrated that they possess the political skills necessary to win an election. Quality candidates are valued by a party trying to upset an incumbent and feared by incumbent politicians, partly because they tend to win about 25 percent of races they enter, compared to around 5 percent for nonquality candidates.

Because most quality candidates would have to give up their current office to run for a House seat, they typically do not emerge to face sitting incumbents unless that incumbent is perceived as electorally weak or is beset by personal or professional scandal. As Figure 3.3 indicates, fewer than 20 percent of House incumbents typically face a quality challenger in each election year, although this percentage can vary by party. Large gains by one party in an election can often be predicted in advance because of disparities in the quality of candidates running under each label. As Figure 3.3 demonstrates, fewer than 15 percent of

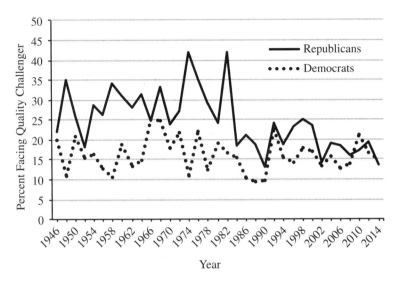

Figure 3.3 Percentage of House Incumbents Facing a Quality Challenger, 1946–2014.
Source: Data shared by Gary C. Jacobson.

Democratic incumbents faced quality challengers in 2006 and 2008, but more than 20 percent did in 2010.

Other measures of incumbent success provide a statistical adjustment for the incumbency advantage based on how well the candidate did in the last election and how advantaged or disadvantaged his or her party is nationwide. Such a measure indicates the advantage of incumbency corrected for the local and national advantages enjoyed by the incumbent and his or her party. Using a more refined measure, the House incumbency advantage shifted upward from 1964 to 1966. In the 1950s and early 1960s, the incumbency advantage was something less than five percentage points in most elections. For much of the late twentieth century the incumbency advantage averaged close to ten percentage points, but has fallen somewhat in recent years as elections have become more party centered.

Senators' constituencies are often larger and more diverse than representatives' constituencies, and thus Senate races are often more competitive than House races. Incumbent senators find it more difficult than do incumbent House members to build a large base of support that will sustain them from election to election. The long six-year term may contribute to the interelection variability in support for senators. Whatever the reason, Senate incumbents face a much higher probability of defeat than do their House counterparts.

In contrast to the pattern in elections involving incumbents, contests for open seats have become more competitive in recent decades. Between 1946 and 1964, only 20.3 percent of House open-seat contests produced a change in the party that controlled the seat; between 1966 and 2000, the percentage rose to close to 30. The trend is sharper in Senate open-seat races – 41.3 percent yielded party change between 1954 and 1964, and more than 50 percent did so between 1966 and 2000. In 2008, all three open Senate seats saw a change in party control.

EXPLAINING THE INCUMBENCY ADVANTAGE

Political scientists have worked hard to identify the causes of the declining competition for seats held by incumbents and have discovered that many factors contribute to it. Influences include the declining importance of party identification in voting, an expanding incumbent advantage in campaign resources, more nonpartisan constituency service, imbalances in campaign funding, the quality of the candidates challenging incumbents, and more contact with voters.

The Decline and Resurgence of Party Identification

A major factor in incumbents' success is that their party holds the advantage in the district or state they represent. Democratic constituencies tend to elect and reelect Democrats; Republican constituencies tend to elect and reelect Republicans.

The decline of party identification in the general electorate in the latter half of the twentieth century probably contributed to incumbents' advantage. As voters' psychological attachment to a major party weakened, the proportion of the electorate voting for congressional candidates in a reflexive, partisan way declined. This enlarged pool of "floating" voters and weak partisans produced more ticket splitting. The proportion of the electorate voting for the candidate of one party for one office and the candidate of the other party for another office – whether measured for House-Senate splits or House-president splits – nearly tripled from the 1950s through the 1980s but has declined markedly in recent elections. There is now a very high level of congruence between House election results and presidential results in each district.

For congressional incumbents, weak partisanship and ticket splitting presented both danger and opportunity. The danger was that incumbents' natural base of support among fellow partisans was weakened, as there were fewer votes guaranteed for their party. This shift made the electorate more unpredictable. In fact, for much of the 1960s through the 1980s, there was more election-to-election volatility in incumbents' vote margins than there was in the 1950s – so much more that it nearly offset the average incumbent's margin of victory. The increase in volatility accounted for the fact that incumbents were receiving a larger share of the vote but not actually winning at a much higher rate. It is interesting to note that with partisan attachments growing in recent election cycles, the fate of incumbents is much more tied to national trends in voting. This has likely contributed to the volatility we saw in the 2006, 2008, and 2010 congressional elections.

Expanded Perquisites of Office

The decline in party loyalty in the 1960s–1980s certainly contributed to the incumbency advantage, but incumbents have continued winning even in this era of renewed partisanship. Another important factor is that incumbents exploit their individual resources to combat electorate volatility and expand their base of support into the enlarged pool of independent voters. Their resources, which are discussed in Chapter 4, include a sizable personal staff distributed between their Washington and home offices, their committee staffs, office and stationery budgets, the use of the frank, a travel allowance, access to and influence over the White House and executive agencies, access to the media, and the expertise of the congressional support agencies.

All of these resources have grown since the 1960s, and legislators can use them to attract favorable publicity at home. Staff members, often with the assistance of experts in support agencies, help members write legislation and timely amendments that are popular at home. Committee and subcommittee staffs assist their bosses in organizing hearings, some of which are held away from Washington and many of which attract media attention. Stationery allowances and the frank permit members to send mass mailings directly to their districts or states. Travel allowances make it easier for members to return home more frequently to appear before groups. Congress's own radio and television facilities now permit members to make live and taped appearances on local television more frequently.

Expanded Constituency Service

Incumbents' official resources also can be used to improve their personal standing with their constituents. Additional home offices and staff have allowed members to provide personal services to constituents. Many of these services fall under the heading of "casework" – efforts to solve constituents' and local governments' problems with federal agencies. Perhaps the most common problem involves a constituent's eligibility for Social Security benefits. The expansion of federal programs since the mid-1960s has fostered this ombudsman role for members. Unlike legislating, which forces legislators to take sides on controversial issues, casework is a nonpartisan activity for which members can gain credit.

Of course, the expansion of members' resources and the growth of constituency service have another side. In a large country with a large, complex federal bureaucracy, members perform a genuine service on behalf of constituents who have real problems with government agencies. Legislators often justify their resources on the grounds that they are meeting the needs and expectations of their constituents. It is not surprising that members advertise their good works and get credit from voters for doing them.

Redistricting

One seemingly obvious explanation for the increase in the incumbency advantage is redistricting. With the Supreme Court ruling in *Wesberry v. Sanders* (1964) that districts had to approximate a "one person one vote" standard, many states had to redistrict for the first time in decades. In 1962, Michigan's largest district contained more than 800,000 residents, whereas the smallest contained less than 200,000. This massive wave of redistricting in the wake of *Wesberry* is timed almost perfectly with the increase in the incumbency advantage.

Congressionally Speaking . . .

Political scientists often use the *swing ratio* to gauge the bias and responsiveness of an electoral system. The swing ratio is the additional percentage change in seats won by a party for a 1 percent increase in its nationwide vote. In a system of perfect proportional representation, the number of seats a party wins is proportional to the number of votes received, so the swing ratio is 1.0. A party winning 55 percent of the vote, for instance, would win 55 percent of the seats. Such a system would have no bias, but low responsiveness.

For single-member districts, a small percentage increase in the vote for a party may produce a large increase in the number of seats it wins – a responsive system. The swing ratio for House elections has been about 2.0 in the past few decades, indicating that a party gains 2 percent more seats for each additional 1 percent of the nationwide vote it gains. In the 2008 elections, Democrats received 55.5 percent of the two-party House vote and held 59 percent of the seats in the House. In 2010, Republicans saw the vote swing 8.9 percent in their direction, which they translated into 55 percent of the seats in the chamber, which is consistent with a swing ratio of approximately 2.

For many years political scientists were unable to demonstrate that redistricting in the aftermath of *Wesberry v. Sanders* was responsible for the increased incumbency advantage. Recently, the political scientists Gary Cox and Jonathan Katz have demonstrated that redistricting in the 1960s played a significant role. They point out that redistricting was dominated by Democrat-controlled state legislatures and federal courts staffed by Democratic judges. These authorities "packed" Republican voters into a few overwhelmingly Republican districts while spreading Democratic voters across more districts so as to increase the number of seats Democrats could be expected to win. This packing of Republicans produced a large number of seats that were virtually guaranteed to elect Republican members, but it decreased competition for many other seats that were controlled by Democrats. Cox and Katz conclude, therefore, that the increase in incumbency advantage was largely attributable to this increase in the number of safe Republican seats.

The decade of the 2000s showed that the best laid redistricting plans can be foiled by political events and shifting population. Many asserted that the post-2000 census redistricting "locked in" a small Republican majority by eliminating most competitive seats. By one count, 75 percent of the seats that had been competitive in 2000 were no longer competitive after redistricting. The most extreme of these "incumbency protection acts" was the new districting system in California, where all fifty-three districts had at least an eight percentage point registration advantage for one party. This account seemed to be accurate in the 2002 and 2004 elections, but as noted at the outset of this chapter, 2006, 2008, and 2010 were three of the most volatile elections in recent memory, with numerous seats shifting in partisan control. Many observers have also claimed that the redistricting that took place following the 2010 census could lock in a Republican House majority for the next decade. This may prove to be true, as the Republicans currently have filled a majority of House seats for both elections held this decade despite earning fewer votes than the Democrats in 2012. But population shifts and changing political fortunes can upset the most carefully laid districting plans.

Biased Campaign Funding

Changes in campaign finance laws and the introduction of PACs have been a mixed blessing for incumbents. The expanded resources and activities of party committees and PACs create a potential threat to incumbents. By recruiting, funding, and providing campaign services to challengers and even organizing mass mailings and media campaigns against incumbents, PACs and party committees can neutralize some of the advantages of incumbents. Republicans have proved to be especially adept at this strategy, but the Democratic Party successfully used it against them in 2006. Representative Rahm Emmanuel (D-Illinois) and Senator Charles Schumer (D-New York) successfully recruited and raised funds for many of the candidates who were key to the Democrats' gaining a majority in the 2006 elections.

Of course, incumbents generally do not sit idly by as potential challengers are recruited and trained. In fact, by using their committee and subcommittee chairmanships, party posts, and other sources of influence, incumbents have done a good job of staying ahead of challengers. The incumbency advantage over challengers in PAC contributions, as well as in total contributions, is huge and has been growing since the 1970s.

Additionally, as the competition over majority control in Congress has intensified, the parties themselves have turned more attention to bolstering the resources of their own incumbents. Following the controversy surrounding the impeachment of President Bill Clinton in 1998–1999, then–House Majority Whip Tom DeLay (R-Texas) created a fund-raising plan dubbed ROMP (Retain Our Majority Program) in which incumbent Republicans donated more than $1.5 million to the campaign funds of Republicans who were thought to be vulnerable during the 2000 election cycle. The stated goal of ROMP was to insure that vulnerable incumbents had enough money to "scare off potential challengers." Democrats instituted a similar program in 2004 called Frontline, which sought to funnel money from members in safe seats to endangered Democratic incumbents. In attempting to keep their newly expanded majority beyond the 111th Congress (2009–2010), the Democratic Party had identified twenty-one endangered incumbents for the Frontline program by February of 2009 – more than nineteen months ahead of the 2010 election!

The flip side of contributions is expenditures. Figure 3.4 shows the historical record of spending by congressional candidates. The incumbent-challenger spending ratio increased from 1.5:1 in 1978 to 3.7:1 in 1990 for House races and from 1.9:1 to 2.1:1 in Senate races for the same years. By the year 2000, challengers improved their competitiveness, reducing the ratio to 2.2:1 in House contests and 1.6:1 in Senate contests; but in 2014 both ratios exceeded 5.0. In Senate campaigns, the gap between incumbents and challengers has grown, but generally it is not quite as large as the gap for House campaigns. Expenditures by open-seat candidates for the House show increases that parallel those of

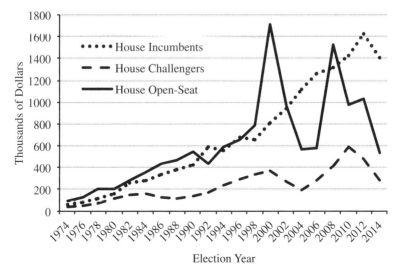

Figure 3.4 Candidate Spending in Congressional Elections, 1974–2014. Source: Data collected by the authors from FEC data and the Center for Responsive Politics.

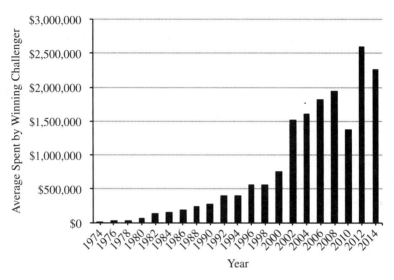

Figure 3.5 Average Spent by Winning House Challenger, 1974–2014. Source: Center for Responsive Politics.

incumbents. In fact, open-seat candidate spending consistently runs ahead of incumbent spending. Without an incumbent to scare away candidates, open-seat races tend to attract quality candidates and stimulate more spending on both sides.

The fund-raising capacity of incumbents gives them a tremendous advantage over challengers. In fact, incumbents now raise large sums early to deter potential opponents from entering the next race and to protect themselves against unforeseen challenges. Incumbents' emphasis on deterrence and risk avoidance is evidenced in their efforts to raise far more money than they end up spending. These surpluses, along with fund-raising efforts initiated just after an election, give the incumbents a huge – and growing – head start on any potential challengers for the next election. Figure 3.5 shows just how costly it has become to defeat a House incumbent. In 2000, the average winning House challenger spent approximately $750,000, but in the 2012 and 2014 elections the average winning challenger to an incumbent spent more than $2 million!

All of the spending figures previously discussed have to be considered in a different light in the wake of the extraordinary growth in outside or independent expenditures discussed earlier. In many races in 2010–2014, outside spending was a major component of overall spending. Outside groups – excluding party groups – spent more than $23 million on the 2010 Colorado Senate race, more than $37 million on the 2012 Virginia Senate race, and more than $5 million on House races in Ohio, Illinois, Florida, and Pennsylvania. In 2002, outside spending was less than $30 million; in 2014, it totaled more than $565 million – a twentyfold increase in just more than a decade.

Contact with Voters

Incumbents' increasing advantage appears to be the product of several mutually reinforcing developments in the electorate's partisanship, incumbents' resources and behavior, campaign finance practices, and the decisions of potential candidates.

The incumbency advantage, the competitiveness of open-seat elections, and House-Senate differences are all revealed by patterns in voters' contacts with candidates. Voters have somewhat more contact with small-state Senate incumbents than with House incumbents, but the big difference lies between House and Senate challengers. Voters report far less contact with House challengers than with most Senate challengers, reflecting the vast difference in visibility and campaign resources for challengers at the two levels. In fact, Senate challengers do not lag much behind Senate incumbents in voter contact. One reason for this is the notoriety of many Senate challengers. People of wealth, celebrities, and well-known politicians make up a larger proportion of Senate challengers than House challengers. Many Senate challengers simply have a head start on their House counterparts.

The form of voter contact for which incumbents enjoy the biggest advantage over challengers is contact through the mail. This is true of both House and Senate incumbents, which suggests that incumbents' franking privilege and funding for mass mailings give them an important edge over the competition. Open-seat candidates have more contact with voters than do challengers, but they have less contact than do incumbents. This is expected. After all, in comparison with challengers, open-seat candidates tend to be better qualified, more familiar to voters, and more successful at raising campaign funds. For the same reasons, Senate open-seat candidates are more successful than House open-seat candidates in reaching voters.

NATIONAL PATTERNS IN CONGRESSIONAL ELECTIONS

Although the local candidates and their personal and political characteristics are the major determinants of congressional election outcomes, as noted at the beginning of the chapter, national forces appear to be an influence worth at least several percentage points in some congressional races. Such a small effect may seem quite unimportant, but it is more than enough to determine the outcome in many close contests. The state of the national economy, the public's evaluation of the president's performance, and the public's tendency to be conservative are typically strongly related to which party is most successful in congressional elections. When the economy is weak, the president's performance ratings are low. When the public mood is out of sync with administration policy, candidates of the incumbent president's party are less successful. By influencing the outcome in at least a few races, such forces can shape the partisan and ideological balances in the House and Senate.

National forces may be felt in congressional elections in several ways. Voters and financial contributors sometimes reward or punish congressional candidates for national conditions. To the extent that they do, potential candidates have reason to assess the odds of winning. In any given year, potential candidates of one party may decide to stay out of congressional races when conditions do not seem favorable, reducing the pool of quality candidates that the party is able to field. Weak candidates, of course, attract few contributions, build ineffective campaigns, and are not likely to win. Thus, anticipated and actual choices made by voters, contributors, and potential and actual candidates combine to reward the candidacies of the party credited with good times and to punish the party blamed for bad times.

This description of the influence of national forces has one serious weakness: It cannot account for the frequency of divided party control between Congress and the presidency. The influence of national conditions generally pushes voters in the same direction for congressional and presidential elections. To be sure, idiosyncratic factors – a presidential scandal, for example – might occasionally produce a Congress and president of different parties. In twenty-one of the thirty-three two-year Congresses between 1952 and 2014, however, divided party control existed. All of the Republican presidents in that period served with a Democratic House and, usually, a Democratic Senate. In 1995–2000, Democratic President Clinton served with a unified Republican Congress. President Obama enjoyed a Democratic 111th Congress (2009–2010) but faced a Republican House in the 112th and 113th Congress, and a Republican House and Senate in the 114th Congress (2015–2016). It turns out that the effects of national forces, including presidential popularity, on congressional elections are not invariant. In fact, important changes have occurred in recent decades.

Midterm Elections

For congressional elections held in the middle of a presidential term – called midterm elections – there is no concurrent presidential contest. For House midterm races, however, the number of congressional seats the two parties win is well predicted by the state of the economy and the public's evaluation of the president's performance. Candidates of the president's party are not credited or blamed for economic conditions in midterm contests as much as they are in presidential election years, when the choice of a presidential candidate is also on voters' minds. In Senate midterm elections, economic conditions are even more weakly related to partisan seat gains or losses than they are in the House.

Midterm elections are distinctive for two reasons. First, turnout among voters is lower in midterm elections than in presidential elections. Without the stimulus of a highly visible presidential contest, turnout is often 10 to 15 percentage points lower in a midterm election. In 2014, less than 35 percent of the nation's voting-age population voted compared to more than 53 percent in 2012, which was a presidential election year. Turnover varies widely among states and districts, however, and surges in midterm election turnout are related to the competitiveness of congressional races. Incumbents must be wary of challengers who can stimulate turnout and create uncertainties about the size and composition of the November electorate in midterm elections.

Second, for most of the twentieth century, political scientists could safely predict that the president's party would gain seats in Congress in presidential election years but would lose seats in midterm elections. This pattern held for House seats in every midterm election from 1938 to 1994 and for Senate seats in all but three midterm elections during the same period. Between 1946 and 1996, the president's party suffered an average loss of about twenty-four seats in midterm elections, compared with an average gain of about nine seats in presidential election years.

The election outcomes in 1998 and 2002 bucked this familiar trend. In 1998, Democrats managed to win a net gain of five House seats and lost no Senate seats, whereas in 2002 Republicans gained seven House seats and three Senate seats. The common thread running through both of these elections is that both occurred while the president enjoyed extraordinarily high public approval ratings.

Furthermore, the president's party tends to lose more House seats in the midterm election of the president's second term than in the president's first term. By one estimate, which took into account other factors that influence House elections, the president's party does about twice as poorly in the second term as in the first term. The 2006 and 2014 elections were excellent examples of this principle

A reasonable explanation of the difficulty confronted by the president's party in midterm elections is the exposure thesis. This thesis holds that the more a party gains in one election above its average or natural level for recent decades, the more seats it is likely to be holding in states and districts that generally favor the other party. The party that gains in a presidential election year becomes vulnerable to losing seats two years later in the midterm election. The number of seats won in the presidential election year that are above the party's average indicates how "exposed" the party will be to seat losses at the midterm. Actual results are influenced by national conditions and the president's popularity.

CONCLUSION

The electoral arena has changed in important ways in recent decades. New laws and court decisions have greatly complicated the rules governing congressional elections and are sure to continue to do so in the coming years. The power of the president's coattails has declined, and outside groups and parties have taken on a greater role in financing campaigns. Campaigns have become more expensive and more focused on national issues. Despite all the changes, congressional incumbents, particularly House incumbents, have retained important advantages over challengers.

Although congressional elections are primarily contests between local candidates, they have had critical national consequences. Time and again, national conditions and elections have altered the ideological alignment between the House, the Senate, and the president. Since the mid-twentieth century, elections have regularly produced divided party control of government, which has increased conflict between the branches of government and has made it more difficult to assign credit and blame for government performance.

SUGGESTED READINGS

A. The following books discuss the mechanics of congressional elections.

Abramowitz, Alan I., and Jeffrey Segal. *Senate Elections.* Ann Arbor: University of Michigan Press, 1992.

Carson, Jamie L., and Jason M. Roberts. *Ambition, Competition, and Electoral Reform: The Politics of Congressional Elections across Time.* Ann Arbor: University of Michigan Press, 2013.

Cox, Gary, and Jonathan Katz. *Elbridge Gerry's Salamander: The Electoral Consequences of the Reapportionment Revolution.* New York: Cambridge University Press, 2002.

Gronke, Paul. *The Electorate, the Campaign, and the Office: A Unified Approach to Senate and House Elections.* Ann Arbor: University of Michigan Press, 2000.

Jacobson, Gary, and Samuel Kernell. *Strategy and Choice in Congressional Elections.* New Haven, CT: Yale University Press, 1983.

B. The following books discuss the connection between elections and policy making.

Fenno, Richard, Jr. *Congress at the Grassroots: Representational Change in the South, 1970-1998.* Chapel Hill: University of North Carolina Press, 2000.

Masket, Seth E. *No Middle Ground: How Informal Party Organizations Control Nominations and Polarize Legislatures.* Ann Arbor: University of Michigan Press, 2009.

Mayhew, David. *Divided We Govern: Party Control, Lawmaking, and Investigations, 1946-1990.* New Haven, CT: Yale University Press, 1991.

Sulkin, Tracy. *Issue Politics in Congress.* Cambridge: Cambridge University Press, 2005.

DISCUSSION QUESTIONS

1 How does the increased correlation between congressional and presidential voting affect the incumbency advantage?

2 What factors make it more difficult for Senate incumbents to win reelection?

3 How does divided government affect policy making?

4 Compare and contrast the effects of various types of primaries – open, closed, jungle – on polarization and candidate quality.

4 Members, Goals, Resources, and Strategies

House members of the 114th Congress (2015–2016) are sworn in on the House floor, January 6, 2015.

In today's world, we make several reasonable assumptions about members of Congress. We assume that most of them will seek reelection, and, if they do not, it is because they are seeking another elective office or are retiring. We expect that legislators have the ability to get back to their districts and states on most weekends to attend civic functions and meet with constituents. We take for granted that legislators can communicate efficiently with constituents, resolve constituent problems, and meanwhile address the policy concerns of House districts that average more than 700,000 people and states that average more than 6 million people.

These assumptions are fairly accurate, but Congress has not always been this way. Only in the past few decades have legislators consistently sought reelection.

In the late 1800s, it was common for two-thirds or less of House members to run for reelection. Even in the 1940s, two out of ten legislators sat out the next election. In recent Congresses, however, 90 to 95 percent of incumbents have run for reelection. Moreover, the technology, resources, and staff required to make frequent trips home and to be responsive to ever-expanding constituencies are of recent vintage. Since the 1950s, office budgets have quadrupled and personal staffs have doubled in size.

This chapter looks at Congress from the members' perspective. Legislators exhibit a range of personal goals, but most modern legislators see politics as a career and view reelection as essential to the achievement of their goals. Over time, they have granted themselves the resources to pursue their electoral, policy, and other objectives simultaneously. Legislators, however, do not pursue all goals all the time but exploit resources and opportunities selectively. We will see that there are important patterns and generalizations that can be made.

SETTING PERSONAL PRIORITIES

Legislators have well-established policy attitudes by the time they arrive in Washington for the first time. For example, most members can be characterized as liberals, moderates, or conservatives, with some variation on specific issues. Those attitudes are the product of many factors – personal experience, a track record in politics, the necessities of the campaign, and so on. In general, the voting behavior of most members is quite predictable (see box "Modeling Voting Behavior"). However, members face many decisions for which their general ideological outlook offers little guidance – how to vote on hundreds of roll call votes on narrow issues, which committee assignments to request, how to allocate staff, which issues to emphasize, and how much time to spend in Washington versus the home state or district. Members' choices about these matters mold their legislative careers.

Members have wide latitude in setting their personal priorities and choosing strategies for pursuing their goals. No party leader or president dictates how members vote, what issues members pursue, how much time members spend in their home districts and states, or how members organize their staffs. To be sure, members are subjected to pressure from leaders, presidents, and many other people and groups, but members of the modern Congress are remarkably free to shape their priorities and determine their own strategies.

There is a catch. Because time, staff, and budgets are limited, members must exercise care in allocating their resources. New members face the most difficult choices. They must worry about organizing a staff, selecting and arranging new offices, requesting committee assignments, and responding to appeals from senior members competing for leadership posts – all while trying to find a place to live in a new city. In addition, in recent Congresses, party leaders expect incoming members to dedicate several hours a day to fund-raising and strategic outreach. Members do these things with incomplete information. In requesting committee assignments, for example, a member might like to know the career plans of committee and subcommittee leaders – whether they plan to retire soon or to run for higher office will affect how quickly the member might rise to chair a committee or subcommittee. In hiring staff, a member might like to know what issues will be hot in the coming years so that he or she can appoint people with relevant expertise. In nearly every aspect of setting priorities, a member would like to know who future opponents are likely to be and whether economic and world conditions will favor his or her party. In addition, most members would like to know if and when opportunities to run for higher office will arise. With the passage of time, members gradually resolve some uncertainties, acclimate themselves to others, and settle into routines that reflect their personal priorities, campaign experience, and style.

Modeling Voting Behavior

Many political scientists measure members' voting positions using something called NOMINATE scores. These measures were introduced by the political scientists Keith Poole and Howard Rosenthal in the early 1980s and are used widely in legislative research. There are a number of different variations on these scores that allow researchers to, among other things, compare the scores across time and chambers. The scores range from -1 to 1, with negative scores indicating policy liberalism and positive scores representing policy conservatism. The technical details of the measure are beyond the scope of this text but can be found elsewhere for those interested.

NOMINATE scores capture the complexity of legislative decision making by measuring members' positions in two dimensions. This, quite simply, suggests that there are multiple forces that ultimately influence members' decision making. If, for instance, you are deciding between multiple restaurants for dinner this evening, you might consider both

(*continued*)

Modeling Voting Behavior (*continued*)

their food options and their cost (i.e., two dimensions of consideration). The first, or primary, dimension in NOMINATE scores is the left-right dimension on economic issues. The second dimension has changing explanations across time, but represents important cross-cutting considerations, such as social issues.

Importantly, NOMINATE scores have an impressive capability to predict legislative behavior. This means that NOMINATE scores, which measure members' voting patterns, have a high degree of accuracy in correctly identifying on which side of a vote a member will fall. In fact, Poole and Rosenthal show that throughout congressional history, the first dimension alone correctly classifies about 87 percent of members' votes, with consideration of the second dimension offering small improvements to this percentage. Therefore, members' voting behavior is extremely predictable. Once elected to office, they adopt policy positions that are relatively stable, although important deviations from these positions can and do occur.

MEMBERS' GOALS

Members of Congress tend to be purposeful in their professional activities as elected officials. Most of what they do as legislators is connected to some goal or goals – political scientists would label this instrumental behavior. They do not always articulate their goals, but they usually can explain how particular decisions affect their own political objectives. Moreover, they usually see connections between their goals and what they do every day. They try to use their limited resources effectively, if not always efficiently, and consciously move toward achieving their personal political goals. In recent decades, political scientists have increasingly adopted the view that legislative behavior can be understood as the outgrowth of members strategically pursuing their goals (see box "Rational Choice Theory and Members' Goals"). To be sure, not every move is calculated, but members generally think and act in ways that make it reasonable to characterize them as strategic politicians.

What are members' goals? For our purposes, it makes sense to focus on the political goals that members mention when explaining their many decisions. The political scientist Richard Fenno, in studying differences among members sitting on different committees, found that three categories – reelection, good public policy, and influence – account for most of the goals expressed by members.

Reelection

Members of Congress are like the rest of us – most of them want to keep their jobs. They gain personal satisfaction from making contributions to public policy and serving the interests of people they care about, as well as from the prestige of holding high public office. Perhaps a few members like the income, have a craving for power, enjoy the attention given to them by lobbyists and others, or simply like to see themselves on television.

Members face a test for retaining their jobs that most of us do not. Periodically, at times fixed by law, they must seek the approval of a very large number of citizens they do not know personally. The opinions that voters hold of their representatives and senators can turn on factors beyond the members' personal control (e.g., the economy, mood about Congress, and so on). In addition, campaigning, even for members who have won by wide margins in the past, involves a large commitment of time, money, and energy. Most of the rest of us do not face such unusual demands to retain our jobs.

We should not be surprised that many, if not most, members make obtaining reelection a high priority in their daily activities. In the view of critics, members care too much about reelection. Some critics assert that members ignore the general welfare of the country while pursuing the narrow interests of financial contributors, the special interests of organized groups, and the parochial interests of their home constituents. Furthermore, critics contend that the reelection drive has become more intense in recent years. Supporters of term limits, in particular, claim that members have become obsessed by reelection, have become excessively insular in their political outlook, and have built up staffs and perks – the resources that come with their office – that virtually ensure their reelection. However, the desire for term limits is not shared by all (see box, 'The Case against Term Limits").

The Case against Term Limits

Some pundits, voters, and scholars have sung the merits of congressional term limits. In fact, a recent Gallup poll found that 75 percent of Americans would support a law limiting the number of terms representatives and senators could serve. Legislation proposing congressional term limits has even been introduced in Congress, but to no avail. Those favoring term limits have suggested that turnover in membership is essential to keeping members in touch with their constituents. Others argue that the incessant drive for reelection has led members to pursue narrow interests at the nation's expense.

Surely there is some validity to these claims. However, it is also worth considering the potential downsides to term limits. Political scientists have shown that members of Congress are more active and successful in legislating as they acquire seniority. That is, members gain knowledge, expertise, and connections as tenure increases, which in turn helps them achieve policy goals that could benefit their constituents. Related to this point, some have argued that the loss of members with institutional knowledge would simply impair the ability of Congress to effectively legislate. Moreover, studies have also shown that once members sever the electoral connection, their participation falls and so too does their dedication to constituent preferences. In other words, members may be less faithful to the wishes of their constituents when the electoral incentive is eliminated.

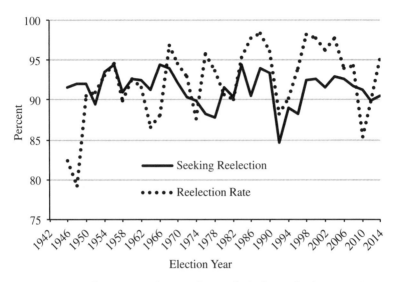

Figure 4.1 Percentage of House Incumbents Seeking and Winning Reelection, 1946–2014.
Source: Norman J. Ornstein, Thomas E. Mann, Michael J. Malbin, Andrew Rugg, and Raffaela
Wakeman, *Vital Statistics on Congress, 2014* (Washington, DC: Brookings Institution and American
Enterprise Institute, 2014).

Even scholars often assume, at least for the sake of argument, that members
are single-minded seekers of reelection. And for good reason: In recent decades
nearly all members of Congress seek reelection, and most are successful in their
efforts (see Figure 4.1). Therefore, much of what members do is best explained
by their drive for reelection. Requesting assignment to committees with jurisdictions affecting their constituents, introducing popular legislation, winning federal funds for projects in their states and districts, solving constituents' problems
with federal agencies, evaluating legislation for its impact on their constituencies, and soliciting media attention are common activities that members pursue
to enhance their chances of reelection. The political scientist David Mayhew
neatly categorized these activities as credit claiming, position taking, and advertising. Moreover, the political scientist R. Douglas Arnold has shown how
congressional leaders take into account the electoral calculations of members
when designing strategies for building majority coalitions.

Still, great care must be exercised in declaring reelection to be members' sole
motivation. Reelection is probably better viewed as a means to an end rather
than as an end in itself. As we see it, people seek election and reelection to Congress primarily because they value membership in Congress in some way. If other
goals were not served by membership, or if running for office were too onerous,
few people would make the effort. Those other goals, whatever they may be,
surely influence members' daily activities as well.

Moreover, for many of members' decisions and activities reelection considerations play a more limited role. Many committee and floor votes have no electoral

consequences; after all, legislating involves many activities that are unseen and unappreciated at home. David Price, a political scientist and a Democratic representative from North Carolina, explains that "most members of Congress, most of the time, have a great deal of latitude as to how they define their roles and what kind of job they wish to do. If they do not have the latitude, they can often create it, for they have a great deal of control over how their actions are perceived and interpreted."[1]

Congressionally Speaking . . .

The *pork barrel* is the term used in politics for local projects funded by Congress. The term is thought to originate in the pre–Civil War practice of serving slaves salted pork from large barrels. When the barrels were set out, the slaves would rush to grab as much of the pork as possible. In the early twentieth century, journalists began to comment that members of Congress behaved similarly in an effort to distribute pet projects to their constituents.

Each year Congress approves funding for hundreds of local projects ranging from a university building to a youth center to a new dam or bridge. Legislators take credit for the projects by issuing press releases, including stories in their newsletters, and appearing at ground-breaking and opening ceremonies. Because these structures are nonpartisan public works, almost everyone at home appreciates the "pork" projects and the legislators' efforts, a perfect combination for members eager to please voters.

Earmarks are provisions in bills or committee reports that direct funding to individual projects. They have come under attack in recent years. In 2007, the House and Senate passed rules changes requiring committees and other sponsors of legislation to list earmarks and their sponsors in accompanying reports. Moreover, the chambers now compel members to certify that they do not have a personal financial interest at stake in an earmark they sponsor. In 2009, the House also passed a rule prohibiting appropriations conference committees from inserting additional earmarks. More recently, House and Senate Republicans renewed their vow to ban earmarks for the duration of the 114th Congress (2015–2016).

One way in which a member gains latitude in terms of his or her legislative behavior is to earn the trust of constituents. Richard Fenno observes that trust is earned only over time, as a member's constituents come to see him or her as qualified, as a person who identifies and empathizes with them, and as someone who can credibly defend his or her actions in Washington. In seeking to win such trust, members develop distinctive strategies for presenting themselves to their constituents, referred to by Fenno as a "home style." This style is tailored to their own personalities and skills and to the nature of their constituencies.

For a former member of the House, Barney Frank (D-Massachusetts), wit was a trademark. During his reelection campaign of 1992, a year in which a large

---

1 David E. Price, *The Congressional Experience: A View from the Hill* (Boston: Little, Brown, 1973), 146.

number of members retired from office, Frank wrote a letter to supporters in which he said:

> I feel somewhat apologetic about what I am going to tell you: I do not plan to quit Congress. As I read the praise which the media lavishes on my colleagues who are retiring, I'm afraid my eagerness to keep working on a broad range of public policy issues may be taken as a character defect. So I hope that as character defects go, this one will be considered sufficiently minor for you to overlook.[2]

Apparently, it was. Frank was reelected in 1992 with 72 percent of the vote and won reelection in each of the following ten House elections by decisive numbers.

Given that nearly all members of Congress seek reelection, it is reasonable to assume that their concern about reelection plays in the decisions that legislators make. Because it is a goal that must be achieved periodically if a legislator is to continue pursuing other goals in public office, it is not too surprising that reelection dominates all other considerations. For most members, however, reelection does not explain everything.

Good Public Policy

Among the other goals that members pursue is to make good public policy. The cynics are wrong. Most, if not all, members care about the country's future. Many members come to Congress with preexisting policy interests and often are deeply committed to certain policy views. These commitments influence members' committee preferences, staffing decisions, and legislative activities.

A good illustration of a legislator's background shaping his or her legislative interests is Representative Carolyn McCarthy (D-New York), who had developed a national reputation as a staunch advocate of gun control. In 1993, McCarthy's husband was killed and her son seriously injured by a gunman on the Long Island Railroad. When McCarthy's representative, Dan Frisa (R-New York), voted against a federal ban on assault weapons, she decided to run for office. Despite being a lifelong Republican, she ran under the Democratic label in 1996 and won by a decisive margin. Between the time of her election in 1997 and her retirement in 2013, she sponsored or cosponsored dozens of bills proposing more stringent regulation of guns and ammunition, and served as a vice chair on the House Gun Violence Prevention Task Force.

Political scientists have shown that personal experience motivates involvement in the legislative process. For example, studies demonstrate that African American members of the House of Representatives devote more legislative effort to the issues that are particularly important to African Americans even when the composition of their home districts is taken into account. Similar findings are reported for women, but, on the whole, their behavior is not as distinctive as that of African

---

2 Quoted in Craig Winneker, "That Was The Year That Was . . . Whew!" *Roll Call* (December 21, 1992):15.

Americans in Congress. More casual observations about other groups – farmers, veterans, business leaders, and so on – are also made with some frequency.

Many legislators acquire policy interests, sometimes quite accidentally, while serving in Congress. It could hardly be otherwise. Members are introduced to many subjects in the process of listening to constituents, sitting through committee hearings, and discussing issues with colleagues, staff, and outside experts.

Political Influence

Many members also want political influence. Influence may be an end in itself, or it may be a means for pursuing certain policy goals, constituency interests, or even reelection. Most members try to develop a base of power within Congress so that they have more influence than other members do.

Influence can be acquired in many ways, but earning formal party and committee positions is particularly important in Congress. Party and committee leaders often enjoy certain procedural prerogatives and additional staff, both of which may give them an edge in influencing policy outcomes. Members striving for broad influence pursue party leadership posts by first seeking appointment or election to low-level party positions, in the hope of gaining a top post in the future. Holders of committee and subcommittee chairs also are advantaged, at least within the jurisdiction of their committees and subcommittees. Members also might try to gain a seat on committees with broad and important jurisdictions, such as House Appropriations and Ways and Means. Because the work of these types of committees is important to all members of Congress and many special interests, a spot on one of them puts a member in a position to help fellow members. As Representative Norm Dicks (D-Washington) described the House Appropriations Committee: "It's where the money is. And money is where the clout is."[3]

Serving Constituents

Many members feel a strong obligation to look out for the interests of their home constituents, even when doing so has little effect on their reelection prospects or when there is little connection between their constituents' needs and their own policy interests. Political scientists have sometimes called the duty to behave in accordance with the wishes of constituents the delegate role. The delegate role is often contrasted with the trustee role, in which the member exercises independent judgment about questions of public policy. Of course, members seldom make a conscious philosophical judgment about whether to act as a delegate or as a trustee. For many members, behaving as a delegate comes naturally, at least on many issues. After all, most members grew up in the districts or states they serve.

3 As quoted in Christopher J. Deering and Steven S. Smith, *Committees in Congress*, 3rd ed. (Washington, DC: Congressional Quarterly Press, 1997), 67.

They often identify and empathize with their constituents, and believe that their constituents deserve good representation; but because their constituents have opinions about only a small fraction of the many policy questions Congress must confront, every member must behave like a trustee much of the time, no matter how committed he or she is to serving constituents' interests.

Christopher Cooper, a political scientist, and Representative Daniel Lipinski (D-Illinois), a former professor of political science, suggest that members strategically communicate their dedication to the delegate role. Using rhetoric, members signal to constituents the extent to which they are acting as a delegate or trustee, although the rhetoric may not be an accurate depiction of their true legislative behavior. The use of rhetoric for this purpose appears to be systematic. Members are more likely to emphasize the delegate role when they are in their first term or when they represent a district that contains a large percentage of blue-collar workers, senior citizens, or friendly partisan voters – groups that appear to prefer a more home-oriented form of representation.

Not all constituents are of equal importance to members though. It goes without saying that virtually every member would prefer a happy constituent to an unhappy one, but members know that they are choosing which constituents to give priority to when they select their committee assignments, set their personal policy emphases, and cast votes on divisive issues. Members naturally give priority to constituents who supported them when they were forced to make tough choices, and this makes it difficult for the outside observer to distinguish between members who are genuinely committed to their constituents' interests and members who are motivated by reelection alone.

Higher Office

Higher office is on the minds of many members of Congress. They may not see their current position solely as a stepping-stone to higher office, but many members are clearly ambitious. In the 114th Congress (2015–2016), for example, 53 senators previously served in the House. In fact, a substantial number of House members have pursued higher office in recent decades. By one count, a total of 261 House members ran for the Senate between 1960 and 2014; and this surely understates the number of members with progressive ambition over this period of time. Counting only those who ran for higher office overlooks the potentially sizable number of members who desired higher office but made the strategic decision not to run, at least for the time being. Figure 4.2 details the highest previous elective office held by members of the 114th Congress. Progressive ambition is quite apparent. In both chambers, the vast majority of members bring to their current positions experience in elective office, with approximately 66 percent of sitting representatives and 84 percent of sitting senators having previously served in elective office. From Figure 4.2, it is relatively

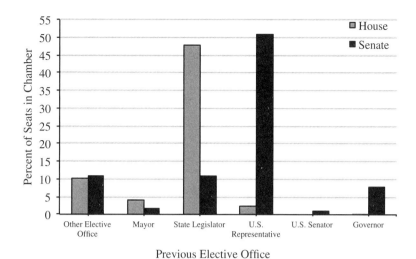

Figure 4.2 Highest Previous Elective Office of Representatives and Senators, 114th Congress (2015–2016). Source: Congressional Biographical Directory. Coding done by authors.

clear that the state legislatures are the springboard for the House, and the House is likewise for the Senate. Ambition does not stop there. For the presidential elections between 1960 and 2012, thirty-one of the fifty-six major party nominees for president and vice president had served in the Senate.

Several factors contribute to a member's decision to run for higher office – in particular, the comparative value of the higher seat to the current seat, the probability of winning the higher seat, and the cost of running for the higher seat. The relative value of seats is an important aspect in any member's decision to run for higher office, and it is often visible in senators' determination whether to run for governor. Incumbent senators seldom run for small-state governorships but are more inclined to run for large-state governorships. The probability of winning is a factor that is frequently illustrated after the redistricting of House seats. House members who find their district lines changed radically anticipate that gaining reelection to their seat may be difficult and often choose to run for higher office.

Legislating

The work of legislating seems to have an intrinsic appeal to many legislators. The legislative game can be fun. Formulating strategies, mastering complicated issues, learning the complexities of the policy-making process, building majority coalitions against talented opponents, making a lasting contribution to public policy, and associating with other bright and energetic people appear to motivate many members. Former senator Dan Quayle (R-Indiana) is a case in point. A close observer of Quayle reports that "in recounting his first year's activities [as a senator] he exuded enthusiasm for legislative work in general. 'I had fun on all of them,' he said after canvassing his first-year interests. 'There was no one highlight. The highlight is getting involved and accomplishing a whole lot of things.'"[4]

Multiple Goals

Most Congress members appear to be motivated by more than one goal. In fact, much of what they do is consistent with pursuing several goals. After all, the more goals a particular activity or decision serves, the more valuable it is likely to be. For example, using a committee hearing to draw attention to a policy problem and to oneself may simultaneously further a member's reelection chances, prospects for higher office, and public policy objectives. Furthermore, the media attention generated by a hearing may help to influence colleagues' views about a member's intelligence and leadership ability as well as their own views on the issue at hand.

Members can pursue a multifaceted strategy to avoid having to select among competing goals. For example, members often seek a mix of committee assignments that satisfy both constituent and personal interests. However, it is unrealistic for members to achieve all their goals all the time. With limited time, money, and staff, members often face making trade-offs among goals. Generally, representatives face more severe trade-offs than senators do. With fewer committee assignments, a smaller staff and office budget, and a shorter term of office, representatives must carefully allocate resources among the various activities they would like to pursue. Fortunately for them, over the past few decades, all members have benefited from an expanding base of resources.

MEMBERS' RESOURCES

Pursuing goals requires resources. A member's most important resource is the power to vote – in subcommittee, in committee, on the floor, or in conference. Members also have many nonprocedural resources. As managers of numerous offices – personal, committee, and perhaps even party offices – with their sizable staffs and budgets, members might even be thought of as heading small political enterprises.

Over the long term, a member's resources may expand. As a legislator takes on more important party or committee leadership positions, he or she will gain more influence and additional budget and staff support. Because many committee

4 Richard F. Fenno, Jr., *The Making of a Senator: Dan Quayle* (Washington, DC: Congressional Quarterly Press, 1989), 29.

Numbered chips are placed in order before the start of the room lottery draw and selection for the incoming members of the 114th Congress (2015–2016).

leadership posts are allocated on the basis of seniority, these additional resources are acquired by winning reelection repeatedly. In this way, the value of a House or Senate seat – to the member and to home constituents – increases with time.

Personal Office and Staff Allowances

For the first time in 1893, the House voted to permit the use of government funds to hire personal staff assistants. Until then, members either paid for assistants with their own funds or relied on family members, usually wives and daughters. Even committee aides were rare until the mid-nineteenth century. Only after office buildings were built adjacent to the Capitol early in the twentieth century did rank-and-file members acquire personal offices. Before then, only top party leaders and committee chairs were given separate rooms in the Capitol.

In the modern Congress, a spending bill for the legislative branch is passed each year. It specifies a certain amount of money for members' personal offices. In recent decades, members in both chambers have been given more discretion over the use of these funds. In 1987, the Senate adopted reforms that consolidated senators' office and staff allowances into a single, fungible account called the Senators' Official Personnel and Office Expense Account (SOPOEA). Whereas the previous system limited the portion of a senator's total personal budget that he or she could allocate to staff or office expenses, the reforms lifted those constraints. Senators now receive a single allowance from which they can determine the mix of resources that best suits their needs. In 1996, the House followed the Senate's lead by putting into place the Members' Representational Allowance (MRA) system. Prior to the MRA, members were required to pay for resources from three separate accounts – the clerk-hire allowance, the official expenses allowance, and the official mail allowance. The MRA puts these allowances under a single, flexible account and permits members to interchange funds freely.

Rational Choice Theory and Members' Goals

Rational choice theory is a school of thought that posits that human behavior is purposive. In other words, when individuals make decisions, they select the alternatives that yield the greatest returns. This perspective, which took root in political science in the 1970s, offers a basis for generalizable theories of politics. Rather than viewing political behavior as unique to the social circumstances, rational choice theory views it as the product of goal-oriented actors who seek to maximize privately held values. Using basic assumptions regarding the goals of political actors, one can deduce the expected behavior of legislators individually and collectively.

Although we certainly cannot know the motivations of all political actors in all circumstances, there are political goals that are common to legislators that offer considerable leverage in predicting legislative behavior. As discussed in this chapter, we know that most legislators desire reelection in the modern era. Reelection, therefore, serves as a central goal in many rational choice models of Congress. In addition, legislators might be assumed to have policy preferences and to pursue legislative strategies that yield policy outcomes as close to those preferences as possible. The spatial theory outlined in the Appendix is based on this kind of rational choice theory.

Although members in both chambers have a single account, the different needs of the members require that components of the accounts be calculated separately. In the House, members are allocated identical amounts for personnel, and are entitled to hire up to twenty-two employees – eighteen full-time and four part-time. That limit is up from eight in 1955, ten in 1965, and eighteen in 1975. Although there are a few restrictions on how office funds may be used, representatives are largely free to allocate staff as they see fit. The office and mailing expense components of the account vary from member to member depending on a variety of factors, such as the cost of traveling to his or her district from Washington, long-distance phone costs to the district, and the cost of renting office space in the district. In calendar year 2014, the MRAs ranged from $1,195,554 to $1,370,009, with an average of $1,255,909.

In the Senate, there is no explicit limit to the number of staff aides a senator can hire. Personal staff funding varies according to state population. Senators from large states have funding to hire many more staff assistants than do senators from small states. In addition, each senator receives an equal amount of funds above the clerk-hire allowance for the hire of three legislative assistants. Senators also have an official expense allowance to cover office, telephone,

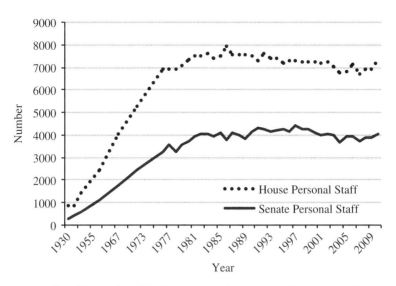

Figure 4.3 Number of Personal Staff in the House and Senate, 1930–2010. Source: Norman J. Ornstein, Thomas E. Mann, Michael J. Malbin, Andrew Rugg, and Raffaela Wakeman, *Vital Statistics on Congress, 2014* (Washington, DC: Brookings Institution and American Enterprise Institute, 2014).

travel, and mailing costs. This allowance varies from one senator to another, as it does in the House. In fiscal year 2015, these accounts ranged from to $2,984,433 to $4,722,299, with an average of $3,235,422.

In addition to their personal staffs, many members enjoy sizable staffs in their capacity as committee leaders – chairs or ranking minority members. Committee staffs are particularly important to senators, nearly all of whom are committee or subcommittee leaders. From time to time, members shift staff between their committee and personal offices in response to changing priorities. The combined personal and committee staffs responsible to a member can be quite large. A large-state senator who chairs a committee can have more than one hundred staff assistants reporting to him or her.

The total number of congressional staff workers grew steadily between the 1930s and the 1980s. The 1960s and 1970s marked a period of particularly rapid expansion of personal and committee staff in both chambers. The numbers have remained relatively stable since the early 1980s, as shown in Figure 4.3. The Senate, having a smaller membership, employs fewer total staff, although senators have more personal and committee staff per capita than representatives have. In fact, the per capita advantage held by senators is substantial. In 2010, for example, the average senator had approximately 2.4 times more personal staff than the average representative.

One of the first decisions new members face is how to divide their staff between their home and Washington offices. Since the 1960s, as the size of lawmakers'

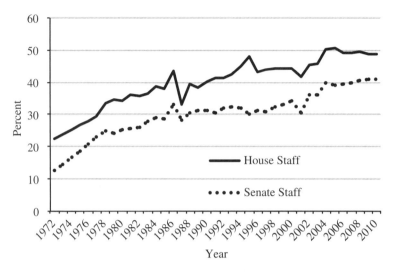

Figure 4.4 Percentage of Personal Office Staff Located in District or State Offices, 1972–2010. Source: Norman J. Ornstein, Thomas E. Mann, Michael J. Malbin, Andrew Rugg, and Raffaela Wakeman, *Vital Statistics on Congress, 2014* (Washington, DC: Brookings Institution and American Enterprise Institute, 2014).

personal staffs has increased, more members have placed staff aides in their home district or state. New members have led the way in exploiting larger staff allocations to develop a more visible presence at home. As seen in Figure 4.4, the percentage of personal staff working in district or state offices has gradually

Representative Charlie Dent (R-Pennsylvania) hosts a town hall meeting at a train station in Kutztown, Pennsylvania, to meet with his constituents.

increased since 1970. In recent years, approximately half of the personal staff of House members and more than two-fifths of the personal staff of senators have worked in district or state offices. Members have shifted more responsibility for constituency service to their home-office staffs, allowing their Washington staffs to devote more time to legislative and policy work. Senators, having larger staffs, keep a higher percentage of their staff in Washington.

Enlarged staffs have helped members meet increased demands for casework while more vigorously pursuing their legislative activities in Washington. Of course, members still differ in how they allocate their staff resources. First-term members seeking to solidify their hold on their seat often concentrate staff in their district. Senior members, who developed their staffing practices when members could not hire as many assistants and now have greater responsibilities in Washington, are often accustomed to having fewer local offices and tend to devote more staff resources to their Washington offices. In the House, a few committee and party leaders focus their personal staffs almost exclusively on constituency service and rely on committee or leadership staffs for their legislative work.

Types of Congressional Staff

There are numerous types of congressional staff. Because legislators organize their own office staffs, there is tremendous variation in organization and titles. Some positions (e.g., legislative counsel) are quite rare in personal offices but quite common in committee staffs. Among the most common types of staff positions on Capitol Hill are chief of staff, legislative director (LD), legislative assistant (LA), constituent services representative or caseworker, and legislative correspondent (LC).

The top personal aide to a member is usually a chief of staff or administrative assistant (AA). The holder of this position oversees the entire operation and manages all staff. The legislative director supervises the policy staff and typically works closely with the member to devise legislative strategies. Legislative assistants are responsible for the legislator's work on specified policy areas and assist with committee work. Those charged with responding to constituent communications are often given the title of legislative correspondent.

All personal offices have constituent service representatives or caseworkers. These assistants are primarily dedicated to *casework*, the term used to describe constituents' problems that members are asked to solve. Casework ranges from solving a problem with Social Security checks to arranging for a leave for a soldier who just had a death in the family. These assistants usually are located in district or state offices where they can deal with constituents directly. They communicate electronically with federal agencies and the Capitol Hill office. Most legislators consider an effective caseworker essential to building a good

TABLE 4.1. Frequency of staff titles in personal staff offices and location of staff, 2010

Position title	Mean number per office	Typical location of staff member
Chief of Staff	1.08	Capitol Hill Office
Legislative Director	1.03	Capitol Hill Office
Senior Legislative Aide	1.29	Capitol Hill Office
Legislative Assistant	1.86	Capitol Hill Office
Legislative Correspondent	1.11	Capitol Hill Office
Office Manager/Executive Assistant	1.02	Capitol Hill Office
Press Secretary	1.14	Capitol Hill Office
Financial Administrator	1.00	Capitol Hill Office
Scheduler	1.15	Capitol Hill Office
Systems Administrator	1.00	Capitol Hill Office
Staff Assistant (D.C.)	1.10	Capitol Hill Office
Staff Assistant (District)	1.25	District Office
Constituent Services Representative	3.09	District Office
District Director	1.12	District Office
Field Representative	1.92	District Office

Source: "2010 House Compensation Study," Chief Administrative Officer, U.S. House of Representatives, 2010.

reputation. As can be seen in Table 4.1, members adopt a wide range of strategies in choosing staff.

Travel and Recesses

Just as an increase in staff has reduced the severity of the trade-offs members must make in setting priorities, expanded travel allowances and official recesses have enabled members to spend more time with constituents at home without fear of missing meetings or votes on Capitol Hill. Since the 1960s, the amount of time that incumbents spend in their home districts and states has grown steadily. Before 1970, for example, House and Senate members averaged about two or three days per month at home. By 1980, House members were spending an average of about ten days each month at home, and senators spent an average of six or seven days a month at home – a pace that they have maintained since then. In general, senior members spend less time in their districts, but members of both houses and at all levels of seniority make more trips home during an election year.

Both the House and the Senate have moved to accommodate members' needs to travel to their home districts and states. The House, for example, rarely holds votes on Mondays or Fridays. Members are thus free to fly home on Thursday evenings and return to Washington in time for Tuesday votes. Members of the "Tuesday-Thursday club" can maximize their time at home among constituents without great cost to their performance in Washington. The 2015 House calendar, for example, scheduled only fifteen Friday sessions, which represents a 30 percent drop compared to 2011, the first session of the 112th Congress (2011–2012). Former House Majority Leader Eric Cantor (R-Virginia), asserted that "[t]ime spent in the district between Friday and Monday is essential for meeting with small businesses, employees, seniors, veterans and other local communities during working hours." Travel to home districts has become so frequent that many members of Congress do not even own or rent homes in the Washington area because they spend only two nights a week there. Several legislators have slept in their offices, sometimes for several years, before finding a residence in the D.C. area.

Living Away from Washington

There appears to be a trend among new House members to avoid establishing residence in Washington, D.C. A survey of the freshman members in the 112th Congress (2011–2012) showed that only one of the forty-six new members interviewed would relocate his or her spouse and children to Washington. Others suggested that they would stay in Washington only for those days in which there was legislative business. One member, Representative Chris Gibson (R-New York), stated that he would be sleeping on a blow-up mattress in his Washington office and would "hightail it back" to his district on the weekends.

It could be argued that members who reside almost exclusively in their home districts have greater opportunity to interact with their constituents. This might yield more faithful representation of constituent preferences. Moreover, to members themselves, keeping their primary residence in their home districts helps them avoid the image of becoming Washington "insiders."

In contrast, some observers suggest that these living arrangements could have negative implications for lawmaking. In particular, it is argued that a quality legislative process requires lawmakers to know and respect each other. Meaningful relationships are developed when members get to know one another outside of work and when their families socialize. Senator Trent Lott (R-Mississippi) once commented that when a lawmaker cultivates such a relationship, "it's impossible to go up on the floor of the Senate or in the media and blast him the next day." Perhaps this trend has been a contributing factor to the partisan polarization and hostilities witnessed in recent Congresses.

Source: Lisa Miller, "The Commuter Congress," *Newsweek*, January 3, 2011.

In both chambers, but particularly in the House, the number of official recess days increased significantly in the late 1960s and has remained high since then. In most years, official recesses now consume more than 100 days, not including weekends. The houses compensate for the increased number of recess days by concentrating their sessions into somewhat longer days, as shown in Figure 4.5.

The figure presents the number of hours that the chambers were in session between the 82nd and 113th Congresses (1951–2014). There is a noticeable

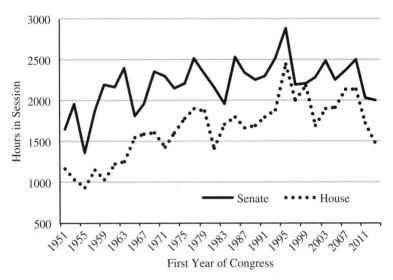

Figure 4.5 Hours Spent in Session in the House and Senate, 1951–2014. Source: Résumés of congressional activity.

increase in the number of hours in session for both chambers. For instance, the 113th House and Senate (2013–2014) were in session approximately 408 and 194 more hours, respectively, than the average Congress in the 1950s (82nd to 86th). No committee markups or floor sessions are held during recesses, so members know that they are free to go home.

Congressional Mail

Mail is a resource members use to remain visible in their districts between elections. By placing their signature where a stamp would go on an envelope (the frank), members of Congress may send mail through the U.S. Postal Service. Congressional offices are given budgets for this specific purpose. Members can maintain a presence at home by sending their constituents franked mail at the taxpayers' expense. Since World War II, the amount of mail sent by House and Senate members has grown steadily. Mail totals surge during election years and then drop in off years, a pattern that reflects members' efforts to advertise themselves as elections draw near. Figure 4.6 documents the total pieces of mass mail (1997–2008) and communication (2009–2012) by fiscal year in the House. We observe a sawtooth pattern to members' communication behavior, with the peaks occurring in even years (i.e., election years).

Some of the increase in mail from Capitol Hill in recent decades is the result of an increase in constituents' opinion letters and requests for assistance from congressional offices (casework). As the population grows and constituencies become larger, legislators must respond by mail to a larger volume of demands;

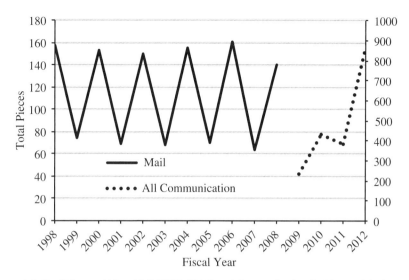

Figure 4.6 Total Pieces of Mass Mail (1997–2008) and Communication (2009–2012) in the House (in millions) by Fiscal Year. Source: Matthew Eric Glassman, "Franking Privilege: Mass Mailing and Mass Communications in the House, 1997–2012," CRS Report RL34458.

but that is only part of the story. Members more actively solicit opinions and casework in their newsletters and personal appearances – they are happy to be of service to voters. Moreover, most of the increase in outgoing mail is because of the vast increases in mass mailings from members' offices to their home districts and states. In fact, by one estimate, more than 90 percent of the mail sent by Congress consists of mass mailings of newsletters. Critics of the practice frequently cite the use of the frank for campaign-related publicity as an unfair incumbent advantage, and there is some evidence to support their view. Incumbents, on the other hand, argue that newsletters are essential for keeping their constituents informed about members' activities as their representatives. Despite lawsuits that have called into question the constitutionality of the franking privilege, the practice has withstood legal scrutiny.

Those Nasty Letters from Constituents

Most famous among the many witty responses that members and their staff have devised for constituents is the standard reply to critical letters issued by Ohio Representative Wayne Hays:

Dear Sir:

Today I received a letter from some crackpot who signed your name to it. I thought you ought to know about this before it went further.

Source: Neil MacNeil, *Forge of Democracy: The House of Representatives* (New York: D. McKay, 1963), 141.

Other Resources: Party Organizations and Support Agencies

The resources made available to legislators (at public expense) have expanded in many dimensions. A very conspicuous development is the expansion of House and Senate radio and television studios. Legislators use satellite up-link equipment to make appearances on local stations without leaving Capitol Hill. The congressional parties also have their own facilities, which are used heavily – most members send regular radio programs to district stations. These programs are aired mostly, if not exclusively, by small-town stations with limited budgets and staff to purchase or produce their own programming. In addition, members sometimes can convince local television stations to use video news releases beamed in from Washington.

The addition and expansion of congressional support agencies (see box "The Changing Congress: Congressional Support Agencies") have made more expertise available to members seeking assistance and advice on policy questions. The assistance of policy analysts, scholars, lawyers, and other professionals in the support agencies makes it easier for rank-and-file members without large committee staffs to write bills and amendments, conduct studies, and meet constituents' requests for information.

Members are further aided by the computerization of Capitol Hill. Information networks give members and their staff instant electronic access to the texts of bills and amendments, to legislative summaries and analyses prepared by the Congressional Research Service, and to a variety of databases on economic and social conditions and government programs. Computers also allow members to transmit large volumes of information among their Washington and home offices; in addition, social networking sites, like Facebook and Twitter, open up additional pathways of communication between members and their constituents.

The tremendous expansion of the interest group community in Washington has also bolstered rank-and-file members' access to experts and information. By various counts, the number of lobbyists and others employed by interest groups doubled during the 1970s and 1980s, after having grown substantially in the preceding decades. Interest groups regularly distribute valuable information and make policy and legal expertise available to friendly members. Think tanks – nonprofit organizations that produce studies and policy recommendations – also have expanded the availability of expert advice and assistance.

INFLUENCES ON MEMBERS

Members act strategically. Their actions are a product not only of their own preferences and resources but also of the actions and anticipated actions of others. Members care about other political actors – constituents, interest groups, party and committee leaders, presidents, and colleagues – because members rely on these actors to achieve their goals. Similarly, other actors place demands on members of Congress because the members have something they want: influence over policy choices affecting them. The nature of the demands placed on members is the subject of this section.

Constituencies

Most members share the perspective of most of their constituents on major issues. This connection between legislators and their constituents is perhaps the most important force in congressional politics. It originates in the process by which legislators are selected. Voters tend to favor candidates whose views are close to their own. Just as liberal, Democratic districts tend to elect liberal Democrats to Congress, conservative, Republican districts tend to elect conservative Republicans. As a result, legislators represent their constituencies' views fairly well simply by following their own political dispositions. In this way, legislators' personal views, the views of their constituents, and even partisanship tend to be mutually reinforcing influences on members' decisions. Figure 4.7 shows the correspondence between the policy positions of House members serving in the 113th Congress (2013–2014) and their districts' partisanship. There is a clear positive relationship, with increasingly conservative districts electing members who pursue increasingly conservative policy positions. Note that the absence of members located in the middle of the ideological spectrum is a testament to the rising levels of polarization in the modern era.

Defining the interests and preferences of a legislator's constituency is, however, no simple matter. After all, the public rarely speaks with one voice and is

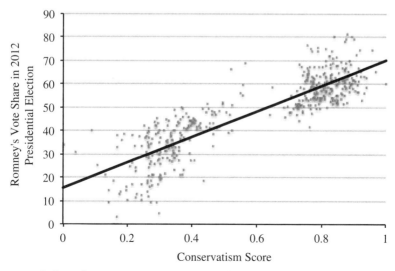

Figure 4.7 Ideology of House Representatives Serving from 2013 to 2014 by District Partisanship. Source: Ideal points estimated by authors using roll call data from the 113th Congress available at voteview.com.

rarely attuned to what is going on in Congress. Richard Fenno proposes that members perceive constituents in four categories that can be conceptualized as concentric circles (see box "Members' Perceived Constituencies"). A member's strongest political friends (intimates) are at the center, and they are encircled by a larger group of constituents who support the member in primary elections. Next is an even larger group that supports the member in general elections but whose support is more tenuous. The entire district population stands as the fourth, or geographic, constituency. Fenno observes that legislators develop styles – home styles, he calls them – for relating to each of these constituencies. Moreover, it is increasingly difficult for members to assess the preferences of voters in the outmost circles.

The Changing Congress: Congressional Support Agencies

Congress has created a number of support agencies within the legislative branch to provide a variety of functions that are not conveniently provided by standing committees and their staffs. These units serve as nonpartisan servants of Congress and cost more than a half billion dollars each year.

Congressional Budget Office (CBO). Created in 1974, the CBO provides economic forecasts, cost estimates for legislation, and other fiscal policy studies. The CBO works most closely with the budget, appropriations, and tax committees and has approximately 235 employees.

Congressional Research Service (CRS). Created in 1970 from the Legislative Reference Service, the CRS provides policy research in nearly all policy areas and functions as a library reference service. The CRS has nearly 600 employees. It responds to requests from committees and individual members and often lends policy experts to committees.

Government Accountability Office (GAO). Created in 1921 as the General Accounting Office (renamed in 2004), the GAO audits executive branch agencies, sets government accounting standards, settles certain claims against the government, gives legal opinions, and conducts policy studies as requested by formal acts of Congress, committees, and individual members. The GAO has approximately 3,000 employees.

Concern about how activities in Washington will play at home often preoccupies legislators. Members have to anticipate whether a roll call vote or other public action will come back to haunt them in a future campaign. Party and coalition leaders, lobbyists, and presidents seeking support from a member must consider how that member's vote will be regarded back home. All participants know that high-profile issues – abortion, tax increases, Social Security, and congressional pay raises – always attract a more attentive public whose views must be considered. Taking a position at odds with one's constituents can result in a member being punished at the polls in the next election. For instance, research has shown that incumbents who supported health care reform in early 2010 were perceived by their constituents as being out of step with their preferences (i.e., excessively liberal), and therefore these members faced electoral consequences in that year's election.

This could, in part, explain the staggering losses experienced by the Democrats in that election cycle. On some issues, only a narrow constituency takes an interest, but its interest may be so intense that members are compelled to pay attention to it. On other issues – perhaps, even on most matters that come before Congress – members need not be overly concerned about the electoral consequences of their decisions. However, the uncertainty of electoral consequences may still keep some members guessing about the political costs and benefits at home of their actions.

Representatives and senators have several ways to gauge constituents' opinions. When a particularly controversial issue comes up, a wave of letters, phone calls, and e-mails is likely to flood members' district and Washington offices. Much of the incoming post takes the form of preprinted letters or cards supplied by lobbying groups. Because it takes little effort to send that kind of mail, legislators may not put much stock in it. However, members are attentive to groups of constituents with intensely held preferences. In such cases, members usually take note of where the letters are coming from and bear in mind the level of interest expressed.

Members' Perceived Constituencies

The political scientist Richard F. Fenno, Jr., observes that many members view their constituencies as a set of concentric circles, ranging from their closest political confidants (the intimates), to their strongest supporters in the electorate (the primary constituency), to voters who vote for them (the reelection constituency), to their whole state or district (the geographic constituency). A great source of uncertainty for members is the variable composition of the primary and reelection constituencies.

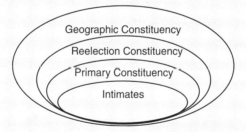

Source: Richard F. Fenno, Jr., *Home Style: House Members in Their Districts* (Boston: Little, Brown, 1978).

Members also learn constituents' opinions from interacting with them at home and in Washington. Most members hold town meetings or other forums in their district to give constituents a way to express their views. While at home, attentive members are almost always asking questions of and listening to their constituents. In Washington, many members schedule regular events, such as a weekly coffee, to provide an additional outlet for constituents to voice their opinions. The Internet has facilitated the interaction between members and constituents by reducing the need for the two to communicate in person (see box "The Changing Congress: Members and Social Media"). With increasing frequency, legislators commission public opinion polls with campaign funds, most often at campaign time.

Interest Groups and Lobbyists

For many people, lobbyists and interest groups represent the unseemly, even corrupt, side of congressional politics. "Money talks," "the best Congress money can buy," and "the golden rule of politics – whoever has the gold rules" – are among the clichés that capture common fears about who really runs Congress. Just where the line between legitimate representation and bribery falls is one of the ambiguities confronting every democratic system of government. On the one hand, lobbying is protected by constitutional guarantees of free speech, free association, and the right to petition the government for redress of grievances. Lobbying often involves building support for a position by bargaining, providing assistance to legislators, and even providing timely campaign contributions. On the other hand, lobbying can cross the line into bribery when cash or other material considerations are traded for certain official actions, such as introducing a bill or casting a particular vote. To many, the whole business of lobbying seems tainted.

Perhaps the most important change in Washington in recent decades has been the great expansion and fragmentation of Washington's interest group community. The best study of the subject indicates that most interest groups were formed after World War II, that the formation of groups has accelerated in recent decades, and that more and more groups are locating in Washington, D.C. (see Chapter 11). Many single-issue groups have been created, and nearly every industry group has professional representation in Congress. In the health care industry, for example, the older American Medical Association is joined by associations for hospitals, medical schools, medical equipment manufacturers, health insurance companies, and a variety of professional associations of nurses, dentists, and others.

The Changing Congress: Members and Social Media

Social media has become an invaluable resource to members of Congress, as outlets such as Facebook, Twitter, and the like provide a relatively low-cost means for members to interact with their constituents. A recent survey of the senior staff and social media managers in congressional offices found that social media has become a central means of communicating with constituents. In fact, approximately 64 percent of those surveyed indicated that Facebook was an important tool for understanding constituents' views and opinions, 42 percent said the same about Twitter, and 34 percent indicated such about YouTube. In addition, social media outlets offer members another platform for disseminating an image or message. The aforementioned survey also found that 74, 51, and 72 percent of those surveyed viewed Facebook, Twitter, and YouTube, respectively, as important means for members to communicate their views and activities to their constituents.

While members have begun to capitalize on the proliferation of social networking websites, their use is not without restrictions. Until 2008, there had been a long-standing rule prohibiting members of Congress from posting official communication on websites outside of the house.gov and senate.gov domains, in part because third-party websites may contain advertising and politicking. Led by Representative John Culberson (R-Texas), who openly violated the rule during a debate over offshore oil drilling by tweeting, "I just learned the Dems are trying to censor Congressmen's ability to use Twitter QuikYouTubeUtterz etc – outrageous and I will fight them," the House and Senate changed their rules to allow members to post communication on external websites provided that the members and the websites themselves abide by certain guidelines. Nearly all legislators now have official Twitter accounts, and the website TweetCongress.org provides a convenient interface to follow members who tweet. YouTube has also launched *House Hub* and *Senate Hub*, which allow members to create and manage their own channels. However, there is a prohibition on members posting personal or campaign information to their social media accounts. Posting such information would constitute an ethics violation, although the House Ethics Committee has yet to sanction a member for doing so. To avoid violating the rules, many members set up separate, unofficial, social media accounts to post personal and campaign information.

Particularly noteworthy is the rise of "citizens' groups" or "public interest groups," organized around a general cause rather than a narrow economic interest. Good-government groups such as Common Cause, environmental groups such as the Sierra Club, and consumer product groups such as the Consumers' Union are examples. About one-fifth of all lobbying groups counted in 1980 were citizens' groups. In addition, more corporations, state and local governments, universities, and other organizations have established Washington offices for in-house lobbyists. By one estimate, the number of corporations with Washington offices increased tenfold between 1961 and 1982. One consequence of this expansion in Washington-based representation of organized interests is that the clout of individual lobbyists and groups has actually declined. Often, large coalitions of lobbyists and interest groups pool their resources to overcome the fragmentation in the interest group community.

Party Leaders

Party pressures in congressional politics are weaker in the United States than in most other national legislatures. Representatives and senators rarely are dependent on party organizations – national or local – to secure reelection. Moreover, party leaders in Congress have relatively few ways to compel rank-and-file members to comply with their wishes. In fact, party leaders generally want their party colleagues to pursue legislative strategies that will enhance their chances of reelection. When members of a congressional party vote in unison, it is more often a product of their shared policy views and similar constituency expectations than of pressure from party leaders.

Still, partisan pressures are ever-present in Congress. In fact, we see evidence of a more assertive party leadership in the modern Congresses – one that is

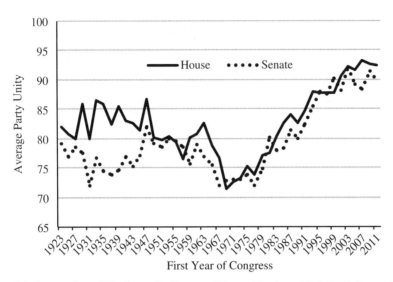

Figure 4.8 Average Party Unity Scores for House and Senate Members, 1923–2012. Source: Party unity scores by member available at voteview.com. Averages calculated by authors.

willing to punish members for disloyalty. Because many decisions that members make have no direct electoral consequences, members are generally free to meet the demands of party leaders. This may be partially responsible for the high levels of party loyalty across time. Figure 4.8 shows the average party loyalty for representatives and senators by Congress. In the 112th Congress (2011–2012), for instance, representatives and senators voted with their party on divisive votes 92 and 90 percent of the time, respectively. Although this may conjure the image that party leaders are forcing members to cooperate with their party, much of the influence of party on legislators' behavior is indirect. For example, party leaders set the floor agenda and, particularly in the House, shape the alternatives from which members must choose. Occasionally, however, particularly on close votes, the direct pressure of party leaders can be critical. Even then, the leaders target just a few members whose votes will make the difference between winning and losing.

The President

Presidents need support from legislators for their own legislative programs, and they can wield considerable influence in their efforts to gain it. Much of the support that presidents receive from lawmakers comes from their partisan ties to members. Because members' own electoral fortunes are affected by the popularity of the president, members of the president's party have a stake in the president's success and thus provide a natural base of support. The size of that base of support depends on past congressional election outcomes, the diversity within party coalitions, and the president's popularity. Every member must decide when to stick with the president and when it is safe to ignore the president's wishes.

A president can also influence members' choices by influencing the congressional agenda. By pushing major legislative proposals, a president can help define the issues that dominate the congressional agenda and how the major alternatives are debated. A successful president draws the attention of the media, the public, and legislators away from issues that hurt him and toward issues that help him. An effective president also knows that his influence over the congressional agenda is tenuous. Presidents, after all, cannot require either house of Congress to vote on their proposals, or even to take their proposals seriously.

The task of presidents is primarily one of persuasion. Presidents have a variety of tools for influencing individual legislators (see Chapter 9). Presidents' primary source of influence is their formal power to sign or to veto legislation, which gives them a source of leverage over members who want to see their own legislation enacted into law. Presidents' ease of access to the media gives them an advantage over members and other actors in shaping public opinion. In addition, their influence on agency decisions, which can have widespread implications for policy implementation, gives presidents more clout. That clout can be used to coax interest groups to work in support of presidents' legislative proposals or to prod legislators whose constituents are affected by executive branch decisions.

Staff

A popular theory is that members of Congress have been captured by their staffs. Michael Malbin's book, *Unelected Representatives*, lends credence to this view. Malbin, a political scientist who worked for many years as a Capitol Hill reporter and staff member, argues that "the staffs – individually well educated, hard working, and, in general, devoted to what they perceive to be the public good – collectively create a situation in which many of the elected members fear they are becoming insulated administrators in a bureaucratized organization that leaves them no better able to cope than they were when they did all the work themselves."[5]

Malbin observes that staff assistants do a good job of representing their bosses, but, he continues, members delegate to their aides too much authority to initiate legislation, negotiate compromises, and narrow the range of policy choices offered to them. Staff assistants have created more work for members, distanced members from one another, and turned members into office managers. Staff influence is pervasive in Congress, and it is felt both in the early stages of the legislative process, in the setting of members' and committees' agendas, and at the late stages when the final details of legislation are worked out.

5 Michael J. Malbin, *Unelected Representatives: Congressional Staff and the Future of Representative Government* (New York: Basic Books, 1980), 5.

CHOOSING STRATEGIES

Political scientists have no comprehensive theory to explain how members' goals, resources, and political environment combine to produce their strategies. Nevertheless, they have done a reasonably good job of describing and explaining members' behavior in one decision-making arena: roll call voting on the floor. A newer area of research looks at policy leaders' coalition-building strategies, which focuses on how members solicit support from their colleagues. This section briefly reviews what we know about the typical member's approach to roll call voting and coalition leadership and contrasts the strategies in these two areas of legislative activity.

ROLL CALL VOTING ON THE FLOOR

Casting roll call votes is one activity that members consider mandatory. Members want a good attendance record so that future opponents will not be able to charge that they are shirking their responsibilities. Maintaining a good attendance record is not easy, and maintaining a perfect record is nearly impossible. In the 113th Congress (2013–2014), for instance, the average member voted on slightly more than 96 percent of the roll call votes held, which is a typical percentage in recent Congresses. Figure 4.9 shows the number of recorded votes taken in both chambers between the 82nd and 113th Congresses (1951–2014). In

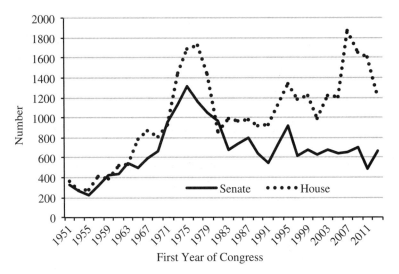

Figure 4.9 Number of Recorded Votes per Congress in the House and Senate, 1951–2014.
Source: Résumés of congressional activity.

modern Congresses (since 1991), senators and representatives have faced an average of 662 and 1,297 roll call votes per Congress, respectively (the difference is partially attributed to the greater ease of recorded voting in the House). Plainly, members are forced to cast votes with such frequency that they cannot possibly study each issue with care. They are, however, aware that they may have to explain a vote to some constituents, perhaps in response to a challenger's charges in some future campaign, or to some party or committee leader. Therefore, most members develop a general strategy for how to approach roll call voting.

From time to time, members are confronted with particularly difficult choices. Over the course of 2012, Democrats and Republicans were locked in a bitter budget battle. Failure to reach an agreement on the budget before January 1, 2013, would send the nation over the proverbial "fiscal cliff," resulting in widespread tax increases and spending cuts to defense, unemployment benefits, and other valued programs. Just after the January 1 deadline, Congress reached a temporary deal that avoided some, but not all, of these punishing spending cuts and tax increases (H.R. 8). For some Republicans, however, particularly those representing the most conservative districts, the agreement created a real predicament. A vote *against* the bill would convey the message that they were not team players and were willing to risk the dangers of going over the fiscal cliff, whereas a vote *for* the bill would implicitly endorse the largest tax increase in the past two decades without any long-term spending cuts. In the end, the bill passed both chambers despite the opposition of a majority of House Republicans. Although the bill passed by unanimous consent in the Senate, 151 House Republicans voted against the bill. Not surprisingly, the members voting against the bill hailed from districts that were considerably more conservative than the districts represented by members who voted in favor of the bill (see Figure 4.10). In fact, Republicans voting against the bill represented districts in which Republican presidential nominee Senator John McCain (R-Arizona) received, on average, 56.5 percent of the two-party vote share in the 2008 presidential election. Compare this to the 50.1 percent of the vote that McCain received, on average, in districts represented by Republicans who voted in favor of the bill. Therefore, for a majority of House Republicans, the electoral concerns of voting for a bill that was out of step with their constituencies outweighed the potentially unfortunate consequences of a failed agreement.

The political scientist John Kingdon conducted an ingenious study of the vote decision and reported the results in his book *Congressmen's Voting Decisions.* Kingdon interviewed members about how they had made up their minds on a series of fairly important votes on controversial issues that had been the subject of substantial political activity. Kingdon asked a simple question about each vote: "How did you go about making up your mind?" He then noted whether the members mentioned their constituencies spontaneously, only in response to a follow-up question, or not at all. For most of the members, the votes concerned

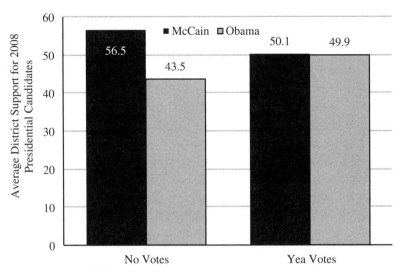

Figure 4.10 Average District Partisanship by Vote for House Republicans on the 2013 Fiscal Cliff Agreement (H.R. 8).

issues that fell under the jurisdiction of committees on which they did not sit. Therefore, most members interviewed by Kingdon had not had the benefit of listening to expert testimony in hearings.

Members' responses to Kingdon's questions show several important patterns (see Table 4.2). First, constituency considerations are frequently involved but are not always the most important factor. Members mentioned constituencies spontaneously 37 percent of the time. Although members spontaneously mentioned fellow members more frequently than they did constituents, constituents ranked above every other group in this category. Members mentioned constituencies in response to probes 50 percent of the time and failed to mention constituencies altogether only 13 percent of the time.

TABLE 4.2. The frequency with which legislators mentioned political actors as factors in their voting decisions (percent of voting decisions)

	Constituency	Fellow members	Interest groups	Administration	Party leaders
Mentioned spontaneously	37	40	31	25	10
Mentioned in response to a question	50	35	35	14	28
Not mentioned	13	25	35	60	62

Source: John Kingdon, *Congressmen's Voting Decisions*, 2nd ed. (New York: Harper & Row, 1981).

Kingdon also found that the more salient the issue, the more likely members were to consider constituents' wishes to be of major importance in making their decisions. Consequently, they were more likely to vote in agreement with the constituency opinion they identified. Even on issues of low or medium salience, members were likely to give weight to, and vote in agreement with, constituency opinion. On most issues, members rely on trusted colleagues for cues about how to vote. In response to Kingdon's questions about their voting decisions, members mentioned their colleagues either spontaneously or after prompting 75 percent of the time (Table 4.2). As one member noted, "On a run-of-the-mill vote, on an obscure bill, you need some guidance. You don't know what's in it, and don't have time to find out." Fellow members serve as informants who reduce uncertainty about the policy and political implications of a roll call vote.

With so many staff assistants and lobbyists circulating on Capitol Hill, why do members rely so heavily on one another? Members turn to certain colleagues because they trust that their fellow representatives and senators, professional politicians with problems similar to their own, will make comparable calculations about which course of action to pursue. In fact, members tend to rely on colleagues from the same party, state, and region – colleagues who can help them assess the political consequences of their votes – and on committee members who know the issue well. Fellow legislators also are in the right place at the right time – on the floor as roll call votes are being conducted.

Members obtain guidance from fellow members in many ways. One way is to read the "Dear Colleague" letters that are routinely sent to all members, explaining bills and soliciting support for amendments. These letters are usually concise arguments in favor of a bill, and they often explain how a bill's opponents plan to distort the bill's true intent. For more detailed information on a bill, members or their staffs are likely to turn to the written reports that accompany most bills when they are reported by committee.

After constituents and fellow members, interest groups and the administration rank as the most important influences on members' voting decisions. Most interest group influence, Kingdon found, came from groups connected to members' constituencies. For example, farm groups played an important role for members from agricultural districts. Presidential influence is greater for members of the president's party – members who are politically connected to the president and have the highest stakes in the president's success.

Finally, party leaders and staff aides appear to have influence only at the margins. In more recent years, party leaders probably have become more important than Kingdon found in the late 1960s, when he conducted his study (Chapter 5 describes the revitalization of party leadership in Congress). Similarly, as roll call votes have become more numerous, other burdens on members' time have grown, and staffs have expanded in the decades since Kingdon's study. Thus, members may have become more dependent on staff assistants for guidance.

In summary, members adopt strategies in response to the unique character of individual voting decisions. Roll call voting is repetitive, very public, consumes little time and few resources, is well documented, and is considered politically compulsory. Members rely on cues from colleagues to simplify their decision-making process and assess the political risks of specific votes. Members appear to be heavily influenced by constituency opinion and electoral considerations, which they assess by seeking advice from trusted colleagues and information from interest groups. At the same time, constituency considerations are seldom the sole or even the decisive influence on members' votes.

Coalition Leadership

Serving as a coalition leader on a legislative issue lies at the other end of the spectrum of legislative activities. In contrast to roll call voting, assuming a leadership role on an issue may not be very visible to the general public, is difficult to document, consumes more time and resources, and is normally discretionary. Consequently, the strategies of policy leaders may be shaped by a different mix of considerations than are voting decisions.

The political scientist David Mayhew observes that the goal of reelection, although nearly universally held by members, motivates little leadership activity within Congress. The effort to mobilize colleagues for or against legislation is worthwhile for a reelection-oriented member only if constituents or important financial contributors are paying close attention to the member's behavior. On most matters, merely advertising one's position and token efforts – citing speeches made, legislation introduced, and amendments offered – may be all that is required to receive maximum electoral benefit from an issue. Certainly, members do not actually have to win legislative battles as long as the people who affect their reelection prospects – people with votes, money, or endorsements – believe that they have put up a good fight.

If Mayhew is right, most genuine leadership is motivated by goals beyond reelection. A member aspiring to higher office may seek special distinction and media attention by championing a legislative cause. A committee chair, seeking to preserve a reputation for influence, may assume the lead in writing legislation and soliciting support simply to avoid being overshadowed by a rank-and-file member who would otherwise take over. That same rank-and-file member may pursue a policy leadership role because no one else seems equally committed to his or her policy views.

Senator Pete Domenici (R-New Mexico), who was a prominent legislator in budgeting and fiscal policy, is a good example of a policy leader motivated by objectives beyond reelection. Fenno, in his book about Domenici's rise as a Senate leader, explains:

From the beginning of his Washington career, Pete Domenici's most transparent goal was to become a policy-making "player" inside the Senate. The chairmanship [of the Budget Committee] brought him that influence. His first two years in that position, he said later, "made me a senator." He wanted to keep or expand the policy influence he had gained. A second goal – institutional maintenance – has been imposed on him by this chairmanship. And Domenici adopted that one, too – to protect and to preserve the budget process itself. The two goals did not always lead to the same decision. In the two years ahead, he would often be forced to choose between his desire for inside policy influence and his desire to keep the budget process alive.[6]

Domenici's reelection prospects, Fenno recounts, were greatly enhanced by his prominence in the Senate. He was elected to six consecutive terms (1973–2008), often winning by large margins.

Domenici's story seems typical in many respects. Electoral concerns did not seem to drive his leadership activity in Washington, even though that activity paid dividends at home. Therefore, partly by good fortune and partly by personal skill and dedication, Domenici's multiple goals of obtaining influence, making good public policy, and gaining reelection were served by his leadership activities. His goal of reelection, however, cannot account for the priority he gave to his chairmanship and the legislative tactics he pursued as chairman.

Some relevant evidence about members' goals in pursuing leadership responsibilities is available. In one study, a political scientist asked top legislative aides of a sample of 121 members of both houses to identify issues on which their boss had taken a central leadership role and to offer explanations for their boss's involvement in those issues.[7]

All aides reported that their boss had taken a leading role on some issue, large or small, but few members had taken on more than two or three issues at one time. Senators' aides tended to mention more issues than did representatives' aides, reflecting important differences between the two chambers. In the Senate, members have more committee assignments and staff, and they receive more demands from larger, more diverse constituencies.

For each issue raised by the aides, the researcher asked them, "Why did (Senator/Representative –) take the lead on this issue?" The respondents often indicated several reasons. For 52 percent of the issues mentioned, the aides noted its importance to the member's district or state, but reelection or some other constituency-related reason was the sole motivation given for only 17 percent of the issues. For 72 percent of the instances of policy leadership described, the aides mentioned their boss's personal interest or policy commitments as a motivating

---

6 Richard F. Fenno, Jr., *The Emergence of a Senate Leader: Pete Domenici and the Reagan Budget* (Washington, DC: Congressional Quarterly Press, 1991), 134.

7 A report on the Senate aides' responses can be found in Steven S. Smith, "Informal Leadership in the Senate," in *Leading Congress*, ed. John Kornacki (Washington, DC: Congressional Quarterly Press, 1990), 71–83. Most respondents were members' legislative directors or were administrative assistants.

factor. In addition, 28 percent of the issues pursued by members were related to their responsibilities as committee or subcommittee leaders. Only 3 percent of the instances of policy leadership were described as being connected to a member's pursuit of higher office.

We are led to this conjecture: Leaders – whether they are party, committee, or self-identified coalition leaders – are motivated by more than reelection, whereas their followers are motivated primarily by reelection. Followers, most of whom are not sufficiently motivated to assume a leadership role on most issues, allow their default goal – reelection – to orient their behavior. Of course, if members' reelection prospects seem unaffected by a particular issue, as they often are, they are free to pursue policy positions for other reasons. Nevertheless, it seems fair to say, coalition building on most important issues typically involves interaction between policy- or influence-oriented leaders and reelection-oriented followers.

Concluding that members ignore their reelection interests when they pursue other objectives would be a mistake. On the contrary, members often discover issues that fit them well – issues that allow them to pursue multiple goals simultaneously, including reelection. In fact, 47 percent of the staff assistants in the study readily identified more than one goal served by their boss's policy leadership activities. Forty-eight percent reported that reelection in combination with some other goal, usually good public policy, had motivated policy leadership activities.

Taking on a policy leadership role is far more discretionary than casting a roll call vote. In addition, assuming a leadership role on an issue requires an investment of resources far in excess of those involved in casting a vote. Members cannot afford to take on more than a handful of issues at a time. Because such efforts may have only small direct electoral benefits and take up time and resources that could be devoted to other activities, the potential value of the effort must be high in terms of policy objectives, personal influence or reputation, or other goals.

CONCLUSION

In this chapter, we have viewed the legislative process from the perspective of the individual member. Members' goals, resources, and strategies combine to shape their policy positions and political careers. We have seen how those goals, resources, and strategies evolve as a function of members' own choices, changes in members' institutional positions, and the evolution of Congress's political environment.

The roll call voting and policy leadership examples in this chapter illustrate the two broad political purposes of members' strategies – avoiding blame and claiming credit. Avoiding blame seems to be the dominant situation in roll call voting. The fact that roll call voting is politically mandatory creates many hazards for members. Particularly in the House, where individual members have little control over the issues on which they must vote, members must frequently choose between groups of constituents in casting their votes. In contrast, claiming credit is the more dominant motivator in policy leadership. Importantly, the opportunistic combination of goals, resources, and strategies can give a member more control over the choices he or she confronts.

Since the late 1970s, members' opportunities for policy leadership have declined as budget constraints have limited new policy initiatives. As a result, members have found that it is more difficult to counter the inevitable criticisms associated with voting by promoting one's own legislative successes. It certainly has contributed to the greater dissatisfaction with service in Congress that members have expressed in recent years and has intensified pressure on leaders to structure floor decision making more carefully.

SUGGESTED READINGS

A.   The following readings address representation from the perspective of members by exploring how members perceive their constituents and pursue their goals.

Fenno, Richard, Jr.*Home Style: House Members in Their Districts.* Boston: Little, Brown, 1978.

Lazarus, Jeffrey. "Giving the People What They Want: The Distribution of Earmarks in the U.S. House of Representatives." *American Journal of Political Science* 54, no. 2 (2010): 338–353.

Miler, Kristina C. *Congressional Representation in Congress: The View from Capitol Hill.* New York: Cambridge University Press, 2010.

Wawro, Gregory. *Legislative Entrepreneurship in the U.S. House of Representatives.* Ann Arbor: University of Michigan Press, 2000.

B.   The following readings address representation from the perspective of constituents by examining how voters respond to legislative behavior.

Canes-Wrone, Brandice, David Brady, and John Cogan. "Out of Step, Out of Office: Electoral Accountability and House Members Voting." *American Political Science Review* 96 (2002): 127–140.

Carson, Jamie L., Gregory Koger, Matthew J. Lebo, and Everett Young. "The Electoral Costs of Party Loyalty in Congress." *American Journal of Political Science* 54 (2010): 598–616.

DISCUSSION QUESTIONS

1   What are the consequences of a legislative body in which its members increasingly pursue and win reelection?

2 If we observe member behavior that aligns with outside influences (e.g., special interests), can we conclude that these influences "caused" members to behave in this fashion?

3 As communication between constituents and representatives improves, giving constituents easier access to members, should we expect to observe a change in legislative behavior?

4 What can we learn about members' goals by studying the way they use their resources? How might members with different goals allocate their staff?

5 Parties and Leaders

From left, House Minority Leader Nancy Pelosi (D-California), now Senate Majority Leader Mitch McConnell (R-Kentucky), now Senate Minority Leader Harry Reid (D-Nevada), and Speaker of the House John Boehner (R-Ohio), join hands to sing "We Shall Overcome" during a ceremony in 2014.

Congressional parties and their leaders have been subject to severe criticism in recent years. The two parties are blamed for dysfunctional governance in Washington and an ugly turn in American political discourse. Their top leaders are vilified in commentary and blogs and even in floor debate by the other side. Once considered to be too similar to provide meaningful alternatives for the American public, the parties are now condemned for failing to compromise in the interest of conducting the public's business. Rather than being an important means for aggregating interests and opinions to facilitate governing and encourage accountability, they are disparaged for adhering to radical beliefs about government, shirking responsibility, playing games with public policy, and casting blame rather than solving problems.

With partisanship running so hot and many Americans deeply frustrated with congressional parties, it may challenge our patience to try to understand the changing role that parties play in congressional policy making. It is worth the effort. Parties and their leaders are now far more central to policy making in Congress than they were a few decades ago. Party leaders, whose primary function in the mid-twentieth century was to facilitate the work of the standing committees, are now regularly involved in both shaping the content of major legislation and formulating political strategy. Committees remain important, but their work is now frequently guided by policy and political considerations that are the responsibility of central party leaders to negotiate. Congressional policy making, once a committee-centered process, is now a party-oriented process; a once decentralized process now is a centralized one.

Driving the reorientation of congressional decision-making processes is the polarization of the parties. In Chapter 1, we outlined the forces in American politics that have produced the polarization of congressional parties. The dramatic changes in the partisan alignment of the South and New England, the changing composition of political activists in the two parties, the emergence of a partisan media, and the strategies of legislators themselves contributed to partisan polarization. After introducing the important features of the parties in Congress and reviewing the major functions of party leaders, we return to that subject in this chapter.

THE NATURE OF CONGRESSIONAL PARTIES

Congressional parties exist to serve the interests of their members. The Constitution does not mention congressional parties. Just as candidates and their supporters created electoral parties outside of Congress to effectively compete in elections, legislators created congressional parties to serve their ends. The four congressional parties (House Democrats, House Republicans, Senate Democrats, and Senate Republicans) convene separately before each new Congress begins, and they meet with some frequency while Congress is in session. No formal joint organization of House and Senate Democrats or House and Senate Republicans exists, although party leaders of the two chambers often discuss matters of mutual concern.

Congressional party organizations are independent of the national and state political parties. Members of Congress have chaired and served in other capacities on the parties' national committees, but the four congressional parties have no formal relationship with the national party committees. Moreover, members of Congress usually are considered important party leaders in their home districts and states, but they are seldom officials of their local party organizations. Members' candidacy for office usually is endorsed by the local party organizations, but winning the party primary, not the endorsement, gets them on the general election ballot in November. The bond between the local party and an incumbent representative or senator can be weak. National committees, congressional party organizations, and local party organizations do not directly control who is nominated through primaries and eventually elected to Congress. Party organizations may recruit candidates, contribute money, and offer campaign advice and expertise. They do not have the power to prevent someone from running in party primaries and gaining a seat in Congress.

A reasonable characterization of congressional parties is that they are relatively stable, but loose, coalitions of legislators that exist to serve the common interests of their members. Both electoral and policy interests appear to motivate party activity.

Common Electoral Interests

Members of each congressional party share a party label – with few exceptions, they are either Democrats or Republicans. The label serves as a political "brand name" that holds meaning for voters and influences their decisions at the polls. In sharing the same brand name, members of the same party have an incentive to build and maintain a positive reputation for their party. This collective interest encourages legislators to develop congressional party organizations and select leaders who work to enhance their parties' images. Leaders choose issues to emphasize, develop public relations strategies, and work with presidents and committee leaders to shape the content of legislation. They also work more directly to aid election campaigns by raising and contributing money, making appearances at fund-raising and campaign events, disseminating information, and playing a role in recruiting candidates. In election years, top leaders spend several weeks traveling to support the electoral efforts of fellow partisans.

By building a favorable party reputation, leaders help their colleagues get reelected and help their party gain and maintain majority party status. A majority party controls committee and subcommittee chairmanships, has more influence over the agenda, and, with more votes, is more likely to win legislative battles. Electoral failures have caused the defeat of some party leaders or led them to resign (see box "Electoral Trouble for Leaders").

Leaders are expected to promote their party's electoral interests, but tensions sometimes arise between leaders and rank-and-file members whose personal or political interests motivate them to vote differently than most of their party colleagues would like. Even party leaders, whose job it is to rally support for their party's policy positions, are sensitive to the personal political needs of deviant colleagues. After all, most party leaders would rather give a deviant party member some leeway to vote as he or she chooses than lose that member's seat to the other party. Imperfect support for party positions is the typical pattern for most members. Differences in members' home constituencies are an important source of conflict over party strategy within all congressional parties.

Shared Policy Preferences

Members of each party hold distinctive views on most important policy questions. The shared policy views among legislators of the same party are grounded in the similarities in the views of their home constituencies. Liberal-leaning districts tend to elect more Democrats than conservative-leaning districts, which elect more Republicans. Shared policy views create an incentive for members to choose leaders and coordinate their strategies.

Majorities of the parties have taken opposing positions on roll call votes about two-thirds of the time in most recent Congresses, up from just over two-fifths of the time in the early 1970s. Figure 5.1 indicates the percentage of roll call votes that were party votes – those on which a majority of Democrats voted against a majority of Republicans. In the recent past, party voting has tended to be higher in odd-numbered years than in even-numbered years, particularly in the House. This trend may reflect political pressures associated with the two-year electoral cycle of the House. In the odd-numbered years immediately after congressional elections, the winning side may feel emboldened to push a partisan agenda. As

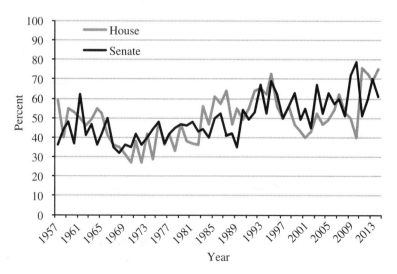

Figure 5.1 Percentage of All Votes That Were Party Votes, 1957–2013. Source: Congressional Quarterly.

another election approaches, members and party leaders may avoid issues that polarize the parties and create problems at home for some members.

Electoral Trouble for Leaders

Members of Congress expect their leaders to guide their parties to electoral success. Major failures, or even unexpected losses, as well as other embarrassing developments, can lead to the resignation or retirement of a leader, as is evident in several episodes described in the following section.

After his party suffered unexpected losses in the 1998 elections, House Speaker Newt Gingrich (R-Georgia) took the extraordinary step of resigning from the speakership and Congress. His party had lost five seats in the House of Representatives, narrowing the Republican advantage to 223, just five more than a majority of 218. Rarely does the party opposing the president lose seats in a midterm election. In fact, 1934 is the only other midterm election of the twentieth century in which the president's party won additional seats. Gingrich was blamed for failing to provide needed leadership.

In 2002, just after his party failed to win seats in the midterm election, Democratic Minority Leader Dick Gephardt chose not to seek reelection as the party leader. Gephardt soon announced his intention to run for president, but many viewed his decision to retire from the post a wise move. Gephardt had served as party leader since 1994, when the House Democrats lost their majority for the first time since 1954, yet he had not managed to lead the party back to majority status.

After his party regained a majority of Senate seats in the 2002 elections, Senate Republican Minority Leader Trent Lott (R-Mississippi) was expecting to become the majority leader as soon as the new Congress convened in January 2003. However, in December a video recording of Lott's comments at a birthday party for retiring Senator Strom Thurmond (R-South Carolina) were aired on television. The recording showed Lott saying that the country would have been better off if Thurmond had won the presidency when he ran in 1948. Thurmond was the pro-segregationist candidate of the Dixiecrats in 1948. It was soon learned that Lott had made similar comments two decades earlier. The public uproar caused by these disclosures led many of Lott's colleagues to conclude that he had to step down as party leader. Lott stepped down as party leader but remained in the Senate.

After 2014 elections, in which Democrats lost their Senate majority, some dissatisfaction was quietly expressed about Senate Democratic leader Harry Reid (D-Nevada), but he faced no serious opposition.

The percentage of party votes has been high in recent decades. We consider this trend later in this chapter. But why are not even more votes in Congress aligned along party lines? The primary reason is that Congress addresses many dozens, even hundreds, of programs and issues that do not involve partisan considerations, such as the merchant marine, veterans' health programs, and flood insurance. Congress considers a greater volume of legislation – and more detailed legislation – than do most other national legislatures. Most of the legislation enacted into law each year is routine or concerns matters about which there is a consensus on how to legislate.

Factionalism within Congressional Parties

Intraparty factionalism in Congress is reflected in the presence of named groups. In the Senate, owing to its smaller size, members appear to see less benefit and some cost in becoming associated with formally organized factions. In recent years, a handful of Senate Democratic liberals formed the Democratic Study Group, a bipartisan group of moderates formed the bipartisan Senate Centrist Coalition, and a group of Senate Democratic centrists and their staff met on a regular basis. Only the Steering Committee, the informal organization of Republican conservatives, has been in existence for long. A Tea Party caucus formed with three conservative Republicans in 2011, and a few Senate Republicans have been affiliated with the caucus in recent years.

In the House, factions representing liberals, moderates, and conservatives have formed and re-formed in both parties. Liberal Democrats make up the Progressive Caucus, which had more than seventy-five members in 2015 and is the largest of the Democratic member organizations. The New Democratic Coalition, organized in 1997 by a group of self-proclaimed centrists, had about forty-five members in 2015. The Blue Dog Coalition is an organization of conservative or moderate Democrats with about fifteen members in 2015. In addition, the Congressional Black Caucus (forty-six members in 2015) and Hispanic Caucus (twenty-seven members in 2015) represent Democrats who generally are liberal.

On the Republican side in the House, the Republican Study Committee, which dates back to 1973, is the major faction; it calls itself the "caucus of House conservatives" and includes about two-thirds of the party. In 1994, Republican centrists organized the Tuesday Group, which numbered about thirty in 2011 and appeared to have fewer members by early 2015. Both the Republican Study Committee and the Tuesday Group hire staff aides to assist the groups.

In 2010, nearly fifty House Republicans formed the Tea Party Caucus under the leadership of Michele Bachmann (R-Minnesota). Membership in this group of the most conservative members of the party appeared to rise to sixty in 2011. The group became largely dormant for a couple years as Bachmann lost interest, although conservatives continued to meet informally. At this writing in early 2015, an effort to reinvigorate the group is underway.

After the 2014 elections, about thirty Republicans formed the House Freedom Caucus, which appears to have become the leading organization for the most conservative wing of the party. Dissatisfied with the Republican Study Committee and the Tea Party Caucus, the group has carefully limited its membership to representatives who are willing to keep pressure on their party leadership to pursue conservative strategies. The group is intended to be large enough in 2015 to deny the Republican leadership a House majority on legislation (without Democratic votes).

The one interchamber group of prominence is the Main Street Partnership, created in 1993 and comprised of Republican moderates from both houses. In 2015, three senators and fifty-three representatives were members.

Even on votes that generate partisan divisions, the two parties are seldom perfectly cohesive. In recent Congresses, an average of 80 to 90 percent of members have voted with a majority of their party on party votes – meaning that a 20 to 30 percent rate of defection is common even when party majorities oppose each other. Indeed, nothing in the way that members are elected or reelected guarantees

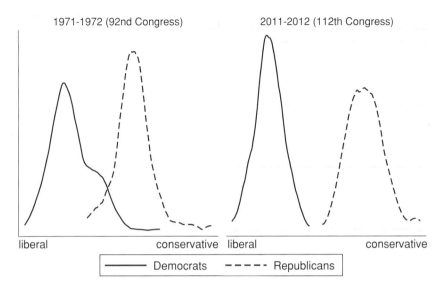

Figure 5.2 The Liberal-Conservative Distribution of Democrats and Republicans, 1971–1972 and 2011–2012. Source: Common space scores from voteview.com.

that members of the same party will agree with one another on important issues or that Democrats and Republicans will take opposing views. To the contrary, variation in the political views of members' constituencies promotes variation in the voting behavior of members of the same party. Factionalism often has made it difficult to use the party organizations to promote policy ideas and solicit support.

Nevertheless, the party divide has grown. Figure 5.2 shows the distribution of Democrats and Republicans on a liberal-conservative scale drawn from all roll call votes in two Congresses, the 92nd Congress (1971–1972) and the 112th Congress (2011–2012), which is typical of recent Congresses. The figure combines members of the House and Senate into one graph on the same scale. For the Congress of the early 1970s, there was a substantial overlap between the parties. In fact, members located between the most conservative Democrat and most liberal Republican could exceed 50 percent of the total membership in those years. In some recent Congresses, there has been no overlap between the parties.

Party Identification

Most members, like most political activists and many citizens of the United States, have a psychological attachment to their parties. This attachment reinforces a sense of group identification and enhances group cohesiveness. These bonds lead members to turn to party colleagues for cues on how to vote and for other forms of assistance and advice. Party leaders further strengthen party bonds by emphasizing common loyalties, policy commitments, and personal ties in their appeals for support from their colleagues.

Furthermore, most members of Congress face another reality: Legislators are dependent on voters who, for the most part, share the same partisan affiliation and vote in party primaries. Members who vote against their party's position on major issues or, even worse, actively work to undermine their party's institutional position may face challenges from within their party in a primary. Few members are willing to take such a risk. In this way, the partisan connection between a member and his or her electoral base constrains members who might otherwise vote against the majority of his or her party in Congress.

Most Common Coalitions

Although congressional parties are not perfectly cohesive, they have important advantages over other groups that might seek to influence legislative outcomes: They are the most common basis for building majority coalitions and benefit from significant institutional advantages. Most legislators are accustomed to working with fellow partisans to attract support for their legislative causes. Rules and precedents give formally elected leaders in both houses of Congress critical procedural advantages for setting the agenda, appointing members to committees, and controlling resources valued by members. By using these advantages granted to them by their parties, leaders are in a better position than other legislators to build support for or opposition to legislation.

In recent decades, all legislators who are elected to the House or Senate as independents or with a party label other than Democrat or Republican choose to caucus with one of the two major parties. They then are treated as Democrats or Republicans with voting privileges at party meetings and benefit from gaining committee assignments and seniority within the party. These members believe that they are better off joining an enduring party organization than operating as freelance legislators. In the past, the very few who have not caucused with one of the two major parties have struggled to gain important roles within their chambers.

Stable but Loose Coalitions

For all of these reasons, the House and Senate depend on party leaders to perform many basic organizational functions but do not give them too much independent power. Members of the *majority* party choose the presiding officers of both chambers (the Speaker of the House and, to preside in the absence of the vice president, the Senate president pro tempore), select committee leaders, and assume responsibility for scheduling activity at all stages of the legislative process. The parties assign members to standing committees and subcommittees as well as to all select, joint, and conference committees. The majority party in each house reserves for itself the majority of seats on nearly all committees. And within the committees, most activity is organized by party – the questioning of witnesses at hearings, the hiring of staff, even the arrangement of seats in committee rooms. Seating on the House and Senate floors is also arranged by party: The Democrats are on the left and the Republicans are on the right when facing the front desk. Partisan elements pervade the organization of the modern Congress and have done so since the first half of the nineteenth century.

Yet even with their current state of deep polarization, American congressional parties are not as strong as parties in many other national legislatures. Congressional parties in the United States usually are not as cohesive on questions of public policy as are parties in other systems. U.S. congressional party leaders have little power over who is elected under their party's label and few resources to compel loyalty from members once they are in office. Equally important, state and national party leaders have no formal authority over members of Congress.

Congressional party leaders sometimes struggle to balance the diverse policy and electoral interests of their party colleagues. In their efforts to do so, they may delay action on a bill until the timing is more convenient for a legislator or urge their colleagues to be tolerant of a legislator whose political circumstances necessitate a vote against the party position. Still, there are situations when leaders seek the vote of every party member. Such situations usually involve legislation that is a high priority for a president of the same party, whose success or failure will reflect on the party, and for which there are not enough supportive members of the opposition party to muster a majority. Leaders may try to accommodate some members by compromising provisions of the legislation or by promising certain actions on unrelated legislation. Explicit or implicit threats of retribution for disloyal behavior are sometimes issued, typically in the form of warnings about future committee chairmanship or appointment decisions made by party committees and leaders. These trade-offs reflect the loose organization and discipline of congressional parties and the long-term importance of party affiliations to members.

Congressionally Speaking . . .

Among the four congressional parties, only House Democrats call their organization a *caucus*. House Republicans, Senate Democrats, and Senate Republicans call their organizations *conferences*. The difference in labels dates back to the 1910s, when the House Democrats used their caucus, the so-called King Caucus, to make policy decisions and required party members to support those positions. The Democrats' binding caucus was so distasteful to House Republicans that they chose an entirely different label for their organization. Senate parties followed suit and use the term "conference."

PARTY ORGANIZATIONS

Each of the four congressional parties (two in each house) has three major organizational features: a caucus (or conference) that includes all party members
in the chamber, party committees, and elected and appointed leaders. All four
party caucuses meet in late November or early December after each election to
organize for the new Congress, which begins in January. They elect their leaders, may adopt or revise their rules, and begin to make assignments to standing
committees. In recent Congresses, the four caucuses have met weekly or biweekly
while Congress is in session. These meetings usually serve as forums for the
discussion of party strategies. To facilitate candid discussion and avoid media
reports of party infighting, caucus meetings are generally not open to the public
or the press.

Each party has a set of committees (see Table 5.1). The policy committees
discuss (and, infrequently, endorse) policy positions; the campaign committees
provide advice and money to party incumbents and candidates; the committees
on committees assign party members to standing committees. For several decades, the policy committees of the House and Senate Republicans have sponsored
weekly luncheons that serve as forums on matters important to the party. Senate
Democrats adopted the practice of weekly luncheons in 1990.

Party staffs provide a wide range of services to members. Services include
timely reports on floor activity, briefing papers on major issues, media advice
and technical assistance, newspaper-clipping services, recorded messages on
current floor activity, personnel services, and limited research assistance. The
Senate parties operate closed-circuit television channels that provide senators
and their staffs with informative details about floor action. They also provide
radio and television studios that allow senators to appear live on home-state
stations. Over the last few decades, most new party leaders have found additional services to promise and deliver to the membership. As a result, the party
staffs have become large and expensive, with nearly all of the funding provided
through appropriations.

The most important recent development is that both House and Senate Democrats have made communications a more visible element of party organization.
In the complicated world of cable television, talk radio, and social media, competition between the parties to frame the issues and legislative activity to their
advantage has intensified. Both Democratic party caucuses have made communication the prime responsibility of a party committee, which has the effect of
formally assigning public relations responsibilities to a party committee chair
and its members. The top leaders remain the chief spokespersons for their parties,
but the formal assignment of public relations activity to a party committee reflects the high priority that modern congressional parties give to public relations.

TABLE 5.1. Party committees, 114th Congress (January 2015)

House Democrats

Steering and Policy Committee	Makes committee assignments; sometimes endorses policy positions; discusses party strategy
Policy and Communications Committee	Public relations for the caucus
Democratic Congressional Campaign Committee	Provides money and other assistance to Democratic House candidates
Organization, Study, and Review	Recommends changes in party organization and rules

House Republicans

Steering	Makes committee assignments
Policy	Discusses and recommends policy proposals
National Republican Congressional Committee	Provides money and other assistance to Republican House candidates

Senate Democrats

Steering and Outreach	Makes committee assignments; formulates political strategy
Policy and Communications	Recommends policy priorities; provides a forum for conference discussion; staff provides research and communication tools
Democratic Senatorial Campaign Committee	Provides money and other assistance to Democratic Senate candidates

Senate Republicans

Committee on Committees	Makes committee assignments
Policy	Discusses and recommends policy proposals; staff provides research; sponsors weekly policy lunch for party
National Republican Senatorial Campaign Committee	Provides money and other assistance to Republican Senate candidates

Source: Collected by authors.

PARTY LEADERS

The Constitution provides for presiding officers in Congress but says nothing about parties or leaders. It states that the members of the House "shall choose their Speaker," makes the vice president of the United States the president of the Senate, and requires that the Senate select a president pro tempore ("president for the time being") to preside over the Senate in the absence of the vice president. Although the Constitution does not explicitly require the Speaker or the Senate president pro tempore to be members of Congress, all have been.

Only in the House is the presiding officer, the Speaker, also the top leader of the majority party (Table 5.2). At the start of each Congress, the majority and minority parties nominate their top leaders for Speaker. The majority party's leader is then elected Speaker, usually on a party-line vote. In the Senate, presiding over daily sessions is normally a routine activity, so the vice president

TABLE 5.2. Top party leaders, 114th Congress (January 2015)

House Democrats

Minority Leader	Nancy Pelosi, California
Minority Whip	Steny Hoyer, Maryland
Assistant Leader	James Clyburn, South Carolina
Caucus Chair	Xavier Becerra, California
Caucus Vice Chair	Joseph Crowley, New York

House Republicans

Speaker	John Boehner, Ohio
Majority Leader	Kevin McCarthy, California
Majority Whip	Steve Scalise, Louisiana
Conference Chair	Cathy McCorris Rodgers, Washington
Conference Vice Chair	Lynn Jenkins, Kansas

Senate Democrats

Minority Leader (and Conference Chair)	Harry Reid, Nevada
Assistant Floor Leader (Whip)	Richard Durbin, Illinois
Conference Vice Chair	Charles Schumer, New York
Conference Secretary	Patty Murray, Washington

Senate Republicans

Majority Leader	Mitch McConnell, Kentucky
Assistant Floor Leader (Whip)	John Cornyn, Texas
Conference Chair	John Thune, South Dakota
Conference Vice Chair	Roy Blunt, Missouri
Senate President Pro Tempore	Orrin Hatch, Utah

is seldom present. Since the 1940s, the majority party has named its most senior member president pro tempore. The president pro tempore is often busy as a committee chair and assigns the duty of presiding over the Senate to junior senators of the same party. All four parties choose a floor leader (known as a majority or minority leader), assistant floor leader (or whip), conference chair, and other leaders.

Major Responsibilities of Party Leaders

Few specific statements about party leaders' jobs can be found in chamber or party rules. Leaders' jobs have evolved in response to their colleagues' expectations that leaders must promote the common electoral and policy interests of their parties. These responsibilities are primarily assigned to the top leader in each party, although the burden is shared among the top three or four leaders in each party.

BUILDING COALITIONS ON MAJOR LEGISLATION. Building coalitions in support of party policy positions is a large part of the job of leaders. Because the majority party is often divided to some degree on controversial issues, such majorities do not automatically materialize. Rather, leaders carefully count votes, craft legislation, and use various means of persuasion to try to unify their own party and attract votes from members of the opposition party to pass or block legislation. Leaders also work to build majority coalitions in committees and conference committees from time to time, but, at least on legislation that is not of great importance to the party, they tend to be deferential to committee leaders at those stages.

Extra-large majorities must often be mustered as well. In the Senate, sixty votes must be secured to invoke cloture on a filibuster, unless the matter concerns the Senate's standing rules, in which case a two-thirds vote (sixty-seven, if all senators vote) is required. On a few other occasions in the Senate, such as to waive a budget restriction, a sixty-vote majority must be found. In both chambers, a two-thirds majority of members present and voting is required to override a presidential veto. In such cases, support from at least a few minority party members is usually required for the majority party leaders to win.

MANAGING THE FLOOR. Managing floor activity is primarily the responsibility of the majority party leadership. This responsibility includes scheduling sessions of the chambers and arranging for the consideration of individual pieces of legislation. The stark differences between House and Senate floor scheduling practices are noted in Chapter 7. In the Senate, minority members' power to obstruct proceedings requires that the majority leader work closely with the minority leader, if possible. In fact, if the minority is not too obstructionist, there is nearly continuous consultation between the two leaders and their staffs. A much more distant relationship between the majority and minority party leaders is common in the House.

SERVING AS INTERMEDIARY WITH THE PRESIDENT. Congressional leaders of the president's party often have dual loyalties. Their most immediate obligation is to their congressional colleagues who elected them, but they also feel an obligation to support the president. Tensions frequently arise as congressional leaders seek to balance the competing demands of the president and their congressional party colleagues.

Serving as intermediaries between the congressional party and the president has been a regular duty of party leaders since the early twentieth century. Leaders of the president's party normally meet with the president once a week while Congress is in session. They often report on those meetings at party luncheons or caucuses. On matters central to the president's legislative agenda, the leaders work closely with executive branch officials to build majority support in Congress.

Leaders of the out party – the party that does not control the presidency – meet sporadically with the president, usually to be briefed on foreign policy matters. The relationship between a president and out-party leaders is not often one of genuine consultation, for obvious reasons. Occasionally, political circumstances or personal friendship may strengthen the bond. Senate Republican leader Everett Dirksen, for example, was a confidant of Democratic president Lyndon Johnson during the 1960s, and Dirksen's support for Johnson's civil rights and Vietnam War policies was crucial to the president's legislative success.

ENHANCING THE PARTY'S REPUTATION. Public relations is a central leadership responsibility in the modern Congress. Skillfully managing media relations is now considered an essential element of a good legislative strategy. The objectives are to win public support for legislative positions, to persuade undecided legislators of the political support for party positions, and to persuade voters that the party's legislative efforts deserve to be rewarded at election time.

Media skills were seldom a major consideration in leadership selection in the 1950s, 1960s, and early 1970s. Service to colleagues, mastery of the mechanics of the legislative game, and the interests of party factions were given greater weight. Perhaps because of their weak institutional position and lack of national media coverage, only House Republicans made media skills much of an issue in leadership contests. In general, party leaders took a back seat to committee leaders as opinion leaders on matters of policy. In fact, the foremost studies on party leadership of the 1960s did not catalog service as party spokesperson or anything similar among the major functions of party leaders.

Leadership PACs

Starting in the 1970s, a few of the top congressional party leaders created political action committees (PACs) to raise funds that they could donate to the campaigns of colleagues. This allowed a powerful leader, who had the influence with wealthy individuals, to assist colleagues' campaign efforts and gain some credit with colleagues whose support may be needed in the legislative arena. Soon, ambitious members who were seeking leadership posts found it useful to raise and spend funds on their colleagues' campaigns. That practice continues. A leadership PAC can contribute to any other congressional campaign, subject to the contribution limits for PACs (Chapter 3), and can make unlimited independent expenditures.

Unfortunately, critics argue, the use of leadership PAC funds has expanded far beyond elections and politics. They have become all-purpose slush funds created by dozens of members who have no obvious interest in leadership offices. Under Federal Election Commission rules, these "leadership" PACs can be formed by any member or former member of Congress and can accept donations from individuals and other PACs – up to $5,000 per election cycle. A member's leadership PAC cannot spend funds on his or her own campaign, but it may fund consultants, polling, travel, and other "noncampaign" expenses. In fact, leadership PACs are funding a wide variety of recreation activity – expensive golf trips, parties at casinos, outings to professional sports events, and much more. Legislators often justify these events as fund-raising or campaign events. Leadership PACs spend a considerable amount on fund-raising for themselves.

As a result of the few limits on leadership PAC spending, more members of Congress have created them. The number of leadership PACs has increased from a handful of leadership PACs established by top leaders in the 1980s to nearly five hundred in the 2014 election cycle. The top leaders still have the largest PACs. House Speaker John Boehner's PAC, Freedom Project, raised $3.6 million and contributed about $1.2 million to House candidates. Freedom Project also helped to support the salaries of Boehner's "political team."

Reformers have urged Congress to ban leadership PACs from spending on personal activities and even to limit their spending to contributions to other candidates' campaigns. Congress has shown little interest in enacting such new legislation or rules.

Source: opensecrets.org (accessed February 2015).

Expectations have changed. The importance of television as a medium of political communication, the president's domination of television news, and the around-the-clock cable news programs seem to have intensified demand for leaders adroit in public relations. Since the mid-1960s, out-party congressional leaders have sought and been granted time on the television networks to respond to presidential addresses. By the early 1980s, the role of party spokesperson had become so prominent as to warrant listing it among leaders' primary responsibilities. Since the 1990s, the use of social media, blogs, and websites has expanded the range of media efforts in which the party leaders and their staffs are engaged.

Congressional party leaders realize that to compete with the president, television pundits, interest group leaders, radio talk show hosts, and other opinion leaders, all of whom actively court public opinion in an effort to generate pressure on legislators, they need to have media strategies of their own. All top leaders have daily contact with reporters from print, radio, television, and online news outlets. The House Speaker and Senate leaders usually have brief press conferences before their chambers' daily sessions. They sometimes commission their own public opinion polls to gauge how well their party's message is being received. In addition to their own press secretaries and speechwriters, they all have party committees charged with devising and implementing media strategies in important legislative battles.

Switching Parties, Changing Party Control

In late May 2001, Senator Jim Jeffords (I-Vermont) announced that he was leaving the Republican Conference, becoming an Independent, and joining with the Democrats for the purpose of organizing the Senate. Since the 1880s, there have been twenty-five instances of party switching in the Senate, but Jeffords's move was the first time that such a switch

(*continued*)

caused a party to lose majority status in either chamber. The Senate had been divided 50–50 between Democrats and Republicans, but the Republican vice president Dick Cheney allowed the Republicans to be considered the majority party, the Republican floor leader to be recognized by the presiding officer as the majority leader, and the Republicans to control the committee chairmanships.

Republicans attempted to keep Jeffords in the party by offering more money for education programs, his favorite cause; giving him a seat in the leadership circle; and granting him an exemption to the party conference rule limiting the number of terms he could serve as chair of the Health, Education, Labor, and Pensions Committee. The new Democratic majority gave Jeffords a committee chairmanship. In the 2002 elections, the Republicans gained additional seats and reassumed majority status. Jeffords lost his chairmanship, and he did not seek reelection in 2006.

There have been more than eighty instances of party switching in the House since the 1880s.

CAMPAIGNING. Providing campaign support to colleagues is a regular part of congressional leaders' activity. All modern leaders help their colleagues raise money and join them at campaign events. Leaders' efforts are not altruistic, of course. Party leaders want to see their party colleagues reelected in order to maintain or gain a majority for their party, and they hope that their kindness will be repaid in loyalty. In fact, most candidates for top leadership posts now spend time and money on their colleagues' campaigns both to attract support and to demonstrate the kind of leaders they will be. All leaders, and most aspirants for leadership posts, form political action committees, known as "leadership PACs," so that they may receive contributions that they can donate to the campaigns of their colleagues.

All four congressional parties have campaign committees, whose chairs and staff take the lead in recruiting and consulting with candidates. The campaign committees raise funds that are then directed to the parties' candidates. The chairs are elected by the party caucuses and are considered to be a part of the leadership. As the fourth-ranking leader, a campaign chair often sees the post as a step to higher leadership positions.

MANAGING THE PARTY AND THE CHAMBER. Organizing the party and chamber is an important duty of party leaders. Obvious political aspects of this job include making committee assignments and appointments to various party positions. More administrative in character are the selection and supervision of chamber officers and other employees. For example, the majority party leaders in the two houses nominate and supervise the chief clerks and sergeants at arms, whose appointment must be approved by the houses, and they share responsibility for choosing a director for the Congressional Budget Office.

Selection of Leaders

The party caucuses elect their top leaders. The leaders are not chosen on the basis of seniority, although most recent leaders have been very experienced members. A candidate's place among factions and regional groups within the party, record of service to colleagues, personal friendships, intelligence and policy expertise, and other factors play a role in leadership contests. Members who have experience in lower party posts often are advantaged in contests for top posts because they have been in a position to demonstrate their skills and perform favors for colleagues.

Only in the ascension to House Speaker is there much routine in leadership selection. A vacancy in the speakership is typically filled by the previous floor leader – the majority or minority leader – without opposition. The majority or minority leader generally has won several leadership elections and has substantial support for the move up to Speaker. Challenging the heir apparent would be pointless. Serious challenges from within the majority party to the party's choice for Speaker have not occurred since 1923, when Progressives delayed the election of a Republican Speaker until the eventual winner agreed to some procedural reforms.

Republican Speaker John Boehner (R-Ohio), who moved from minority leader to Speaker after the Republicans won a House majority in the 2010 elections, faced some opposition from disgruntled Republicans in 2013 and 2015. The unhappy Republicans (numbering 13 in 2013 and 25 in 2015) were showing their dissatisfaction with Boehner's occasional interest in bargaining with President Obama on important legislation. In neither year did the dissenting Republicans become so numerous that they put in doubt Boehner's reelection as Speaker, but they did demonstrate the continuing importance of "Tea Party" Republicans as a faction in the House (more on party factions will follow).

For other party offices (whip, conference chair, and so on), contested races are common, usually to fill vacancies. As contests among fellow partisans, the races are often filled with intrigue. The behind-closed-doors campaigning and secret-ballot voting always generate a great deal of speculation and second-guessing among Washington insiders. They involve intense campaigns as the candidates make personal appeals to colleagues in soliciting support. Organized factions sometimes choose a favorite; in fact, faction leaders often are the candidates. Wild speculation, personal grudges, and conspiracy are standard fare. These contests generate so much interest because they often place the winners on track to take top positions in the future.

Challenges to incumbent leaders occur only occasionally. Most incumbent leaders do the kind of job their party colleagues expect. Challenges to an incumbent tend to be particularly divisive, and even disgruntled members

Speaker of the House John Boehner (R-Ohio) holds his weekly press conference in the Capitol in early 2015.

usually try to avoid a fight within the party family. Of course, taking on an incumbent may be risky. Leadership contests are expensive in terms of time and effort. Running and losing may undermine future leadership hopes, to say nothing of incurring the wrath of the winner.

HOUSE PARTY LEADERS

Today's House party leaders are much more visible and active than were their predecessors of the mid-twentieth century. Legislators expect their leaders to be aggressive and media savvy in an era with polarized parties and a 24-hour news cycle. Members of the House certainly do not want their leaders to take a back seat to Senate leaders.

The Speaker of the House

The Speaker of the House possesses more formal authority than any other member of Congress. House rules and precedents grant the Speaker important prerogatives concerning floor scheduling and procedures, bill referrals, and appointments to select and conference committees and to various commissions. One of the Speaker's newest prerogatives is the power to remove a member from a conference committee delegation and replace him or her without the approval of the House, a power that is intended to make majority party members of a conference delegation accountable to their party's top leader. In addition to the rules of the House, both parties' internal rules give their top leaders control over the party's appointments to the Rules Committee, extra influence over other committee assignments, and power to make appointments to party committees. It is the combination of powers granted under House and party rules that make the Speaker more powerful than the Senate's majority leader, who enjoys few special powers under Senate rules.

Term Limits for Leaders

Since the early 1990s, term limits for party leaders and committee chairs have been a popular reform proposal. Congressional Republicans have moved further in adopting limits than Democrats.

House Republicans led the way among congressional parties to set limits on the number of terms a legislator could serve in a particular leadership post. Soon after they gained a majority in the 1994 elections, the House Republicans limited all party leaders to six-year terms in any given office, with the exception of the speakership for which an eight-year limit was established. House Republicans eliminated the limit on the Speaker in 2003, and it has not been reinstated. Some observers argue that a term limit for the speakership would violate the Constitution, which provides that the House shall choose a Speaker without mentioning any limit on the Speaker's term of office.

Senate Republicans have no term limit for the floor leader or, when they are in the majority, for the president pro tempore, but they limit a senator to six years for holding any other leadership position.

House Democrats limit their caucus chair, caucus vice chair, and elected regional whips to two consecutive terms but do not set term limits for other party leaders.

Senate Democrats have not imposed term limits of any kind on party or committee leadership posts.

The Speaker's most important source of power is control of the flow of business on the House floor. By precedent, the Speaker has the power to recognize members on the House floor without appeal. That means that the Speaker may choose to ignore members who seek recognition to call up legislation that the Speaker prefers to consider later or to block. Scheduling prerogatives give the Speaker control over the timing of floor action, which may affect the legislative outcomes and political impact of House votes. Among other things, the Speaker can keep from the floor legislation he or she opposes or wishes to delay. There are ways to circumvent a Speaker, such as by using a discharge petition to force floor action, but they are difficult to use.

As presiding officer of the House, the Speaker rarely votes or makes floor speeches. He or she votes on matters of symbolic importance and occasionally when a vote makes a difference in the outcome. A Speaker makes a floor speech on only a few occasions each year, usually during debate on momentous

TABLE 5.3. Recent Speakers and party divisions in the House of Representatives

House Speaker	Party	Congress	Years	Party division D-R-I[a]
Thomas P. "Tip" O'Neill (MA)	D	95th	1977–1979	292–143
"	D	96th	1979–1981	279–156
"	D	97th	1981–1983	243–192
"	D	98th	1983–1985	270–165
"	D	99th	1985–1987	255–180
James C. Wright (TX)	D	100th	1987–1989	259–176
"	D	101st[b]	1989	262–173
Thomas S. Foley (WA)	D	101st[b]	1989–1991	
"	D	102nd	1991–1993	267–167–1
"	D	103rd	1993–1995	258–176–1
Newton L. "Newt" Gingrich (GA)	R	104th	1995–1997	206–228–1
"	R	105th	1997–1999	207–226–2
J. Dennis Hastert (IL)	R	106th	1999–2001	211–223–1
"	R	107th	2001–2003	205–229–1
"	R	108th	2003–2005	213–220–2
"	R	109th	2005–2007	205–229–1
Nancy P. Pelosi (CA)	D	110th	2007–2009	233–202
"	D	111th	2009–2011	257–178
John A. Boehner (OH)	R	112th	2011–2013	193–242
"	R	113th	2013–2015	201–234
"	R	114th	2015–2016	188–247

[a] Democrats-Republicans-Independents.
[b] Wright resigned in June 1989, and Foley was elected.

legislation. When the Speaker addresses the House from the floor, he or she is accorded the privilege of speaking last.

Recent Speakers (see Table 5.3) have been more active in using their formal powers than were the Speakers of the middle decades of the twentieth century. After his party gained a House majority for the first time since the mid-1950s, Republican Newt Gingrich, elected Speaker in 1995, became the most proactive Speaker since the first decade of the twentieth century. A well-developed agenda, called the Contract With America, provided an unusually concise ten-point policy platform for Gingrich. Gingrich was given much of the credit for these developments – he had championed aggressive Republican strategies in the House, coauthored the Contract With America, raised money, and recruited candidates to challenge the incumbent Democratic majority. Gingrich, backed by his House Republican colleagues, became the leading spokesperson for his party, dominated the selection of committee leaders and other committee appointments, directed the actions of committees, set the floor agenda, and pushed legislation associated with the Contract With America through the House in the first 100 days of the 104th Congress (1995–1996).

Gingrich's speakership was a lightning rod for partisanship and ended in political tragedy. His political downfall began with his 1995 strategy to hold hostage debt-ceiling increases and funding for executive departments in order to get President Bill Clinton's approval of the Republicans' budget plan. Clinton refused to budge, and eventually the Republican Congress accepted Clinton's compromise legislation. The episode produced sharply weaker approval ratings in public opinion polls for Gingrich and much stronger ratings for Clinton. After that point, Gingrich became far less aggressive, setting aside his confrontational strategies. Following Clinton's reelection in 1996, Gingrich maintained a low public profile and appeared to be somewhat less heavy-handed in directing the work of the House, an approach that received mixed reviews from his colleagues. In the summer of 1997, after he was the subject of serious ethics charges, there was discussion among senior Republicans of replacing him. Gingrich continued to be criticized for ineffective leadership, and he eventually resigned his post in the aftermath of the 1998 elections.

In 1995, the Republicans instituted a new House rule limiting the number of consecutive terms that a member could serve as Speaker. In December 1994, newly elected Republicans had proposed a three-term limit for the Speaker, just as they proposed for committee chairs. At Gingrich's insistence, they approved a four-term limit instead, which was incorporated into the House rules in January 1995. Gingrich did not serve long enough for the rule to apply to him.

Gingrich's successor, Republican Dennis Hastert, exhibited a style that contrasted sharply with Gingrich's, at least at first. Hastert consulted more frequently with his fellow partisans and granted more independence to committee chairs. He successfully healed some of the rifts among Republicans left from the Gingrich years, and, for a while, he held regular meetings with the Democratic leader. He campaigned endlessly for his colleagues, earning their respect and indebtedness, and, in the view of some observers, used this support to gain the upper hand with other party and committee leaders.

However welcome Hastert's more accommodating style was initially, by late 2002 Hastert became more aggressive in his enforcement of party loyalty. He denied committee chairmanships and choice committee assignments to several Republicans who had opposed the leadership position on campaign finance reform, patients' bill of rights, and other issues. He endorsed Majority Leader Tom DeLay's (R-Texas) proclamation that a Republican member who voted against the party on any procedural matter would be excused from any party or committee leadership post.

After the Democrats won a majority of House seats in the 2006 elections, they elected their floor leader, Nancy Pelosi, the first woman Speaker. Pelosi, a liberal

Democrat from San Francisco, had worked hard as minority leader to build support among moderate and conservative Democrats. During her first few months in the speakership, she proved to be an aggressive leader who set the agenda for her party and showed a willingness to work around committee chairs who were not in sync with her agenda. While she worked hard to win the support of fellow partisans on controversial issues, she created more opportunities for the minority party to offer alternatives and gave her own partisans somewhat more freedom to vote as they chose. Nevertheless, Pelosi proved quite willing to have the most important legislation developed within her party, with little minority party participation.

Republican John Boehner, elected Speaker in 2011 after the Republicans won a new majority in the 2010 elections, renewed the commitment to give more leeway to committee leaders and, perhaps with more credibility than Gingrich and Hastert, promised a more collegial leadership style. At the start of his service, he deliberately tried to distinguish himself from the partisan brinksmanship of his Republican predecessors, but, like all Speakers, he faced the problem of balancing the demands of his party colleagues with his own view of the party's electoral and policy interests. From time to time, Boehner has struggled with Tea Party Republicans in his conference who have advocated less compromising tactics in bargaining with President Obama and the Democrats.

House Floor Leaders

Both House parties elect a floor leader – that is, a majority leader or a minority leader who takes the lead in managing the party's affairs on the House floor – at the start of each Congress. As the label suggests, floor leaders are the chief spokespersons for their parties on the House floor. The majority leader is considered the second-ranking leader of the party, just behind the Speaker. The minority leader is the minority party's top leader and is always that party's (losing) nominee for Speaker at the beginning of each Congress.

There are few duties formally assigned to the majority leader in party rules. Recent Speakers have relied on the floor leader to receive and screen requests to schedule legislation for floor consideration. The majority leader consults with the Speaker (normally several times a day), works with the Speaker and others to promote party unity, and increasingly serves as a party spokesperson. Recent majority leaders have been loyal to the Speaker and have seldom publicly disagreed with him or her. As the person who is next in line to become Speaker, and an individual with a strong voice in scheduling and all other leadership decisions, the majority leader is considered very powerful.

The minority leader generally is the minority party's chief spokesperson and strategist. The minority leader sometimes consults with the majority leader about the floor schedule, although more often he or she is merely informed of the

House Minority Leader Nancy Pelosi (D-California) holds her weekly press conference in the Capitol in early 2015.

majority leadership's scheduling decisions. Keeping the minority party united and attracting majority party votes are the central tasks of the minority leader's job. The job is made easier when the minority leader's party controls the White House, and the president's resources can be drawn upon. The minority party can do little to obstruct a cohesive majority in the House, so the minority floor leader's job tends to be quite frustrating. The minority leader, like the Speaker, is an ex officio member of the Permanent Select Committee on Intelligence.

House Whips and Whip Organizations

The third-ranking majority party leader and second-ranking minority party leader in the House are the whips. Both whips are now elected (until late 1986, the Democratic whip was appointed by the majority leader). Both whips head large whip organizations that have the purposes of collecting information for the leadership and persuading colleagues to support party positions. To facilitate the communication process, the whip offices maintain systems of recorded messages and e-mail about floor actions, issue whip notices about the upcoming schedule, and use automated telephone and paging systems to reach members about pending votes. Whips also try to keep track of the whereabouts of members, particularly on days when important, close floor votes are expected.

Congressionally Speaking . . .

The term *whip* originated in the British House of Commons. It is derived from the term *whipper-in* – the fellow who keeps the dogs in line during an English foxhunt. In the American Congress, the use of the term reflected the responsibility of the whip to get party members to the floor on time. Today the term is often used as a verb – as in "the undecided members were whipped" – to refer to the process of persuasion and arm-twisting.

The Democratic whip organization has been large for many years. In recent Congresses, the House Democrats had as many as 11 chief deputy whips, 12 deputy whips, and 70 at-large whips, all appointed by the whip. In addition, there have been 24 regional whips elected by groups of Democrats from specific regions and one ex officio whip (the ranking Democrat on the Rules Committee), for the nearly 100 members in the whip organization. Since the 1970s, the whip system has grown as the top leaders have responded to demands for whip appointments from party factions and individual members.

The Democratic leaders often appoint task forces to collect information and generate support on specific issues. This approach has been called a "strategy of inclusion," because it gives a large number of members an opportunity to work closely with the leadership. By working hand in hand with the party rank and file, party leaders are able to persuade some members who otherwise might oppose the leadership to join the team.

The House Republicans have a more modest whip system, although it also has expanded in recent years. The Republican whip system has comprised a chief deputy whip and about 17 deputy whips – all appointed – and nearly 50 assistant whips elected by groups for regions of the country. The Republican whips meet irregularly. The Republicans maintain several subcommittees on their Policy Committee that serve purposes similar to Democratic Caucus task forces.

Appointment or election as a whip or member of a policy subcommittee or task force gives a member some prestige, an additional office to add to his or her letterhead, and access to informative weekly whip meetings. For some members, service in these party posts provides an opportunity to prove their leadership abilities to their colleagues, which can be important to a member who aspires to the top leadership posts. For all members, these posts provide an opportunity to learn more about the politics of key issues and of their party. Nearly all members advertise at home their election or appointment to these party positions.

Evolving Party Organizations

Congressional party organizations have become much more elaborate in the past generation, a result of competitive pressures and the desire to include more members in party activities. A good example is the elaboration of the Senate Democratic leadership in recent years. Senator Charles Schumer (D-New York) was praised by his party colleagues for recruiting candidates, raising money, and aiding in the creation of a new Democratic majority. He was rewarded by Majority Leader Harry Reid (D-Nevada) with an appointment to a new party position, conference vice chairman, that Reid created for him. Reid said that the position would be the third-ranking leadership post under the majority leader and assistant majority leader (whip). Schumer continued to hold the position in 2009. After the 2010 elections, in which the Democrats lost six seats, Reid appointed Schumer to chair the Democratic Policy Committee and to run a new Democratic Policy and Communications Center, which combines the staffs of the Policy Committee and Reid's communications operation, so that legislative and public relations strategies could be better coordinated.

Another example is the appointment in 2011 of co–vice chairs of the House Democratic Steering and Policy Committee. With the top Democratic leaders exceeding seventy years of age and concern about getting new talent into the leadership following the Democrats' loss of majority control in the last elections, Democratic leader Nancy Pelosi created the new positions and appointed Debbie Wasserman Schultz of Florida and Henry Cuellar of Texas. Wasserman Schultz is a popular guest on television programs and represents liberal interests. Cuellar is a member of the Blue Dog and Hispanic Caucuses and represents more moderate interests in the party.

Also in 2011, just after her party lost its House majority, Democratic leader Pelosi created a new party position – assistant Democratic leader – that was given to James Clyburn (South Carolina). Clyburn is African American and had become a respected spokesperson for the party. He had been Democratic whip, but the loss of majority status meant that the former Speaker Pelosi would be minority leader and that former majority leader Steny Hoyer (D-Maryland) would seek to be elected minority whip. To avoid a contest for whip between Hoyer and Clyburn and to keep Clyburn in the leadership, the new post was formalized. The assistant leader serves as a formal liaison to groups within the party and attends leadership meetings. Clyburn continued to hold the position in 2015.

SENATE PARTY LEADERS

Traditionally, the Senate's smaller party organizations have had fewer formal leadership posts, committees, and staff than have their House counterparts, although Senate party organizations have become more elaborate in recent years. The Senate's chief leaders are the majority leader and the minority leader. These two leaders have historically been prominent politicians, frequently mentioned in the newspapers and seen on television.

Senate Floor Leaders

The majority leader is the principal leader of the Senate (see Table 5.4 for a list of recent majority leaders). The majority leader does not preside over sessions of the Senate; that is the responsibility of the vice president, who serves as president

TABLE 5.4. Recent majority leaders and party divisions in the Senate

Senate majority leader	Party	Congress	Years	Party division D-R-I[a]
Robert C. Bryd (WV)	D	95th	1977–1979	**61**–38–1
"	D	96th	1979–1981	**58**–41–1
Howard H. Baker, Jr. (TN)	R	97th	1981–1983	46–**53**–1
"	R	98th	1983–1985	45–**55**
"	R	99th	1985–1987	47–**53**
Robert C. Byrd (WV)	D	100th	1987–1989	**55**–45
George J. Mitchell, Jr. (ME)	D	101st	1989–1191	**55**–45
"	D	102nd	1991–1993	**56**–44
"	D	103rd	1993–1995	**57**–43
Robert J. Dole (KS)	R	104th[b]	1995–1996	48–**52**
Trent Lott (MS)	R	104th[b]	1996–1997	
"	R	105th	1997–1999	45–**55**
"	R	106th	1999–2001	45–**55**
"	R	107th[c]	2001–2003	50–**50**
Thomas A. Daschle (SD)	D	107th[c]	2001–2003	**50**–49–1
William H. Frist, Sr. (TN)	R	108th	2003–2005	48–**51**–1
"	R	109th	2005–2007	44–**55**–1
Harry M. Reid (NV)	D	110th	2007–2009	**49**–49–2[d]
"	D	111th	2009–2011	**57**–41–2
"	D	112th	2011–2013	**51**–47–2
"	D	113th	2013–2015	**53**–45–2
A. Mitchell McConnell (KY)	R	114th	2015–2016	44–**54**–2

[a] Democrats-Republicans-Independents.
[b] Dole resigned in June 1996 and was replaced by Lott.
[c] In 2001, the Republican vice president broke the tie to make the Republicans the Senate maority. After Senator James Jeffords (VT) left the Republican conference, became independent, and joined the Democratic conference in May 2001, the Republican leader Lott became minority leader and the Democratic leader Daschle became majority leader.
[d] The Independent and Independent Democrat caucused with the Democrats.

of the Senate, and the president pro tempore and his or her appointees in the absence of the vice president. Instead, the majority leader operates from his or her desk on the floor, making motions or working through a trusted lieutenant to direct the business of the Senate. The Senate majority leader is elected by fellow party conference members, unlike the Speaker of the House, who is nominated by his or her party but elected by the full House.

The majority leader sets the Senate's schedule and plans the order of business for the Senate floor. Critical to that function is a procedural advantage granted to the majority leader by precedent: the right of first recognition. The presiding officer recognizes the majority leader to speak or to offer a motion before recognizing any other senator, a practice that dates back to the 1930s.

Like House Speakers, Senate majority leaders vary in their assertiveness. Lyndon Johnson (D-Texas), who served as Democratic leader from 1955 to 1960, set the modern standard for aggressive leadership. Recent majority leaders of both parties have played a more important role in enacting major legislation – negotiating the content of many important bills, pushing committees to bring legislation to the floor, and taking a leading role in managing controversial legislation on the floor.

A majority leader's ability to set the floor agenda depends on the cooperation of his or her Senate colleagues. To call up a measure for consideration on the floor, the majority leader normally must gain approval of a "motion to proceed." Although the motion requires only a simple majority for approval, it also may be debated and so may be subject to a filibuster. Thus, on a controversial measure, the majority leader may require sixty votes to invoke cloture on the motion to proceed and get a measure to the floor for debate and amendment. Once the motion to proceed is adopted, the measure itself or any amendment to it may be filibustered. Consequently, the Senate's schedule is often quite unpredictable.

The majority leader usually seeks to limit debate and often seeks to limit amendments without going as far as invoking cloture. But to do so, the leader must receive unanimous consent – that is, the leader's request will be rejected if one senator objects. Objections are common from senators who want to protect their right to speak, do not want to give up opportunities to offer amendments, or simply do not want to be inconvenienced. Of course, leaders of both parties entertain requests from colleagues not to allow certain measures to be called up for consideration on the floor. As a result, scheduling in the Senate is much less routine and more a process of negotiation among senators and between the parties than it is in the House.

The minority leader represents his or her party in consulting with the majority leader on scheduling matters. The minority leader protects the parliamentary prerogatives of party members when the majority leader seeks unanimous consent to call up measures, schedule floor action, or limit debate and amendments. Like majority leaders, minority leaders differ in their aggressiveness, and their success depends on the size and cohesiveness of their parties. Unlike the House Speaker and floor leaders, the Senate floor leaders may retain committee assignments. Both Senate leaders are ex officio members of the Select Committee on Intelligence. Floor leaders do not hold full committee leadership positions, however.

Time for Reform?

Senator Robert C. Byrd (D-West Virginia), who died at age ninety-two in 2010 in his ninth term in office, was president pro tempore of the Senate from 1989 to 1995, 2001 to 2002, and 2007 until his death, as the most senior member of his party when in the majority. Byrd served a record 17,327 days in the Senate and, combined with his three terms in the House, was the longest-serving member in the history of Congress. He was in poor health in his last few years and seldom presided over the Senate.

The 1947 presidential succession act provides that the Senate's president pro tempore is third in line to the presidency behind the vice president and Speaker of the House. Because of the modern practice of giving the position to the most senior member of the majority party, the president pro tempore often is quite old and may not be capable of managing the duties of the presidency. In 2001, Strom Thurmond served as president pro tempore at age ninety-eight and surely would not have been an effective president. Concerns about an act of terrorism incapacitating national leadership have stimulated new questions about the age of presidents pro tempore, but there has been no serious effort to change the informal seniority practice or the 1947 law.

In late 1996, Senate Republicans set a three-Congress term limit for party leadership positions except for the floor leader and president pro tempore. The term limit forced several leaders to give up their positions for the first time at the end of 2002. Senate Democrats are alone among the four congressional parties in not placing term limits on any leadership positions.

Senate Whips and Whip Organizations

Both Senate parties call their whips "assistant floor leaders" to reflect their chief responsibility: standing in for the floor leader in his or her absence. The Senate whips conduct few formal head counts. One reason is that bill managers – committee leaders or others who take the lead in the floor debate – often do their own head counting, owing to the Senate's smaller size. Senate whips' specific duties depend on the needs of individual floor leaders. Senate party whips have sometimes named assistant or deputy whips to help with head counts and floor duties, but, as a general rule, the deputy whips have not played a regular or important role in the smaller Senate, where the top leaders, bill managers, and their staffs can manage most duties.

PARTY LEADERS' RESOURCES

In addition to their team of elected and appointed leaders, top party leaders have several resources that they use to influence policy outcomes: (1) their parties' voting strength, (2) the procedural powers granted them by the formal rules of their chamber and party, (3) the tangible rewards that they can grant to members, (4) information, (5) their access to the media, and (6) the effort and expertise of their staffs. Generally, the combination of party strength and formal powers accorded to him or her makes the House Speaker the most powerful member of Congress, followed in descending order by the Senate majority leader, the Senate minority leader, and the House minority leader.

Strength in Numbers

The relative size of the parties' delegations in Congress determines their majority or minority status and thus which party will enjoy the procedural advantages conferred to the majority. Figure 5.3 shows the percentage of House and Senate seats held by the Democrats since 1900 (Republicans held the remaining seats). In Congresses in which the percentage of Democrats is over 50, Democrats were the majority party; when less than 50 percent were Democrats, Republicans were the majority party. Of course, a party's ability to pass or block legislation involves more than its size alone. A majority party must also be fairly cohesive, or at least able to benefit from a fractured opposition, for its potential strength to be realized. Seldom are majority parties so large that they can afford to lose many votes from their own ranks and still win on the floor.

Votes that require supermajorities, such as the two-thirds majority required to override presidential vetoes or the three-fifths majority required to overcome a Senate filibuster, are particularly troublesome for majority parties (lines corresponding to the supermajority thresholds are shown in Figure 5.3). As a general rule, there is uncertainty about a majority party's prospects of prevailing on

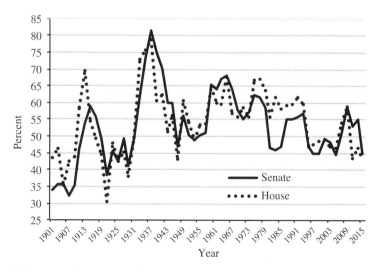

Figure 5.3 Democrats' Percentage of Seats, 1901–2015.

important issues, and there is even more uncertainty when a supermajority is required. In most Congresses, the majority party is not large enough to win votes that require supermajority majorities without support from some minority party members. Hard work is required to build winning coalitions on most important legislation. Not all party colleagues can be trusted to support their leadership, and ways of attracting support from members of the minority party often must be found.

Procedural Advantages

The standing rules of the House and Senate, as well as the written rules of the congressional parties, grant party leaders certain procedural advantages over other members. Of the four top leaders, the Speaker of the House is, by far, the most advantaged by standing rules and precedents. The Speaker enjoys powers that far exceed those of the most comparable Senate leader, the Senate majority leader.

THE SPEAKER OF THE HOUSE. In the early 1970s, the formal power of the House Speaker was bolstered under the rules of the Democratic Caucus and under the rules of the House. Perhaps most important, the Speaker was granted the power to nominate the party's members of the Committee on Rules. The Rules Committee writes resolutions that, when adopted by a majority of the House, provide for the immediate consideration of important legislation and may limit debate and amendments on those measures (see Chapter 7). By controlling the Rules Committee and recognizing its members to offer its resolutions (known as "special rules") on the floor, the Speaker has effective control over the floor agenda.

In the House rules, at about the same time, the Speaker was granted the power to refer legislation to multiple committees or to propose the creation of an ad hoc or temporary committee. Previously, the Speaker was required to refer each measure to the single committee that had predominant jurisdiction over it. The Speaker now may send legislation to committees sequentially, with one committee identified as the primary committee, or can split legislation into parts to send to different committees. The Speaker may set time limits on committee action when more than one committee is involved. This flexible referral rule has substantially enhanced the Speaker's ability to control the flow of legislation in the House – even to direct legislation toward friendly committees and away from unfriendly committees. On only one occasion, for a large multifaceted energy bill in 1977, whose content spanned the jurisdiction of many committees, has an ad hoc committee been used successfully.

The powers granted to the Speaker created the prospect of a more centralized, Speaker-driven, policy-making process in the House. That possibility certainly was not fully realized in the 1970s. Speakers Carl Albert and Tip O'Neill continued to defer to committees and did not attempt to manipulate committees by using their referral powers. To the contrary, the 1970s were a period of remarkably fragmented, decentralized policy making. This was the product of simultaneous reforms that diffused power from full committee chairs to subcommittee chairs (see Chapter 6). And it reflected the expectations of rank-and-file Democrats. Only in the last year or two of the 1970s did Speaker O'Neill begin to use his new referral powers with some vigor.

The power of the Speaker was enhanced in 1993 when the House, over the objections of minority party Republicans at the time, adopted a rule that allows the Speaker to remove members and appoint additional members to select and conference committees after initial appointments have been made. The new rule, which covers minority party appointees as well as majority party appointees, is aimed at majority party conferees who pursue positions that will obstruct outcomes favored by the leadership. Such conferees cannot be confident that their place on a prominent select committee or important conference committee will be protected once they have been appointed. Instead, the Speaker is free to correct errors in judgment made at the time of the initial appointments. In practice, the Speaker is likely to continue to defer to the minority leader on the appointment of minority party members to select and conference committees. The Republicans retained the rule once they became the majority party after the 1994 elections, and it has remained in place since then.

With respect to intraparty rules and practices, the House parties allow their top leaders considerable power. In addition to giving their top leaders the power to nominate their parties' members of the Rules Committee, they give their leaders strong influence over their party colleagues' assignments to other committees and to appoint members to a variety of party positions. In combination, the powers granted under House and party rules make the Speaker exceptionally influential.

THE SENATE MAJORITY LEADER. It bears repeating that the Senate does not grant its presiding officer the same power that the House grants the Speaker. Because the vice president serves as president of the Senate, may not be of the same party as the Senate majority, and, as a general rule, is a lieutenant of the president, senators have not given their presiding officer much power. The Constitution grants the vice president a vote when a tie vote occurs, but otherwise the Senate gives its presiding officer little power. Even rulings on procedural matters can be overturned by a Senate majority.

The most powerful senator is the majority leader, but the majority leader's procedural powers are more limited than those of the House Speaker. The primary procedural advantage of the Senate majority leader is the right of first recognition. The right of first recognition, which is not written in the Senate's rules but is a well-established practice, gives the majority leader an opportunity to offer a motion before any other senator is recognized by the presiding officer to do so.

With recognition to speak or offer a motion, the majority leader can attempt to set the agenda by moving that the Senate consider a bill or nomination, offering an amendment, or making some other motion. In this way, the Senate majority leader has a power that parallels the House Speaker's ability to recognize a member to make a motion without appeal.

The difference between the House Speaker and the Senate majority leader rests on the ability to win votes to set the agenda. With limits on debate in the House and a unified party, the Speaker can set the agenda by majority vote. In the Senate, a motion to set the agenda can be checked by a cohesive minority that can filibuster legislation (Chapter 7). Without backing from a sixty-vote majority, the Senate majority leader's effort to set the agenda may be blocked. As Figure 5.3 shows, the Senate majority leader usually needs the support of minority party senators to overcome a filibuster. The majority leader may have to promise policy concessions or opportunities to offer certain amendments, or even promise to bring up unrelated legislation, as concessions to the minority in order to overcome a filibuster, or a threatened filibuster, on a bill. Similar concessions are seldom required in the House, where a simple majority gives the Speaker the power to move legislation through the stages of the legislative process with only the votes of members of his or her own party.

Congressionally Speaking . . .

The predicament of the Senate majority leader is illustrated in the practice of holds. A *hold* is an objection to considering a measure on the Senate floor. Senators usually communicate their objections by letter to their party's floor leader. For several decades, these communications were considered confidential so that the name of the senator placing the hold often was not known to his or her colleagues. When senators place holds on measures, they sometimes merely want advance warning of floor action, but at other times they seek to change the bill or even prevent Senate action on the bill.

Working to remove holds is time-consuming and involves bargaining with contending factions. Holds are not formally recognized in Senate or party rules, but rather are effective because they constitute notices to object to a unanimous consent request to move to the consideration of a bill or other measure. A leader may call the bluff of a colleague and seek to bring up a bill without clearing the hold, but leaders generally observe holds because they need the cooperation of their colleagues on other matters.

In 2007, a provision requiring public disclosure of the name of the senator placing a hold was included in ethics reform legislation. The sponsors hoped that disclosure would limit the practice by allowing the public and fellow senators to hold accountable those senators who place holds. The rule proved toothless (requiring senators to disclose their hold *after* an objection to considering a measure was made), with many more holds placed on presidential nominations in recent years. Filibusters and gaining cloture proved to be far more serious problems for the majority leader.

Favors to Grant

Party leaders have a few resources at their disposal that provide direct political benefits to their colleagues and can be used to reward friends and punish enemies. Influence over committee assignments is the most prominent of these resources. An assignment to a committee with jurisdiction over legislation relevant to a member's home constituency or to well-financed special interests may be important to the member's electoral prospects. Other committees are coveted because of their jurisdiction over key legislation and because they place their members in the middle of the most important legislative battles. Because party leaders play a major role in their parties' committees on committees, where committee assignments are made, they can offer or withhold favors from colleagues.

Tangible rewards come in many other forms, too. The expanded use of task forces by the congressional parties has increased the number of opportunities for leaders to bestow special status on party colleagues. Leaders can appoint members to special commissions and approve international travel plans.

Leaders can be supportive of their colleagues' campaign efforts. They can influence the allocation of funds from the party campaign committees. In recent decades, party leaders have created political action committees of their own and contributed to colleagues' campaigns. Even candidates for leadership posts seek to demonstrate their leadership abilities by raising money that is directed to their colleagues' campaigns. And in recent years, leaders have become very active in attending the fund-raising events of their colleagues, sometimes even choosing not to attend an event to make clear their dissatisfaction with a member's behavior. In a few cases, leaders have intervened to discourage primary challenges to an incumbent colleague.

Procedural Cartels and Party Loyalty

In recent Congresses, several dozen of the most conservative House Republicans associated with the Tea Party Caucus and the new House Freedom Caucus have opposed their own party leaders on important issues, including the election of John Boehner to the speakership. In 2012, Speaker John Boehner persuaded the House Republican Steering Committee, which he chairs, to take away key committee assignments from four conservative Republicans who had opposed the party position on critical legislation. Boehner's problems with the most conservative Republicans did not end there. He struggled to get sufficient party support on several issues in the following years and faced votes against his reelection as Speaker in 2014. In early 2015, party leaders and several committee chairs announced their expectation that Republicans chosen as subcommittee chairs would be loyal to the party on all procedural matters. The message was clear: Accepting a prestigious position from the majority party came with an obligation to support the party on procedural matters and most important policy issues.

(continued)

Procedural Cartels and Party Loyalty (*continued*)

The political scientists Mathew McCubbins and Gary Cox called legislative parties "procedural cartels" to capture the idea that party members seek to control the procedural features of the House and Senate that they consider vital to their collective interests. Top leaders are expected to defend those interests – even when it requires that they create disincentives for disloyal behavior on the part of mid-level committee leaders.

The threats voiced in 2015 were part of a pattern dating back to the 1970s. In the early 1970s, several Democratic full committee chairs lost their positions for being too uncooperative with the liberal majority of the party. In the early 1980s, Democratic subcommittee chairs were explicitly warned that holding their positions was conditional on supporting the party on important issues. And in the mid-1990s, Republican Speaker Newt Gingrich made loyalty to the party leadership a clear expectation for committee and subcommittee chairs.

Some independence from the party is tolerated. If voting against the party from time to time helps a member get reelected, some disloyal behavior is expected. However, disloyal behavior on important matters, particularly those involving procedural control over the floor agenda, undercuts the value of being in the majority party and causes leaders some embarrassment. Thus, from time to time, majority party leaders reinforce the expectation of loyalty, particularly for members who have been given committee leadership posts.

Their Information Network

Information is critical to legislative success. Devising effective legislative strategies requires information about the specific policy issues and alternatives that will arise during the Congress, the administration, the other key players, the policy preferences of the membership, and how others plan to act. Advantages from chamber or party rules, or even from party strength, remain only potential sources of leadership power if they are not matched by useful and timely information.

The top leaders navigate in a sea of information. With the help of their colleagues and staff, leaders collect and absorb information about committee schedules and actions, floor scheduling, presidential requests, members' political circumstances, and interest group activity. The top leaders do not have a monopoly over most kinds of information, of course, but they are uniquely placed to assimilate information from many different sources. Requests are made of them on such matters as scheduling, committee assignments, and campaign assistance, and leaders can sometimes pry information from members, lobbyists, and others who want something from them. The whip systems and party task forces are often activated to gather and disseminate information. The time they spend on or near their chamber floor gives leaders and their staffs opportunities for casual conversations and informal exchanges of information.

Because information flows to the top leaders so readily, few other members can compete with party leaders as coalition builders. To be sure, committee leaders and bill sponsors master information relevant to their own legislation, but from time to time even committee leaders turn to party leaders for assistance in gathering and distributing information. By exercising care in granting access to their information, party leaders can affect the strategies of other important players.

Leaders' informational advantage is stronger in the House than in the Senate owing to the House's larger size. In the House, the seemingly simple task of counting members planning to vote for or against something is onerous. For the majority party, this means reaching more than 218 members, many of whom are likely to be away from Washington, when the information is needed. Consequently, House bill managers often must rely on the party leadership – whip offices and task forces – for timely information. In contrast, Senate bill managers are more self-reliant because they need to count fewer heads. Thus, Senate whip organizations are not critical to the collection and dissemination of information on most important matters.

The overall trend in recent decades has been toward a diffusion of information across Capitol Hill. Junior members have benefited from the expansion of committee, personal, and support agency staffs and from the growth of the interest group community and informal members' caucuses. Party leaders are no longer as advantaged in their command of information as they were just a few decades ago.

Another Story of Switching Parties

In 2004, with no advance notice, Louisana freshman Representative Rodney Alexander, who had been elected in 2002 as a Democrat, filed for reelection to his seat as a Republican. Not only were House Democratic leaders surprised, they soon became upset when Alexander did not promptly return approximately $70,000 in contributions that he had received from the political action committees of several Democratic colleagues. Democratic leaders threatened a lawsuit against him for fraud after failing to hear from Alexander for a month. Alexander began to refund the contributions about two months later, just a month before the November elections, which, at least one Democrat complained, was so late that it limited the value of redirecting the money to other campaigns. Alexander won the election and was rewarded by his new party with a seat on the prestigious Appropriations Committee, a move up from the Committee on Agriculture and the Committee on Transportation and Infrastructure assignments he had had as a Democrat. Alexander was reelected in 2006, 2008, 2010, and 2012 as a Republican, always with more than 75 percent of the vote. In 2010, Alexander joined the Tea Party Caucus. In 2013, he gave up his seat to serve as secretary of the Louisiana Department of Veterans Affairs.

Getting Out the Message

Although top party leaders cannot compete with the president for media attention, they enjoy far better access to the media than do most other members. The media often turn to top leaders for their reactions to events or to presidential decisions or statements. This phenomenon is natural: Leaders are presumed to represent their parties and to be in a position to act on their views. Even when there is no breaking story, leaders' routine press conferences attract reporters on the chance that the leaders will say something newsworthy. Few other members can count on such attention. Thus, leaders gain media attention because they are powerful and, at least in part, they are powerful because they gain media attention.

One Name, Two Parties

House and Senate Democrats and House and Senate Republicans have separate organizations and elect their own leaders, but there are still good reasons for fellow partisans in the two houses to coordinate their activities. In fact, periodically a party's House and Senate leaders promise to work together on an agenda and public relations. For the party of the president, the White House staff often is involved in planning sessions on the legislative agenda. Over the course of a Congress, coordination tends to fade as leaders in each house struggle to get legislation passed and meet the expectations of their separate party conferences.

Party leaders' media access is an important resource in the legislative game. Leaders can share their access with colleagues: They can mention a colleague's legislation, invite a colleague to join in a press conference, or refer reporters and television producers to a colleague. They can selectively divulge information about the plans of friendly and unfriendly factions. They also can increase the ease or difficulty of reaching compromises by softening or intensifying the rhetoric of claiming credit and avoiding blame.

Until recently, Senate leaders generally had an advantage over House leaders in their access to the media. Speakers of the mid-twentieth century often shunned the media and were not particularly good on radio or television. The greater public prestige of the Senate and greater public interest in senators than in representatives may have encouraged the national media to pay more attention to Senate leaders. The advent of televised floor sessions in the House in 1979, about seven years before the Senate permitted television coverage of its sessions, seemed to make little difference.

Recent Speakers have promised to be effective at public relations, and most have been quite visible in the media. These House Speakers – particularly Wright, Gingrich, Pelosi, and Boehner – have been as active in efforts to create daily media messages for their party and as visible on network news programs as the top Senate leaders. For a couple of years in the mid-1990s, Speaker Gingrich was second only to the president in media visibility. The House minority leader generally lags far behind other top leaders in media visibility, reflecting the limited influence of most House minority leaders. In contrast, the power of the Senate minority to obstruct bills, coupled with the Senate's prestige, gives the Senate minority leader a big advantage over his or her House counterpart in attracting media attention.

Recent party leaders in both houses have made a concerted effort to shape the message communicated through the media to the general public. They have expanded their press office operations, hired media specialists, consulted pollsters, formed party committees or task forces to shape party messages, and sought new ways to communicate to the public. All recent top leaders have sought to fashion coherent policy programs, to advertise their programs, and to develop a common argument or theme for the parties on major issues. In recent years, most House leaders, or at least their staffs on their behalf, have been active on social media, particularly on Twitter, with followers numbering well over a half million.

The Assistance of Sizable, Expert Staffs

Top leaders' staffs have expanded as leaders have sought to meet colleagues' expectations and extend their own influence. These staffs now include policy and political specialists, along with public relations personnel, speechwriters, experts in parliamentary procedures, and people who assist the leaders with daily chores. Both Senate leaders manage the activity of the party secretaries, who are staff members, and the secretaries' assistants, who can be seen sitting at tables on the Senate floor. With the help of expanded staffs, leaders can more carefully follow committee deliberations, more rapidly respond to political events, and more frequently take a leading role in the negotiation of legislative details.

A NEW PARTY ERA

The emergence of stronger, polarized parties in Congress would have surprised most observers of the Congress in the 1960s. At that time, the House and Senate caucuses had remarkably diverse memberships, the caucuses of the majority party Democrats seldom met, and the top majority party leaders were deferential to committee leaders on the content of legislation. Because it was led by whatever committee happened to have jurisdiction over a bill, the policy-making process within the House and Senate looked very decentralized. Today, the parties in each house are deeply polarized. Each party in each house meets regularly to discuss policy and politics. And party leaders are expected to take the lead in devising legislation and designing strategies with the collective policy and political interests of their parties in mind.

These developments are due primarily to changes in the composition of the two parties. The policy or ideological makeup of each congressional party is more homogeneous now than it was fifty years ago, which is primarily the result of who gets elected to Congress. Most new members arrive on Capitol Hill with a general ideological outlook and many specific policy commitments that are a product of a selection process that involves, in some cases, being recruited to run for office by party activists, attracting support from key party groups to raise money and win primary elections, and motivating partisans to get out to vote in a general election. That process now produces more uniformly liberal Democrats and more uniformly conservative Republicans than it did a generation ago.

Party Realignment

There are multiple, reinforcing causes of party polarization in Congress, some of which we noted in previous chapters. The realignment of partisan preferences in the electorate is, perhaps, the most important cause. Figure 5.4 shows darker

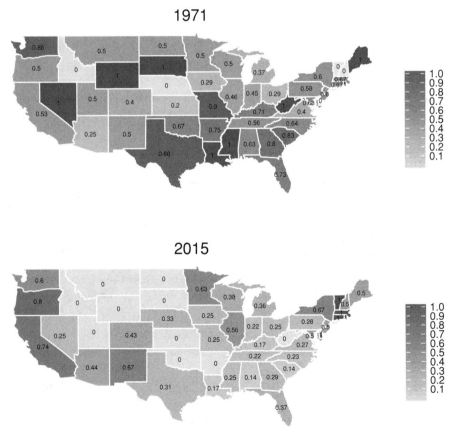

Figure 5.4 Democrats' Proportion of Seats, by State, 1971 and 2015 (darker shade indicates higher proportion of Democrats).

shades to indicate the percentage of House seats from each state won by the Democrats, comparing 1971 on the top with 2015 on the bottom. The lighter shades of the lower map reflect the fact the Republicans became much more successful in winning House seats over the last forty years.

In the 1970s and 1980s, the South, which was long a conservative region, shifted from majority Democratic to majority Republican in many congressional districts and states. As a result, the conservative, southern Democrats began to disappear as they were replaced with conservative Republicans. Across the "rust belt" states from the Midwest to New England, moderate Republicans were replaced by liberal Democrats. For both parties, the most important sources of centrist legislators dried up. Republicans made gains in the mountain West states, which produce conservative Republicans, and the Democrats made gains in the Pacific coast states, which produce liberal Democrats. Fewer centrists, along with many more conservative Republicans and a few more liberal Democrats, yielded more polarized congressional parties.

The regional shifts in partisan preferences are only a part of the story. Throughout the country, Americans sorted themselves into liberal and conservative camps. The sorting has been imperfect, but in recent years Americans, like members of Congress, are more likely to hold liberal or conservative views across a wide range of issues – taxes, the environment, civil rights, abortion, immigration, and so on – than they did a generation ago. The liberals more regularly support Democratic candidates for Congress, and the conservatives support Republican candidates more than they did previously. This sorting process, which took place in the 1990s and 2000s, appears to have made the voters who support each party more homogeneous. In turn, fewer Democratic and Republican legislators have an incentive to oppose their own party in Congress and, if they do so frequently or on important issues, they can expect trouble in winning their next primary at home.

What Caused the Realignment?

Simple political manipulation of congressional district lines, some argue, is the central cause of partisan polarization. That is, the parties and their ideological backers redrew district lines so that Democratic and Republican incumbents could get reelected easily, play only to partisans on their side, and pursue extremist policy agendas without worrying about losing the support of moderate voters or alienating opposition partisans. If the manipulation of district boundaries, known as gerrymandering, was eliminated and legislators had to compete for support from middle-of-the-road voters, extremism would end and partisan polarization would diminish, the argument goes.

The gerrymandering argument is wrong. There is evidence that the drawing of district lines provided a net advantage to Republicans in recent decades, but claims about the effects of gerrymandering on partisan polarization in Congress are misguided. Gerrymandering had only a small role in the regional realignment of party support. The sorting of political attitudes and partisanship in the electorate occurred nearly everywhere, with and without redrawn district lines. And the polarization is evident as much in the Senate, where state lines have not been redrawn, as for House district lines.

Unfortunately, the story behind party polarization in Congress is not as simple as pointing to gerrymandering. The social upheaval of the 1960s – including, but not limited to, the anti–Vietnam War movement, the civil rights movement, the women's movement – recast the thinking of many Americans about the two parties and spurred the emergence of the Christian right movement in the 1970s. These developments had a profound effect in the South, but their effect was not limited to the South. They served as a foundation for leading Republicans to appeal to both economic and social conservatives, which expanded the Republican base and made the party more competitive. Republican elites, led by some members of Congress like Newt Gingrich, deliberately sharpened the differences between the parties with the expectation, they argued, that a natural conservative majority in the country would elect Republican majorities to Congress. Their success was reinforced by the emergence of stronger activist groups and wealthy individuals who influenced primary election outcomes, the growth of talk radio, and, with the spread of cable television and Internet access, the development of "narrowcasting" to targeted political audiences. The demonization of the other side, always common in politics, reached new levels of meanness.

Important features of this process are cues given by political elites, including leading members of Congress, about how issues, ideology, and partisanship match up. The demise of centrists in both parties changed the mix of signals the public received and the perceived alternatives at election time. Without experiencing a traumatic political event, Americans appeared to draft to one side or the other, realigning their policy views to the perspectives they observed among elites and sorting themselves into partisan camps. Surviving politicians, running through the selection process of endorsements, campaigns, and elections, tended to appeal to one side or the other, with appeals to supporters of the other party deemed useless.

If you think that deeply polarized parties are a problem, this account of congressional politics of the last few decades leads to the conclusion that solutions are not readily devised. The polarization rests deep in the relationship between voters and members of Congress, all of whom operate in a polarized environment shaped by political money, commentators, and party activists. Thus, calls for more effective leadership from the elected leaders of Congress probably represent an overly optimistic view of the power of those leaders over the legislators who elected them and an unrealistic view of the political pressures placed on rank-and-file legislators.

Leadership in Another Era

Sam Rayburn (D-Texas) was, perhaps, the most beloved Speaker of the House. He served as Speaker from 1940 to 1961, with the exception of four years when Republicans controlled the House. Rayburn listened well and was always kind to his colleagues, and because he was sheepish about his bald head, he shied away from cameras. He exercised his power quietly. A biographer reported an incident on the floor of the House that was typical of the way Rayburn ruled:

> [W]hen a bill providing for a cooling-off period to stave off labor strikes came to the House floor, Rayburn wanted it debated fully. Experience and instinct told him that with feelings running high an attempt might be made to shut off debate and go directly to a vote. This proved correct when Jennings Randolph of West Virginia, a member of the Labor Committee, won recognition and started to make a motion to do this.
>
> While he was still talking, Rayburn walked down from the dais and headed toward him. With each approaching step Randolph's voice grew weaker. Finally he stopped talking when Rayburn reached him and put a hand on his shoulder. For a short time, with his face set sternly, Rayburn spoke in a low, gruff tone to Randolph, whom he liked. Then still talking, he removed his hand, plunged it into his jacket pocket, and his body rocked back and forth from his heels to his toes. Then he turned suddenly and walked back to the rostrum.
>
> Laughter swept the chamber as embarrassment crossed Randolph's face. When silence came, Randolph announced he was withdrawing his motion, and he added, "As a legislative son I am always willing to follow the advice of my legislative elders."

Rayburn was special, to be sure, but no recent Speaker, in an age of televised floor sessions and independent-minded members, would have dared embarrass a colleague in that way.

CONCLUSION

The environment of the late twentieth century and early twenty-first century pushed congressional party leaders to the forefront of policy making. Party leaders are now central strategists and coordinators of policy development in Congress. It has not always been so. In the mid-twentieth century, party leaders coordinated the floor schedule and worked closely with committee leaders on strategy, but, for the most part, they left the development of legislative details to the standing committees and their chairs.

Party leaders are not all-powerful. Far from it. Party leaders still lack the capacity to deny nomination or election to Congress and so have limited influence over their members, far less influence than exists in most other national legislatures. To be sure, the parties elect leadership, organize the standing committees, and structure floor and conference action. Moreover, congressional parties' internal organizations and staffs have become more elaborate. And in the last two decades leaders have been prime movers in the legislative process on major issues. Nevertheless, diverse constituency interests across a large, heterogeneous country, the weakness of the parties in candidate selection, the fragmentation of American party organizations across several levels of government, and the difficulty of coordinating House and Senate activities stand in the way of party-directed policy making over the long term.

Even so, party leaders are now central to the policy-making process. They are far more than servants of committee leaders, as it sometimes appeared in the mid-twentieth century. For the majority party in each house, central party leaders take the lead in setting the agenda, often have a direct role in writing important legislation, and frequently take the lead in negotiating with the president and the other chamber. Their parties expect them to do so.

SUGGESTED READINGS

A.   The following books provide theoretical accounts of the creation and development of parties.

Aldrich, John H. *The Origin and Transformation of Political Parties in America*. Chicago: University of Chicago Press, 1995.

Cox, Gary W., and Mathew D. McCubbins. *Setting the Agenda: Responsible Party Government in the U.S. House of Representatives*. Cambridge: Cambridge University Press, 1995.

B.   The following books discuss the causes and consequences of polarized parties in the House and Senate.

Sinclair, Barbara. *Party Wars: Polarization and the Politics of National Policy Making*. Norman: University of Oklahoma Press, 2006.

Smith, Steven S. *The Senate Syndrome: The Evolution of Procedural Warfare in the Modern U.S. Senate*. Norman: University of Oklahoma Press, 2014.

C.   The following books provide thorough discussions of party influence in Congress.

Lee, Francis E. *Beyond Ideology: Politics, Principles, and Partisanship in the U.S. Senate*. Chicago: University of Chicago Press, 2009.

Smith, Steven S., *Party Influence in Congress*. New York: Cambridge University Press, 2007.

DISCUSSION QUESTIONS

1   Why do legislators create and maintain party organizations and leadership positions?

2   What resources do leaders employ to influence the behavior of rank-and-file members? Generally, can party leaders in Congress compel compliant behavior by members of their parties?

3   Why have parties become more important to congressional policy making in recent decades?

6 The Standing Committees

Treasury Inspector General for Tax Administration J. Russell George and former Commissioner of the Internal Revenue Service Steve Miller face a wall of cameras before the start of a House Ways and Means Committee hearing to investigate an IRS scandal involving the targeting of conservative groups.

One of the most visible and enduring features of Congress is its committee system. From hearings to investigations to legislative activity, committees are the congressional darlings of the mass media. Considering the central role that committees play in modern-day lawmaking and oversight, there is little wonder why they garner so much attention. Most important legislation originates in a standing committee, most of the details of legislation are approved in committee, and standing committee members usually dominate floor and conference action. When legislation dies, it usually does so in committee.

The significance of standing committees in the policy-making process varies over time. In the mid-twentieth century, committees were often described as nearly autonomous policy makers (see Chapter 2). The tremendous growth in government and the power of the presidency that characterized the New Deal and World War II era of the 1930s and 1940s led Congress to reevaluate the way it did business. The Legislative Reorganization Act of 1946 reduced the number of standing committees, provided detailed written committee jurisdictions, guaranteed a professional staff for each committee, and directed committees to conduct oversight of executive agencies. As a result of the 1946 act, most of the key features of the modern committee system were put into place. Moreover, the leadership of the internally divided Democratic majority usually preferred to defer to committees rather than risk open divisions on the House and Senate floors. In fact, prescriptive norms of deference to committees and senior committee leaders were articulated by leaders to bolster the power of committees.

In recent decades, committees have lost much of the autonomy they had gained in the middle of the twentieth century. A more assertive membership, increasingly polarized parties, stronger party leadership, and new checks on committee leadership, among other factors, reduced the level of independence once held by committees and their leaders. Committees, however, retain a considerable amount of power within their issue domains; they process the vast majority of legislation that is approved by the House and Senate. In this chapter, we profile the House and Senate committee systems and then examine the foundations of committee power and how these powers have evolved over time.

TYPES OF COMMITTEES

Modern congressional committees have two formal functions: (1) collecting information through hearings and investigations, and (2) drafting and reporting legislation. Committee hearings are Congress's primary means for formally receiving the testimony of representatives of the executive branch, organized interest groups, independent experts, the general public, and, occasionally, movie and TV stars. Congress usually relies on committees to investigate disasters (natural or human-made), scandals in government or elsewhere, and policy crises. Informally, congressional hearings provide opportunities for legislators to publicize causes and receive media attention. Figure 6.1 shows the frequency of congressional hearings between 1946 and 2010. On the legislative side, the vast majority of bills and other legislation introduced by members are referred

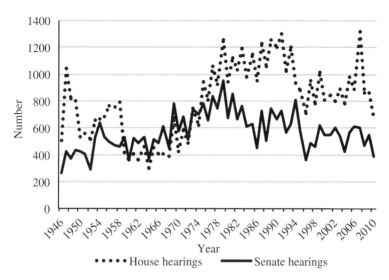

Figure 6.1 The Frequency of House and Senate Committee Hearings, 1946–2010. Source: Data from the Policy Agendas Project available at http://www.policyagendas.org.

to the committee or committees with the appropriate jurisdiction. In committee meetings for considering legislation, called markups, the details of legislation are reviewed or written.

The House and Senate have developed several types of committees to perform these informational and legislative functions. All committees can hold hearings and investigate policy problems that fall within their jurisdiction. However, not all committees have the right to receive and report legislation, and not all committees are considered to be standing or permanent committees (Table 6.1).

Standing committees have legislative authority and permanent status (standing committees for the 114th Congress [2015–2016] are listed in Table 6.2). Their legislative jurisdiction is specified in chamber rules and precedents, and they write and report legislation on any matter within their jurisdiction. Committee members, and particularly chairs, are territorial about their committees' jurisdictions and resist efforts to reduce or reallocate their jurisdictions. As a result, with a few important exceptions, changes to the committee systems of the House and Senate have been incremental.

TABLE 6.1. Types of committees

| Permanent status? | May report legislation to the floor? | |
	Yes	No
Yes	standing committees	some select committees, joint committees
No	conference committees, most select committees, ad hoc committees	

TABLE 6.2. Standing committees of the House and Senate, 2015–2016

House of Representatives name (number of subcommittees)	Dems[c]	Reps[c]
Agriculture (6)	19	26
Appropriations (12)	21	30
Armed Services (7)	26	36
Budget (0)	14	22
Education and the Workforce (4)	15	22
Energy and Commerce (6)	23	31
Ethics[b] (0)	5	5
Financial Services (5)	26	34
Foreign Affairs (6)	19	25
Homeland Security (6)	12	18
House Administration (0)	3	6
Judiciary (5)	16	23
Natural Resources (5)	18	26
Oversight and Government Reform (6)	21	25
Rules (2)	4	7
Science, Space, and Technology (5)	17	22
Select Committee on Intelligence[a] (4)	9	13
Small Business (5)	10	14
Transportation and Infrastructure (6)	25	34
Veterans' Affairs (5)	10	14
Ways and Means (6)	15	24
Senate name (number of subcommittees)	**Dems[c, d]**	**Reps[c]**
Agriculture, Nutrition, and Forestry (5)	9	11
Appropriations (12)	14	16
Armed Services (6)	12	14
Banking, Housing, and Urban Affairs (5)	10	12
Budget (0)	9	12
Commerce, Science, and Transportation (6)	11	13
Energy and Natural Resources (4)	10	12
Environment and Public Works (6)	9	11
Finance (6)	12	14
Foreign Relations (7)	9	10
Health, Education, Labor, and Pensions (3)	10	12
Homeland Security and Governmental Affairs (3)	7	9
Indian Affairs (0)	6	8
Judiciary (6)	9	11
Rules and Administration (0)	8	10
Select Committee on Ethics[b] (0)	3	3
Select Committee on Intelligence[a] (0)	7	8
Small Business and Entrepreneurship (0)	9	10
Veterans' Affairs (0)	7	8

[a] The two intelligence committees are officially named select committees but have authority to report legislation.
[b] The House Committee on Ethics may report legislation; the Senate Committee on Ethics does not have legislative authority.
[c] Numbers include full members of the chamber and vacant seats allotted to the party.
[d] Independent Senators Bernie Sanders (I-Vermont) and Angus King (I-Maine) are counted among the Democrats.
Source: www.house.gov; www.senate.gov.

Ad hoc committees may be created and appointed to design and report legislation, but they are temporary and often dissolve either at a specified date or after reporting the legislation for which they were created. Since 1975, the Speaker of the House has been permitted to appoint ad hoc committees with House approval. Although this authority has been used infrequently, it extends additional referral alternatives to the Speaker.

Conference committees are temporary and have legislative responsibilities. They are appointed to resolve the differences between House and Senate versions of legislation. The Constitution requires that legislation be approved in identical form by both chambers before it is sent to the president. Although the Constitution is silent as to how the two chambers are to resolve their differences, conference committees were an almost immediate solution to this problem in the earliest Congresses. Although inter-chamber differences can be resolved in other ways, conference committees have historically been used for most important legislation. Conference committees have wide, but not unlimited, discretion to redesign legislation in their efforts to gain House and Senate approval. In theory, conference committees are bound to the differences between the House and Senate legislation. In practice, however, it is not uncommon for conference committees to insert provisions into legislation that did not appear in either chamber's final legislation and remove provisions that were agreed on by both chambers. When a majority of House conferees and a majority of Senate conferees agree, a conference committee issues a report that must be approved by both houses before the bill can be sent to the president. Conference committees dissolve as soon as one house takes action on the conference report.

Joint committees are permanent but lack legislative authority. Joint committees are composed of members from both chambers, and the chairs alternate between the chambers from Congress to Congress. The Joint Economic Committee frequently conducts highly publicized hearings on economic affairs, and the Joint Committee on Taxation serves primarily as a holding company for a respected staff of economists whose economic forecasts and reports on fiscal policy matters are frequently cited. The Joint Committee on Printing performs the more ministerial duty of overseeing the Government Printing Office; the Joint Committee on the Library oversees the Library of Congress. Bills are not referred to joint committees, and joint committees cannot report legislation to the floor. The Joint Committee on Atomic Energy (1946–1977) was the only joint committee to date with authority to report legislation.

Select, or special, committees are, in principle, temporary committees without legislative authority. They may be used to study problems that fall under the jurisdiction of several standing committees, to symbolize Congress's commitment to major constituency groups, or simply to reward particular legislators. Select committees have been used for seven prominent investigations since 1970, including the Senate's 1973 investigation of the Watergate break-in and cover-up and the 1987 House and Senate investigation of the Iran-Contra affair. Major reforms of congressional rules and organizations have originated in select committees.

Unfortunately, committee nomenclature can be misleading. For example, the House and Senate have each made their Select Intelligence Committee permanent and granted it the power to report legislation. Moreover, some standing committees, such as the House Committee on Homeland Security, began as select committees and gained standing status later. In 1993, under pressure to streamline the legislative process and reduce spending, the House abolished its Select Committee on Aging, Hunger, Narcotics Abuse and Control and its Select Committee on Children, Youth, and Families. The Senate maintains a Special Committee on Aging, which studies issues relevant to the elderly, in addition to the Select Committee on Ethics, which handles ethics violations by senators and staffs.

Standing committees are the primary concern of this chapter. In the modern Congress, standing committees originate most legislation, and their members manage the legislation on the floor and dominate conference committees. Unless otherwise indicated, the following discussion concerns standing committees.

THE NATURE OF CONGRESSIONAL COMMITTEES

The Constitution makes no provision for congressional committees. However, committees emerged early in congressional history. Over time, the committee system has undergone considerable change. At different points in history the House and Senate have adopted rules to expand and reduce the number of committees, as well as to modify their structure and authority. Given the emergence and longevity of committees, it is clear that the division of labor that allows each chamber to pursue multiple hearings and legislative efforts simultaneously has proven useful.

To whom are committees responsible? What interests do committees serve? Such questions have motivated an important literature in political science. Three prominent perspectives offer rationale for the existence of committees – the information perspective, the distributive perspective, and the partisan perspective.

Informational Politics: Committees Governed by Floor Majorities

One view of congressional committees is that they are designed to meet legislators' demands for information about policy problems and solutions. Given

Congress's large workload and the complexity of issues, it is unrealistic to expect members to have the capacity to make informed decisions on all matters. By focusing on the issues before their own committees, legislators gain expertise that is applied in a committee setting to improve the fit of policy solutions to policy problems. The expertise serves the interest of the larger membership by generating information that is useful to all legislators as they make various policy decisions.

In this view, committee experts serve the interest of a majority of the parent chamber. If committee recommendations diverge too much from the preferences of the floor majority or prove misleading, floor majorities will reject committee recommendations and may even reform the committee system. Under normal circumstances, the better-informed arguments of committee experts will guide the behavior of other legislators.

Distributive Politics: Autonomous Committees

A classic view of congressional committees is the distributive theory. This perspective emphasizes that legislators seek to distribute the benefits of public policy to their districts and states. In the case of Congress, a system of committees institutionalizes "gains from trade" – members acquire policy benefits for their home constituencies in exchange for supporting benefits for other legislators' constituencies. Committees are created to address the legislative interests of constituencies who are important to legislators' reelection efforts. The multiple committees of each chamber allow legislators to gain membership on the committee or committees most relevant to their own constituencies. By empowering committees, a chamber gives legislators with the strongest constituency interest in a policy area the most influence over legislative action in that area. Because members represent diverse constituencies, the committee system institutionalizes a mutually beneficial arrangement for legislators who want to do favors for home audiences. Public policy is then the product of a giant "logroll," whereby each committee of legislators gets what it wants.

From the perspective of distributive politics, committees serve the interests of individual legislators and their home constituencies (see box "The Earmark Moratorium: End of Distributive Politics?"). Therefore, the committee system reflects the pluralism of American politics and permits legislators to focus on the political interests that matter most to them. The distributive perspective considers committees to be relatively autonomous units to which parties and the parent chambers defer. Each committee operates in a community of executive branch agencies and interest groups with similar interests. The larger public interest may suffer as the demands of the disparate constituencies are addressed by committees.

Partisan Politics: Committees Governed by the Majority Party

The partisan perspective posits that parties create committees to better ensure the success of party programs. On committees whose jurisdictions matter to the majority party, party leaders make committee assignments to enhance the party's policy prospects. This, along with expectations of loyalty, constrains the behavior of committee members. Because the majority party has a numerical advantage on committees, it ultimately dictates the policies that emerge.

From this perspective, committee members serve the interests of the parties. Although each chamber approves committee membership lists, each party determines which of its members are on each committee list. Parties structure the internal organization of committees – the majority party assumes the chairmanships and controls most staff. The majority party leadership also schedules committee legislation for action on the floor.

The Earmark Moratorium: End of Distributive Politics?

At the outset of the 112th Congress (2011–2012), House and Senate Republicans, along with the Senate Appropriations Committee, agreed to a moratorium, or temporary ban, on earmarks – a pledge that Republicans in both chambers have renewed since. This moratorium has not been without some critics on both sides of the aisle. Simply put, critics of the moratorium understand that earmarks bring electoral benefits and potentially are a tool for achieving consensus on divisive, but important, legislation. House Speaker John Boehner, discussing the difficulties of coalition building in the aftermath of the earmark ban, commented, "It's made my job more difficult in terms of how to pass important legislation, because there's no grease, I've got no grease." But does the moratorium mean the end of distributive politics as we know it? Not exactly . . .

Stories from recent Congresses suggest that the earmark moratorium has been less prohibitive than intended. Legislators have still found ways to send money back to their districts. One such way of circumventing the moratorium has been the practice of creating special flexible funds in spending and authorization bills. For instance, the 2012 budget for the Army Corps of Engineers included twenty-six separate funds, amounting to $507 million, to be spent by the corps for various construction, maintenance, and other projects. This total is quite close to the $534 million in earmarks included in the 2010 budget for the Army Corps of Engineers, prior to the adoption of the moratorium. Critics of this practice suggest that these special funds, which come with minimal guidance on how they are to be spent, are simply a way for members of Congress to have agencies distribute pork on their behalf. "It appears Congress was able to get the administration to do some of the earmarking dirty work for them," claimed Steve Ellis, a vice president for the budget watchdog Taxpayers for Common Sense. As part of this practice, legislators often petition federal agencies to allocate agency funds to projects in their districts. This, of course, places agencies in a difficult position considering that they rely on members of Congress for their funding.

Congress also continues to distribute pork to favored constituents by way of tax expenditures. Tax expenditures are changes to the tax code that extend special accommodations (e.g., exemptions, deductions, credits, etc.) that reduce tax liabilities for certain individuals. Because tax expenditures do not involve explicit spending, they go largely unnoticed, despite the fact that they have the same net effect on the federal government's financial bottom line. The Simpson-Bowles deficit commission estimated that these forms of earmarks represent approximately $1.1 trillion in spending every year.

Source: Ron Nixon, "Congress Appears to be Trying to Get Around Earmark Ban," *New York Times,* February 5, 2012; Ron Nixon, "Lawmakers Set Aside Money for Construction," *New York Times,* February 8, 2012.

In Practice: Committees Governed by Multiple Principals

In practice, committee members must balance conflicting demands placed on them by their parent chambers, parties, and constituencies. While seeking to satisfy the expectations of constituents, they must stay on good terms with party colleagues to retain important committee positions and must meet chamber majorities' expectations to get legislation passed. Fortunate legislators find that the demands of constituents, party leaders, and the chamber majority are aligned most of the time, but real-world politics require many committee members to take risks, balance interests, and struggle with difficult choices.

The extent of independent committee influence over policy outcomes varies over time and across committees. Three sets of factors stand out for their impact on the relationship between committees and their principals: the character of the policy agenda, party strength, and institutional context.

SIZE AND SALIENCE OF THE POLICY AGENDA. The size and salience of the congressional agenda affects the importance of committees to the parties and all chamber members. A large policy workload requires the division of labor that a system of committees provides, but only issues that are salient to a large number of legislators will attract the attention of party leaders or rank-and-file members on the floor. Committees with jurisdictions that affect narrow constituencies are unlikely to be supervised by party leaders or given serious scrutiny on the floor.

MAJORITY PARTY STRENGTH. Political scientists have observed that when parties lack cohesiveness because of internal divisions over policy, less authority is extended to party leaders to pursue partisan objectives. Under these conditions, strong-arm tactics are not tolerated and will alienate large numbers of partisans. Committee delegations will recognize party leaders' weaknesses and operate with little fear of retribution. In contrast, a cohesive majority party will expect its leaders to work proactively for party positions and pressure committee chairs and members to support the party.

INSTITUTIONAL CONTEXT. The House and Senate operate under very different rules. The larger, more unwieldy House has a stronger presiding officer and relies more heavily on formal rules than the Senate does. Senate rules protect each senator's right, on most legislation, to offer amendments on any subject and to conduct extended debate. In doing so, Senate rules protect individual initiative and create more opportunities to resist committee- or party-imposed policy choices. As a result, senators have more bargaining leverage with committee and party leaders than do representatives.

THE POWER OF MODERN COMMITTEES

Committees' powers are expressly or implicitly granted to them by the parent chambers and parties. Their continued existence and parliamentary privileges depend on the sufferance of those two entities. The parent chambers formally approve all committee assignments, but the parties construct the committee lists that are routinely ratified by the chambers. This function gives the parties a source of leverage with committee members and allows the parties – and, most important, the majority parties – to regulate the behavior of committee members through formal and informal rules (see box "Boehner's Committee Shakeup"). For the most part, committees must function procedurally and substantively in ways that are consistent with the expectations of their parent chambers and parties.

The Legislative Power of Committees

Evaluating the power of committees is difficult. It is very difficult to determine the influence of a committee on any given measure without knowing what the outcome would have been in the absence of committee involvement. Nevertheless, it is reasonable to infer that committees exercise real power in the modern Congress. Much of their power stems from the indifference of most members about the details of most legislation. Committees are extended considerable autonomy because most matters over which they have jurisdiction are of some importance to committee members and little, if any, importance to most other members. Parties and leaders focus on the few issues each year that are likely to affect the parties' reputations and electoral prospects. Members do not and cannot take an interest in the details of much, and probably even most, of the legislation that is considered on the floor.

Boehner's Committee Shakeup

Republican Speaker John Boehner (R-Ohio) began the 113th (2013–2014) and 114th (2015–2016) Congresses with a series of controversial committee decisions. He announced that several members who had demonstrated a willingness to challenge the Republican leadership were to lose coveted committee seats. At the outset of the 113th Congress, Representatives Justin Amash (R-Michigan) and Tim Huelskamp (R-Kansas), who had served on the House Budget Committee, and Representatives David Schweikert

(R-Arizona) and Walter Jones (R-North Carolina) from the House Financial Services Committee lost their committee seats. Each of these members had developed a reputation for bucking Republican leaders. In particular, Amash and Huelskamp, both Tea Party loyalists, voted against Paul Ryan's 2013 budget plan in committee and on the floor, claiming that the plan was not sufficiently aggressive in cutting spending. Their "no" votes on the Ryan budget in committee led to the slimmest margin of victory for the Republicans – a nineteen to eighteen vote. Similarly, Boehner removed Representatives Daniel Webster (R-Florida) and Richard Nugent (R-Florida) from the prestigious Rules Committee at the beginning of the 114th Congress. This decision was unsurprising considering that Webster had challenged Boehner for the speakership and Nugent had been an outspoken supporter of Webster's candidacy. When considering committee assignments, the Republican Steering Committee – the committee responsible for determining committee assignments and chaired by the House Speaker – in recent Congresses has reportedly reviewed a spreadsheet that lists how often each Republican member voted with the leadership. The aforementioned members did not fare well on this scale. It remains to be seen whether shakeups like these will help Republican leaders shore up loyalty from members and committees in years to come, but Republicans leaders have made it clear that disloyalty will not be tolerated. In fact, early in the 114th Congress at least three committee chairs were instructed to issue formal warnings to subcommittee chairs that if they planned to vote against the party on procedural motions, they should give up their seat.

Even when members are not indifferent, committees still have advantages that give their members disproportionate influence over policy outcomes. Mounting real challenges to their power can be difficult. Generally speaking, threats to strip a committee of jurisdiction, funding, or parliamentary privileges, or to retract members' committee assignments, are rare and usually not credible. Such actions set precedents that members of other committees would not like to see established. In this way, an implicit, self-enforcing pact among members underpins committee power. The most practical means for keeping committees in check is to reject their policy recommendations.

It is convenient to consider two forms of committee power:

- Positive power is the ability of committees to gain the approval of legislation opposed by others.
- Negative power is the ability of committees to block legislation favored by others.

On both counts, committees have substantial advantages over other players.

POSITIVE POWER. At first glance, committees appear to have no positive power. Under the Constitution, legislation can be enacted only by the full House and Senate. Neither chamber has rules that permit a committee to act on the chamber's behalf with respect to final approval of legislation. Therefore, positive power for committees must come from sources other than the explicit provisions of chamber rules.

Standing committees start with considerable discretion in writing and reporting legislation. They are free to act as they see fit on most legislation that is referred to them. They may simply refuse to act, or they may hold hearings but take no legislative action; they may amend the legislation in some way or accept the legislation without change. They may also write their own legislation, or they may vote to report legislation with a recommendation that it pass, with no recommendation, or with a recommendation that it be rejected.

Nevertheless, committees are not guaranteed that their legislation will receive favorable consideration on the House and Senate floors. To gain passage of legislation that might not otherwise pass, committees may exploit four sources of potential positive committee power: (1) *persuasion* on the basis of superior argument and information about the merits of legislation, (2) *leverage* acquired through threats of unfavorable action on members' bills if they fail to cooperate with a committee on its agenda, (3) *strategic packaging* of unpopular legislative provisions with more popular provisions to win floor majorities, and (4) *domination of conference committees* to gain chamber endorsement of policy provisions favored by the committee. Each of these deserves a brief mention.

First, committees can usually gain a tactical edge by being better informed than their opponents. Committee members sit through hearings, participate in discussions with lobbyists and executive branch officials, and often have previous experience with the issues their committee deals with. Committees' large, expert staffs and their extensive networks of allies in the executive branch and interest group community further enhance their informational advantage over competitors. Traditional norms such as serving an apprenticeship before actively participating, developing expertise in the jurisdiction of one's committees, and deferring to committee specialists reflect the importance of informational advantages for committee power.

Second, the ability of committees to obstruct action on some legislation can be used to gain leverage with members whose support is needed on other legislation. Particularly in the House, where circumventing a committee is neither easy nor convenient, obstructing action on legislation can be used as a threat to win support for committee recommendations.

Third, within the bounds of their broad jurisdictions, committees may package provisions addressing multiple subjects in legislation. By doing so, they can combine the unpopular provisions with more popular provisions to win support for bills. In the House, this power is enhanced when a committee can acquire a special rule from the Rules Committee that limits amendments to the unpopular provisions when the legislation is considered on the floor.

Fourth, members of committees gain positive power through their domination of conference committees. Conference negotiations between the House and Senate give conferees considerable flexibility to alter chamber decisions. The conferees know that they are free to exercise such discretion provided that they can attract majority support for the conference report – which cannot be amended on the House or Senate floor – when it is returned to the two chambers for final approval. The ability of conferees to choose any policy outcome that is at least preferred to no bill by the two chambers often renders opposition to the committee's preferences futile (see box "The Ex Post Veto").

NEGATIVE POWER. The negative power of standing committees rests in their ability to control newly introduced legislation and to obstruct alternative routes to the floor. The ability to obstruct action is often called "gatekeeping" in theories of politics. Committees' negative power is much stronger in the House than in the Senate.

In the House, negative power is supported by rules that give committees near-monopoly control over newly introduced legislation and make circumventing committees difficult. House Rule 10 requires that all legislation relating to a committee's jurisdiction be referred to that committee, a rule that has been in place since 1880. Before 1975, the single committee with the most relevant jurisdiction would receive the referral, a process that often involved direct conflicts between committees with related jurisdictions. Since 1975, the rule has provided for multiple referrals by granting to the Speaker the authority to refer legislation to each committee with relevant jurisdiction. Monopoly control by single committees was broken by the new rule, but the practice of referring nearly all legislation to committee remains in place.

The Ex Post Veto

The political scientists Kenneth Shepsle and Barry Weingast introduced the concept of the *ex post veto* in their seminal work exploring the source of chamber deference to standing committees. It has long been of interest to political scientists why standing committees are able to exert positive power, because formal rules do not explicitly grant such power to committees. Shepsle and Weingast argued that the ability of standing committee members to dominate conference committees effectively gives them the final move in determining the location of policy outcomes. Because the agreements reached in conference are protected against amendment when they return to the floor for final consideration and are rarely rejected, standing committee members are given wide discretion to adjust the legislation at the conference stage. Because rank-and-file members can foresee this outcome, they instead grant standing committees considerable discretion in the earliest stages of the legislative process. This generates the appearance that the floor simply defers to the preferences of standing committees.

In practice, the discretion exercised by conferees is constrained. It is constrained by the need to gain the approval of the other chamber's conferees and both parent houses. Particularly in recent Congresses, in which the parties have been polarized and the leaders very assertive, the work of conference committees is supervised by party leaders and scrutinized by rank-and-file members. Conferees who move too far from the expectations of their parent parties are likely to have a difficult time gaining reappointment to senior committee positions or even getting party support for their reelection efforts.

Committees' blocking power is enhanced by their domination of conference committees. The wide latitude extended to conferences to design the final form of legislation gives committee members another opportunity to wield negative powers. Committee members appointed to conference can, and frequently do, delete provisions they find objectionable. Because conference reports cannot be amended when sent to the House and Senate floors, it is difficult to reverse a conference committee's surgical removal of legislative provisions. Conferees also can take the more drastic step of refusing to file a conference report, thus blocking the legislation in its entirety, at least temporarily.

Circumventing House committees is difficult but not impossible under House rules. The House operates under a germaneness rule that requires a floor amendment to be relevant to the section of the bill or resolution it seeks to modify. Therefore, it is difficult to bring to the floor as an amendment a policy proposal relating to a subject that has not been addressed in legislation reported by a committee. The germaneness rule can be waived, but only if a special rule from the Rules Committee is approved by a majority on the House floor. The Speaker's control of the Rules Committee means that this approach is unlikely to work without the Speaker's cooperation.

House rules provide additional means for bringing legislation to the floor. At certain times, members may move to suspend the rules to consider a measure blocked by a committee. Going this route is usually not feasible without the consent of the party leadership and relevant committee because the member must be recognized by the Speaker to make the motion and two-thirds of the House must support it.

Another route is to gain a special rule from the Rules Committee to discharge a measure from committee. This route requires Rules Committee support and majority support in the House for the special rule. The Speaker's cooperation is typically required to gain Rules Committee action on such a rule.

Alternatively, party leaders occasionally circumvent committees by drafting legislation themselves or by delegating this responsibility to task forces or special committees. Task forces are ad hoc panels typically created by party leaders to carry out legislative duties. Party leaders may use task forces if they are concerned that a committee with jurisdiction will perform unsatisfactorily. For example, they may fear that the committee will not reach an agreement in a timely fashion or that it will produce a bill that either cannot pass the chamber or will not satisfy majority party members. When legislation is drafted in a task force, party leaders determine which members are charged with drafting the legislation and, in the House, can and often do exclude minority party members from the process.

Finally, House members may seek to discharge a measure from a committee that fails to report it within thirty days of referral. Any member may file a discharge petition, which requires the signatures of 218 members. Once the petition receives the necessary number of signatures, it is placed on the Discharge Calendar for consideration on the second or fourth Monday of the month following a seven-legislative-day waiting period. On eligible days, any member who signed the discharge petition may be recognized to offer the motion to discharge, although norm dictates that the member who filed the petition will likewise offer the motion. Should a majority of the members present vote in favor of the motion, the committee is discharged of the given measure. At this point, a subsequent motion may be offered that calls up the discharged measure for immediate consideration. Many members are hesitant to encourage the use of discharge petitions because doing so threatens the power of their own committees. Nevertheless, there has been more interest in discharge petitions since late 1993, when the House voted to make public the names of the members who sign them. Public disclosure makes it easier to generate public or interest group pressure on members to sign petitions.

The discharge petition may appear to be the most promising route for circumventing committees because it does not require the assistance of the Rules Committee or the Speaker. In fact, between 1931 and 2014, 654 discharge petitions were filed, but the petitions gained the required number of signatures only forty-eight times. Of the forty-eight instances in which discharge petitions gained the necessary 218 signatures, the motion to discharge carried on only twenty-six occasions, and the discharged measure went on to pass the House only nineteen times. However, the threatened use of discharge petitions, special rules, and suspension of the rules occasionally has stimulated committees to act in accordance with the floor majority's preferences. For example, between 1931 and 1994 there were fifteen cases in which the needed 218 signatures were acquired on a discharge petition but the majority leadership called up the legislation for consideration by other means.

The Senate's rules create weaker blocking power for its committees. Senate committees lack much of the negative power that House committees enjoy. Although measures are routinely referred to Senate committees after their introduction, a senator can easily object to a referral and keep a measure on the calendar for floor consideration. Furthermore, the Senate lacks a germaneness rule for most measures, so senators are able to circumvent committees by offering whole bills as amendments to unrelated legislation. Senators often hesitate to support efforts to bypass a committee in this way, but it is a procedural route that is used much more frequently than are the more complicated House procedures for circumventing committees. Moreover, most conference reports are potentially subject to filibusters in the Senate, giving Senate minorities a source of bargaining leverage over committee members at the conference stage that does not exist in the House.

Nevertheless, in practice, Senate committees retain some blocking power. Calling up a measure from the calendar requires the cooperation of the majority leader, who usually sides with the committee chair on procedural matters. If the majority leader cooperates, committee members, like all senators, may filibuster or threaten to filibuster unfriendly legislation. Consequently, successful circumvention of a committee on a controversial matter often requires the support of at least sixty senators, the number needed to invoke cloture.

Nongermane amendments are troublesome for Senate committees, but they can often be set aside by a motion to table. A successful motion to table kills the amendment. Because a tabling motion is not debatable (and therefore cannot be filibustered) and is a procedural question, it often attracts more votes than would be cast against the amendment itself. Moreover, the members of conference committees have an opportunity to drop adopted nongermane amendments in conference. In short, under most circumstances, committees in both chambers – but especially in the House – exercise considerable negative power. Circumventing committees requires special effort and is usually possible only with the cooperation of the majority party leadership.

Oversight and the Investigative Power of Modern Committees

Central to the legislative power of committees and vital to the power of Congress as an institution is the ability of committees to oversee and investigate governmental or private activity that is or might be the subject of public policy. Courts have ruled that Congress's power to compel cooperation with its investigations is implicit in its constitutional functions of legislating and appropriating funds. Without broad powers to investigate and compel cooperation, Congress would not be able to exercise its legislative powers effectively.

Throughout the history of Congress, committees have been the vehicle for conducting congressional investigations. Select or special committees have been appointed for many important investigations. In the past few decades, major investigations of the Watergate break-in and cover-up, the involvement of the Central Intelligence Agency in assassinations, and the Iran-Contra affair were conducted by select committees.

Since the passage of the Legislative Reorganization Act of 1946, standing committees have been assigned the duty of maintaining "continuous watchfulness" over executive branch activities within their jurisdictions. The 1946 act also created two committees with government-wide oversight duties, now called the House Committee on Oversight and Government Reform and the Senate Committee on Homeland Security and Governmental Affairs. Both committees attract members who want to participate in hearings on and investigations into a wide range of government activity.

Chairman Chuck Grassley (R-Iowa) reacts as ranking member Pat Leahy (D-Vermont) pulls out a large gavel from his tenure as chair of the Agriculture Committee during the ceremonial handing over of the gavel to the new chair of the Judiciary Committee.

Congressionally Speaking . . .

As part of their oversight and investigative powers, committees and subcommittees are authorized by House and Senate rules to issue *subpoenas* – formal writs compelling a recipient to testify or produce documents (or both) to the committee or subcommittee from which they originated. Typically committees/subcommittees receive the information they need without forcing compliance. Should the president invoke executive privilege or an official simply refuse to cooperate, however, subpoenas help equip committees to carry out investigations.

The decision rules for issuing a subpoena vary across committees, as they are not codified by chamber rules and parent bodies extend considerable autonomy to committees in determining their internal proceedings. House rules require only that a quorum (majority) be present at the time that the subpoena is agreed to. House rules also allow the committee/subcommittee to delegate subpoena power to full committee chairs. At the outset of the 114th Congress (2015–2016), seven standing committees in the House voted to empower their committee chair with unilateral subpoena-granting power. Senate rules provide even less guidance. It is important to note, however, that federal courts have established basic requirements that subpoenas must satisfy to be recognized as legitimate.

The 1946 act was reinforced by stronger directives to committees in the Legislative Reorganization Act of 1970, which required most committees to write biennial reports on their oversight activities. Moreover, during the 1970s, both ssigned oversight responsibility for several broad policy areas to ..uple committees to encourage oversight. Furthermore, the House instructed many committees to create oversight subcommittees and allowed them to add an oversight subcommittee beyond the limit for the number of subcommittees that would otherwise apply. With these developments, committee staffs devoted to oversight expanded greatly in the 1970s, which enabled committees and sub-committees to organize more hearings and more extensive investigations.

Issa's (Frequent) Use of the Subpoena

Representative Darrell Issa (R-California) served as the chair of the House Oversight and Government Reform Committee from 2011 to 2014, when he vacated the chair because of term limits. During his time as chair, the committee led investigations into such matters as the Fast and Furious scandal, the Affordable Care Act, and the IRS scandal, among others. In his time as chair, Issa reportedly issued in excess of 100 subpoenas, many of which were carried out unilaterally. While this number pales in comparison to the more than 1,000 subpoenas issued by former Representative Dan Burton (R-Indiana), who was chair of the committee during the investigations of the Clinton administration, Issa's use of the subpoena outpaced that of his three predecessors *combined*. Moreover, previous committee chairs had purportedly sought the support of the ranking minority member or a majority of the committee before issuing subpoenas. Critics of granting unilateral subpoena authority to committee chairs suggest that the practice paves the way for members to carry out political vendettas. To this effect, the former chairman of the House Oversight and Government Reform Committee, Henry Waxman (D-California), wrote: "In the past 60 years, only three chairmen have embraced issuing subpoenas without obtaining bipartisan or committee support: Sen. Joe McCarthy, R-Wis., Rep. Dan Burton, R-Ind. and Rep. Darrell Issa, R-Calif. It is not a coincidence that these men led the most discredited, partisan and unfair congressional investigations in modern history"

Source: ("Congressional Chairmen Shouldn't Be Given Free Rein over Subpoenas," *Washington Post*, February 5, 2015). Yet others who support the practice suggest that it is necessary in order to rein in the corruption of government.

Oversight has become an increasingly important part of committee activity. In 1961, less than 10 percent of committee meetings and hearings were devoted to oversight; by 1983, more than 25 percent were devoted to oversight. The big-gest surge occurred in the 1970s and appears to have been the product of several factors: the new independence of subcommittee chairs to pursue oversight, the expanded capacity of larger committee and subcommittee staffs to conduct oversight activities, tensions between a Democratic Congress and a Republican administration, and a generally more assertive Congress. The proportion of meet-ings and hearings dedicated to oversight continued to rise throughout most of the 1990s, as congressional Republicans aggressively investigated the Clinton administration. By 1997, nearly 34 percent of all committee hearings and meet-ings were devoted to oversight. In 2009, the House changed its rules to require each standing committee to hold at least one oversight hearing during each 120-day period on waste, fraud, abuse, or mismanagement in the programs and agencies under the committee's jurisdiction.

DECLINING COMMITTEE AUTONOMY

Committee power has been under siege since the early 1970s. Although committees continue to draft the details of nearly all legislation and their members remain central players in nearly all policy decisions, they have become less autonomous as their parent houses and parties have exercised more control over their operations and policy choices. Change has been most dramatic in the House of Representatives, where committees appear to have dominated policy making during the middle decades of the twentieth century. The forces producing changes in the role of committees in recent decades are similar to the forces that have been active throughout Congress's history – the policy agenda, strength of congressional parties, and the institutional context.

Changing Policy Agenda

Changes in the policy agenda have led to a decline in the autonomy of committees in recent decades. Many new and salient issues arose in the 1960s and 1970s, such as consumer protection, civil rights, and numerous others. Some of the emerging issues, like energy and the environment, were interconnected, sparked controversy, and stimulated the growth of interest groups. These issues energized outsiders to seek influence over committees' policy choices and pitted powerful committees against one another. As a result, more controversy spilled out of the committee rooms and onto the chamber floors. Since the late 1970s, the struggle with budget deficits has led Congress to adopt rules that limit the policy discretion of most congressional committees. As we report in Chapter 12, the effect of the budget rules has been a shift in emphasis from authorizing to appropriating committees and increased control over committee action by party and budget leaders.

Changing Party Strength

The increasing polarization of congressional parties (see Figure 6.2) has generated demands for central leaders to become more assertive. Therefore, party leaders have clamped down on committee autonomy. Furthermore, the rank-and-file members of the parties, particularly in the House, have become less tolerant of committee and subcommittee chairs' deviating from party policy positions.

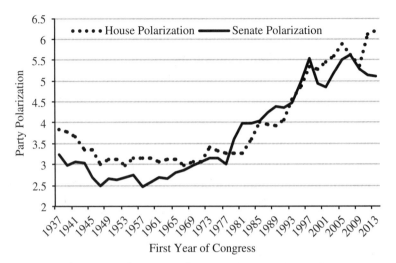

Figure 6.2 Party Polarization in the House and Senate, 1937–2014. Source: Common space scores from www.voteview.com/dwnl.htm. Calculations by the authors. Note: The measure of polarization is taken from Ryan J. Vander Wielen and Steven S. Smith, "Majority Party Bias in U.S. Congressional Conference Committees," Congress and the Presidency 38(3) (2011): 271–300.

Following the Republican takeover of 1994, Republican and Democratic majorities alike have been particularly aggressive in expressing their expectations of committee leaders. For example, the Senate Democratic conference changed its rules in 2011 to upend the seniority system and require committee chairs to stand for election at the beginning of every Congress.

The increase in activity by the party organizations and leaders during recent years is noted in Chapter 5. The party organizations now provide more opportunities for meaningful participation in policy making outside of members' assigned committees. The parties have provided forums, such as task forces, for those members outside of committees to challenge the committees and their leaders and even to devise legislation for floor consideration. In the House, party leaders have frequently negotiated legislation after a committee has reported a bill and placed the negotiated provisions in the bill through use of a special rule from the Rules Committee.

Committee Chairs Push Back

As the strength of congressional parties grows, the corresponding decline in the power of committees and committee chairs in recent Congresses has been undeniable. For instance, former House Ways and Means Committee Chairman Dave Camp (R-Michigan), according to some sources, played little role in crafting the fiscal cliff agreement reached on January 1, 2013. This is a shocking turn of events when one considers the influence that Ways and Means chairs once wielded. To make matters worse for Camp, party leaders reportedly pressured him to publically advocate the bill's passage, despite his lack of input and the dismal support for the bill from within his party. Senator Max Baucus (D-Montana), who chaired the Senate Finance Committee, was also noticeably excluded from these negotiations.

Committee chairs in both chambers bemoan the lack in recent Congresses of "regular order," whereby committees play a pivotal role in the legislative process. In fact, according to some senior aides, there was not a single significant bill introduced in the 112th Congress (2011–2012) that followed the textbook legislative path. Committee chairmen, however, are not sitting quietly. Some chairs have begun pushing legislation without the approval of party leaders, and others have even created their own vote-counting operations to bypass leadership. For instance, Camp reportedly forwarded several drafts of tax reform measures despite Speaker John Boehner's (R-Ohio) disapproval. In addition, Baucus advocated a series of tax reforms that were not revenue generating – a position expressly opposed by then Senate Majority Leader Harry Reid (D-Nevada).

Source: Paul Kane, "Congress's Committee Chairmen Push to Reassert Their Power," *Washington Post*, February 13, 2013.

Changing Institutional Context

Committee autonomy has been further undermined by rules changes that either directly regulated committee behavior or made it easier for members to challenge committee recommendations. These new rules were pursued by members who were unhappy with the nearly dictatorial control that some full committee chairs exercised over legislative proceedings. They reflected an effort to make committees – and especially committee leaders – more accountable to rank-and-file members of the parent chamber and to make members less dependent on committees for information and advice.

SUNSHINE RULES. Sunshine rules – rules that open congressional activity to public scrutiny – have contributed to the diminishing autonomy of standing committees. One such rule requires that roll call votes cast in committee be recorded in documents that are open to the public. Another rule dictates that committee markups be held in public sessions (except for meetings concerned with national security matters) unless a majority of committee members cast a recorded vote in favor of closing a meeting. Even conference committees are required to hold their meetings in open sessions unless, as the House rule requires, a majority of the parent chamber approves the use of closed meetings. The rules were intended to make committee members more accountable, both to outside constituencies and to their colleagues. In recent Congresses, committees have voted more frequently to close meetings to the public, and they have become more creative in their efforts to sidestep the rules. In some cases, members appear to have allowed staff to negotiate legislative details to avoid holding official meetings subject to open-meeting rules. Party leaders, however, have attempted to reinforce the sunshine rules by requiring that committees accommodate television and radio broadcasts and still photographers whenever a meeting is open to the public.

BILL REFERRAL RULES IN THE HOUSE. In 1974, the Speaker of the House was granted the authority to send legislation to committees jointly, sequentially, or in parts. Before 1974, the Speaker was required to assign legislation to the single committee that had the most relevant jurisdiction, a practice that guaranteed monopoly referral rights to a single committee in each policy area. Under the current rule, adopted in 1995, sending a bill jointly to more than one committee is no longer possible, but the Speaker may still establish a sequence of committees for consideration or split a bill into parts that are referred to different committees (sequential and split referral). In fact, in recent Congresses, about one-fourth of the workload for the average House committee has consisted of multiply referred legislation. In the Senate, all three forms of multiple referral are possible following a joint motion of the majority and minority leaders. Multiple referral remains far less common in the Senate than in the House, perhaps because committees can more easily protect their jurisdictional interests by seeking to amend legislation on the floor.

Multiple referral in the House generates greater interdependence among committees and with the Speaker, reducing committee autonomy. Multiple referral also creates more potential conflicts among committees and increases the number of legislators with some role in committee action on the affected bills. Sometimes the conflict among committees spills onto the House floor, where party leaders are asked to intercede. Perhaps most important, multiple referral substantially strengthens the Speaker's influence over committee decisions. The Speaker determines, without appeal, the referral of legislation to multiple committees and may set deadlines for committee action in such cases. In designing such arrangements, the Speaker is in a position to advantage some committees, speed or delay committee action for strategic purposes, and send strong signals about his or her policy preferences.

VOTING RULES. Weakening committee autonomy and the demise of deference to committees are reflected in the record of floor-amending activity since the mid-1950s. In terms of the absolute number of floor amendments, the number of amendments per measure, and the proportion of measures amended on the floor, floor-amending activity increased in both chambers during the 1950s and 1960s and surged upward in the 1970s. In the Senate, the number of floor amendments nearly tripled between the mid-1950s and late 1970s, with most of the increase occurring in the 1960s. The number of House floor amendments more than quadrupled between the mid-1950s and the late 1970s, with most of the increase occurring in the early 1970s after the introduction of recorded electronic voting. Previously, recorded votes were not possible on most amendments, which made it difficult to bring public pressure to bear and enhanced the influence of powerful insiders, particularly committee chairs.

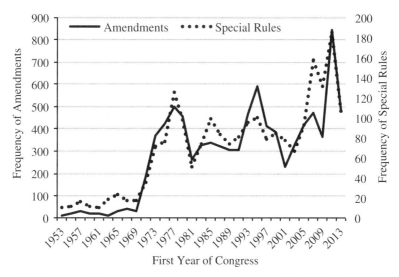

Figure 6.3 Frequency of House Roll Call Votes on Amendments and Special Rules, 1953–2014.
Source: For the period 1953–2012: Political Institutions and Public Choice dataset available at
www.poli.duke.edu/pipc.data.html. For the period 2013–2014: voteview.com.

Floor-amending activity was perceived to be a more serious problem in the
House, and therefore the House majority party changed its practices in response.
The most important response was the expanded use of special rules to limit floor
amendments. In fact, historical trends in amendment votes and the use of special
rules are generally congruent (see Figure 6.3). Most rules have not foreclosed
floor amendments, but they have required that amendment sponsors notify the
Rules Committee in advance, which permits the Rules Committee to arrange for
their order of consideration and allows committee leaders to prepare against
unfriendly amendments (see Chapters 7 and 8).

No effective constraints on floor-amending activity for the purpose of enhancing committee autonomy are possible in the Senate. The minority would
prevent a vote on any reform that would put it at a disadvantage. In only two
areas, budget measures and certain trade agreements, has the Senate moved to
limit debate and amendments. In general, therefore, a majority of senators have
no way to insulate committee bills from unfriendly or nongermane amendments
whose sponsors are committed to offering them.

CONFERENCE RULES. The ability of committees to control conference negotiations on behalf of their chambers has long been a vital source of power. In the
House of the 1970s and 1980s, challenges to committee autonomy were accompanied by challenges to committees' monopoly over appointments to conference
delegations. New rules were adopted imploring the Speaker to appoint delegations that represented House preferences, to include members who had sponsored
major components of the legislation in question, and to require conferences to

hold their meetings in public sessions. The rules were targeted at senior commit-tee members who had dominated conferences for decades. The Speaker's control over conference delegations was reinforced in 1993 when the House adopted a rule giving the Speaker the power to remove a member from a conference del-egation at any time. In spite of these rules, few members not sitting on the stand-ing committees originating legislation are appointed to conference committees. In recent Congresses, conference committees have been used less frequently as party leaders have taken a more dominant role in structuring intercameral agree-ments (see box "The Changing Congress: The Disappearing Conference").

RANK-AND-FILE RESOURCES. Individual members now have far more sources of information at their disposal than they once did in the mid-twentieth century, so the traditional advantage enjoyed by committee members over rank-and-file members – greater access to expertise and staff assistance – has been reduced. Over the years, changes in House and Senate rules have allowed members to ex-pand their personal staffs. Much of a member's personal staff is devoted to non-legislative duties such as answering the mail and handling constituents' problems with the federal agencies. Nevertheless, the great expansion in members' personal staffs has allowed legislators to draw on staff for assistance in developing leg-islative proposals, making arguments, and soliciting support – often in opposi-tion to committee positions. Furthermore, members may utilize the congressional support agencies. These agencies often conduct studies for or delegate staff to congressional committees, but they also respond to requests for information from individual members and their staffs. As a result of the increased availability of these varied sources of information, an enterprising member can equip himself or herself to challenge committee members' arguments. Therefore, seldom does a committee now command deference on the basis of policy expertise alone.

The Changing Congress: The Disappearing Conference

Conference committees are used with less frequency in modern Congresses than they once were. In fact, the decline in their usage has been quite dramatic. In the 93rd Congress (1973–1974), one-fourth of all public laws went through the conference stage, whereas just over one percent of public laws cleared conference in the 113th Congress (2013–2014).

Some critics of this trend have suggested that the decline of conferences has contributed to a more clandestine way of lawmaking. Others, however, contend that in an era of such considerable party polarization there is little incentive to include minority party members in the conciliation process because legislators of the two parties are unlikely to engage in serious deliberations with each other. Although the decrease in conference usage may well appear a recent phenomenon, their decline as an open and deliberative body coincides with the increasing partisan divide. As early as 1995, just after Republicans gained majorities in both chambers, reports began to surface that Democrats were being closed out of conference negotiations. Even when conferences included Democrats, the minority members were often precluded from offering input. When asked about his experience on the Sarbanes-Oxley conference committee in 2002, Representative Luis Gutierrez (D-Illinois) retorted: "I never got a word in."

Instead of using conference committees to reconcile chamber differences, the chambers have drawn on a variety of alternative methods. For one, party leaders have increasingly turned to private negotiations with their counterparts in the other house. In addition, the chambers often exchange amendments, such as when the House accepts a Senate amendment to a House amendment to a Senate bill. This has come to be known as the "ping-pong" process in recent Congresses. The simplest method for reconciling chamber differences without conference has been for one house to acquiesce to the other house's version – in most cases, this has been the House accepting the Senate's version. Particularly on contentious legislation on which a filibuster is likely to occur in the Senate, a House amendment to a Senate bill would compel the Senate to once again achieve a sixty-vote majority for cloture.

Scholars point to the increasing partisanship of Congress, and, relatedly, the growing power of party leaders, as a cause for the decline in conference committees. In short, alternative means of resolving intercameral differences may often be necessary to overcome the heightened conflict between the parties that exists in the chambers. Since conference reports – the agreements reached by conference committees – must go back to the chambers for final consideration, these agreements may encounter additional opposition. This is particularly problematic in the Senate, where the conference report can be filibustered. Therefore, party leaders in recent Congresses have increasingly turned to other methods of resolving differences between the chambers.

Source: Edward Epstein, "Dusting Off Deliberation," *CQ Weekly,* June 14, 2010.

COMMITTEE MEMBERSHIP

At the start of each new Congress, members of the House and new members of the Senate seek committee assignments that will shape their daily schedules and perhaps their electoral and legislative futures. Returning members are routinely reappointed to their former committees, following the "property right" norm, unless they seek to improve their situation by transferring to other committees, as a few always do. State delegations, intraparty factions, and lobbyists work to maximize their influence over policy by getting friendly members onto the right committees.

Committee Size and Party Ratios

Majority and minority party leaders negotiate the number of Democratic and Republican seats on each committee, with the majority leaders having the upper hand because of their ability to win a floor vote on the resolutions that provide for the allocation of seats to each party. With important exceptions in the House, seats on most committees are allocated roughly in proportion to the size of each party. The exceptions tend to be the House Appropriations, Budget, House Administration,

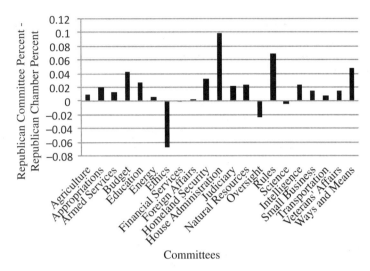

Figure 6.4 Difference between the Percentage of Republicans on Committees and in the House, 2015–2016.

Rules, and Ways and Means Committees; because these are particularly important committees, the majority party reserves a larger-than-proportionate number of seats for itself. Figure 6.4 shows the difference between the percentage of House Republicans on the committees and in the chamber for the 114th Congress (2015–2016). Therefore, the bars above zero indicate committees on which the majority party claimed more seats than warranted by the party ratio in the chamber. As can be seen, the majority's seat advantage on the aforementioned committees exceeds their advantage across most other committees as well as in the chamber, which the committee ratios should, in theory, resemble. The House and Senate Ethics Committees are the only committees on which there is an equal number of majority and minority party members. Moreover, the disparity between the committee and chamber advantages for the majority seems to be on the rise in recent Congresses.

Committee Assignments

In each chamber, committee seats are filled on the basis of recommendations from each party. For example, the House rule states that "the House shall fill a vacancy on a standing committee by election on the nomination of the respective party caucus or conference." To accomplish this, each House and Senate party has its own committee on committees, which is responsible for making committee lists. Assignment decisions depend on the number of vacancies, the number of members competing for assignments, and the rules on the number and type of assignments each member may hold. New members and returning members seeking new assignments must compete for support from the members of their party's committee on committees to gain assignment to the committees they want.

THE HOUSE. For the first time in 1995, as proposed by the new Republican majority that year, the House adopted a rule restricting the number of committee assignments its members may hold. The two parties had had internal rules, but the Republicans imposed the new rule and it has remained in place since. The rule prohibits a member from holding more than two standing committee assignments and more than four subcommittee assignments on standing committees. The two parties supplement this restriction by treating five committees (Appropriations, Energy and Commerce, Rules, Ways and Means, and Financial Services) as "exclusive" committees. Members serving on these committees are not permitted to hold seats on other committees. Both parties also identify two "exempt" committees (Select Committee on Intelligence and Ethics) that do not count against a member's committee membership limit.

In recent years, both House parties have become less inclined to grant exemptions to their limits on assignments. Traditionally, members have received exemptions with relative ease and have been allowed to maintain them indefinitely. However, leaders of both House parties grew frustrated with the number of members who expected to receive exemptions and retain coveted extra seats. Minority Leader Nancy Pelosi (D-California) has strictly applied party rules limiting committee assignments, having refused to grant members waivers to the limits in a number of notable cases. House Republicans have been equally judicious. In fact, they approved a party rule in 2004 that requires members who have received a waiver to committee assignment limits to reapply every two years. Moreover, the Republicans require members who wish to sit on multiple committees to receive the approval of the chairs of the committees involved in addition to the approval of the steering committee. For both parties, restricting exemptions allows party leaders to distribute desirable committee assignments to more members.

THE SENATE. Since the 1970s, Senate rules have restricted the number and type of committee assignments that senators may receive. A senator may sit on no more than two of the twelve most important committees and the Select Committee on Intelligence ("A" committees) and is limited to an appointment to only one of four other standing committees, the Special Committee on Aging, or the Joint Economic Committee ("B" committees). There is no restriction for seats on the Select Committee on Ethics, the Committee on Indian Affairs, and the Joint Committee on Taxation ("C" committees). See Table 6.3 for the list of committees in the 114th Congress (2015–2016) by their classification. A senator may sit on no more than three subcommittees of any "A" committee (Appropriations members are exempt from this restriction) and no more than two subcommittees of any "B" committee. Moreover, a senator cannot serve as a chair or ranking member of more than two subcommittees. Both parties have adopted rules that

TABLE 6.3. Senate committees by type, 114th Congress (2015–2016)

A Committees	B Committees	C Committees
Agriculture, Nutrition, and Forestry	Budget	Select Committee on Ethics
Appropriations	Rules and Administration	Indian Affairs
Armed Services	Small Business and Entrepreneurship	Joint Committee on Taxation
Banking, Housing, and Urban Affairs	Veterans' Affairs	
Commerce, Science, and Transportation	Special Committee on Aging	
Energy and Natural Resources	Joint Economic Committee	
Environment and Public Works		
Finance		
Foreign Relations		
Health, Education, Labor, and Pensions		
Homeland Security and Governmental Affairs		
Judiciary		
Select Committee on Intelligence		

further restrict membership on "A" committees. Senators are not permitted to sit on more than one of the "Super A" or "Big Four" committees, which include Appropriations, Armed Services, Finance, and Foreign Relations (for Republicans only). Both parties also stipulate (by rule for the Republicans and by tradition for the Democrats) that same-state senators cannot serve on the same committee when they belong to the same party. The Senate occasionally grants exemptions to these assignment limitations at the request of the parties. Since the 1950s, both Senate parties have observed the practice of granting every senator a seat on one of the top four committees before any senator gets two such seats. The practice is called the "Johnson rule," after Lyndon Johnson (D-Texas), the Democratic leader who initiated the practice.

INFLUENCES ON ASSIGNMENTS. Many factors influence the committee assignment decisions of party leaders and the committees on committees. The legislators' political needs, claims by individual states or regions for representation on certain committees, geographic considerations, party loyalty, views on specific issues, and seniority are among the most important factors. In the House, members supported by the largest state delegations are at a distinct advantage. In 1992, for example, New York's delegation lost all three of its members on House Appropriations through retirement or defeat, but it managed to regain all three seats (two Democratic and one Republican) for its members when new appointments were made. There are, however, few guarantees – New Jersey Democrats lost their representation on both Appropriations and Ways and Means (one seat each), but failed to gain a replacement.

Only for Senate Republicans has seniority historically been a decisive consideration. Until recently, seniority had been the sole determinant in both the allocation of committee seats and the ascension in the committee hierarchy for Senate Republicans. In 2004, reflecting a desire to strengthen their leader's influence with party colleagues, Senate Republicans approved, by narrow margin (a 27–26 vote), a change in party rules to grant the floor leader the authority to make influential committee appointments without regard to seniority. The rule permits the Republican leader to appoint at least half of the party's committee assignments on "A" committees. As a result, the leader has considerable say in the appointments to committees such as Agriculture, Appropriations, Armed Services, Finance, Foreign Relations, and Judiciary. For Senate Democrats, seniority has been an important, but less decisive, factor in committee assignment decisions.

Similar to the Senate Democrats, the House parties consider seniority along with many factors when making committee assignments. Having an established record of party loyalty, trustworthiness, and skill gives a more senior member an edge over newcomers. In recent Congresses, party leaders have increasingly taken into account members' contributions to party campaign efforts when distributing committee seats. Particularly when a large class of new members enters Congress, however, party leaders make sure that a few first-year members are named to the top committees. The 112th Congress (2011–2012) is noteworthy not only for marking a change in party control of the House but also for having such a large class of new Republicans. The transition in party control gave the Republicans twenty-five new seats on the exclusive committees. The party allocated fourteen of those seats to freshmen, a very large number by historical standards. Given the comparatively smaller freshman class in the 114th Congress (2015–2016), only five first-year members were given seats on exclusive committees (two on Appropriations and three on Financial Services). One of these new members, Representative David Young (R-Iowa), gained a seat on the Appropriations Committee after his predecessor, who served on the committee, had retired.

LEADERSHIP PREROGATIVES. Assignments to the House Committee on Rules and the House Committee on House Administration are unique cases. The Rules Committee's primary function is to consider, devise, and report "special rules," which are resolutions that provide for the floor consideration of measures, usually reported by other committees, that would otherwise not receive timely consideration under the standing rules. In the 1960s and early 1970s, the independence of Rules Committee members was troubling to the majority party Democrats. Ultimately, both parties transferred the power to appoint Rules members to their top party leaders, making members of the Rules Committee agents of their party leadership.

In late 1994, both House parties also gave their top leaders similar power to name the members of the House Administration Committee. Because the House Administration Committee has jurisdiction over the internal administrative affairs of the House, including the way important resources are distributed to committees and members, the top leaders wanted to assert more control over it than they had in the past. The committee also has jurisdiction over election and campaign finance law – subjects of the highest partisan significance.

The Pecking Order

The appeal of committees to members varies. We can learn about the value of committees to members by examining the committees that members choose to leave or join. Because members have the ability to stay on the committee that they served on in the previous Congress (because of the norm of "property rights"), we can assume that members choose to transfer to a different committee because they consider it more desirable. This is especially likely to be true because of the costs members incur for leaving a committee on which they have accumulated seniority. Table 6.4 shows the ranking of committee values for the House and Senate derived from the study of members' transfers off and on committees. Committees receive a higher ranking when members systematically leave their existing committee assignments for them. When members transfer to new committees, it signals that they value the new committee more than their present one *even* with the power they have accrued on it.

House Ways and Means (taxes, Social Security, trade), Energy and Commerce (health, regulation of interstate commerce), Appropriations (spending authority), and Rules (special rules) have jurisdictions of exceptional breadth and importance and attract the interest of many members. Competition for assignment to these committees is intense. Because of these committees' importance, party leaders expect loyalty from members assigned to them. In late 1992, a House insider reported that the Democratic leadership was holding applicants to Appropriations and Ways and Means to a high standard of loyalty. Leaders were telling members that "[t]here may be a time your leader and your president will need your support. It may be difficult for you to vote for it. Will you be with us?" Such anecdotal evidence illustrates the significant role of party as a cue to members on committees of prestige.

As a general rule, first-year members have difficulty gaining assignment to the top committees. Only when an extraordinary number of new members are elected does the leadership become eager to demonstrate a commitment to appointing a fair share of freshmen. Moreover, freshmen tend to be emboldened to demand their share of top assignments only when their numbers are large. The

TABLE 6.4. Popularity of House and Senate committee values, 1979–2012

Ranking	House Committees	Senate Committees
1	Ways and Means	Finance
2	Energy and Commerce	Appropriations
3	Appropriations	Rules and Administration
4	Rules	Armed Services
5	Armed Services	Foreign Relations
6	Foreign Affairs	Veterans' Affairs
7	Post Office and Civil Service	Homeland Security and Governmental Affairs
8	House Administration	Health, Education, Labor, and Pensions
9	Judiciary	Budget
10	Ethics	Small Business and Entrepreneurship
11	Budget	Judiciary
12	Financial Services	Banking, Housing, and Urban Affairs
13	Natural Resources	Commerce, Science, and Transportation
14	District of Columbia	Energy and Natural Resources
15	Merchant Marine and Fisheries	Agriculture, Nutrition, and Forestry
16	Transportation and Infrastructure	Environment and Public Works
17	Education and the Workforce	
18	Oversight and Government Reform	
19	Veterans' Affairs	
20	Agriculture	
21	Science, Space, and Technology	
22	Homeland Security	
23	Small Business	

Source: Charles Stewart III. "The Value of Committee Assignments in Congress since 1994," paper presented at the 2012 Annual Meeting of the Midwest Political Science Association.

difficulty of gaining access to one of these committees as a freshmen was evident in the 114th Congress (2015–2016), in which only five freshmen (all Republicans) were able to get a seat on Appropriations, Ways and Means, Rules, Energy and Commerce, or Financial Services.

Beyond the common desire for assignment to one of the top committees, members vary widely in their preferences for committee assignments. Differences among members reflect their personal interests and political goals. As a consequence of these differences, many committees are not very representative of their parent house. Sometimes this imbalance is manifest in the policy preferences held by committee members. For example, the House Armed Services Committee, which attracts members disproportionately from districts with military bases, has historically been more conservative than the House as a whole.

However, many committees are distinguished from the rest of their chamber less by their policy views than by their degree of interest in the subject matter. The House Agriculture Committee, for example, overwhelmingly attracts legislators from rural farming districts.

Committee Bias?

Differences in the policy preferences of committees and their parent chambers are not easy to measure, but it does appear that the political balance on some committees is quite different from the balance in their parent chamber. Committee medians on a liberal/conservative scale (larger numbers imply increasing conservatism) for the Republican-controlled House and Democratically controlled Senate of 2013–2014 are shown along with the chamber medians in Figure 6.5. We would expect to observe committees that generally favor the majority party, and they did, but there still is substantial variation among committees. In the House, those committees with a larger proportion of Republicans are consistently among the most conservative – Appropriations, Budget, House Administration, Judiciary, Rules, and Ways and Means. It is not entirely surprising that these are the committees that often deal with legislative matters most central to the success of the majority party. Therefore, the majority party has an incentive to ensure that the outcomes produced by these committees reflect the majority's preferences.

The biases of congressional committees, as well as subcommittees, are also evident in the character of the witnesses they call to their hearings. A study of congressional hearings between 1945 and 1986 on four issues – nuclear power, drug abuse, smoking, and pesticides – found large, predictable bias in the mix of industry and public interest group representatives appearing before them. Committee majorities chose to listen to more witnesses that confirmed their views than opposed their views.

COMMITTEE LEADERS

The most powerful member on most committees is the full committee chair. The chair exercises considerable control over the agenda, schedules meetings and hearings of the full committee, and, in recent Congresses, approves the scheduling of subcommittees' meetings and hearings. Furthermore, the committee chair controls the committee budget, offers party leaders recommendations regarding the composition of conference committees for legislation falling under the committee's jurisdiction, supervises a sizable staff, and often serves as a spokesperson for the committee and party on issues under the committee's jurisdiction. The

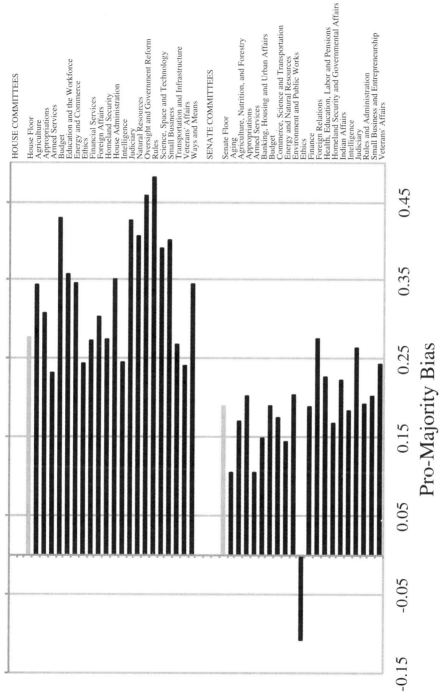

Figure 6.5 Median Conservative Score for Standing Committees, 2013–2014. Source: Common space scores from www.voteview.com. Committee medians calculated by authors.

chair also reports legislation to the floor on behalf of the committee and makes requests of the majority leadership and, in the House, the Rules Committee to schedule the legislation for action on the floor. In exercising his or her formal powers, the chair benefits from years of experience in dealing with the policy problems and constituencies of the committee. Consequently, the support of the full committee chair can be critical to bill sponsors and opponents. However, full committee chairs no longer dominate their committees as they once did. Understanding why is important.

The Seniority System

Both the majority and minority parties designate a formal leader for each committee and subcommittee. The majority party names the chair of each committee and subcommittee, and the minority party appoints a ranking minority member for each committee and subcommittee. The seniority norm dictates that the party member with the longest continuous service on the committee serves as chair or ranking minority member, although there are limitations on the number and type of chairmanships a member may hold. Subcommittee chairs and ranking minority members are chosen, in most cases, on the basis of seniority within the committee. Accruing seniority toward leadership posts is one reason members are reluctant to transfer to other committees, where they must start at the bottom of the seniority ladder.

The seniority norm came to be recognized in the House in the late nineteenth century and was observed in both chambers, virtually without exception, in the middle decades of the twentieth century. The norm was weakened in the 1970s by party rules that required a secret ballot election of full committee chairs and ranking minority members. Senate Republicans led the way in 1973 by requiring that their ranking member on each committee be elected by the Republican members of the committee, although the full Republican conference retains the right to reconsider a committee contingent's decision. House Democrats followed by requiring that all committee chairs or ranking members and the chairs or ranking members of subcommittees on the Appropriations Committee stand for election in the Democratic Caucus at the start of each Congress. They later required the chairs of Ways and Means subcommittees to stand for caucus election as well. The new rules had an impact. Three full committee chairs were deposed in 1974, an Appropriations subcommittee chair was replaced in 1977, and four more Democratic committee chairs were ousted later. The other two congressional parties, House Republicans and Senate Democrats, adopted rules in the mid-1970s allowing separate votes on the ranking committee members in their conferences.

The reforms have been extended. In 1992, House Republicans, then in the minority, adopted a new party rule to limit the tenure of their full committee and subcommittee leaders to three consecutive Congresses, forcing rotation in the top committee posts every six years. In 1995, the Republicans made this a House rule for committee and subcommittee chairmanships. Although term limits were temporarily repealed during the 111th Congress (2009–2010), they were reinstated in 2013 and remain in place during the 114th Congress (2015–2016). House rules exempt the Rules Committee chair from the limit. A Republican conference rule also applies term limits to ranking committee and subcommittee leaders when the party is in the minority. Since the adoption of the term limits, party leaders have granted few exemptions to the limit.

Testing Term Limits

A combination of chamber and conference rules restrict House Republicans from serving more than six consecutive years as a committee chair or ranking member. The Republican conference rule states that "[n]o individual shall serve more than three consecutive terms as Chairman or ranking member of a standing, select, joint, or ad hoc Committee or Subcommittee beginning with the 104th Congress [1995–1996]."

This rule was important to committee chair selections at the beginning of the 114th Congress (2015–2016), when Republican leaders had to decide what to do with five committee chairs who were subject to the six-year term limit. Only one of the term-limited chairs, Representative John Kline (R-Minnesota), a close ally of Speaker John Boehner's, was granted a waiver to stay on as committee chair. The conference rules have not always been well received by all within the party. Some have argued that counting continuous service across different positions (i.e., ranking member *and* chair), goes against the spirit of the rule. Others have argued that imposing terms limits also puts inexperienced, and perhaps less qualified, chairs in place. In this vein, some point to the decision of the term-limited Ways and Means Committee chair Dave Camps (R-California) to retire at the end of the 113th Congress (2013–2014) as evidence that term limits remove an incentive for experienced members to contribute to committees and even to pursue reelection. However, the party leadership has been largely diligent in upholding the limits. Term limits are viewed by many as an effective way to ensure that committee chairs remain independent of the interests and agencies that their committees are charged with overseeing.

Senate Republicans also adopted a rule governing the election of committee leaders. Rather than allowing the Republicans on each committee to elect their committee chair or ranking minority member, as they had been doing for many years, the 1995 rule requires secret ballot votes within each committee and then by the full Republican conference, making the chairs and ranking members more accountable to the full conference. As a result, some Republican senators have had to overcome substantial opposition from within their party conference to retain or gain chairmanships. More recently, Senate Democrats have followed suit by similarly adopting party rules in 2011 that require committee chairs to stand for reelection by the entire party conference at the beginning of every Congress.

Formal reforms have been reinforced by changes in practice. After the Republicans won a House majority in the 1994 elections, Speaker Newt Gingrich assumed responsibility for appointing committee chairs even before his conference had an opportunity to meet. For three committees, Gingrich bypassed the most senior committee Republican and backed a more assertive or conservative member as chair. At the same time, House Democratic leader Dick Gephardt chose a close political ally to be ranking member on the House Oversight Committee (now House Administration), dumping the former chair, who had challenged Gephardt for his leadership post. Speaker Dennis Hastert followed Gingrich's lead by considering member loyalty to be an important element in the selection of committee chairs when vacancies occurred. Speaker Nancy Pelosi made it quite clear prior to the Democratic victory in 2006 that seniority would be only one of the factors considered in determining committee assignments. In fact, the Democratic Caucus rules drafted by the House Democratic leaders stated that the steering committee "shall consider all relevant factors, including but not limited to merit, seniority, length of service on the committee, degree of commitment to Democratic principles and the Democratic agenda, and the diversity of the caucus." After shaking up the committee membership at the beginning of the 113th Congress (2013–2014), Speaker John Boehner, likewise, declared that the steering committee takes under consideration a wide range of factors when determining committee assignments.

Selecting Subcommittee Chairs

THE HOUSE. The means for selecting House subcommittee chairs have come full circle. Before the 1970s, full committee chairs appointed subcommittees and their chairs. That procedure was transformed into a more egalitarian process in the 1970s. Starting in the mid-1970s, House Democrats required that Democratic committee members bid for subcommittee leadership posts, chairs, or ranking minority member status in order of seniority and that appointments be ratified by a majority vote of the party members on the committee. Although seniority generally is observed, this procedure gives party members on a committee the right to reject the most senior member and elect someone else, as has happened more than a dozen times. House Democrats also bar full committee chairs or ranking members from serving as chair or ranking member of a subcommittee. To make the most important subcommittee leaders accountable to the party, House Democrats require subcommittee leaders of three committees – Appropriations, Energy and Commerce, and Ways and Means – to receive majority approval of the full House Democratic

Caucus and, since early 2004, require those subcommittee leaders to first receive approval of the party's Steering and Policy Committee, which is chaired by the party leader.

In contrast, the House Republicans leave the appointment process to each committee's chair (or ranking minority member), although a majority of the Republican members on the full committee can override the chair's decisions. Like the House Democrats, the Republicans require that subcommittee leaders of the Appropriations Committee receive full approval of the party conference. In practice, nearly all of the Republican subcommittee leaders are selected on the basis of committee seniority. As a part of their late 1992 reforms, the House Republicans adopted a party rule prohibiting most chairs or ranking members of full committees from serving as chair or ranking member of any subcommittee. This party rule was made a rule of the House in 1995. These rules spread committee and subcommittee leadership posts among more members and limit the influence that any one member can enjoy by holding multiple leadership posts.

THE SENATE.   Both Senate parties allow committee members to select their subcommittee chairs or ranking members in order of seniority. Less conflict over subcommittee chairs has arisen in the Senate than in the House, perhaps because nearly all senators can count on having at least one subcommittee leadership post. Senate rules merely prohibit any member from holding more than one chair on a single committee. With most senators serving on three standing committees, they may have up to three subcommittee chairs (or two if they hold a full committee chair on one of those standing committees). In the 114th Congress (2015–2016), nearly 80 percent of majority party members held at least one subcommittee chair, and several held two or three subcommittee leadership posts.

LIMITING THE POWER OF FULL COMMITTEE CHAIRS

Compared with their predecessors of the 1950s and 1960s, today's full committee chairs face more effective competition for control over policy choices. Rank-and-file legislators are more likely to appeal to central party leaders and their party caucus to hold committee leaders accountable to them, and the parties have adopted changes in their rules to limit the service of committee leaders and to force chairs to face party approval periodically. Moreover, as discussed earlier, rank-and-file legislators now have larger staffs and can turn to outside groups for assistance in challenging the handiwork and arguments of committees and their leaders.

House Committee Chairs

We have noted a few of the changes affecting the power of full committee chairs, but it is useful to review the two waves of reforms that altered the role of House committee chairs. First, the House Democratic majority of the early 1970s adopted rules to reduce the influence of full committee chairs over the decisions of their committees:

- chairs were required to stand for election by the Democratic Caucus at the start of each Congress,
- committees with fifteen or more members were required to form at least four subcommittees,
- subcommittees were empowered with written jurisdictions and provided with staffs,
- proxy voting by chairs and ranking members was restricted (see box "Congressionally Speaking . . ."),
- the minority party contingents on committees were guaranteed staff,
- committees were required to open their meetings to the public unless a majority of committee members agreed to close them,
- committee members were empowered to call meetings (on a majority vote) so that chairs could no longer refuse to hold meetings, and
- chairs were required to report legislation promptly after it was approved by their committees.

Furthermore, as discussed earlier, House Democrats adopted a new procedure for subcommittee assignments so that full committee chairs could no longer stack important subcommittees with their supporters. Therefore, the ability of full committee chairs to block legislation favored by their committees was curtailed.

Second, following the Republican takeover in 1995, the House passed a series of reforms that would increase the power of the majority party at the expense of both committee and subcommittee chairs. First, and, perhaps most visible, House rules reduced the number of committees by three and the number of subcommittees by twenty-eight. The elimination of these committees and subcommittees resulted in a loss of 484 seats. Additional reforms were passed that placed the majority party leadership at the center of decision making and further constrained the behavior of committee chairs:

- six-year term limits were placed on committee chairs,
- committees were limited to forming five subcommittees (some exceptions granted),
- proxy voting was banned (see box "Congressionally Speaking . . ."),
- TV and radio coverage had to be accommodated for all committee meetings that were open to the public, and
- overall committee staff budgets were cut.

Congressionally Speaking . . .

Attendance at committee meetings has been a problem for many years. Members often have multiple committee meetings or hearings scheduled at the same time and must fulfill other obligations – meet with constituents, vote on the House floor – while their committees are meeting. Therefore, members often grant their committee leaders authority to cast proxy votes in their absence.

To control abuses of proxy voting, the House adopted rules on their use. An old House rule provided that a majority of committee members must actually be present at the meeting for a committee to report legislation to the floor. If a majority were not present, a point of order could be raised against a bill when it reached the floor, which would lead the Speaker to rule a bill out of order.

But getting a majority of committee members to show up at one time and circumventing points of order can be troublesome. House Democrats moved in 1993 to minimize the problem. Their rule allowed for a "rolling quorum," which counted as "present" any member who voted in committee even if no majority was actually present at the same time. Moreover, no point of order could be raised on the House floor unless it was raised at the appropriate time in committee.

House Republicans banned proxy voting and rolling quorums after they gained a majority in the 1994 elections. They reinstituted the requirement that a "majority of the committee be actually present." Since that time, attendance has continued to be a problem for committee chairs, some of whom have suggested returning to some form of proxy voting. Despite persistent problems with committee attendance, the rules remained intact today.

Furthermore, party leaders have become more involved in committee chairmanship fights and creating task forces and other forums for writing legislation.

Senate Committee Chairs

The Senate also adopted rules to provide guidelines for the conduct of committee meetings, hearings, and voting and to require committees to publish additional rules governing committee procedures. Unlike in the House, however, Senate chamber and party rules have never specified internal committee organization in any detail and are silent on the functions of subcommittees; in fact, most Senate committees' rules are very brief. In the majority of cases, the full committee chair is assumed to have great discretion, although even that is left unstated. For nearly all Senate full committees, the referral of legislation to subcommittees and the discharge of legislation from subcommittees remain under the formal control of the committee chair.

Senate Republican Party rules specify limitations on the number and type of committees that Republicans can lead. In 1995, after the Senate Republicans regained a majority, they joined their House counterparts in placing even stricter limitations on committee chairs in party rules. The Senate Republicans adopted a party rule prohibiting full committee chairs from chairing any subcommittees and further barring any Republican senator from chairing more than two subcommittees. Both rules were intended to spread chairmanships among as many senators as possible and to limit the special influence that any one senator might enjoy through multiple chairmanships. The rule soon proved to be a hardship for the party, however. On a few committees, the Republicans found themselves without a sufficient number of eligible senators to take another subcommittee chairmanship, so they began to grant waivers to the rule. Senate Democrats have not adopted similar rules.

Subcommittees

Subcommittees became more common after the Legislative Reorganization Act of 1946 consolidated committee jurisdictions and reduced the number of standing committees in both chambers. The number of subcommittees continued to grow into the 1970s, as individual committees responded to new policy problems and as members demanded their own subcommittees. Currently, of the committees with authority to report legislation, the only ones without subcommittees are the House Administration, Budget, and Ethics Committees, and the Senate Budget, Rules and Administration, Indian Affairs, Intelligence, Small Business and Entrepreneurship, and Veterans' Affairs Committees.

THE HOUSE. In the House, the resistance of some full committee chairs to create legislative subcommittees was eventually overcome by a 1974 rule that provides that "each standing committee . . . except the Committee on the Budget . . . that has more than twenty members shall establish at least four subcommittees." As a result, subcommittees proliferated to the extent that more than one hundred twenty-five subcommittees existed in 1980. Later, problems associated with the growth in the number of House subcommittees – jurisdictional squabbles between subcommittees, scheduling difficulties, and the burden of subcommittee hearings on executive officials – led the Democratic Caucus in 1981 to limit the number of subcommittees. The 1981 rule was supplanted by a new House rule, adopted in 1993, limiting the number of subcommittees to five per committee, unless a committee maintains a subcommittee on oversight (in which case the committee may have six subcommittees). The 1993 rule permitted only two committees to exceed the subcommittee limit – Appropriations (which may have thirteen subcommittees) and Oversight and Government Reform (which may have seven). The rules changes adopted in 1993 required the abolition of sixteen subcommittees, and additional changes introduced by the Republicans in 1995 further scaled back the number of subcommittees. Cumulatively, these changes brought the House back to the 1955 level of about eighty subcommittees. The number of subcommittees has crept up since then, as rules changes have granted additional exemptions on subcommittee limits to Armed Services (which may have seven), Foreign Affairs (which may have seven), and Transportation and Infrastructure (which may have six).

Congressionally Speaking . . .

One of the earliest intensive book-length studies of Congress was Woodrow Wilson's *Congressional Government*, written in 1883 and 1884 when Wilson was a graduate student at Johns Hopkins University. He penned two frequently quoted phrases – "Congressional government is *committee government*" (emphasis added) and "Congress in session is Congress on public exhibition, whilst Congress in its committee-rooms is Congress at work." Wilson later became president of the United States.

   The power of subcommittees was enhanced during the early 1970s, leading observers to look for new ways to label Congress. The political scientists Roger Davidson and Walter Oleszek characterized the House as *subcommittee government* in their 1977 book *Congress against Itself*. Neither Davidson nor Oleszek has exhibited ambition for high public office.

THE SENATE. The Senate and the Senate parties do not have formal rules on the number of subcommittees. Instead, the Senate's limits on the number of subcommittee assignments that individual senators may hold effectively restricts the number of subcommittees that can be created. In 1985, compliance with the limits on subcommittee assignments led to the elimination of ten subcommittees. Republicans further reduced the number of subcommittees after taking majority control of the Senate in 1995. In 1997, the Senate had sixty-eight subcommittees, down from nearly ninety ten years earlier. The number of Senate subcommittees has changed little since that time, with sixty-nine subcommittees in 2015.

Checking the Power of Subcommittees in the House

In the Democratic House of the 1970s, subcommittees became very important in committee decision making. The House and the Democratic Caucus adopted rules in the early 1970s that substantially weakened the ability of full committee chairs to control subcommittees. Consequently, decision-making processes within House committees became more decentralized than they had been in the 1950s and 1960s. Most legislation originated in subcommittees, the vast majority of hearings were held in subcommittees, about half of all committee staff was allocated to subcommittees, and subcommittee chairs usually served as the floor managers for legislation originating in their subcommittees. The House and Democratic Party rules together created substantial uniformity across House committees in their re-liance on subcommittees for initial action on legislation. The pattern in the House led some observers to label House decision making "subcommittee government."

   Subcommittee government evaporated with the new Republican majority in 1995. House subcommittees were no longer guaranteed that legislation sent to their parent committees would be referred to them. In addition, as noted previously, the Republicans forced most House committees to reduce the number of their subcommittees from six to five (with the exception of those committees maintaining an oversight subcommittee and those granted explicit exemptions), and they returned to the full committee chairs control over subcommittee appointments and over all committee and subcommittee staff. When they cut committee budgets, a disproportionate share of the resulting staff cutbacks occurred in subcommittee staffs. Whereas subcommittee chairs once had the authority to hire one staffer, House rules now give full committee chairs the authority to determine the staff allotted to subcommittees. Subcommittee staff now constitute less than 40 percent of all committee staff, down nearly 10 percent from the 1980s. The consequence of these changes has been the reemergence of variation across House committees in the way they use subcommittees.

The Senate and its parties never adopted rules granting subcommittees the kind of independence that House subcommittees enjoyed under the Democrats in the 1970s and 1980s. The lack of formal rules empowering subcommittees in the Senate has produced great variation among committees in their reliance on subcommittees. Several Senate committees hold no or only a few hearings in subcommittee, and only a few Senate committees use subcommittees to write legislation. Subcommittee government never fit the decision-making processes in most Senate committees.

Committee Staff

Committees in the early nineteenth century worked without staff assistance, which meant that committee chairs personally managed the administrative details of committee business. The growing workload of the mid-1800s, however, rendered this practice infeasible. In 1856, the House approved committee assistance for the Ways and Means Committee, and the Senate did the same for the Finance Committee. Expansion in committee assistance following this was slow; it was not until 1890 that the total number of committee employees in both chambers exceeded 100. See Figure 6.6 for a detailed account of changes in numbers of committee staff in both chambers across time.

The Legislative Reorganization Act of 1946 was a significant turning point in the history of committee staffing as it established statutory provisions for the allocation of staff. Specifically, it granted standing committees in both chambers the authority to hire four professional staff assistants and six clerical aides. The number of professional assistants was raised to six (totaling twelve statutory positions) in 1970 by the second Legislative Reorganization Act. In addition, committees were extended the opportunity to make annual requests for committee staff beyond the statutory allotments. This gave way to a rapid expansion of committee staff, particularly in the nonstatutory category (referred to as "investigative"). After the 1970 Legislative Reorganization Act, committee staffing has followed different courses in the two chambers.

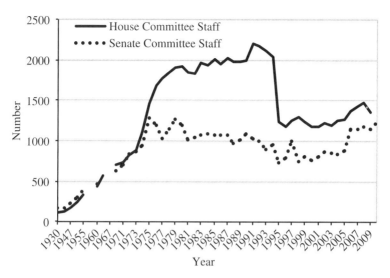

Figure 6.6 Number of Committee Staff in the House and Senate, 1930–2010. Source: Norman J. Ornstein, Thomas E. Mann, Michael J. Malbin, Andrew Rugg, and Raffaela Wakeman, *Vital Statistics on Congress, 2014* (Washington, DC: Brookings Institution and American Enterprise Institute, 2014).

THE HOUSE. In 1974, the House increased the personnel limit for committees to eighteen professional assistants and twelve clerical aides, where it remains today. The number of committee staff in the House exploded in the 1970s, primarily as a result of the growth in subcommittees. Although growth leveled off in the House during the 1980s, the total number of committee staff employed continued to rise through the early 1990s. By 1990, only one House committee had a staff smaller than forty, and six committees had more than one hundred assistants.

THE SENATE. Although growth in committee staff was more gradual in the Senate, Senate committees, like their House counterparts, took advantage of the 1970s' procedures permitting investigative staff. The adoption of a 1980 Senate resolution, however, eliminated the distinction between statutory and investigative staff, and moved to annual funding (changed to biennial funding in 1985) of committee staff. As is now the practice, committees were directed to draft budget requests to be packaged and voted on by the chamber.

REPUBLICAN CUTS RESTORED. As they had promised, the Republicans elected to Congress in 1994 cut committee budgets and staff. House committee (full and subcommittee) staff dropped from more than seventeen hundred to less than eleven hundred; Senate committee staff dropped from nearly one thousand to less than eight hundred. Republican leaders packaged these cuts as a money-saving measure, but many have suggested that this was also an effort by Republican leaders to centralize power. Since the mid-1990s, committee staff in each chamber has risen to approximately thirteen hundred, although the House numbers are still considerably lower today than they were before these cuts.

Both chambers guarantee the minority party a share of the staff. Senate rules state that the allocation of committee staff "should reflect the relative number of majority and minority members of committees." The standing rules of the House are less favorable to the minority than in the Senate. The House guarantees to the minority only ten staff members, or one-third of the committee staff, whichever is less.

CONCLUSION

Committees are a central but changing feature of legislative policy making. Changes in the role of committees are primarily the products of:

- the emergence of new and salient policy problems,
- fluctuations in the strength of congressional parties, and
- the character of the existing institutional arrangements.

When interest in an issue is narrow, the policy outcome satisfies most members and the issue has little impact on party fortunes; autonomous committees are tolerated and even revered. However, when an issue is more complex and few members are indifferent to the outcome, as appeared to happen more frequently in the 1970s, committees become constrained by their parent chambers and must rely on formal procedural safeguards to preserve their control over legislative details. When the parties' electoral fortunes are tied to the issue and the policy outcome, as happened on budget matters in the 1980s and again more recently, party leaders and their functionaries assume decision-making responsibilities that subvert the powers of committees.

The direction of change over the past three decades – toward less autonomous committees and a less committee-oriented process – must not be confused with the degree of change. The changes reported in this chapter, particularly those in the House, appear to be quite sweeping. Many of the procedural sources of committee power seem to have been weakened. Developments affecting committee assignments, bill referrals, floor debate, conferences, and the budget process have reduced committee autonomy. Additionally, the informal norm of deference to committee recommendations certainly is much weaker today than it was in the 1950s and 1960s.

But some care must be taken in drawing inferences about these changes. Most legislation comes from a single committee in each chamber, receives few or no floor amendments, and does not require a conference. Necessary conferences are managed by conferees chosen nearly exclusively from the committee of origin. Moreover, committees have devised a remarkable variety of legislative tricks to minimize the effect of budget constraints. With the creative use of special rules and large omnibus measures in the 1980s, committees have actually recovered some of the autonomy they lost in the 1970s.

SUGGESTED READINGS

A.   The following readings offer competing theories regarding the central purpose of congressional committees.

Cox, Gary, and Mathew McCubbins. *Legislative Leviathan.* 2nd ed. New York: Cambridge University Press, 2007.

Krehbiel, Keith. *Information and Legislative Organization.* Ann Arbor: University of Michigan Press, 1991.

Maltzman, Forrest. *Competing Principals: Committees, Parties and the Organization of Congress.* Ann Arbor: University of Michigan Press, 1997.

Weingast, Barry, and William Marshall. "The Industrial Organization of Congress; or, Why Legislatures, Like Firms, Are Not Organized as Markets." *Journal of Political Economy* 96 (1988): 132–163.

B.   The following readings address the politics of committee assignments.

Krehbiel, Keith. "Are Congressional Committees Composed of Preference Outliers?" *American Political Science Review* 84 (1990): 149–164.

Londregan, John and James Snyder. "Comparing Committee and Floor Preferences." *Legislative Studies Quarterly* 19 (1994): 233–266.

Vander Wielen, Ryan J., and Steven S. Smith. "Majority Party Bias in U.S. Congressional Conference Committees." *Congress and the Presidency* 38 (2011): 271–300.

C.   The following readings offer an overview of the committee system and explore the strategies of members serving on committees.

Deering, Christopher J., and Steven S. Smith. *Committees in Congress.* 3rd ed. Washington, DC: Congressional Quarterly Press, 1997.

Evans, C. Lawrence. *Leadership in Committee: A Comparative Analysis of Leadership Behavior in the U.S. Senate.* Ann Arbor: University of Michigan Press, 1991.

Fenno, Richard, Jr. *Congressmen in Committees.* Boston: Little, Brown, 1973.

DISCUSSION QUESTIONS

1   Who or what are committees responsive to according to the information, distributive, and partisan theories of congressional committees?

2   Do you think that one of the theories of committees captures the behavior of all committees all of the time? How about one committee all of the time, or all committees some of the time?

3 What can we learn about a member's goals on the basis of his or her committee assignment?

4 Why do we observe a struggle between parties and committees? In other words, why does the strengthening of one typically result in a weakening of the other?

5 Imagine that you are a party leader who wishes to pass a bill that is important to your party; however, you know that the committee with jurisdiction over this bill is opposed to it. What strategies might you employ to win passage, and what are the implications of the various strategies?

7 The Rules of the Legislative Game

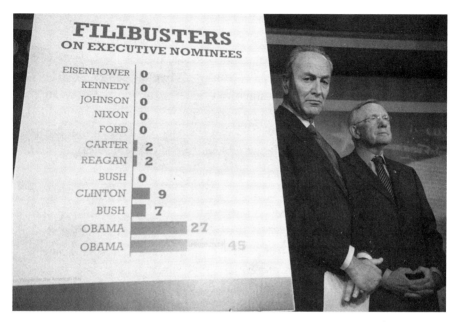

Senator Charles Schumer (D-New York), *left*, and then-Senate Majority Leader Harry Reid (D-Nevada), *right*, attend a news conference in the Capitol after a historic vote in the Senate to end the minority's ability to filibuster and kill most presidential nominations.

Congressional politics often has the flavor of a game – albeit a very important game – as the contending factions vie for control over public policy. The game is characterized by bargaining, procedural maneuvers, close votes, and uncertainty. When the interests and rights of large groups in society are at stake, the game is emotionally charged. The game is made more compelling by the personalities of the players. Members of Congress, presidents, staff aides, lobbyists, and other participants in congressional politics are ambitious people. Many of them hate to lose. Skilled players are masters of the rules; they are proficient in strategy and tactics and take pleasure in anticipating the moves of their opponents. Their knowledge of the rules and their aptitude for strategy do not guarantee success, but it can give them an advantage. Even for spectators, mastering the rules and strategy is essential to appreciating and enjoying the game.

The rules of the game change – and legislators do the changing. Each chamber of Congress is empowered by the Constitution to enact its own rules. The rules of the House of Representatives extend to more than sixty thousand words, but the Senate's rules are less than half that long at around thirty thousand words. The differences in the length of the rules reflect not only the differences in the sizes of the two chambers, with the larger House requiring more formalities to keep order, but also the different paths that the two chambers took at critical junctures in their parliamentary histories. The Senate, at a very early point in its history, eliminated the means to limit debate, which created the possibility of preventing a vote on a measure by refusing to stop talking. As a result, controversial changes in the rules can be blocked by a minority in the Senate. The House, in contrast, adopted a means to limit debate by a simple majority vote, which allowed even small majorities to impose new rules on that chamber. The result is that the House gradually accumulated a much larger and more detailed set of rules.

LEGISLATIVE RULES IN PERSPECTIVE

Perhaps the most remarkable feature of the legislative process is how much it is stacked against the enactment of new law. Typically, getting a major bill passed involves attracting majority support in successive stages – first in a subcommittee, then in the full committee, then on the floor, then perhaps in conference, and then on the floor again for the conference report. This must be done in both chambers and usually requires the cooperation of both the minority and the majority party leadership in the Senate and, in the case of the House, the majority party leadership and the Rules Committee. Once congressional passage is acquired, presidential approval or the support of an extraordinary majority in both chambers must be obtained. Success, then, depends on finding support from multiple groups and subgroups that are not likely to have identical policy preferences. Proponents of a new program or project usually must successfully pilot the necessary legislation through the process twice – once for an authorization bill to create the program and once for the related appropriations bill to fund the program.

Often, the members of Congress and other players in this game take the rules as they are and adjust their strategies accordingly. However, the players also seek to shape and create rules that suit their political needs, which change over time. The existing rules are seldom reevaluated in their entirety. Instead, their weaknesses or biases are considered individually and solutions are adopted piecemeal. New options, limitations, and contingencies have been added incrementally, making the rules more elaborate and altering the strategic context within which legislative factions must compete for majority support. Over the more than two centuries that Congress has been making law, a remarkably complex set of rules, further elaborated by precedents and informal practices, have evolved to shape the legislative process.

It would be a serious mistake to infer that the rules are so detailed and biased that they dictate policy outcomes. They are not. Rules are typically created to facilitate action, not determine outcomes. With a few exceptions, rules do not stipulate the issues to be considered by Congress. National and international events shape those issues, and much of the legislative struggle involves getting new issues on the congressional agenda. Moreover, rules do not determine the policy preferences of the players. Who gets elected is the most important factor in determining what policies will be favored by Congress, although interest groups, presidents, and others influence members' policy choices as well. In addition, the rules do not determine which of the interest groups, local government officials, political commentators, and others exercise the most influence on policy decisions. Larger social forces are more important than the legislative rules in this regard. Generally, the rules are not so detailed and biased that they can compensate for a scarcity of support and votes.

Nevertheless, the rules of the legislative game do matter. Some rules restrict or expand the options available to members by placing certain bills in order on the floor at certain times or by regulating the amendments that may be offered. Other rules set the decision rule – requiring a majority or supermajority for certain kinds of motions or measures – and others specify which members have the right to make a motion or to speak at certain times. Members know that Congress's rules matter and often regret that the general public does not appreciate their importance. Robert Michel (R-Illinois), the House Republican leader from 1981 to 1994, once lamented the difficulty of attracting public attention to the plight of the minority party under House rules:

> Nothing is so boring to the layman as a litany of complaints over the more obscure provisions of House procedures. It is all "inside baseball." Even among the media, none but the brave seek to attend to the howls of dismay from Republicans [then the minority party] over such esoterica as the kinds of rules under which we are forced to debate. But what is more important to a democracy than the method by which its laws are created?
>
> We Republicans are all too aware that when we laboriously compile data to demonstrate the abuse of legislative power by the Democrats, we are met by reporters and the public with that familiar symptom best summarized in the acronym "MEGO" – my eyes glaze over. We can't help it if the battles of Capitol Hill are won or lost before the issues get to the floor by the placement of an amendment or the timing of a vote. We have a voice and a vote to fight the disgraceful manipulation of the rules by the Democrats, and we make use of both. All we need now is media attention, properly directed to those boring, but all-important, House procedures.[1]

1 Robert H. Michel, "The Minority Leader Replies," *Washington Post*, December 29, 1987, A14.

Representative Michel was well aware that misconceptions about congressional rules abound. Some believe that "if there's a will, there's a way" – legislators' efforts, not rules, determine outcomes. Others see congressional procedures as arcane and deeply biased against action – "the outcome is rigged by the rules." Particular rules become critical factors in shaping policy choices only in combination with the preferences of the players. If all members of Congress support a particular bill, it doesn't matter whether only a simple majority or a supermajority is required to pass it. As divisions emerge, however, the particular rules under which bills are crafted and brought to a vote may influence the outcomes. The ability to offer an amendment at a crucial moment, to delay action until more support can be attracted, or to gain enactment with a simple majority rather than a supermajority can be critical to the final policy outcome.

Knowledge of the rules can be an important resource. The former House Energy and Commerce chair John Dingell (D-Michigan) once said, "If I let you write the substance and you let me write the procedure, I'll screw you every time." In both chambers of Congress, the rules and precedents are sufficiently complex that most members do not master them in their entirety. Instead, they rely on knowledgeable colleagues, staffers, the parliamentarians, and others to advise them. A member who masters the rules is valuable to other members, more likely to be consulted, and more likely to be viewed as fit for a leadership position.

The rules governing the legislative process have two main sources: the Constitution and Congress itself. The Constitution sets a few basic but critically important rules (see Chapter 2). The chambers themselves, however, are a source of rules in three ways. First, the rules adopted by the House and Senate supplement the constitutional requirements. Second, several statutes or laws passed by Congress set procedural requirements for the two chambers of Congress (although most of these allow the House and Senate to supplement or supplant the statutory requirements with their own rules). Third, the two chambers of Congress have a large body of procedural precedents, built up over their more than two hundred-year history, that govern many aspects of congressional operations not addressed elsewhere. This chapter outlines the rules that are critical to understanding legislative politics.

BEYOND THE CONSTITUTION: HOUSE AND SENATE RULES

The Constitution outlines the fundamental rules of the legislative game but leaves out important details. How legislation is to be prepared for a vote in the House and Senate is left undefined, as are the means for resolving differences between the House and Senate. The Constitution makes the vice president the presiding officer of the Senate and specifies that an elected Speaker shall preside over the House, but it does not mention the specific powers of these presiding officers. The Constitution also does not mention how the president is to decide what to recommend to Congress or the degree to which the president will rely on departments and agencies to speak for the executive branch.

The details of legislative procedure have been filled in by the evolution of informal practices and the accumulation of recognized precedents. In both chambers of Congress, however, a sizable number of formal rules have been established as well. Such rules both reflect and shape the distribution of power within Congress and between Congress and the president.

The framers of the Constitution anticipated the need for rules of procedure. The Constitution's Article I, Section 5 provides that "each house may determine the rules of its proceedings." As a result, each chamber has devised a complex set of standing rules. They concern the committee systems, procedures for amending and voting on legislation, ethics regulations for members and staff, and many other matters. It is important to keep three things in mind: (1) each chamber has its own set of rules, (2) each chamber may change its rules whenever it desires, and (3) each chamber may waive its rules whenever it desires.

Formally, the House dissolves at the end of each two-year Congress and must reestablish its rules as one of its first items of business at the start of each new Congress. In nearly all cases, this is done with a few amendments sponsored by the majority party and approved on a party-line vote. The Senate, in contrast, considers itself to be a continuous body because at least two-thirds of its members continue to serve from one Congress to the next. For that reason, the Senate's rules remain in effect from Congress to Congress unless the Senate votes to change them.

In addition to their own standing rules, the House and Senate are guided by statutes and precedents established by rulings of their presiding officers. When Congress chooses to include certain procedures in new statutes, such as the Congressional Budget and Impoundment Control Act of 1974 (see Chapter 12), these have the force of standing rules. Party rules govern such matters as committee appointments and the selection of party leaders . In some instances, party rules dictate limits on the use of standing rules by party or committee leaders. Rulings of the presiding officers concern interpretations of statutory or standing rules.

THE STANDARD LEGISLATIVE PROCESS

The standard legislative process in the modern Congress is outlined in Figure 7.1. It is called the standard process because it is patterned after the prototypical route that major legislation follows. The chambers are free to alter it for certain

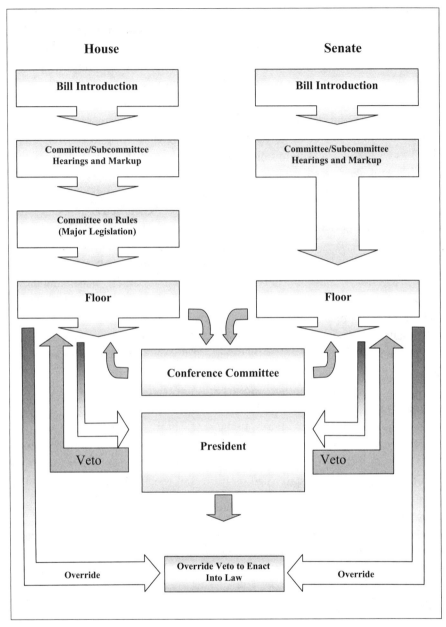

Figure 7.1 The Standard Legislative Process for a Major Bill.

legislation, and they have done so with greater frequency in the past decade or two. Even the standard process has many options that are not used regularly. The standard process involves multiple stages in each chamber, followed by steps for resolving House-Senate differences. The Constitution stipulates that after the House and Senate agree on legislation, the president must approve or veto it, and if it is vetoed, Congress may then attempt to override the veto. The standard process is like an obstacle course in which majorities must be created at several stages among different groups of legislators.

INTRODUCTION OF LEGISLATION

The modern legislative process gives members who are interested in enacting a new law three basic procedural options. First, they can introduce their own bill and work to gain passage in each chamber. Second, they can seek to have their ideas incorporated into legislation drafted by a committee or by other members. Third, they can offer their proposal as an amendment to someone else's legislation. They can even pursue the three options simultaneously.

Legislation can be drafted by anyone – a member and his or her staff, a committee, lobbyists, executive branch officials, or any combination of insiders and outsiders – but it must be introduced by a member while Congress is in session. In the House, a member simply places a copy of the draft legislation in a mahogany box, the "hopper," which is located at the front of the House chamber. In the Senate, members hand their draft legislation to a clerk or gain recognition to introduce it orally from the floor. In both chambers, the chief sponsor of a measure may seek cosponsors. Legislation is designated as a bill, a joint resolution, a concurrent resolution, or a resolution, and is numbered as it is introduced (see box "Types of Legislation").

Although legislation is given a number, it may be known by several names. Each bill is required to have a formal title, which is often quite long. For example, the 2014 Jobs for America Act was "[a] bill to make revisions to Federal law to improve the conditions necessary for economic growth and job creation, and for other purposes." But the bill was also known by a more convenient, short title – the Jobs for America Act – and many participants and observers simply referred to it as the jobs bill. In addition, bills often come to be known informally by the names of their chief sponsors. The Pell Act, which provided grants to college students, was named after Senator Claiborne Pell (D-Rhode Island), who fought hard for student financial aid.

Because lobbyists and other outsiders cannot introduce legislation, they search for members who are willing to champion their causes and introduce legislation they have drafted. Although they would prefer to have influential members introduce their proposals, they also seek members who have the time and interest to give their legislation some priority. The right mix is often found in a majority party member of mid-level seniority who sits on the committee with jurisdiction over the bill. It is usually advantageous to gain the sponsorship of several members willing to work together on behalf of the legislation.

Better still is a group of cosponsors who are known as serious legislators and who represent a range of views in both parties. Of course, sponsors also are sought in both chambers so that companion bills can be introduced at about the same time.

Members sometimes introduce measures "on request," as a courtesy to the president or someone else. When this is done, it is indicated next to the sponsors' names at the top of the first page of the legislation, signifying that the sponsor does not endorse the provisions of the bill. Similarly, legislation is often introduced by a committee chair on behalf of his or her committee, usually after the committee has drafted and approved the details. The chair is the formal sponsor, but the bill is recognized as a "committee bill."

Types of Legislation

There are four types of legislation. In each Congress, legislation of each type is generally numbered in the order it is introduced, although sometimes members request that specific numbers be reserved for their bills.

Bills are designated H.R. (number) or S. (number). Public bills change public law. If enacted into law, public bills are published in a volume entitled *Statutes at Large* and given a public law number, such as P.L. 114–2 (114th Congress, 2nd public law). Private bills address matters affecting individuals, such as an immigration case, and are not reported in *Statutes at Large*.

Joint resolutions are designated H.J. Res. (number) or S.J. Res. (number). Most joint resolutions are the same as bills for all purposes – they change public law and, if enacted into law, are published in *Statutes at Large* and given a public law number. By tradition, certain kinds of legislation, such as special appropriations measures, are labeled joint resolutions. A special class of joint resolution is proposed constitutional amendments, which – if passed by Congress – do not go to the president but go directly to the states for ratification.

Concurrent resolutions are designated H. Con. Res. (number) or S. Con. Res. (number) and do not change public law. They concern matters affecting both chambers, such as certain changes in congressional procedures, and so must be adopted by both chambers. They sometimes are used to express the "sense of Congress" about certain issues or events.

Resolutions are designated H. Res. (number) or S. Res. (number) and do not change public law. They concern matters affecting only one chamber, such as most standing rules, and so are adopted only by that chamber. They sometimes are used to express the "sense of the House" or the "sense of the Senate" about certain issues or events.

REFERRAL TO COMMITTEE

After draft legislation is introduced, the Speaker of the House or the Senate's presiding officer refers it to the appropriate committee(s). In practice, the

House and Senate parliamentarians inspect the content of proposed legislation and recommend referral to the committee or committees with the appropriate jurisdiction. Careful drafting of legislation may favorably influence the referral decision.

Because committees sometimes share jurisdiction over a measure's content, legislation may be referred to more than one committee, an action called "multiple referral." Multiple referral has become quite common in the House. Since 1974, the Speaker of the House has been authorized to send legislation to multiple committees. The current rule requires that the Speaker identify a "primary" committee, except in "extraordinary" cases when the Speaker may identify more than one committee as primary. The Speaker may send a bill in whole or in part, reflecting the different jurisdictions of committees, to one or more additional committees either before or after consideration by the primary committee. The Speaker also may set time limits for committee action. In recent Congresses, about one in five House measures has been multiply referred, with a higher proportion of important measures, closer to one in three, being so referred.

Most referrals are routine, but occasionally referrals can become controversial. Committee members care about referrals – staking a claim and winning a dispute over jurisdiction may expand a committee's area of authority and influence for years to come. Large, complex bills – such as major health care reform and telecommunications bills – often generate competition among committees with jurisdictions relevant to the legislation. Bills dealing with issues not anticipated by the existing rules governing committee jurisdictions are especially likely to stimulate competing jurisdictional claims. On some matters, the composition of the committee that receives a bill may affect the nature of the legislation it eventually reports to the floor, so bill sponsors and outside interests care about which committee receives the referral. On occasion, protracted negotiations among bill sponsors, committee leaders, and party leaders will precede introduction and referral of draft legislation.

COMMITTEE ACTION

Formally, committees have many options concerning how to process most of the legislation referred to them. They may approve the legislation and report it back to the parent chamber, with or without amendments; reject the measure outright; simply not consider it; or set it aside and write a new bill on the same subject. In practice, most proposed legislation does not survive committee consideration. Inaction at the committee stage dooms most legislation. In the 113th Congress (2013–2014), 3,712 bills and resolutions were introduced in the Senate and 6,924 were introduced in the House. Only 496 and 667 measures were reported by committees of the Senate and House, respectively – 13.4 and 9.6 percent.

Committees may send a bill to a subcommittee for initial action or hold it for the full committee to consider. Although nearly all committees have sub-committees with well-understood jurisdictions, full committee chairs have substantial discretion in deciding whether to refer measures to subcommit-tees or hold them for full committee consideration. Full committee chairs can also control the scheduling of meetings as a way to expedite or delay action on a bill.

Committees and subcommittees may hold hearings to receive testimony on proposed legislation from members, administration officials, interest group rep-resentatives, outside experts, and others. Hearings may address a general issue related to the legislation or the specifics of the legislation itself. Hearings are perhaps the most important formal information-gathering mechanism for Con-gress and its committees. Some hearings generate little but rhetoric and media coverage – members' questions turn into lengthy statements, celebrity witnesses offer scripted answers, and the television networks later replay a twenty-second exchange between an antagonistic committee member and an acerbic witness. Other hearings are designed more to advertise a bill, raise issues, or draw public attention to a problem than to gather information.

If a committee or subcommittee intends to act on a bill, it normally conducts a "markup" on the legislation – a meeting at which the committee or subcommittee reviews the measure line-by-line or section-by-section and considers amend-ments. Committees may write their own legislation and have it introduced by their chair. When this approach is taken, the chair often proposes a "chair's mark" as the starting point for the markup. Once the markup by the full com-mittee is complete, the measure may be reported to the floor if a majority of the committee votes to do so. Committees are free to report legislation with or with-out amendments or even without a recommendation that the legislation pass. Most important legislation is amended or written as a "clean" committee bill and then recommended to pass.

In the House, a bill reported to the floor from a committee must be accompa-nied by a committee report. Senate committees are not required to write these reports but usually do. Committee reports provide the committee's justification for the bill and are usually drafted by staff members as a routine matter. Com-mittee reports may include a statement of minority views on the legislation. On occasion, committee reports are controversial because they provide further inter-pretations of the bill that might guide later actions on the part of executive agen-cies or the courts. Committee reports sometimes help non-committee members and their aides explain complicated legislation to constituents. In the House, the Ramseyer rule (named after Representative John Ramseyer who proposed it years ago) requires that committee reports specify all changes to existing law that the proposed legislation would make.

CIRCUMVENTING COMMITTEES

Proponents of legislation opposed by a committee have a variety of means for gaining floor action on the legislation without having it reported from the committee. These mechanisms are different in the two chambers. Circumventing committees is more difficult in the House.

Circumventing Committees in the House

In the House, the options for circumventing committees are to move to suspend the rules, to employ a discharge petition, or to gain a discharge resolution from the Rules Committee. To successfully suspend the rules and pass a bill (one motion), a member must be recognized by the Speaker to make the motion to suspend, and then a two-thirds majority must approve the motion. Because the Speaker is usually supportive of committees dominated by members of his or her own party, this approach is seldom a feasible strategy. In addition, a two-thirds majority is unlikely to be obtained for a measure opposed by a committee. In recent decades, committee leaders have used the suspension process to speed floor action or to avoid amendments to committee bills.

The discharge procedure allows any member to introduce a motion to discharge or extract a measure from a committee once the measure has been before the committee for thirty legislative days (i.e., days on which the House meets). After the motion is filed, a discharge petition is prepared and made available for members to sign. If 218 or more members sign the petition, the motion to discharge becomes privileged business on the second and fourth Mondays of the month (except during the last six days of a session). If the discharge motion is adopted by majority vote, a motion to call up the bill for immediate consideration is in order.

Until a rule change in 1993, the identity of members signing a discharge petition was not made public until the 218th signature was added. The secrecy of the signatories made it difficult to hold members accountable and undermined lobbyists' efforts to pressure members to sign. Both before and after the 1993 rule change, however, the discharge process has seldom produced House action on a bill. In fact, only nineteen bills have been discharged and passed by the House since 1931. Two factors may account for this. First, committees are probably more or less in line with the House majority most of the time. Second, members may prefer to discourage a practice that could be used to discharge legislation from their own committees.

Unorthodox Legislating

The committee process is sometimes circumvented on important legislation in order to facilitate top-level negotiations between party leaders, committee chairs, the administration, and sometimes key representatives of outside groups. In 2012, for example, a bill to extend tax cuts was drafted by the top Senate leaders and administration officials. The text of the agreement replaced the text of a House bill pending in the Senate. Quick Senate action was made possible by a unanimous consent agreement providing for the bill's consideration. The House approved the bill with the Senate amendments. On its way to approving the Senate version, the House adopted a special rule for the consideration of the bill that provided for one hour of debate, barred amendments, and waived points of order.

The third approach to circumventing committees involves the Rules Committee's authority to report a privileged resolution that, if adopted, brings a bill to the floor for immediate consideration. The majority party members of the Rules Committee are appointed by the Speaker, so the committee is unlikely to use this power without the support of the Speaker. Again, the Speaker usually works to support the actions of committee majorities.

Circumventing Committees in the Senate

In the Senate, committees can be circumvented by introducing nongermane amendments to bills under consideration on the floor, by placing bills directly on the calendar for floor action, by moving to suspend the rules, or by employing the discharge procedure. Unlike the House, which requires that amendments offered to a bill be germane to the content of the bill, Senate rules are silent on the content of amendments offered to most bills. Consequently, a senator is free to offer his or her bill as an amendment to another measure pending before the Senate, thus circumventing a committee that is refusing to report the bill to the floor. There is no guarantee that a majority will support the amendment, of course, but the mechanism is very easy to employ.

Another approach is to object to the standard procedure of referring a bill to committee. Under Senate Rule XIV, a single senator may object and have a bill placed on the calendar, thereby avoiding delays that might be caused by an unfriendly committee. This action, however, may alienate senators who otherwise might support the bill. Senators also may seek to suspend the rules, but doing this requires a two-thirds vote under Senate precedents, which makes it more difficult to use successfully than a nongermane amendment. Alternatively, a senator can move to discharge a committee, but such motions are debatable and can therefore be filibustered.

FLOOR SCHEDULING

Legislation is listed, in the order it is reported from committee, on one of four calendars in the House and one of two calendars in the Senate. Each chamber has multiple mechanisms for scheduling legislation for floor consideration so that priority legislation will not get backlogged behind less important legislation. Moreover, for certain types of "privileged" legislation – such as budget and appropriations bills – the House allows committee leaders to call up the legislation directly on the floor. In both chambers, the majority party leaders assume primary responsibility for scheduling, but the two chambers have developed very different methods for setting the floor agenda.

Scheduling in the House

Minor legislation and major legislation are treated differently in the House. In recent years, minor bills have been called up most frequently by unanimous consent requests or by motions to suspend the rules. When legislation is called up by unanimous consent, there typically is no discussion. Under a motion to suspend the rules and pass a bill, debate is limited to no more than forty minutes, no amendments are allowed (unless specified in the motion), and a two-thirds majority is required for approval. Although legislation can be brought up under suspension of the rules only on specified days (typically Monday, Tuesday, and Wednesday), this has become a very common means for disposing of bills on the House floor. In recent Congresses, a majority of measures have passed under the suspension procedure, as shown in Figure 7.2.

Major or controversial legislation is more troublesome. Sponsors of a major or controversial bill usually cannot obtain unanimous or even two-thirds majority support, so they go to the Rules Committee to request a resolution known as a "special rule," or simply a "rule." The following box shows a recent rule adopted by the House for a 2014 continuing appropriations resolution. The rule provides for priority consideration of the measure upon the adoption of the rule. The rule further limits general debate on the bill to one hour equally divided and controlled by the chair and ranking minority member of the Appropriations Committee, and it immediately adopts an amendment (printed in part A of the Rules Committee report). Furthermore, the rule only permits the consideration of one additional amendment if offered by Representative Howard McKeon (R-California) or someone designated by him. This amendment (printed in part B of the Rules Committee report) may be debated for six hours, equally divided. This rule also sets aside objections (waives points of order) that may be made to

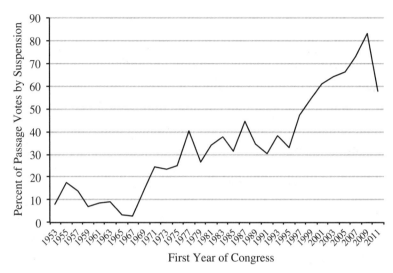

Figure 7.2 The Percentage of Passage Votes by Suspension of the Rules, 1953–2012.

the consideration of the bill or to provisions and/or amendments to the bill that violate House rules. Finally, the rule includes an amendment to the language of a separate House resolution.

Resolved, That upon adoption of this resolution it shall be in order to consider in the House the joint resolution (H.J. Res. 124) making continuing appropriations for fiscal year 2015, and for other purposes. All points of order against consideration of the joint resolution are waived. The amendment printed in part A of the report of the Committee on Rules accompanying this resolution shall be considered as adopted. The joint resolution, as amended, shall be considered as read. All points of order against provisions in the joint resolution, as amended, are waived. The previous question shall be considered as ordered on the joint resolution, as amended, and on any further amendment thereto to final passage without intervening motion except: (1) one hour of debate equally divided and controlled by the chair and ranking minority member of the Committee on Appropriations; (2) the further amendment printed in part B of the report of the Committee on Rules, if offered by Representative McKeon of California or his designee, which shall be in order without intervention of any point of order, shall be considered as read, shall be separately debatable for six hours equally divided and controlled by Representative McKeon of California and Representative Smith of Washington or their respective designees, and shall not be subject to a demand for division of the question; and (3) one motion to recommit with or without instructions.Sec. 2. Section 4(c) of House Resolution 567 is amended by adding the following new paragraph:

"(7) The provisions of paragraphs (f)(1) through (f)(12) of clause 4 of rule XI shall be considered to be written rules adopted by the Select Committee as though pursuant to such clause."

Special rules are highly flexible tools for tailoring floor action to individual bills. Amendments may be limited or prohibited. The order of voting on amendments may be structured. For example, the House can adopt a special rule known as a "king-of-the-hill rule." First used in 1982, a king-of-the-hill rule provides for a sequence of votes on alternative amendments, usually full substitutes for the bill. The last amendment to receive a majority wins, even if it receives fewer votes than some other amendment. This rule allows members to vote for more than one version of the legislation, which gives them the freedom both to support a version that is easy to defend at home and to vote for the version preferred by their party's leaders. Even more important, the procedure advantages the version voted on last, which is usually the proposal favored by the majority party leadership.

If the Rules Committee grants the rule and a majority of the House supports it, the way is paved for floor debate on the bill. Since the mid-1970s, the Rules Committee has been under the direction of the Speaker. In 1975, after years of struggle to get friendly, timely rules from a Rules Committee dominated by conservatives, the House Democratic Caucus granted the Speaker the power to appoint the committee's Democratic members, subject to its approval. Because the Democrats were the majority party and insisted on firm control of the rules, they reserved nine of the thirteen seats on the committee for their party – a ratio that is closely adhered to today. Since the late 1970s, Rules Committee members, often at the direction of the Speaker, have become much more creative in structuring the amendment process on the House floor.

Finally, five House committees (Appropriations, Budget, House Administration, Rules, and Ethics) have direct access to the floor for certain kinds of legislation. Privileged measures – such as appropriations or tax bills – are considered critical to the House as an institution. When other legislation is not pending on the floor, a member authorized by one of these committees can move for immediate consideration of a privileged measure. Special rules from the Rules Committee are the single biggest group of privileged measures. Although privileged bills do not require a special rule from the Rules Committee, their sponsors often seek one anyway to limit or structure debate and amendments or to waive a House rule that might otherwise be used to raise a point of order against the bill.

Special Rules of the House

Since 1979, the House Rules Committee, in partnership with the majority party leadership, has proven remarkably creative in designing special rules to govern floor debate and amendments on major legislation. Different styles of special rules have gained informal names that are widely recognized by the members of the House. All of these creative special rules waive many standing rules of the House governing floor debate and amendments.

Restrictive rules. Three kinds of rules restricting amending activity were known before the 1980s – modified open rules, modified closed rules, and closed rules. Closed rules

(continued)

Special Rules of the House (*continued*)

simply bar all amendments. Modified open rules allow amendments except for a specific title or section of a bill. Modified closed rules bar amendments except for a specific title or section of a bill. Since the early 1980s, restrictions have come in so many combinations that these traditional categories do not capture their diversity. In modern parlance, the Rules Committee itself will label many rules as "structured."

King-of-the-hill rules. Invented by Democrats in the early 1980s and sometimes called king-of-the-mountain rules, these rules provide that the House will vote on a series of alternative versions of a bill (substitutes) in a specified order and that the last version to receive a majority vote (no matter how large the majority on other versions) wins.

Queen-of-the-hill rules. Invented by Republicans in 1995, these rules provide that the House will vote on a series of alternative versions of a bill in a specified order and that the version with the most votes wins. If two versions receive the same number of votes, the last one voted on wins.

Time-limit rules. Invented by Republicans in 1995, these rules provide that all debate and amending activity on a bill will be completed within a specified period of time.

Scheduling in the Senate

Scheduling is one area, and certainly not the only one, in which the Senate is very different from the House. In some respects, floor scheduling is simple in the Senate. Bringing up a bill is a matter of making a motion to proceed to its consideration. This is done by the majority leader, and although the motion technically requires a majority vote, it usually is approved by unanimous consent. The Senate has no committee empowered to report special rules.

What has appeared bizarre to many newcomers to Senate politics was that, until 2013, the motion to proceed was debatable and might be subject to a filibuster (see a discussion of the new filibuster rules below). That is, senators could refuse to allow the majority leader's motion to come to a vote by conducting extended debate. In fact, they might not even have to conduct the filibuster because just the threat of doing so is usually enough to keep legislation of only moderate importance off the floor. The reason is that the majority leader usually cannot afford to create a logjam of legislation awaiting floor consideration by subjecting one measure to extended debate. Under Senate Rule XXII, breaking a filibuster is a time-consuming process that requires a three-fifths constitutional majority – if no seat is vacant, sixty senators – willing to invoke cloture.

A good example of a bizarre filibuster was the one conducted by Senator Alfonse D'Amato (R–New York) in October 1992. D'Amato objected to the fact that a tax break for a Cortland, New York, typewriter manufacturer had been stricken from a bill in a conference committee, so he filibustered the entire bill. D'Amato held the floor for more than fifteen hours, sometimes with the assistance of Senators Patrick Moynihan (D–New York) and John Seymour (R–California). Under the Senate's rules, D'Amato could not sit down or excuse himself to go to the bathroom without yielding the floor. The quality of this extended "debate," which prevented the Senate from completing its business and adjourning for the year, degenerated as time wore on. At one point, D'Amato reported:

> The young lady who works for me in my Syracuse office, Marina Twomey – her parents. She married a young boy who I ran track against in high school – went to Andrew Jackson, met Larry, he went up to Syracuse on a track scholarship, competed. And he married this lovely girl, Marina, who came from Cortland. This is how I came to know Cortland. I visited her and her family.
>
> Fate and life and whatnot, circumstances as we talk, Marina is now one of the two people – the other you know for many years, Gretchen Ralph, who used to be the leader of the symphony or the executive director – and a great community person. She and Marina Twomey run my Syracuse office. We talk about Cortland and knowing and having an affinity.[2]

By the time D'Amato gave up, the filibuster consumed more than eighty-six pages of the *Congressional Record*. This number was not enough to break the record established by Strom Thurmond (R-South Carolina), who spoke for more than twenty-four hours against a civil rights bill in 1957. Filibusters such as D'Amato's, Thurmond's, and the fictitious one depicted in the 1939 movie *Mr. Smith Goes to Washington* are actually quite rare in today's Senate. Most uses of the filibuster today take the form of holds and other less visible stalling tactics (more on this later in the chapter).

The ever-present threat of a filibuster requires that scheduling be a matter of consultation and negotiation among the majority leader, the minority leader, bill sponsors, and other interested senators. These discussions, conducted in private, often yield bargains about how to proceed and may include compromises about substantive policy matters. The agreement, which may include limitations on debate and amendments, is then presented to the Senate. It requires unanimous approval to take effect. The process contrasts sharply with the formal Rules Committee hearings and majority approval of special rules in the House.

Frustration with minority party filibusters along with the angry responses of majority party members have led reformers to devise a variety of proposals to change the Senate's rules in recent Congresses, and modest changes were made in 2013. The problem for reformers was that the minority could prevent consideration of a filibuster reform resolution by filibustering. Under Senate Rule XXII, a two-thirds majority of senators present and voting is required to close debate on a measure to change the standing rules (on most matters, the threshold for cloture is two-fifths of all elected senators). To get around this, many majority party Democrats in the 113th Congress (2013–2014) hoped to gain a procedural ruling that the Constitution implies that a simple majority can get a vote on a change in the rules at the beginning of a Congress. Such a move was considered a radical step by Republicans and by at least some Democrats, so Majority Leader Harry Reid (D-Nevada) negotiated modest reforms with Minority Leader Mitch McConnell (R-Kentucky) that attracted bipartisan support (see box that follows). However, as we discuss later (see box "The Changing Congress: Filibuster Frustrates Majorities"), these reforms were still not sufficient to silence the majority party's concerns about the filibuster.

The 2013 Senate reforms came in two resolutions, one to make a change in the standing rules and the other to adopt procedures exclusively for the 113th Congress (2013–2014). First, the standing rules were revised in two ways to expedite Senate action:

(a) Debate on the motion to proceed (to consider a measure) following a cloture vote (to close debate) was eliminated if cloture is endorsed by the leaders of both parties and at least seven senators of each party. Therefore, if cloture is invoked, and the cloture petition has the requisite signatures, then no additional debate on the motion to proceed occurs.

(b) The previous three motions to go to a conference with the House (a motion to disagree with the House, a motion to request a conference, and a motion to appoint conferees) were combined into a single motion, debate on cloture on the conference motion was limited to two hours, and, if cloture is invoked, no additional debate on the conference motion occurs.

Second, a standing order – a rules change that is in effect for just that Congress – was approved to limit debate on the motion to proceed to the consideration of legislation and on postcloture debate on nominations:

(a) Debate on a motion to proceed was limited to four hours.

(b) The minority and the majority were each guaranteed two amendments to any measure after adoption of the motion to proceed.

(c) Postcloture debate on nominations other than cabinet-level and appellate judicial nominations is limited to eight hours; postcloture debate on district court nominations is limited to two hours.The standing order was not reinstated at the start of the 114th Congress (2015–2016), although Senate Majority Leader Mitch McConnell (R-Kentucky) voted for it in the previous Congress and has signaled continued support for the practice.

FLOOR CONSIDERATION

For most minor and routine legislation that reaches the House or Senate floor, floor consideration is brief, no amendments are offered, and the legislation is approved by voice vote or by unanimous consent. On major legislation, many members usually want to speak and offer amendments, creating a need for procedures that will maintain order and expedite action. The two chambers have quite different floor procedures for major legislation.

Congressionally Speaking . . . The Filibuster

The term *filibuster* is an anglicized version of the Dutch word for "freebooter." A "filibusterer" was a sixteenth- and seventeenth-century pirate. How it came to be the Senate term for talking a bill to death in the nineteenth century is not clear. The political lexicographer William Safire notes that one of the term's first appearances was in 1854, when the Kansas-Nebraska Act was filibustered.

The current Senate Rule XXII provides for cloture (closing of debate) with the approval of a three-fifths majority of the senators duly chosen and sworn. Given that the Senate consists of one hundred elected senators, at least sixty must support a motion for cloture to stop a filibuster. An exception is made for measures changing the Senate rules, for which a vote of two-thirds of those senators present and voting is required.

Floor Action in the House

In the House, committee chairs write a letter to the Rules Committee chair, requesting a hearing and a special rule for major legislation that they are about to report to the floor. Once a special rule for a measure is adopted, the House may resolve to convene "the Committee of the Whole House on the State of the Union" to conduct general debate and consider amendments. The Committee of the Whole, as it is usually abbreviated, consists of the full House meeting in the House chamber and operating under a special set of rules. For example, the quorum required to conduct business in the Committee of the Whole is smaller than it is for the House (100 versus 218), making it easier to conduct business while members are busy with other activities.

A chair appointed by the Speaker presides over the Committee of the Whole. The Committee of the Whole first conducts general debate on the bill and then moves to debate and vote on amendments. Legislation is considered section by section. An amendment must be relevant – germane – to the section under consideration, a requirement that is interpreted very restrictively. For example, an amendment to limit abortions cannot be considered when a bill on water treatment plants is being debated. Amendments sponsored by the committee originating the legislation are considered first for each section and are considered under the five-minute rule. That is, members are each allowed to speak for five minutes on an amendment. The special rule providing for the consideration of the measure may – and often does – alter these standard procedures.

Voting on amendments in the Committee of the Whole can take one of three forms: voice vote, standing division vote, or recorded vote. On a voice vote, members yell out "yea" or "nay," and the presiding officer determines whether there were more yeas or nays. On a standing division vote, members voting "yea" stand and are counted, followed by those voting "nay." Since 1971, it has been possible to get a recorded vote for which each individual member's position is officially and publicly recorded. Under the current rule, a recorded vote in the Committee of the Whole must be demanded by twenty-five members. Since 1973, recorded voting has been done by a computerized system. Members insert an identification card into a small voting box and push a "yea," "nay," or "present" button. This system is used for recording other voting in the House as well.

Once debate and amending actions are complete in the Committee of the Whole, the measure, along with any approved amendments, is reported back to the House. Special rules usually provide that the "previous question" be ordered, preventing additional debate by the House. The amendments approved in the Committee of the Whole may then be subject to separate votes; if no one demands separate votes, however, the amendments are voted on as a group. Next, a motion to recommit the legislation to committee, which by custom is made by a minority party member, is in order. If the motion to recommit is defeated, as it nearly always is, or simply not offered, the House moves to a vote on final passage.

Floor Action in the Senate

The Senate lacks detailed rules or a well-structured process for debating and amending legislation on the floor. What happens after the motion to proceed is adopted depends on whether unanimous consent has been obtained to limit or structure debate and amendments. In the absence of a unanimous consent agreement that provides otherwise, Senate rules do not limit debate or amendments for most legislation. Debate and amending activity may go on for days. In contrast to the House, the Senate has no five-minute rule or general germaneness rule for amendments. The floor schedule becomes very unpredictable. Normally, the Senate muddles through controversial legislation with one or more unanimous consent agreements that limit debate, organize the consideration of amendments, and lend some predictability to its proceedings.

One reason that consent may not be acquired for a time limitation on debate is that some senators may want to have the option of filibustering. A filibuster, and sometimes just the threat of one, will force a compromise. If a compromise is not possible, cloture must be invoked, or the majority leader will be compelled to withdraw the measure from the floor. Once cloture is invoked, thirty hours of debate are permitted (under the current rule), and germane amendments submitted before cloture was invoked can be considered. In fact, cloture is sometimes invoked to avoid the inclusion of nongermane amendments that may require embarrassing votes, complicate negotiations with the House, or risk a presidential veto.

The Changing Congress: Filibuster Frustrates Majorities

Going nuclear is a term used in the Senate to describe a strategy for limiting debate on judicial nominations and other matters. In principle, presidential nominations and treaties can be filibustered. If they are, a three-fifths majority is required to invoke cloture in order to get a vote on them. It has been argued that this practice violates the spirit of the Constitution, which provides that the president may make appointments to top executive and judicial positions with "the advice and consent" of the Senate. If the Senate cannot vote on a presidential nomination, the argument goes, it is not meeting its constitutional obligation under the advice and consent clause.

One possible way to address filibusters is to change the cloture rule, perhaps just for certain types of votes, like nominations and treaties. Proposals to change the cloture rule, however, may be filibustered and would themselves require a two-thirds majority to invoke cloture. Senate majorities have therefore looked for more direct means of reining in filibusters, an approach that the media have described as the "nuclear option."

In short, the nuclear option involves a senator raising a point of order that a simple majority can bring a question to a vote, rather than the supermajority typically required to invoke cloture. At that point, the presiding officer makes a ruling either in favor of or opposed to the use of a simple majority threshold. Those opposed to the presiding officer's ruling then appeal that decision. How the process continues from here depends in part on which side was advantaged by the presiding officer's ruling. Nonetheless, this approach turns on the fact that regardless of the presiding officer's initial ruling, there are subsequent, non-debatable (i.e., not subject to a filibuster) steps that ensure a vote by simple majority on the presiding officer's ruling. Thus, the chamber can decide by simple majority whether to dispense with the filibuster, setting a precedent for certain types of votes to occur by simple majority rule.

For years, Senate majorities had threatened that they would execute the nuclear option if minorities did not restrain their use of filibusters. In fact, Senator Nelson Aldrich (R-Rhode Island) advocated using the nuclear option in 1891. In November 2013, however, the Senate finally did go nuclear. The Republican minority had been holding up three of President Obama's nominees to the D.C. Circuit Court of Appeals. When then-Senate Majority Leader Harry Reid (D-Nevada) called up for consideration one of those nominees, Patricia Millett, the Republicans filibustered her nomination. Reid then raised a point of order that the threshold for cloture should be a simple majority on all executive nominees except for those to the Supreme Court. Acting according to the advice of the parliamentarian, the presiding officer, Senator Patrick Leahy (D-Vermont), ruled that the motion was out of order. Reid then appealed his ruling, and fifty-two senators voted against maintaining the supermajority requirement. In so doing, a simple majority of senators undid the filibuster for the consideration of most executive nominees.

To avoid an unanticipated filibuster, Senate floor leaders seek to learn of possible objections to their plans to bring up a bill on the floor. An informal practice has arisen in recent decades that allows senators to register their objections, usually in writing, to floor action on a bill. An objection is known as a "hold." A hold gains its bite when a majority leader refuses to bring up a measure or nomination on which a hold has been placed or when the minority leader indicates his or her objection to the consideration of a measure or nomination on the basis of a hold that has been registered. Since at least the 1970s, holds have been a source of frustration, particularly for majority leaders and bill managers, and rank-and-file senators of both majority and minority parties have voiced concerns about the practice with regularity. Making holds even more frustrating is the practice of keeping secret the identity of the senator placing a hold. Although floor leaders do not always observe holds or confidentiality, the practice is difficult to avoid as long as the majority leader needs unanimous consent to take up measures and wants to avoid filibusters that would make the floor schedule unpredictable for all senators.

The Senate attempted to make holds a matter of public record under a rule adopted in 2011. The new rule requires a senator to disclose a hold "following the objection to a unanimous consent to proceeding to, and, or passage of, a measure or matter on their behalf" by the floor leader. This exceptionally poorly phrased rule goes on to say that the disclosure – a "Notice of Intent to Object" – must be published in the *Congressional Record* within six session days, which was shortened to two days in the 2011 standing order. In other words, a senator is required to have his or her objection to the consideration of a bill published *after* the objection is first exercised by the leader on the floor. The rule is not enforceable without the cooperation of the floor leaders, who continue to have an incentive to accommodate their colleagues. Only a few notices of holds have been published since the new rule was adopted, and senators continue to complain about the frequency of holds.

The modern Senate does not use a committee of the whole. Floor voting can take one of three forms: voice vote, division vote, and roll call vote. Voice and division votes are similar to those in the House, although the Senate very seldom uses division votes. The Senate does not have an electronic voting system, so recorded votes, which can be demanded by eleven senators, are conducted by a name-by-name call of the roll. The vote on final passage of a bill occurs as specified in the unanimous consent agreement or, in the absence of an agreement, whenever senators stop talking about and offering amendments.

RESOLVING DIFFERENCES BETWEEN THE CHAMBERS

The Constitution dictates that the two chambers must approve identical bills before legislation can be sent to the president. This can be accomplished in several ways. One chamber can accept a measure passed by the other. The chambers may exchange amendments until they agree on them, they may agree to hold a conference to resolve matters in dispute and then send the bill back to each chamber for final consideration, or their party leaders may even informally negotiate a

compromise subject to chamber approval. Conference committees have historically been used to resolve differences on the most important and complex legislation, although there has been a decline in their use in recent Congresses (see
Chapter 6 for more discussion).

Members of conference committees, known as conferees, are appointed by the
presiding officers of the two chambers, usually according to the recommendations of standing committee leaders. Committee leaders take into account potential conference committee delegates' seniority, interest in the legislation, and
other factors, and some committees have established traditions concerning who
shall serve on conference committees, which the leaders observe. Conference
committees may be of any size. Except for the large conferences held for budget
measures, the average conference has roughly twenty-four representatives and
twelve senators.

Congressionally Speaking . . .

The Constitution stipulates that the vice president serve as president of the Senate.
The vice president retains an office in the Capitol, may preside over the Senate, and
may cast a vote in the Senate to break a tie. Because recent vice presidents have had a
policy-making role in the administration and travel frequently, they have not used their
Capitol office on a regular basis and have seldom presided over the Senate.

Eleven vice presidents never cast a vote in the Senate. In contrast, George H. W.
Bush, when he was vice president between 1981 and 1989, cast seven votes, and Albert
Gore, vice president under President Bill Clinton, cast two votes in 1993. The record
belongs to John Adams, the first vice president, who cast twenty-nine tie-breaking
votes during the eight-year presidency of George Washington.

Agreements between House and Senate conferees are written up as conference
reports, which must be approved by a majority of each chamber's conferees.
Conference reports must then be approved by majority votes in the House and
Senate. Once approved by both houses, a bill is "enrolled" by being printed on
parchment paper, signed by the Speaker of the House and either the president
(the vice president) or president pro tempore of the Senate.

Conference committees have become less common in recent years, as Figure 7.3
shows. In the 113th Congress (2013–2014) only three conference reports were
filed, down from twenty-nine in the 109th Congress (2005–2006). Stalemate
between a Republican-controlled House and Democratic-controlled Senate
reduced the number of bills passed by both houses. Moreover, the growing
strength of parties in recent Congresses has led party leaders to take a more
prominent role in resolving House-Senate differences and enacting compromises through informal mechanisms or exchange of amendments rather than
through conferences.

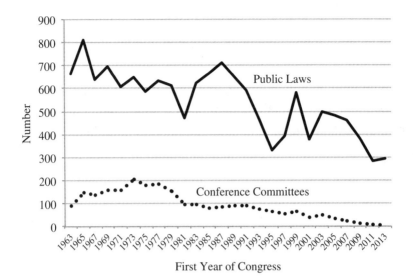

Figure 7.3 The Number of Public Laws and Conference Committees, 1963–2014.

HOUSE AND SENATE RULES COMPARED

The procedures of the House reflect a majoritarian impulse. A simple majority is allowed to take action expeditiously and can do so easily if it is led by the majority party leadership. The House carefully follows established rules and practices, which are quite lengthy. The House makes exceptions to its most important floor procedures by granting and adopting special rules by simple majority vote. Procedures dictating internal committee procedures are elaborate. Debate is carefully limited, and the timing and content of amendments are restricted.

The rules of the Senate are relatively brief. They reflect an egalitarian, individualistic outlook. The right of individuals to debate at length and to offer amendments on any subject is generally protected. Only extraordinary majorities can limit debate or amendments. For reasons of practicality, most scheduling is done by unanimous consent. The majority party usually must negotiate with minority party members to schedule floor action and to bring important measures to a vote. Consequently, Senate decision making is more informal and less efficient than House decision making.

In part, these differences (which are highlighted in Table 7.1) are because of the different sizes of the chambers. The large size of the House requires that its rules more explicitly and stringently limit participation on the floor. Scheduling floor action to suit the needs of individuals is out of the question. In contrast, Senate leaders manipulate the floor schedule through unanimous consent agreements to meet the requests of individual senators. The Senate's smaller size

TABLE 7.1. Major House-Senate differences in rules of practice

House	Senate
Does not allow filibusters	Allows filibusters on most legislation
Has a general rule limiting debate	Has no general rule limiting debate
Bars non-germane amendments	Has no general rule barring non-germane amendments
Uses special rules from the Rules Committee to schedule major legislation for floor action	Relies on unanimous consent agreements to schedule major legislation for floor action
Frequently adopts restrictive special rules to limit the number of amendments and limit debate	Must rely on unanimous consent or cloture to restrict debate and amendments
Uses multiple referral frequently	Rarely uses multiple referral
Committees are not easily circumvented	Committees easily circumvented
Rules permit efficient action without minority party cooperation	Rules do not permit efficient action without minority party cooperation
Considers major legislation in the Committee of the Whole first	Has no Committee of the Whole
Speaker of the House given strong powers by House rules	Presiding officer given little power by Senate rules
Records roll call votes by electronic device	No electronic voting system; roll call votes are tabulated manually

Source: Collected by authors from House and Senate rules.

allows peer pressure to keep obstructionism in check. A senator who objects frequently to unanimous consent requests risks objections to consideration of his or her own bills.

The differences also reflect the unique parliamentary history of each chamber. In their earliest days, the rules of both the House and the Senate contained a previous question motion, a motion to end debate. In modern times, standard parliamentary rules such as *Roberts Rules of Order* provide for a motion that, if passed, forces an immediate debate on the issue before the body. In this way, the previous question motion is a means to bring debate to a close, but in the early Congresses neither chamber used the previous question motion as a tool to end debate. The question took the form of "shall the main question be now put," which was the traditional parliamentary means of putting off discussion on a controversial measure. If the motion failed, discussion was put off; if it passed, discussion continued. The early Senate rarely invoked the motion and eliminated it from its rules in 1806. The House overturned a ruling of the Speaker in 1807 that a successful previous question motion ended debate on a bill, before reversing this precedent in the face of obstruction in 1811. Therefore, from 1811 forward, the House has had an effective means for a majority to end debate on a bill or proposed rule change. In contrast, bound by its lack of a previous question motion, the Senate has never been able to develop an efficient means of ending debate.

The previous question motion played a pivotal role in the development of House and Senate rules. With the previous question motion, House majority parties could get a vote on new rules they wanted adopted. Senate majority parties faced minority filibusters when they proposed rules that advantaged the majority. Consequently, House majority parties have regularly modified and elaborated on their chamber's rules, whereas Senate majority parties seldom seek, let alone achieve, a change in their chamber's rules. The result is that modern House rules are considerably longer than Senate rules. When it has been determined that some limitation on debate is desirable, as for budget measures and trade agreements, special provisions have been written for the Senate to guarantee that debate could be closed. This has happened only when supermajorities favor the change and often has happened as a part of a much larger legislative package.

Not until 1917, 111 years after the Senate dropped the previous question motion from its rules, did the Senate again adopt a rule that provided a means for closing debate. Rule XXII allowed an extraordinary majority to invoke cloture – that is, to force an end to debate. The 1917 rule required the support of two-thirds of the senators present and voting to invoke cloture. The 1975 reform of the rule changed the required majority to three-fifths of all elected senators (60 votes with 100 elected senators), except for matters affecting the Senate's rules, which are subject to a two-thirds majority of elected senators. As a result, a fairly broad base of support is still required to bring a rules change to a vote in the Senate.

Congressionally Speaking . . .

An *engrossed bill* is the final version of a bill passed by one house, including any amendments that may have been approved, as certified by the clerk of the House or the secretary of the Senate.

An *enrolled bill* is the final version of a bill as approved by both houses, printed on parchment, certified by either the clerk of the House or the secretary of the Senate (depending on the house that first passed it), and signed by the Speaker of the House and the president pro tempore of the Senate; it has a space for the signature of the president.

AUTHORIZING AND APPROPRIATING

Under congressional rules, most federal government programs are subject to two types of legislation: authorization bills and appropriations bills. Theoretically, an authorization bill sets the program's organization, rules, and spending ceiling, and an appropriations bill provides the money. House and Senate rules require that an authorization bill creating a federal program or agency be passed before an appropriations bill that provides spending authority for it can be adopted. The authorization bill and the appropriations bill for each program or set of programs both follow the standard legislative process. For most programs, a new appropriations bill must be approved each year.

For example, suppose proponents of a bill that creates a new financial aid program for college students managed to get the measure enacted into law. They would have taken the bill through the House Committee on Education and the Workforce and the Senate Committee on Health, Education, Labor, and Pensions. The bill would specify how the program was to be organized, how financial aid decisions were to be made, and how much – say $400 million – could be spent, at most, on the program in any one year. It is likely that the bill would authorize the program for a specific period of time – say, four or five years. A separate appropriations bill, which would include spending authority for the new program, must be passed before the program could begin operations. The House and the Senate Appropriations Committees might decide that only $250 million should be spent on the program. If the House and Senate went along with the lower figure, the program would be limited to a $250 million budget for the next year.

In the modern Congress, jurisdiction over authorization legislation is fragmented among many standing committees. Jurisdiction over appropriations is consolidated in one appropriations committee in each chamber, although each of the Appropriations Committees has thirteen subcommittees that do most of the work. Jurisdiction over taxes, the major source of federal revenue, falls to one tax-writing committee in each house: the House Committee on Ways and Means and the Senate Committee on Finance. Therefore, power over fiscal policy is not only shared among the House, the Senate, and the president, it is shared among the various committees within the House and Senate as well.

A Major Glitch

In 2008, the House and Senate passed the conference report to an important farm bill in identical form. President George W. Bush vetoed the bill and returned it to the House, with everyone unaware that Title III, which concerns international trade, had not been included in the papers sent to the president. The omission of the title from the fifteen-title bill was made by the enrolling clerk of the House in the rush to complete action on the renewal of farm programs before they expired. No one in the administration reported the missing title when the bill was vetoed. The error was not discovered and reported to the House leadership until the day of the veto-override vote. Minority party members complained, but the House and Senate proceeded to override the veto. To clarify the status of Title III, the two houses repassed the farm bill with all titles in their proper place, the president vetoed the new bill, and the House and Senate again overrode the veto.

The system creates tensions among congressional committees. Tax committees do not like to pass bills increasing taxes to cover spending that other committees have authorized. Authorizing committees often dislike the handiwork of the appropriations committees. A small appropriation can defeat the purpose of the original authorization bill. In response, authorizing committees have pursued a number of tactics, such as including provisions for permanent appropriations for some programs (Social Security is one), to avoid the appropriations process.

Provisions limiting the length of authorizations are known as *sunset provisions*. In principle, sunset provisions force the authorizing committee and Congress to repass authorization legislation periodically, which compels the executive branch to justify the continuation of the programs and gives the authorizing committees additional influence over the executive agencies. In recent years, many authorizations have expired, but the programs have not died – sometimes out of neglect but often because of conflict over the program. Welfare reform, college student financial aid, and federal highway programs are among the dozens of unauthorized programs in recent years. These programs can continue as long as Congress passes their separate appropriations bills. An appropriation is possible by use of a waiver of the House rule, which may be included in the special rule under which the appropriations bills are considered on the House floor. A consequence of this practice is that the authorizing committees do not realize the special influence over the direction of these programs that was expected when the sunset provisions were first enacted.

EVOLUTION OF THE LEGISLATIVE PROCESS

For most of the twentieth century, nearly all major and minor legislative measures have followed the path of the standard processes described in this chapter. The House and Senate were always free to modify their processes and have sometimes handled a bill in a special way. In the last three decades of the twentieth century, nonstandard approaches to preparing legislation for a vote were employed with increasing frequency. Bypassing committees, negotiating details in summits between congressional leaders and representatives of the president, having multiple committees consider bills, and drafting omnibus bills characterize the action on a large share of major legislation considered by recent Congresses. In fact, according to one survey of the processes used by the House and Senate on major legislation since the late 1980s, four out of five measures in the House and two out of three in the Senate were considered under some nonstandard procedure.

Unorthodox legislative procedures have been invented for many reasons. The sheer complexity of some new public policies and legislative measures forces action by many committees. Committee and party leaders are compelled to find new ways to piece together legislation, negotiating a bewildering array of technical provisions and working with the president to avoid a veto. The reforms of the 1970s – which strengthened the House Speaker's procedural options and

reduced the power of full committee chairs – were discovered to have unanticipated uses. Perhaps most important, partisan maneuvering stimulated procedural
innovations as one party and then the other sought parliamentary advantages
when pushing legislation.

Furthermore, both chambers of Congress often devise new rules in response to
new challenges. In some instances, the House and Senate have tailored their procedures to particular kinds of legislation or specific issues. In the past two decades,
for example, Congress has created "fast-track" procedures for considering trade
agreements negotiated by the executive branch with foreign governments. These
procedures limit debate and bar amendments in order to speed congressional approval and limit congressional second-guessing of executive branch decisions.

An even more important class of legislation that has inspired special procedures
concerns fiscal policy: decisions about federal spending, taxing, and budget deficits
and surpluses. The Congressional Budget and Impoundment Control Act of 1974,
often known simply as the Budget Act of 1974, established a process to coordinate
congressional decision making that affects fiscal policy. In the 1980s and early
1990s, skyrocketing federal deficits motivated Congress to set tight rules constrain-
ing fiscal choices and to adopt unique procedures for enforcing the new constraints.

In other cases, special procedures are invented for an individual bill. In the
House, special rules governing floor debate have become more complex, as have
the provisions of unanimous consent agreements in the Senate. Task forces, usually appointed by party leaders, have become an everyday part of decision making in the House. Intercommittee negotiations guided by party leaders sometimes
occur after committees report but before legislation is taken to the floor. In these
ways, the traditional committee-to-floor-to-conference process has become a
less accurate description of the increasingly meandering route that major legislation takes through the modern Congress.

CONCLUSION

Rules matter. Legislative rules, whether they arise from the Constitution or elsewhere, determine procedural advantages among the players, factions, and parties
that compete for control over public policy. The rules also are the foundation
of Congress's major organizational features, such as its leadership positions and
committees, which help the institution manage a large and diverse workload and
are generally designed to serve the political needs of its members.

The House and Senate have evolved to have quite different rules. Compared
with Senate rules, House rules make it more difficult to circumvent committees,
more strictly limit participation on the floor, and give the majority a greater
ability to act when confronted with an obstructionist minority. The House is
more majoritarian; the Senate is more egalitarian. The House is more committee
oriented; the Senate is more floor oriented.

But the rules do not determine the political and policy objectives of legislators. Those objectives are primarily the product of the electoral processes through which people are selected to serve in Congress. Campaigns and elections connect members to their constituencies and lead many members to take a local, sometimes quite parochial, outlook in legislative politics.

SUGGESTED READINGS

A.   The following readings provide useful background on congressional procedures and recent changes in practices.

Oleszek, Walter J. *Congressional Procedures and the Policy Process.* 8th ed. Washington, DC: CQ Press, 2010.

Sinclair, Barbara. *Unorthodox Lawmaking: New Legislative Processes in the U.S. Congress.* 2nd ed. Washington, DC: Congressional Quarterly Press, 2000.

Tiefer, Charles. *Congressional Practice and Procedure.* Westport, CT: Greenwood Press, 1989.

B.   The following readings provide detail on the development of parliamentary procedures in the House of Representatives.

Bach, Stanley, and Steven S. Smith. *Managing Uncertainty in the House of Representatives: Adaptation and Innovation in Special Rules.* Washington, DC: Brookings Institution Press, 1988.

Binder, Sarah. *Minority Rights, Majority Rule: Partisanship and the Development of Congress.* Cambridge: Cambridge University Press, 1997.

C.   The following readings provide useful background on the development of parliamentary procedures in the Senate.

Binder, Sarah, and Steven S. Smith. *Politics or Principle? Filibustering in the United States Senate.* Washington, DC: Brookings Institution Press, 1997.

Smith, Steven S. *The Senate Syndrome: The Evolution of Procedural Warfare in the Modern Senate.* Norman: University of Oklahoma Press, 2013.

DISCUSSION QUESTIONS

1   What are the major differences in the legislative processes of the House and Senate?

2   How are committees circumvented in the House and Senate?

3   What is a "special rule" in the House? What is the importance of a special rule to the majority party?

4   What is a "filibuster" in the Senate? How is it overcome? What is the importance of a filibuster to the minority and majority?

8 The Floor and Voting

The electronic tally board is illuminated in the U.S. House of Representatives to count the votes of the members.

When the gavel fell late on the evening of Tuesday, January 1, 2013, the House had passed H.R. 8, the American Taxpayer Relief Act, otherwise known as the "fiscal cliff" deal. Despite intensive negotiations, the preceding months had failed to produce a workable agreement between the parties. Failure to reach a deal by the January 1 deadline would result in the expiration of the tax cuts passed during the administration of President George W. Bush and the activation of punishing automatic spending cuts agreed to by Congress and President Obama in 2011. As the month of December was coming to a close, it appeared that Speaker John Boehner (R-Ohio) would be unable to hammer out a deal capable of satisfying both his fellow Republicans and the administration. Many House Republicans were simply unwilling to accept a bill that included income tax raises of any sort, even on the wealthiest Americans. In fact, Boehner was forced to pull his own proposal from the House floor on December 20, 2012 – a proposal that called for tax hikes on incomes greater than $1 million – because of a lack of support from within his party. Consequently, a frustrated Boehner left the task of structuring an agreement to Senate Minority Leader Mitch McConnell (R-Kentucky). On the eve of the fiscal cliff deadline, McConnell and Vice President Joe Biden struck a deal that would temporarily ward off the fiscal cliff. In the early hours of January 1, the Senate passed the bill with broad bipartisan support. Many House Republicans, however, were unhappy with the Senate bill. Republican leaders spent hours counting votes and considering the possibility of amending the bill and sending it back to the Senate. Of course, returning an amended bill to the Senate, where it would be subject to a filibuster – the very feature that had proven to be an obstacle to reaching a deal – was far from desirable. At one point, Boehner was heard on the floor saying, "Am I having a nightmare, or what?" In the end, House Republican leaders opted against amending the bill. It subsequently cleared the House by a vote of 257 to 167, despite lacking the support of a majority of Republicans. The uneasy agreement reached by Congress and the president marked the end of a months-long legislative and political struggle.

Although the events leading up to this House vote were dramatic, there was little real doubt as to the outcome of the vote once the bill was brought to the floor. All of the deals had been struck, and the votes had been counted and recounted. In this sense, the proceedings were choreographed and the bill's passage a fait accompli. This is not unusual, as both the House and Senate have developed elaborate committee and party systems that can take much of the policy-making process, deliberation, and compromising off the chamber floors and into more private settings.

During most of Congress's history, responsibility for the details of public policy rested with the standing committees. At times, power over the details of important bills resided in the hands of central party leaders. Most scholars have used this continuum – from decentralized, committee-oriented decision making to centralized, party-oriented decision making – to characterize the decision-making processes and distribution of power within the two chambers. Everything that goes on within the House and Senate is formally subject to the approval of the parent chambers in floor sessions. In principle, the details of all legislation could be written and reviewed on the chamber floors, but in modern practice this rarely happens.

These alternatives are depicted in Table 8.1. If important decisions were made on the chamber floor, all members, in that one place, would have the opportunity to participate effectively in deliberations on all measures. In general, as we saw in Chapter 6, the modern House is more dependent on committees than is the Senate. There have been times, however, when central party leaders

TABLE 8.1. Possible patterns of congressional decision making

Number of units	Number of effective participants	
	Few	Many
Few	Centralized (party leadership)	Collegial (floor)
Many		Decentralized (committees)

dominated the House. Therefore, the House is often characterized as varying along the centralized–decentralized continuum. The Senate is more collegial – more likely to make detailed policy choices on the floor. Both committees and party leaders are important in the Senate, but relative to the House, the Senate has long been far more floor oriented. Neither committees nor party leaders have found the Senate floor predictable or controllable. These differences are obvious every day in the Capitol.

In this chapter, we report on a typical day on the House and Senate floors and explain how differences in floor procedure shape the distribution of power in the two chambers. In addition, the chapter reviews how members' records of floor voting are most commonly analyzed by political scientists, journalists, and interest groups, providing a "consumer's guide" to studies of floor voting. The chapter concludes with a review of the factors that influence the relationship among the parties, the committees, and the floor.

A TYPICAL DAY ON THE HOUSE AND SENATE FLOORS

On a February day in 2013, a fairly typical day when Congress is in session, dozens of committees and subcommittees held morning meetings and hearings in the congressional office buildings while clerks and pages prepared for the opening of the House and Senate floor sessions. In the Senate, this meant distributing various documents to individual senator's desks, which are arranged by party (when facing the front, Democrats are on the left and Republicans are on the right) and seniority (junior members are in the back). In the House, members do not have desks or assigned seats, although, by tradition, the Democrats sit on the left and the Republicans on the right. As the clerks and pages went about their work, tourists went in and out of the galleries, some disappointed that they did not have a chance to see a debate before they hurried off to other sites in Washington. As usual, the Senate session opened before the House session – the Senate at 10:00 AM and the House at 12:00 PM. Prior to the start of its session, the House met for morning hour debates at 10:00 AM . Morning hour debates are an opportunity for members to speak on a wide variety of topics. Members who make advanced arrangements with their party leaders may speak during this period for up to five minutes. Since 2011, morning hour speeches can be held Monday through Thursday, two hours before the beginning of the regular session.

The Day in the House

The House session began when Speaker John Boehner (R-Ohio) assumed the chair. The Speaker does not always preside over House proceedings. Instead, the Speaker frequently appoints other members (Speakers pro tempore) to take his or her place presiding over the House so that the Speaker can conduct business elsewhere. Typically, several members will preside during the course of the day. On this day, Speaker Boehner passed the gavel to Speaker pro tempore Virginia Foxx (R-North Carolina) soon after the opening of the House session.

The session opened with a prayer from Archbishop Emeritus John Quinn of the Diocese of San Francisco, California. The Speaker then announced that he had examined the *Journal* Journal of the House and stated his approval of it. Approval of the *Journal* previously required a vote of the House, but dilatory requests for votes led House Democrats to push through a rule allowing the Speaker to approve the *Journal*. A member may still demand a vote on the *Journal*, but that vote may be postponed until late in the day. Next came the Pledge of Allegiance, which has been recited since 1989. The practice was started the year the Supreme Court ruled that burning the American flag was constitutionally protected speech, and Congress responded with legislation to ban flag burning. House Republicans proposed – and the Democrats did not dare block – a House rule that required that the Pledge be recited after the prayer. After the Pledge, led by Representative Gene Green (D-Texas), Representative Anna Eshoo (D-California) welcomed Archbishop Quinn to the House and gave a brief speech on Quinn's life and accomplishments. The floor session was televised (see box "The Changing Congress: Televising the House and Senate").

The Changing Congress: Televising the House and Senate

The House began televising its floor sessions in 1979. After becoming somewhat jealous of the attention given to the House, the Senate began to televise its sessions in 1986. Congressional employees operate both television systems, and the signal is made available to television networks and individual stations via satellite.

Floor proceedings are carried live on C-SPAN, the Cable-Satellite Public Affairs Network. Most cable television systems carry C-SPAN I, on which House sessions are shown. Many cable systems also carry C-SPAN II, where Senate sessions are broadcast. Many committee hearings, press conferences, and other public affairs programs are shown on C-SPAN when the House and Senate are not in session.

In both chambers, the most obvious consequence of television coverage has been an increase in floor speeches. In the House, one-minute and special-order speeches have become more numerous. One-minute speeches are made at the beginning of the day for about half an hour. Special-order speeches are made after the House finishes its regular business for the day. In 1994, House Democratic and Republican leaders agreed that special-order speeches should be limited to four hours on most days. They also began to experiment with structured, Oxford-style debates. In 1995, "reaction shots" of members on the floor were limited after members complained about being caught in unflattering shots by the floor cameras.

The Senate created a new class of speeches, the aforementioned special-order speeches, which are limited to five minutes. In addition, representatives and senators have made increasing use of large poster charts and graphs to illustrate their points for the television audience. Many senators now also address their chamber from the back row, some distance from their personal desks, so that the camera angle will be less steep and, in the case of male senators, will not expose their bald spots to home viewers.

The Speaker pro tempore announced that up to fifteen members of each party would be recognized to give one-minute speeches. The reservation of time for one-minute speeches gives legislators a brief period to address the House and the nation on any matter they choose. Frequently, members use one-minute speeches to respond to the news of the day, and they often use the opportunity to compliment or criticize the president. Occasionally, a group of members will organize themselves to emphasize a particular theme – and being outrageous or flamboyant increases the chance of getting on the evening news. On this day, there was a mix of speeches; some concerned the impending sequestration, the decaying American infrastructure, and strengthening the middle class, whereas others concerned less controversial topics, such as commending Gainesville, Georgia, for its track record in job creation.

Congressionally Speaking . . .

On the House floor, members engage in a carefully scripted language when debating. When a bill manager wishes to speak about a bill on the floor, he or she will say, "I yield myself such time as I may consume." If another member wishes to interject into the debate, he or she will say, "Will the gentleman [gentlewoman] yield?" If the member holding the floor wishes to yield, he or she will say in return, "I yield two minutes [or another block of time] to the gentleman [gentlewoman] from New Hampshire [the member's state]." The interjecting member will then say, "I thank the gentleman [gentlewoman] for yielding. I rise in support/opposition . . ." Once he or she has concluded, he or she may say, "I yield back the balance of my time." The bill manager will then begin his or her speech again with "Reclaiming my time . . ." This back and forth between floor managers and other members continues until the time allotted for debate is consumed.[1]

1 Information taken from "Pocket Guide to Common Parliamentary Phrases in the House of Representatives," Congressional Research Service.

After roughly twenty minutes of one-minute speeches, the Speaker pro tempore recognized Representative Lou Barletta (R-Pennsylvania), who offered a motion to suspend the rules and pass H.R. 592 to amend the Robert T. Stafford Disaster Relief and Emergency Assistance Act. The House often considers minor or relatively noncontroversial measures under the suspension procedure. This procedure limits debate to forty minutes (twenty minutes for each party) and prohibits amendments to the underlying measure. Suspending the rules and passing the bill occur simultaneously if two-thirds of the chamber agrees. In this case, the bill amended the Robert T. Stafford Disaster Relief and Emergency Assistance Act to make community centers, including tax-exempt houses of worship, eligible for federal funds in the aftermath of a major disaster. At the completion of debate, Speaker pro tempore Foxx brought the floor to a vote on passage, stating that "[t]he question is on the motion offered by the gentleman from Pennsylvania (Mr. Barletta) that the House suspend the rules and pass the bill, H.R. 592." Foxx proceeded to hear the yeas and nays and announced that "in the opinion of the chair" two-thirds had voted in the affirmative. Representative Barletta rose to request a recorded vote, which was granted, as it customarily is. The bill cleared the chamber by a final vote of 354 to 72.

As the day progressed, the House also passed a bill under suspension of the rules to improve hydropower efficiency. Other activities of the House this day included speeches paying tribute to praiseworthy individuals, the election of some members to standing committees, and a one-hour debate on gun violence prevention. The House adjourned at 7:21 PM until 10:00 AM the next morning.

The Changing Congress: The Congressional Record

The proceedings of the House and Senate are published daily in the *Congressional Record*. The *Record* is printed overnight and distributed to Capitol Hill and many other places, including most large libraries. Hardcover, permanent editions are published and distributed periodically.

The *Record* is much more than a report of the words spoken on the chamber floors. Introduced bills, committee meetings, and many other items are listed in the *Record* each day. The texts of bills and conference reports considered on the floor is included, as are the many newspaper articles, scholarly studies, executive agency reports, and other items that members place in the *Record* by gaining unanimous consent of their house. As a general rule, the charts or graphs that members use on the floor cannot be printed in the *Record*, although tabular material may be inserted if the member receives unanimous consent.

The members' ability to alter prose reported in the *Record* after they have spoken has long been a controversial issue. Members are allowed to make nonsubstantive grammatical changes in their prose. As a result, some members appear far more articulate in the *Record* than they do on the floor. Statements and other insertions in the *Record* are supposed to be distinguished by a bullet (•). In the Senate, members frequently seek, and then always receive, unanimous consent to have their statements placed in the *Record* "as though read." Such revision makes distinguishing what was said from what was inserted nearly impossible. Frequently, senators request that their statements be included "at the appropriate place," which is usually done so that the statement does not interrupt the discussion on a pending matter in the *Record*.

The *Congressional Record* tends to be a more faithful record of House proceedings than of Senate proceedings. Representatives frequently seek permission to "revise and extend" their remarks, so many statements reported in the *Record* were not actually read on the floor. The House has more restrictive rules about including extraneous matter and speeches in the *Record* and requires that newspaper articles and other insertions be printed in a separate section, "Extensions of Remarks." The House also has long required that revisions or extensions that are not "a substantially verbatim" account be distinguished by a different typeface. The House adopted an even tighter rule in 1995 that limits changes to corrections of grammar and typographical errors.

The Day in the Senate

The Senate convened at 10:00 AM when Senator Heidi Heitkamp (D–North Dakota) called the Senate to order. The vice president is the president of the Senate but tends to preside only at ceremonial occasions (e.g., when the oath of office is administered to newly elected senators at the start of a Congress) and when a tie-breaking vote might be needed. The Constitution provides for a president pro tempore to preside in the absence of the vice president. However, the president pro tempore, who by tradition is the most senior member of the majority party, is not able to preside on a full-time basis because of other duties. Consequently, the president pro tempore's staff arranges for other majority party senators, usually the most junior ones, to take turns presiding over the Senate.

On this day, following a prayer and the Pledge of Allegiance, Senator Heitkamp requested that the clerk read a letter from the president pro tempore, Senator Patrick Leahy (D–Vermont), appointing Heitkamp as acting president pro tempore. Senator Harry Reid (D–Nevada), the majority leader, was then recognized and detailed the schedule for the day, which included one hour of "morning business" and consideration of the nomination of Judge William J. Kayatta to the First Circuit. Despite the name, "morning business" does not necessarily occur in the morning. During morning business, the Senate conducts routine tasks, such as receiving messages from the House and the president, as well as receiving petitions and memorials, committee reports, and bill introductions.

Prior to the morning remarks, Senator Reid and Senator Mitch McConnell (R–Kentucky), the minority leader, were recognized to speak, and both offered commentary on President Obama's State of the Union Address given the night before. During the period of morning business that followed, senators spoke on the economy and on for-profit schools, and made additional comments on the president's address. Senator David Vitter (R–Louisiana) also asked for unanimous consent to enter into a colloquy, or debate, with Senator Jeff Sessions (R–Alabama) about the topic of immigration reform. The order of business in the Senate is often subject to changes and interruptions for unanimous consent requests.

Unlike in the House, the Senate's presiding officer does not have the power to preempt a member's request by denying him or her the floor. Thus, the Senate often sees multiple requests for unanimous consent to give speeches or consider noncontroversial measures throughout the day. This flexibility in scheduling is a key distinction between the House and Senate. On this day, the Senate would return to morning business, by unanimous consent, on a number of occasions to give senators an opportunity to comment on a wide variety of topics, ranging from a tribute to General Chuck Yaeger to the fiscal challenges facing the nation.

Following the first period of morning business, the Senate moved to executive session for consideration of the Kayatta nomination. The Senate holds executive sessions, as part of the daily session, to consider treaties, nominations, and other business received from the president. The Senate does this to fulfill its constitutional responsibility to provide its "advice and consent." Unlike some other pending nominations at the time, there was broad support for Kayatta's nomination. First to speak on Kayatta's behalf was Senator Susan Collins (R-Maine), from his home state of Maine. Following Collins's speech, the Senate Judiciary chairman, Senator Patrick Leahy, took the floor to offer remarks in support of Kayatta's nomination. The Senate then voted on the question – Will the Senate advise and consent to the nomination of William J. Kayatta, Jr., of Maine, to be U.S. circuit judge for the First Circuit? – and approved the nomination by a vote of eighty-eight to twelve.

Congressionally Speaking . . .

On the Senate floor, *quorum calls* are used to get a temporary break in the action – a time-out. A senator might say, "Mr. President, I suggest the absence of a quorum," and the presiding officer will respond, "The clerk will call the roll." Technically, if a quorum is not discovered, the Senate will have to adjourn. In fact, filibustering senators sometimes note the absence of a quorum to force senators to appear on the floor. Most of the time, however, a quorum call is used as a time-out that gives absent senators time to come to the floor to offer an amendment or speak. At other times, a quorum call is used to give leaders time to work out agreements on issues or procedure.

Later this day, the Senate returned to executive session to tend to procedural matters relating to the nomination of Charles Hagel to be secretary of defense. Majority Leader Reid took the floor to announce that, after speaking with Senator James Inhofe (R-Oklahoma), ranking member of the Senate Armed Services Committee, it was clear that the parties were at an impasse over Hagel's nomination. As a result, Reid filed a cloture motion with the clerk, to be considered the following Friday. By Senate rules, the cloture motion cannot be considered until the second day of session after it was filed. After several speeches were heard regarding the Hagel nomination, intermixed with speeches on other topics, the Senate then confirmed by unanimous consent the nominations of several high-ranking military officials.

As a final order of business this day, Senator Richard Blumenthal (D-Connecticut) moved for the consideration of several noncontroversial resolutions by unanimous consent. The resolutions addressed such matters as recognizing the significance of Black History Month, extending congratulations to the North Dakota State University football team, and commemorating the 150th anniversaries of Emporia State University and Kansas State University. The resolutions were approved en bloc (simultaneously). After dispensing of the resolutions, the Senate adjourned for the day at 6:46 PM.

House–Senate Differences

The events of this day illustrate many of the differences between the two chambers of Congress. Most of the differences are the by-product of one fact: Floor debate and amendments are governed by strict rules in the House but are generally limited only by unanimous consent agreements or supermajority votes in the Senate. Representatives must worry that their floor amendments might not be put in order by a special rule from the Rules Committee. Once a bill is on the House floor, representatives are compelled to conform to the schedule laid out by the Speaker and the special rules. In sharp contrast, senators can introduce amendments freely,

Speaker John Boehner (R-Ohio) signs the Keystone XL Pipeline Approval Act during a ceremony in the Capitol's Rayburn Room, as *from left,* House Majority Whip Steve Scalise (R-Louisiana), Senate Majority Leader Mitch McConnell (R-Kentucky), Senator John Hoeven (R-North Dakota), House Majority Leader Kevin McCarthy (R-California), and Representative Kristi Noem (R-South Dakota), look on, February 13, 2015.

even on subjects unrelated to the bill at hand, and protect their ability to do so by objecting to requests for unanimous consent to limit amendments. Moving the Senate from amendment to amendment and from bill to bill is a constant struggle for the majority leader and bill managers. The House has a schedule that is followed in the main; scheduling in the Senate is often much like fortune-telling.

VOTING PROCEDURE

By the end of that February day in 2013, the House had held two recorded votes, all using its computerized voting system. The Senate held one recorded vote confirming Kayatta. When the Senate conducts a roll call vote, the process is time-consuming. It is an old-fashioned roll call for which a clerk calls out the individual names of the senators in alphabetical order ("Mr. Alexander . . . Ms. Ayotte . . . Ms. Baldwin . . . Mr. Barrasso . . ." and so on) and waits for senators to arrive on the floor and respond. After calling all of the names, the roll call clerk starts from the beginning to call the names of senators who have not voted. The clerk is then interrupted by senators as they appear during the vote to recognize them and hear their votes. The Constitution provides that "the Yeas and Nays of the Members of either House on any question shall, at the desire of one-fifth of those present, be entered upon the Journal." This rule means that twenty senators or eighty-seven representatives (if all members are present) may demand a vote in which each member's vote is recorded. In practice, with few members being present, usually only eleven senators or forty-four representatives are required – one-fifth of a quorum, which is half of the membership of the chamber. Because the quorum requirement is not enforced unless a member makes a point of order that a quorum is not present, the presiding officer will assume that a quorum is present and order the yeas and nays based on the lower threshold. Under the rules of the House, twenty-five members may demand a recorded vote in the Committee of the Whole, where most votes on amendments to bills take place. The Constitution does not specify how the houses should vote in the absence of a demand for the yeas and nays.

House Voting Procedure

In today's Congress, the House votes by three means: voice vote, division vote, and recorded vote. On most motions, the presiding officer (the chair of the Committee of the Whole or the Speaker) first asks for a voice vote. He or she might say, "The question is on the amendment by the gentlewoman from Illinois. All in favor say 'aye,' all opposed say 'no.' The noes have it, and the amendment is rejected." In many cases, this is spoken so rapidly that it is obvious that the number voting each way had little to do with the announcement of the winning side. Sometimes, the issue is not controversial, and the presiding officer is merely reporting the obvious result. In other cases, the presiding officer knows that his or her announcement will make no difference because a member will demand a recorded vote on the issue.

The division, or standing, vote is used little and is virtually never decisive. Any member may demand such a vote, which is conducted by having members voting "aye" stand and be counted and then having members voting "no" stand and be counted. Only the vote tally – the number of ayes and noes – is recorded. Because few members are on the floor for debate on most matters, the result usually shows that less than a quorum of members is present (a quorum is 100 or more in the Committee of the Whole), which leads automatically to a recorded vote. Consequently, this method is seldom used.

Recorded votes are conducted with the assistance of an electronic voting system and nearly always occur upon the demand of the necessary number of members after a voice vote. In the Committee of the Whole, twenty-five members must demand a recorded vote. (The Constitution's requirement that one-fifth of those present demand a recorded vote applies only to requests for recorded votes in the House, not in the Committee of the Whole.)

Each member is issued a voting card about the size of a credit card. To vote, a member uses his or her card in any one of the nearly forty voting boxes scattered around the House chamber (most are attached to the back of the chamber's benchlike seats). With the card inserted, the member presses one of three buttons – yea, nay, or present – and his or her vote is recorded by the computer system. As the votes are cast, they are displayed on panels above the gallery at the front of the chamber, and the running totals can be viewed on computer terminals. Under the House rules, recorded votes take minutes, although the presiding officer often holds the vote open a little longer to allow members to make it to the floor and cast their votes. On a few occasions, the Speaker has held open the vote for several minutes to find the last vote or two his or her side needs to win. The rules do permit the Speaker to postpone votes – to "stack" votes is the jargon used – in some circumstances, such as votes on motions to suspend the rules and pass a measure. Stacked votes are cast in rapid succession in periods of five minutes each, usually near the end of a session, to allow members to vote on several matters without having to make multiple trips back and forth between their offices and the House floor. By the way, the record for the number of recorded votes cast without missing one belongs to Representative William Natcher (D-Kentucky), who cast 18,401 consecutive votes over twenty-two years before he became ill and died in 1994.

Senate Voting Procedure

The Senate, too, has voice, division, and recorded votes, but virtually no division votes are cast in the Senate because of its smaller size. On voice and recorded votes, Senate practice is quite different from House practice. On many, perhaps most, "votes," the Senate does not really vote at all. The presiding officer often brings a matter to a vote when debate appears to have ended by saying, "Hearing no further debate, and without objection, the amendment is agreed to." In this way, even the pretense of a voice vote is not observed in the Senate. Because recorded roll call votes are often ordered in advance, after the successful demand of a senator, no preliminary voice vote is held, as in the House.

Recorded votes in the Senate are properly called roll call votes. The names of the senators are called out, one by one, by a clerk, and senators' responses are recorded by hand. Roll call votes are supposed to take only fifteen minutes, as stipulated by a unanimous consent agreement that the majority leader arranges at the beginning of each Congress. Many, if not most, Senate roll call votes last longer than fifteen minutes, however, to accommodate senators who need more time to make it to the floor. At times, these delays have become so burdensome that majority leaders have promised to insist that the fifteen-minute limit be observed, but the desire to accommodate colleagues seems so overwhelming that votes extending to twenty minutes or more remain common. Former Senator Robert Byrd (D-West Virginia) cast more than 18,680 roll call votes in his fifty-one-year career in the Senate (1959–2010) – a Senate record. Senator Chuck Grassley (R-Iowa) currently holds the record for most time served without missing a vote – his last missed vote was in mid-1993.

The Changing Congress: Long Votes Lead to Controversy

On November 23, 2003, the House of Representatives passed a prescription drug benefit for senior citizens under the Medicare program. Debate on the bill had continued until 3:00 AM at which time presiding officer Richard Hastings (R-Washington) announced that the House would have a fifteen-minute vote. At the end of fifteen minutes, the bill was losing by fifteen votes, and after one hour, the tally stood at 216 to 218. By most accounts, then-Speaker Dennis Hastert (R-Illinois) was resigned to the fact that the bill would fail, but he, along with then-Majority Leader Tom DeLay (R-Texas) and others, continued to try to convince recalcitrant Republicans to vote for the bill. At 5:00 AM, then-President Bush was awakened to begin calling wayward members. The combination of his encouragement and other persuasive activities was enough to secure victory. Democrats cried foul and called for reform. After gaining a majority in the House following the 2006 elections, Democrats enacted a rule banning holding a vote open for the "sole purpose of reversing the outcome."

The new rule did not prevent the Democrats from becoming ensnared in their own controversy over vote outcomes in August 2007 on a motion to recommit. Republicans charged that the vote count was reported incorrectly and that the vote had been closed while members were still trying to change their vote. A Select Committee on Voting Irregularities agreed and urged the House to repeal the apparently unenforceable rule on holding votes open. The House followed the committee's recommendation by striking this language from the House rules at the outset of the 111th Congress (2009–2010).

Changes in Floor Decision Making

On the surface, it might seem that the differences in voting procedures between the two chambers matter little. The record suggests otherwise. House voting procedures changed in the early 1970s – and with important consequences. As earlier chapters have discussed, the early 1970s was a period of remarkable transformation in House politics. Power devolved from full committee chairs to subcommittee chairs, many of whom were inexperienced as bill managers. Personal and subcommittee staffs were growing, which enabled more members to design and promote their own legislation. Additionally, a new breed of member – more media oriented and more insistent on having a meaningful role – seemed to be flooding into Congress. In this context, the House changed its voting rules in such a way that encouraged members to pursue floor amendments more frequently and more actively.

The House voting reforms had two components. First, a new rule extended recorded voting to the Committee of the Whole. Before 1971, no recorded votes took place in the House's Committee of the Whole, where action on floor amendments takes place. That meant that members' positions on most floor amendments also were not recorded. As is still the case, a roll call vote could be demanded on amendments approved in the Committee of the Whole just before the vote on final passage of the bill, but rejected amendments could not be considered again.

Second, the electronic voting system was used for the first time in 1973. Voting "by electronic device," as they call it in the House, nearly completely replaced the old system of teller voting in the Committee of the Whole and the traditional call of the roll in the House. Teller voting was done by having members pass by tellers (members appointed to do the counting), with the yes voters to one side and the no voters to the other. The 1971 reform allowed recorded teller voting, in which members signed green (yes) or red (no) cards, deposited them in a box, and then waited for tellers to count them and turn them over to clerks, who would record each member's individual vote. This cumbersome process discouraged recorded voting in the Committee of the Whole. Automated vote counting by the electronic system allowed both the Committee of the Whole and the House to complete a vote and have the results in fifteen minutes.

Electronic recorded voting produced a surge in amending activity. Being able to put one's position on a particular issue on the record (and forcing one's opponents to do the same) created new incentives to offer amendments, particularly for the minority party. Electronic voting also reduced the burden imposed on colleagues by demands for recorded votes. The result, as Figure 8.1 illustrates, was an increase in the number of floor votes in the House, most noticeably on amendments, beginning in the first Congress (the 93rd, 1973–1974) that used both electronic and recorded voting in the Committee of the Whole. The fact that we do not see an analogous increase in floor votes in the Senate at this time

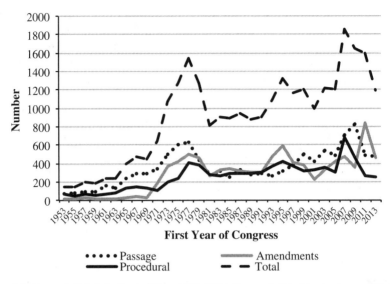

Figure 8.1 House Roll Calls by Type of Vote, 1953–2014. Source: Political Institutions and Public Choice dataset (1953–2010). Data from 2010 to present collected by the authors.

provides evidence that electronic voting was at least partially responsible for the change in floor voting behavior (see Figure 8.2). By the late 1970s, the House floor began to look much more like the Senate floor than it had for a century. Longer daily floor sessions, repetitive amendments, and scheduling uncertainty had become the norm. Worse yet for the Democratic leaders, more freewheeling amending activity made it more difficult for the leaders to enforce deals made in committee and to hold a majority coalition together on the floor.

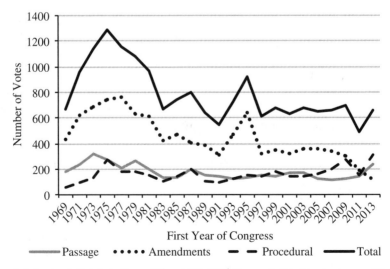

Figure 8.2 Senate Roll Calls by Type of Vote, 1969–2014 Source: Political Institutions and Public Choice dataset (1969–2010). Data from 2010 to present collected by the authors.

House Democrats sought relief in new rules and practices. In 1979, after several aborted attempts, they finally increased from twenty to twenty-five the number of members required to support a request for a recorded vote in the Committee of the Whole. This change seemed to have little effect on amending activity, however. A more important reaction to the increase in amendment votes was an expansion of the number of days each month in which motions to suspend the rules were in order. A motion to suspend the rules simultaneously brings a measure to the floor and passes it. No amendments are allowed and debate is limited to forty minutes, which makes suspending the rules an attractive procedure for bill managers. Although a successful motion to suspend the rules requires a two-thirds majority, Democrats managed to increase the use of suspension motions during the 1970s, a trend that has continued.

The most important response by the Democrats was to have the Rules Committee design more special rules to restrict floor amendments. The change in the content of special rules in the 1980s was quite dramatic. Most special rules continued to put in order at least some, and often many, amendments (open or modified open rules), but Republicans correctly complained that many special rules had been designed to prevent all or most amendments (closed or modified closed rules). Consequently, Republicans made procedural reform a centerpiece of the 1994 congressional campaign. As Figure 8.3 reveals, after becoming the majority party in the 104th Congress (1995–1996), Republicans initially kept their campaign promise to offer more open/modified open rules than had the Democrats, although there was a slight increase in the use of modified closed

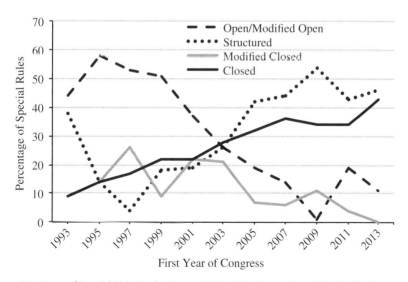

Figure 8.3 Types of Special Rules in the House, 1993–2014. Source: Donald R. Wolfensberger, "Getting Back to Legislating: Reflections of a Congressional Working Group." Data from 2013–2014 gathered by the authors.

and closed rules under the new Republican majority. Structured rules limit the amendments that can be offered to those specified in the special rule; modified closed rules permit only a single amendment, which is usually a minority amendment in the nature of a substitute; and closed rules preclude any amendments whatsoever. The use of restrictive special rules (i.e., structured, modified closed, or closed rules) has changed considerably in recent congresses. Since the 109th Congress (2005–2006), approximately 88 percent of the special rules have been restrictive. The House reached an all-time high in rule restrictiveness in the 111th Congress (2009–2010) when an astounding 99 percent of special rules limited amendments in some fashion. As a result, as Figure 8.4 shows, voting alignments on special rules have become much more partisan. This figure reports the average party difference on special rule adoptions. A value of 0 would mean both parties unanimously approved or rejected the rule; a value of 100 would reflect total partisan disagreement on the rule. As the data show, the average party difference on special rule adoptions has increased from less than 20 percent in the 1970s to more than 90 percent in recent Congresses.

The net result of the more than two decades of adjustments to the voting reforms of the early 1970s has been a more bifurcated process for managing legislation on the House floor. Legislation that is of little importance is not subject to amendments; it is considered under suspension of the rules, or, if it is sufficiently noncontroversial, it is brought up by unanimous consent and passed without a recorded vote. Legislation that is likely to attract even a few amendments tends to be considered under a special rule that limits amending activity in some way, often to the disadvantage of the minority party.

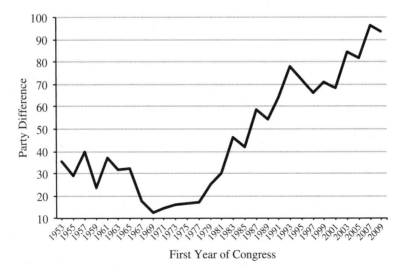

Figure 8.4 Party Difference on Special Rules Votes, 1953–2010. Source: Political Institutions and Public Choice dataset available at www.poli.duke.edu/pipc.data.html.

These changes have renewed the distinctiveness of House floor decision making. Although the number of House floor votes has been similar to that of the Senate in recent Congresses, House floor action is more predictable and more carefully controlled to advantage committees' legislation.

ANALYZING VOTES

Because nearly all members participate in recorded floor votes, floor votes offer a natural basis for comparing members' policy positions. The voting record is available in the *Congressional Record* and a variety of commercial publications. It can even be examined on personal computers through the use of THOMAS, a service of the Library of Congress (http://thomas.loc.gov). Political scientists, journalists, interest groups, challengers to incumbents, and many others have long analyzed the roll call record for scientific, educational, and political purposes. Consequently, the use – and misuse – of the congressional voting record to make inferences about legislators is a subject that recurs in nearly every congressional campaign.

The Problems of Interpreting the Roll Call Vote

A legislator's roll call vote can be thought of as an act based on (1) a policy preference and (2) a decision about how to act on that preference. The policy preference may be influenced by an array of political forces – constituents, the president, interest groups, party and committee leaders, the legislator's personal views, and so on. Therefore, the personal view of a legislator is not easily inferred from a roll call vote. Moreover, whatever the basis for his or her policy preference, the legislator may hold that preference intensely or only weakly.

A member's decision about how to vote can be sincere or strategic. For example, a member may strategically vote against a bill even if he or she prefers the bill to no bill at all, if the member believes that killing the bill will lead to action on an alternative that he or she will like even more. Strategic voting of this variety explains the phenomenon of "ends-against-the-middle" voting patterns, whereby members on opposite sides of the ideological spectrum vote in a similar fashion. For instance, Tea Party opposition to Republican proposals in recent Congresses is less likely the result of these members having more in common with Democrats than with Republicans than it is of their effort to compel more conservative proposals in future versions of the given measure (and other measures). Such strategic voting on the first bill might lead an observer to conclude incorrectly that these members prefer the status quo to the first bill. Members might also cast deceptive votes. An extreme example is a member who holds a strong policy preference and works hard behind the scenes to push his or her point of view, yet votes the other way on the floor to make the folks back home happy.

Plainly, the political and strategic character of members' policy preferences and voting choices is an obstacle to the use of roll call votes as the basis for making claims about legislators' intentions or objections in casting a vote. The situation, however, is not as hopeless as it might seem. Most votes are not strategic or deceptive. They reflect the political preferences of the member fairly well, which makes political sense. Because members know that their votes on important issues may be used against them, they have an incentive to cast votes that are easily explained. In addition, the number of situations that present an opportunity for strategic or deceptive voting is not nearly as large as it could be. Nevertheless, caution is required when making inferences from a particular vote.

The possibility of strategic or deceptive voting is less troublesome in analyzing summary statistics on members' voting records than it is when considering votes individually. Many voting indices summarize members' records over a large number of votes by counting the number of times that they vote in a certain way – for example, in favor of the president's position. Instances of strategic or deceptive voting are not likely to affect the scores assigned to the legislators, but skepticism is in order for scoring based on subsets of the larger voting record. Even still, one should refrain from claiming to infer more than a member's *revealed* policy preferences from his or her aggregate voting behavior.

The Changing Congress: Ends-against-the-Middle Voting

In today's polarized Congress many roll call votes pit one party against the other with very few members of each party voting with the other side. Most votes then are easily classified as one-dimensional, with liberal Democrats voting against conservative Republicans. The emergence of the Tea Party wing of the Republican Party has produced some unusual voting alignments in recent years. For example, the vote on the continuing resolution in December 2014 – the so-called Cromnibus – featured an ends-against-the-middle voting alignment. The bill passed 217–203, with the nay votes coming from extremes of each party and the yea votes coming from the more moderate members of each caucus. Although the liberal Democrats and Tea Party Republicans voted the same way, they likely did so for different reasons. Many Tea Party Republicans thought that the bill did not do enough to fight back against President Obama's actions on immigration, whereas many liberal Democrats thought that the bill went too far by only extending funding for the Department of Homeland Security for three months.

Common Voting Measures

Political scientists and journalists have relied on several indices to characterize members' voting records. The most widely reported measures are those calculated by the research department of the Congressional Quarterly (CQ), which publishes

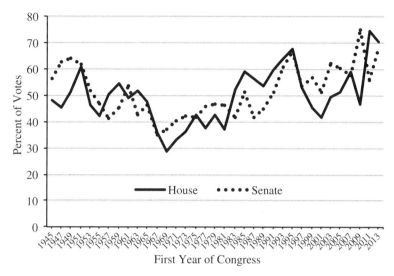

Figure 8.5 Percentage of All Votes. That Were Party Votes, 1945–2014. Data generously provided by Keith Poole.

Congressional Quarterly Weekly Report, a news magazine that provides in-depth coverage of Congress. CQ calculates objective indicators of members' support for and opposition to the president, support for and opposition to their own party's positions, and support for and opposition to the conservative coalition.

Measures of the role that party plays in members' voting decisions are the most frequently used roll call statistics. Many of these measures are based on the party vote, which CQ defines as a vote on which a majority of Democrats oppose a majority of Republicans. The percentage of all votes that are party votes is a common measure of the degree of partisanship in the House and Senate. The historical record for party votes – sometimes called party unity votes – is demonstrated in Figure 8.5. An individual member's overall level of support for his or her party is usually determined by the percentage of times he or she has supported the party's position on party votes. CQ calls these "party unity scores."

CQ's label is a little misleading. Because a party vote occurs any time that a majority of one party votes differently than a majority of the other party, a party vote might occur when the parties actually differ very little. For example, a vote on which 51 percent of Democrats and 49 percent of Republicans voted yea would be considered a party unity vote. This result would hardly be an indication of "unified" parties, and party influences or differences might not have played much of a role in the outcome. Of course, any objective measure requires that some standard be used – if not a simple majority, then perhaps a two-thirds or a 90 percent majority. In addition, some scholars have raised concerns about aggregate measures of party unity voting on the grounds that these measures fail to control for fluctuations in the agenda across time. Specifically, the mix of vote types that are predisposed to promote or depress party voting can change dramatically across Congresses. For instance, amendments are more likely to generate party voting than many other vote types. Therefore, a Congress with more amendments than another is likely to have a higher rate of party unity votes, all else being equal. As a result, the percentage of party unity votes in a Congress is partially the result of changes in the agenda that are unrelated to the dynamics of partisan division. Therefore, some caution is required in using CQ's measure. Nonetheless, it remains one of the best available for examining the frequency of party alignments in Congress over time.

CQ also analyzes congressional votes on bills for which the president has taken a position by examining the public statements of the president and administration officials. CQ calculates a success rate for the president, consisting of the percentage of such votes on which the president's position prevails. Analysts using CQ's scores must rely on the CQ staff's ability to accurately identify the votes and the president's position. They must also hope that CQ is consistent in applying its selection criteria over time. Perhaps because CQ says nothing beyond a single sentence about the president's public statements, no one has effectively challenged CQ's work on this score.

The most obvious weakness of the CQ scores is that they do not take into account the varying importance of the issues behind the votes. One way to handle this problem is to use only votes that are contested – those that show a close division. The argument is that lopsided votes – for example, ninety to ten – are less likely to have been seen as decisive, controversial, or critical to the choices made on issues important to members. In addition, one-sided outcomes do not allow analysts to distinguish among members. Thus, analysts frequently limit their choice of votes to those with less than 75 percent, or perhaps even 60 percent, of the members voting in the majority. Eliminating uncontested or minimally contested votes also serves to stabilize the legislative agenda across Congresses – it controls for the potentially considerable amount of variation in purely symbolic votes from one Congress to the next.

CQ offers an innovation of its own by identifying fifteen to twenty key votes every year for each chamber. The publication first identifies the year's major issues subjectively – identifying those that were highly controversial, were a matter of presidential or political power, or had a great impact on the country – and then, for each issue identified, chooses the vote that was the most important in determining an outcome. CQ does not calculate scores based on these key votes, although political scientists have frequently used key votes for the construction of their own voting measures.

The Ratings Game

Dozens of interest groups regularly report ratings for members of Congress. The wide range of groups that do this includes ideological groups, farmers' organizations, environmental and consumer groups, and large labor and business associations. Not surprisingly, the ratings are used for political purposes. Most interest groups send press releases to the news media in members' home states and districts, praising their supporters in Congress and chastising their opponents. They also use their own ratings as a factor in decisions about campaign contributions. Nearly all groups use their scores to enlighten their memberships about their friends and enemies in Congress. Even incumbents and challengers advertise interest group ratings to substantiate their claims about the policy stances of the incumbents.

Interest groups' ratings of legislators are based on a limited number of votes selected by group officials. The processes by which groups select votes on which to base their ratings vary widely. Some groups do not complete their analyses until their board of directors or some other authoritative group approves the list of votes, whereas others allow low-level staff to identify the pertinent votes. Typically, groups have compiled and published their annual lists at the end of a congressional session. More recently, however, some groups have begun choosing votes prior to their occurrence and sometimes even at the request of individual members or party leaders. In publicizing that a particular vote will be "scored," interest groups seek to influence wavering members to support the group's position. Upon preselecting a vote for scoring and prior to the vote, groups will fax notices to members' offices or distribute cards that are imprinted with the group's logo and position on the vote. In the past few Congresses, House Republicans have often had to pull a bill from the floor or see it go down in defeat because Heritage Action – a conservative group – announced its intention to score the vote.

Groups vary in how narrowly or broadly they define their interests. The AFL-CIO, for example, includes votes in its ratings that concern issues that "affect working people who are not necessarily union members." The National Farmers Union has included in its scales votes on such issues as the MX missile, Social Security financing, and constitutional amendments requiring a balanced budget.

Additionally, the number of votes included in interest group scales varies widely. Sometimes as few as nine or ten votes are included in an interest group's scale, which means that just one or two votes can produce great swings in the scores assigned to legislators. Groups sometimes include several votes on the same issue to give that issue greater weight in their calculations, whereas others carefully avoid doing so. Groups have also been known to alter their selection of votes to get a certain scale that will benefit friends or make enemies look bad.

Further complicating the interpretation of interest groups' ratings of lawmakers is the type of votes these groups select. Quite naturally, because interest groups want to separate supporters and opponents, they tend to choose important votes that show close divisions. Because legislators are likely to be consistent in their policy positions, an interest group's tendency to pick votes with

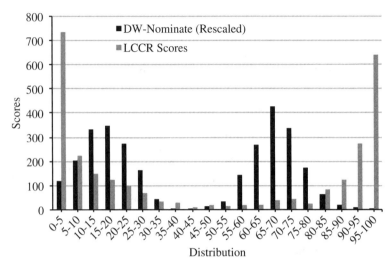

Figure 8.6 Comparing the Distributions of LCCR and DW-Nominate Scores. Source: DW-Nominate scores from www.voteview.com, and LCCR scores from http://www.sscnet.ucla.edu/polisci/faculty/groseclose/Adj.Int.Group.Scores/.

close divisions has the effect of repeatedly counting the same set of members as supporters and another set of members as opponents. As some critics of interest group ratings have noted, this process produces a polarized distribution of scores even when the real distribution of legislators' preferences more closely approximates a normal curve (a bell-shaped curve). For instance, Figure 8.6 shows the distributions of Leadership Conference on Civil Rights (LCCR) scores and DW-Nominate scores in the House for the 107th to 112th Congresses (2001–2012). We adjust the DW-Nominate scores to place them on the same scale as the LCCR scores. LCCR scores are interest group scores intended to assess members' voting records on civil and human rights measures, and they are based on a small subset of votes (typically, twenty to twenty-five votes) per Congress. Conversely, DW-Nominate scores place members on an ideological continuum by utilizing all available recorded votes that involve at least a minimal level of conflict. As can be seen, the distribution of LCCR scores is significantly more polarized and contains more observations in fewer (extreme) categories than does the DW-Nominate distribution.

The lesson is that we should be quite skeptical of claims that legislators' interest group ratings are reliable indicators of their support for particular causes. Anyone seriously concerned about a legislator's support for a cause should seek additional clues. Using the ratings of two or more groups with similar agendas is a good place to start. Sometimes, a better guide than a legislator's specific percentage rating is how that figure compares with other legislators' ratings. The legislator might have a rating of 85 percent support on a group's rating scale but place in only the fiftieth percentile among all legislators on that scale. The latter often is a better indicator of where the member is positioned on the full spectrum of views on a given issue. Moreover, whenever a member's degree of commitment to a cause is at issue, we should look for corroborating evidence – bills sponsored, amendments offered, speeches made, and behind-the-scenes effort – that may be reported in the press or identified by knowledgeable observers.

Interest group ratings, however, retain their special appeal for analysts because collectively they provide a summary of legislators' policy views across a broad array of issue areas. Scholars often argue that the selection of the votes used in the ratings by knowledgeable interest group officials gives the ratings validity as measures of support for various causes. However, convenience, rather than a careful judgment about the ratings' validity, seems to underlie many scholars' use of interest group ratings.

Dimensions, Alignments, and Coalitions

Given the limitations of interest group ratings, asking whether legislators' policy positions can be characterized in more objective ways is natural. They can. Political scientists have developed ways to determine the basic attitudes or dimensions that underlie voting patterns and the nature of the voting alignments in Congress (who votes with whom). Three basic concepts – dimensions, alignments, and coalitions – are important to understand.

Political scientists' techniques involve a search for consistency in voting patterns across a set of roll call votes. The idea is simple: If the legislators' voting behavior exhibits a discernible pattern for a set of votes, then we might assume that a particular mix of political forces was at work on members for that set of votes. A dimension of political conflict is said to be present when a certain alignment of members is visible throughout a set of votes.

For example, liberal and conservative members are often identified as being at opposite ends of an ideological dimension. The usual assumption is that each member holds a fairly stable ideological perspective and is guided by that perspective when deciding how to vote. Of course, members' voting behavior also may reflect the political outlook of their home state or district, the influence of party or faction leaders, and other political forces that produce an alignment of members that appears to have a liberal-to-conservative character. This is one reason politicians often resist being labeled liberals or conservatives. Some members may not even have personal views about the policies at issue on most votes and still demonstrate voting patterns that appear to fit neatly on a liberal-conservative continuum.

In principle, many dimensions of conflict may organize voting patterns, perhaps a different dimension for different sets of votes. In fact, many scholars argue that we should expect many dimensions in congressional voting because Congress operates in a pluralistic political system, one in which a different set of interest groups and constituents wages the legislative battle on each issue. The issues may divide urban and rural Americans, producers and consumers, employers and employees, coastal and middle Americans, retired and not-yet-retired people, and, of course, Democrats and Republicans. The number of possible bases for conflict is large. The analyst's task is to find the important dimensions of conflict without arbitrarily limiting the search to a few of the possible alignments, such as party-based alignments.

Two schools of thought about the dimensions and alignments of congressional voting have emerged. The older school adopts the pluralistic view and emphasizes the multidimensionality of congressional voting. A newer school emphasizes the consistent presence and explanatory power of a liberal-conservative dimension. Some of the difference between the schools can be attributed to differences in the statistical techniques they use. Part of it is because of differences in judgment or taste – just how much must a voting alignment vary from what is thought to be a liberal-conservative division before we count it as something else?

The difficulty of making a satisfactory interpretation is visible in an analysis of Senate votes during the 113th Congress (2013–2014). Senators' scores on two dimensions, calculated by the political scientist Keith Poole, are arrayed in Figure 8.7. The horizontal dimension is related to the general liberal-conservative position on economic, tax, and spending issues; the vertical dimension separates senators according to their behavior on the very few issues that do not cleanly divide senators along liberal-conservative lines, such as free trade, immigration, and abortion. Senators with nearly identical scores on one of the dimensions often have a wide range of scores on the other dimension. In recent Congresses, however, the first dimension

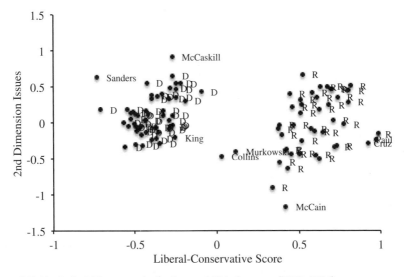

Figure 8.7 Ideological Alignments in the Senate, 113th Congress (2013–2014). Source: DW-Nominate scores from www.voteview.com.

has explained more than 90 percent of the variance in roll call voting. Party leaders, presidents, and lobbyists do not dare ignore such differences. They see important differences among members who operate in a complex world filled with conflicting pressures on legislators.

The alignment of legislators in Figure 8.7 is clearly partisan. Democratic senators are grouped in the upper left and Republicans are grouped in the lower right. We might be tempted to say that the two parties were strong coalitions on the issues confronting Congress. Both parties, however, show substantial internal variation, with some Democrats and Republicans falling closer to each other than they do to some of their fellow partisans. Senators Lisa Murkowski (R-Alaska) and Susan Collins (R-Maine) are situated extremely close to one another on the liberal-conservative dimension but are quite distant from their fellow Republicans Ted Cruz (Texas) and Rand Paul (Kentucky). Although the parties have very different central tendencies, they simply are not tightly knit groups that keep their members from deviating from the position preferred by most party members. To be sure, party leaders and other factors tend to keep party members together, but many other forces lead party members to go their own way from time to time.

The distinction between alignments and coalitions is critical for understanding legislative politics. An alignment merely shows the distribution of policy positions among members, based on their voting behavior. A group of members may vote the same way for different reasons, however, and they may vote alike only because they have similar home constituencies. They can be called a coalition only if they consciously coordinate their voting. Therefore, we simply cannot determine the presence of active coalitions from voting behavior alone.

During the middle decades of the twentieth century, southern Democrats often voted with Republicans, creating policy victories for what was known as the "conservative coalition." There has been some dispute about how much coordination actually took place between Republican leaders and southern Democratic leaders on these votes. That is, just how much of a coalition was the so-called conservative coalition? The answer seems to be that at times genuine coordination took place that affected members' voting behavior, but at most times the alignment of Republicans and southern Democrats against northern Democrats appeared without coordination as members made largely independent judgments about how to vote.

The Floor, Committees, and Parties

This chapter completes the examination of the three major features of congressional organization – the parties, the committees, and the floors. These three components combine to create the policy-making process in Congress. As we have seen, just how the components are combined varies over time between the two chambers and within each chamber. This is a good place to summarize the forces that lie behind those variations – the character of Congress's policy agenda, the distribution of policy preferences among members, and the institutional context.

Issue Agenda

The character of the legislative process is greatly affected by the nature of the issues that Congress confronts. As a general rule, Congress relies more heavily on committees to make policy choices when it must deal with a large number of issues and when the issues it considers are readily separable, recur frequently, or are less salient. Why? A large workload requires a division of labor so that many issues can be addressed simultaneously. A system of standing committees provides such a division of labor. If the issues are separable into distinct categories, committees with distinct jurisdictions work well. Furthermore, if the same issues arise time and again, fixing committee jurisdictions can be done without concern that some committees will become superfluous over time. Moreover, if most issues concern only a few members, committees are a natural place for those members to gather and make the detailed policy choices that do not interest other members.

Alignment of Policy Preferences

Because the process by which decisions are made may influence which choices are made, the contending parties and factions in Congress often seek to shape the decision-making process to their liking. Sometimes party divisions predominate; at other times, cross-party coalitions arise to make the important policy choices. When issues are salient to most members and the members of the majority party share similar policy views, the majority party may centralize policy making in the hands of its leaders. When most members care about the issues, but the majority party is not cohesive, neither committees nor majority party leaders may be trusted. Members then turn to the floor as the place where they can shape policy details.

Institutional Context

Differences in the institutional arrangements in the House and Senate are likely to cause different responses to similar changes in issue agendas and policy alignments. The Senate's rules and practices protect the rights of individual senators to offer amendments and conduct debate on the floor. Consequently, the Senate usually retains a more collegial, floor-oriented decision-making process. In contrast, the rules and practices of the House advantage the Speaker and standing committees. If the majority party is united, the Speaker tends to direct policy making with vigor; if not, the committees are more independent. As a result, House decision making is generally less collegial and less floor oriented. Change in the House tends to come as movement along the centralized-decentralized continuum described previously.

In fact, the constraints on floor amendments under House special rules are the product of cooperation between the traditional centers of power in the House – committees and majority party leaders. Rules Committee decisions about special rules often represent the terms of an agreement between committee and party leaders. Cohesiveness in the majority party enables agreements between committee and party leaders to gain the majority required to adopt restrictive special rules on the floor. In the Senate, the carefully preserved rights of individual members to debate and offer amendments to legislation stand in the way of committee and party leaders who might otherwise seek to structure floor action in a way that would disadvantage the minority party or individual member.

CONCLUSION

The floor is not only a place in which the full House and Senate conduct business, it is also where the most vital stage in the policy-making process, when members exercise their equal voting rights, occurs. We have seen variations between the House and Senate in the degree to which the details of legislation are devised on the floor, but the possible reaction of the floor to the handiwork of committees and parties has always been a central consideration in legislative strategies. Despite similarities in the nature of floor activity in the two chambers, we see obvious interchamber differences – the details of legislation are far more likely to be determined on the Senate floor than on the House floor.

SUGGESTED READINGS

A.   The following readings explore the various dynamics that members' consider when making legislative decisions.

Arnold, R. Douglas. *The Logic of Congressional Action*. New Haven, CT: Yale University Press, 1990.

Kingdon, John W. *Congressmen's Voting Decisions*. 3rd ed. Ann Arbor: University of Michigan Press, 1989.

B.   The following readings offer historical analysis of floor behavior in Congress.

Smith, Steven S.*Call to Order: Floor Politics in the House and Senate*. Washington, DC: Brookings Institution Press, 1989.

Taylor, Andrew J. *The Floor in Congressional Life*. Ann Arbor: University of Michigan Press, 2012.

C.   The following readings explore the implications of the Senate filibuster and equal representation in the Senate.

Binder, Sarah, and Steven S. Smith. *Politics or Principle? Filibustering in the United States Senate*. Washington, DC: Brookings Institution Press, 1997.
Lee, Frances E. "Senate Representation and Coalition Building in Distributive Politics." *American Political Science Review* 94 (2000): 59–72.

D.   The following reading offers a comprehensive historical analysis of roll call voting in Congress.

Poole, Keith, and Howard Rosenthal. *Congress: A Political-Economic History of Roll Call Voting*. New York: Oxford University Press, 1996.

DISCUSSION QUESTIONS

1   Considering that there are important differences between the House and Senate in terms of their floor procedures, how do you think these differences affect bargaining between the chambers?

2   Does the growth of special rules that limit amendments render House minorities powerless in an increasingly polarized Congress? In what ways can the minority remain relevant?

3   Because members determine whether to record votes, which votes would we expect members to record, and why?

4   What exactly can we infer about groups of members who vote together? Is it reasonable to assume that they share the same policy preferences?

9 Congress and the President

President Barack Obama during his 2015 State of the Union address before a joint session of Congress.

The president is an integral part of the legislative process. The basic rules of the legislative game specified by the Constitution provide for three institutional players – the House, the Senate, and the president. The president requires Congress to pass legislation for any policy that requires statutory authorization. In turn, the enactment of legislation necessitates presidential approval unless both chambers of Congress can muster a two-thirds majority to override a veto. Moreover, the Senate must ratify treaties negotiated by the president and must approve the president's choices for top executive and judicial posts. Congress must approve all funding for federal programs. Interdependency, based on shared as well as separate powers, characterizes the relationship among the three institutions.

Interdependency would not be important if the House, Senate, and president held similar policy preferences on important issues. Even when one party controls the House, Senate, and presidency, incumbents of the three institutions are not likely to have identical views. Representatives, senators, and presidents are elected on different cycles and they have diverse constituencies. They are likely to anticipate and react to somewhat different political demands and conditions.

To complicate matters, the framers left ambiguities in the Constitution about congressional and presidential functions and powers. For example, the president is instructed to appoint ambassadors and make treaties with the "advice and consent" of the Senate, but it is unclear how the president is to receive and account for senatorial advice. When the framers granted Congress the power to declare war, they did not anticipate the speed of modern military technology and the scope of the threats, which in some circumstances require the president to make decisions about war without congressional involvement. In addition, when the framers allowed the president to kill a bill after a congressional adjournment by taking no action, they did not define adjournment. In each of these examples of constitutional ambiguity, and in many others, presidents have argued for interpretations that maximize their power at the expense of Congress.

The role of the president in policy making expanded during the twentieth and early twenty-first centuries. Congress has given more power to the president and executive agencies by delegating to the executive branch the authority to determine the details and methods of implementing a wide range of policies. Presidents have asserted their ability to make policy through executive orders and other means. In addition, the enhanced role of the United States in foreign affairs and the increased importance of world events for American life have given the president, who has important advantages over Congress in foreign affairs, a more powerful role.

Whereas presidents have become more important relative to Congress in policy making over the past century, Congress has moved to reassert its own role, at least to some degree. An expanded staff, restrictions on appropriated funds, new approaches to designing programs, and other developments have helped Congress retain a critical role in policy making when faced with aggressive presidents.

THE PRESIDENT AS A LEGISLATIVE PLAYER

The president is central to the legislative process, although he does not always assert himself actively. Many pieces of legislation do not interest the president and are routinely signed into law at the recommendation of trusted administration officials. On some issues, the president chooses to remain silent and inactive for political reasons. When the president chooses to become involved, he usually can have some influence over the outcome by threatening to use his veto power, employing his unilateral powers, and mobilizing support for his position with his considerable political resources.

The President's Formal Role

The Constitution defines a formal role for the president at both the beginning and the end of the legislative process. With respect to the beginning of the process, the Constitution assigns the president responsibility to recommend a legislative agenda. The Constitution provides that the president

> shall from time to time give to the Congress information of the state of the union and recommend to their consideration such measures as he shall judge necessary and expedient; he may, on extraordinary occasions, convene both houses, or either of them, and in case of disagreement between them, with respect to the time of adjournment, he may adjourn them to such time as he shall think proper.

This provision is supplemented by various federal laws that require the president to recommend legislation to Congress.

With respect to the end of the legislative process, the Constitution provides that "Every order, resolution, or vote to which the concurrence of the Senate and House of Representatives may be necessary (except on a question of adjournment) shall be presented to the President of the United States; and before the same shall take effect, shall be approved by him, or being disapproved by him, shall be repassed by two thirds of the Senate and House of Representatives, according to the rules and limitations prescribed in the Case of a Bill." This clause stipulates that any measure that has the force of law must gain either the approval of the president or two-thirds support from both chambers. Presidential veto power – the ability of the president to reject the legislation passed by both chambers of Congress – is not unambiguous and has been a source of controversy between the branches.

AGENDA SETTING. By requiring the president to report to Congress on the state of the union and recommend legislation, the framers of the Constitution expected the president to energize and focus the legislative process. Of course, Congress is not required to consider matters the president brings to its attention. This is true even if the president calls a special session. In fact, the president's powers and duties were designed to spur congressional action without giving the president coercive power over the activity of Congress or the ability to impose new laws unilaterally.

Presidents now address a joint session of Congress early in each calendar year with a speech known as the State of the Union Address. The speech is covered on live, prime-time television. It signals the president's priorities and is designed to generate support for his program. Some recent presidents have sent to Congress longer written versions of their addresses to provide more detail and rationale.

Since the 1970s, a congressional leader of the opposite party has sought network television time after the speech to respond to the president. The major networks have typically given opposition leaders the requested time.

Federal law requires the president to submit a variety of statements and proposed legislation to Congress. Of particular importance is the requirement that the president submit an annual budget message and an annual economic message to Congress. The budget message, required by the Budget and Accounting Act of 1921, specifies the president's taxation and spending proposals for the forthcoming fiscal year. The economic message, prescribed by the Employment Act of 1946, provides a presidential assessment of the state of the U.S. economy and details the chief executive's economic projections for the coming fiscal year. These messages sometimes stir controversy and often shape congressional debate over spending and tax policy each year.

Starting with President Harry Truman in 1948, modern presidents have offered special messages providing additional detail – and often drafts of legislation – for the components of the administration's legislative program outlined by the State of the Union Addresses and the budget and economic messages. The administration's legislation usually is introduced by members of the House and Senate as a courtesy to the president. Since Truman, presidents have devised formal processes within the executive branch for generating, synchronizing, and clearing legislative proposals from the administration.

Formal constitutional rules also grant the president agenda-setting power in negotiating treaties and international agreements. Specifically, the Constitution authorizes the president to make treaties "by and with the Advice and Consent of the Senate." The executive branch customarily initiates treaties and international agreements, although the president does not have exclusive power over the treaty-making process. The president must submit treaties to the Senate and obtain ratification by a two-thirds majority vote. The Senate, however, is under no obligation to act on treaties presented by the president. Furthermore, the president is often dependent on the House for the appropriation of the necessary funds or to modify domestic law to comply with the terms of a treaty. Nevertheless, the power to determine the starting point for policy bargaining on treaties and international agreements gives the president considerable influence over the outcome. It is exceedingly unusual for the president's proposal to fail, and the Senate accepts a majority of treaties without change.

EXECUTIVE ORDERS. The president's implied authority to issue regulations and executive orders to subordinates in the executive branch without the direct authorization of Congress boosts the president's ability to influence policy. Executive orders are directives issued by the president to require or authorize some action of executive branch agencies. Some executive orders are authorized by law, but in most cases they are issued on the basis of the express or implied constitutional powers of the president. This positive power becomes particularly

controversial when the president seeks to interpret laws in a manner inconsistent with the expectations of members of Congress. Presidential actions often
stimulate Congress to clarify its position in new legislation, if such legislation
can survive a presidential veto.

Executive orders can have a significant effect on the structure of the executive
branch and on public policy. For instance, an executive order issued by President
Obama in 2014 protected millions of undocumented persons from deportation.
Some executive orders establish important policy, particularly in areas – such as
civil rights – in which Congress did not enact relevant legislation. President Truman desegregated the military by executive order, and President John Kennedy
created the Presidential Committee on Equal Employment Opportunity by an executive order in which the term "affirmative action" was first used in federal policy.

In theory, the use of executive orders is constrained by the Constitution and
by law, although presidents often justify the use of executive orders by citing
previous executive orders as precedents. Executive orders must be linked to executive authority and must not contradict provisions of the Constitution or a
statute passed by Congress. In fact, during most of the eighteenth and nineteenth
centuries, executive orders were principally used for routine administrative matters. In recent decades, however, executive orders have become quite common,
more important, and, at times, inconsistent with statute. Presidents since the
beginning of the twentieth century have, on average, issued approximately 119
executive orders per year (see Figure 9.1). The prominence of executive orders in
modern politics can be attributed in part to the rise in divisive partisan politics
that make legislative action difficult.

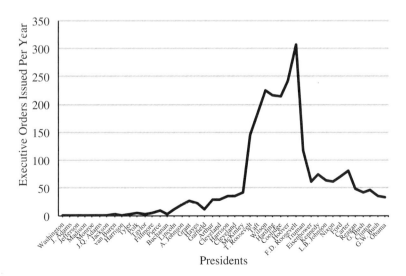

Figure 9.1 Average Number of Executive Orders Issued Per Year by President, 1789–February
2015. Source: The American Presidency Project at the University of California, Santa Barbara.

In the 1980s, the Supreme Court upheld executive orders provided that they do not directly challenge explicit statutory provisions. Because it is unrealistic for statutes to address all contingencies, these decisions grant the president substantial flexibility in policy making. Furthermore, in a few cases, the courts have sided with the president when executive orders and statutes were directly at odds with each other, and the Supreme Court has at times found circumstances in which an executive order or proclamation invalidates a law. Step-by-step, the use of executive orders, and judicial tolerance for it, has expanded presidential power at the expense of Congress.

THE VETO POWER. The power to sign, veto, or take no action on legislation passed by Congress makes the president a critical actor in the legislative process. When the president vetoes a measure (a bill or joint resolution), he returns it to the chamber that first passed it along with a message indicating his objection to the legislation in its present form. If the chamber that first passed the measure is capable of obtaining the votes of two-thirds of the members to override the veto, the measure is then sent to the other chamber. The second-acting chamber also must vote to override the veto by a two-thirds majority before the measure can become law.

The veto power gives the president both the ability to block legislation (subject to a possible override) and a source of leverage with legislators to gain policy concessions. Legislators must necessarily consider both a potential presidential veto and the likelihood of forming a two-thirds coalition to override a veto in their initial legislative decisions. For instance, members interested in passing some form of legislation may choose to make policy concessions to the president if they expect the president to veto their most preferred legislation and they lack sufficient numbers to orchestrate an override. It should be noted, however, that there are instances in which congressional majorities that lack enough support for an override will present the president with legislation they know the president will find unacceptable. Typically, this is a strategic maneuver with the purpose of intensifying partisan differences or forcing the president to expend valuable political capital to win a veto battle.

Congress seldom overrides a presidential veto – since 1789, Congress has overridden just over 4 percent of all vetoes (see Figure 9.2). Recent presidents facing opposing majority parties in Congress have increasingly resorted to vetoes in confronting Congress. President George H. W. Bush (1989–1993) used vetoes rather successfully; only one of his twenty-nine regular vetoes was overridden. Of the thirty-six regular vetoes issued by President Bill Clinton, all during periods of divided government, only two were overridden. Presidents challenge the House and Senate with vetoes much less frequently when their parties have enjoyed majorities in both houses. Although President Clinton issued a number of vetoes during Republican Congresses, he did not veto a single measure passed when Democrats had majorities in both chambers. Republican President George W. Bush

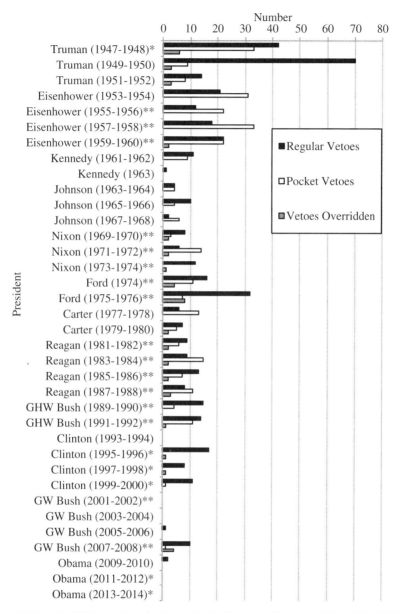

Figure 9.2 Presidential Vetoes: Regular Vetoes, Pocket Vetoes, and Veto Overrides, 1947–2014. *Democratic president with at least one Republican house in Congress; **Republican president with at least one Democratic house in Congress; no asterisk: Unified party control of House, Senate, and presidency. Source: www.senate.gov/reference/reference_index_subjects/Vetoes_vrd.htm.

(2001–2009) vetoed only one bill when dealing with Republican Congresses for nearly six years, but he vetoed eleven bills (ten regular vetoes and one pocket veto) in the last two years of his administration, when he was dealing with a Democratic Congress. Four of those eleven vetoes were overridden by Congress.

In his first six years (2009–2014), President Obama successfully vetoed two bills, neither of which was politically significant. His vetoes represented fewer vetoes per year than any president since President Chester Arthur in 1881 (most of the early presidents seldom vetoed legislation). Polarized parties in Congress contributed to this record low rate. During the first two years of his presidency, Democrats controlled both houses and did not pass disfavored legislation. In the following four years, party control of Congress was divided and the Senate could block legislation that might be vetoed. Cross-party coalitions that might pass significant legislation that the president opposed did not form. With unified Republican control of Congress in the 114th Congress (2015–2016), the Senate serves as less of a gatekeeper than it had been in the previous two Congresses. As a result, President Obama used his veto pen early in the Congress, vetoing the highly salient Keystone XL Pipeline Approval Act.

In some circumstances, the veto is a sign of presidential weakness. Failing to persuade Congress to pass legislation to his liking, the president resorts to a veto. For example, in 1988 President Ronald Reagan – weakened by revelations of the Iran-Contra scandal – vetoed several bills that had broad congressional support, including measures to overhaul the nation's water pollution control and highway funding programs. The vetoes were swiftly overridden.

At other times, a veto is an interim step in a longer bargaining process as presidents use the veto in the hope of forcing additional concessions from Congress. An analysis of vetoed bills between 1946 and 1991 shows that Congress repassed about 35 percent of them in a modified form. Of the repassed bills, 83 percent became law, which reflects the success of the president in extracting policy concessions following a veto.[1]

The pocket veto deserves special mention. The Constitution allows the president to kill a bill by simply failing to sign it if Congress has adjourned within ten days (Sundays excepted) of enacting a measure. If Congress has adjourned and therefore is not in session, its absence prevents the president from returning the bill to Congress with an official veto message. The informal name for such a veto is a "pocket veto."

The pocket veto has been controversial. What counts as a congressional adjournment has been challenged in several court cases. In response to a lawsuit filed by Senator Edward Kennedy (D-Massachusetts), the Ford administration declared in 1976 that pocket vetoes would be used only after the adjournment at the end of a Congress's second session. This move limited the president's ability to use the pocket veto during vacation recesses and the adjournment period between the first and second sessions of a Congress, provided that Congress had made arrangements for receiving veto messages during the intervening periods. President Reagan maintained that such intersession pocket vetoes were constitutional. A federal

---

1 Paul Light, *The President's Agenda*, rev. ed. (Baltimore: Johns Hopkins University Press, 1991), 2.

district judge upheld the president's position, but an appeals court reversed the decision. The appeals court decision stands as the most definitive ruling to date. Fearing an unfavorable ruling from the Supreme Court, the Reagan administration did not appeal further. Because the Supreme Court has yet to rule directly on the issue, presidents continue to argue that midsession pocket vetoes are valid.

The President's Informal Role

Formal institutions place the president firmly in the legislative game. So, too, do the president's fellow partisans, the expectations of the American public, and the president's own commitments and aspirations.

PARTISAN BONDS. The president's service as the recognized leader of his party positions him as a player in the legislative process. Parties often are a means for bridging the gap between the legislative and executive branches, and much of the responsibility of building this bridge is borne by the president. There are powerful incentives for a president and his Capitol Hill partisans to work together. Presidents usually need the support of fellow party members in Congress for their legislative program, and partisans in Congress know that their own political success is affected by the standing of the president. This mutual dependence means that a president and his congressional partisans can influence each other.

The relative weakness of American political parties makes it difficult for the president merely to command support from his party colleagues in Congress. The president does not determine who represents his party in Congress; legislators gain the ballot through primaries and are elected largely on the basis of their own efforts. The president does not select his party's leaders in the House and Senate; legislators elect their own leaders. Consequently, although the president is expected to and generally wants to take the lead in setting legislative strategy for his party, the president must often bargain with legislators of his own party over priorities and the direction of public policy.

PUBLIC EXPECTATIONS. The American people expect presidential leadership on matters of national importance, and legislators often turn to the president to help move legislation through Congress. The emergence of the president as the focal point of an expanding federal government after the Great Depression and World War II was accompanied by heightened public expectations of the president. Increased media concentration on the chief executive, as well as the president's tendency to resort to public appeals for support, has contributed to the president's standing as the most visible elected official in the country. Since World War II, the American public has increasingly expected the president to be the nation's leading policy maker in both domestic and international affairs.

In response to public expectations, presidential candidates and sitting presidents make many public policy commitments. These pledges help attract political support, but – because violating a commitment is likely to alienate some supporters in the electorate and in Congress – policy pledges also may constrain a president while in office. The president's policy objectives are determined in part by the public commitments he makes during campaigns. As presidents have become more likely to try to mobilize public pressure on Congress, their public policy commitments have become more of a double-edged sword for them.

The chief executive's role as a legislative player also is conditioned on public approval ratings. Members of Congress, primarily for electoral reasons, are more willing to pay heed to the legislative proposals and policy positions of a president who has the confidence of the public. A president with high approval ratings cannot, however, be expected to dominate all policy formation. High approval ratings do not translate to presidential influence on all types of legislation. Instead, scholars have found that approval ratings are related to a president's legislative influence on matters that are both salient and complex. When the public is paying little attention to an issue, legislators do not fear electoral repercussions from opposing a popular president.

PERSONAL ASPIRATIONS. Most presidents, and surely all presidents since the 1920s, have had aspirations that required them to take an active role in the legislative process. Whether seeking to move the federal government into new endeavors or to modify or repeal existing policy, presidents have had to work with, and often resist, Congress. Presidents' personal interests, political commitments, and circumstances beyond their control compel them to become engaged.

PRESIDENTS' STRATEGIES

Presidential strategies for influencing legislative outcomes depend on political context. Although executed in a variety of ways, every recent president has confronted decisions about how to structure his legislative agenda, how to generate congressional support, how to employ the veto power, and how to control the bureaucracy in the face of competition from Capitol Hill.

Agenda Setting

Perhaps nothing affects presidential success in Congress as much as a president's decisions about what legislation to recommend to Congress, when to recommend it, and what priority to give each recommendation. The political scientist Paul Light observes that "control of the agenda becomes a primary tool for securing and extending power. Presidents certainly view the agenda as such."[2] The president's legislative choices send a signal to a wide audience – Congress,

2 Citing a study by Christopher Kelley, Charlie Savage, "House Panel Probing Bush's Record on Signing Statements," *Boston Globe*, February 1, 2007.

administration officials, interest groups, the media, and the public – about the president's view of the lessons of the last election, the president's policy preferences, and the president's likely priorities. The president's choices shape the strategies of other legislative players and help set expectations by which the president's own success or failure will be judged.

In most situations, the president cannot force Congress to address his proposals. Instead, he must convince members of Congress to give priority to his legislation. Members of Congress may see national problems differently, give precedence to other issues, or approach problems in a different way. The president must, therefore, motivate Congress by generating support among important members or groups of members, organized interest groups, and the general public. He may employ the full range of presidential resources available to encourage Congress to take his proposals seriously.

Except in times of national crisis, the president's ability to influence the legislative agenda is strongest at the beginning of his first term, followed, perhaps, by the beginning of the second term. At those times, public support, a claim to an electoral mandate, and core congressional support tend to be most in the president's favor. Opponents of the president's programs are likely to have fewer seats in Congress, be more disorganized, and suffer from lower public esteem.

Even in the best of times, the president must carefully calculate which issues to pursue. He almost always wants more than Congress is willing to support. The president must not overload Congress and his own staff with too many proposals. Congress and its committees have a finite capacity to produce major legislation quickly. At the same time, the administration has a limited ability to formulate detailed proposals, lobby Congress, and negotiate compromises in its first few months in office. Moreover, the president is unable to generate media attention and public support for more than a few proposals at a time. Keeping the president's legislative agenda focused has proven more effective than spreading the administration's efforts over many issues.

Among recent presidents, Ronald Reagan appears to have used the early months of his first term most effectively. Reagan moved quickly and set his priorities carefully by defining his agenda as two major bills, one for domestic budget cuts and one for tax cuts. Although both were complex, multifaceted proposals, Reagan was successful in leading the media and the public to focus on the broad effects of his proposals. The approach allowed the Reagan administration to concentrate its resources, stimulate public pressure on Congress for widely recognized proposals, and gain legislative action in its first year in office.

Attracting Congressional Support

On important legislation, modern presidents usually pursue a mixed strategy – both bargaining in Washington with members of Congress and lobbyists and soliciting public support to affect legislators' estimates of the public response to their treatment of the president's proposals. In deciding how to allocate resources to inside and outside strategies, the White House takes into account how many and which members of Congress must be persuaded, the strategies of the opposition, whether public opinion currently favors the president's position, the commitment of resources to other issues, and how much time the president has before Congress makes a decision. Daily, even hourly, tactical adjustments are common in the midst of a tough legislative fight.

A president's legislative strategy is often shaped by the demands of members of Congress. Congressional leaders of the president's party regularly consult with the White House and other administration officials about the substance of policy proposals and legislative tactics. In fact, recent presidents have met with their party's congressional leaders at least once a week while Congress is in session. Committee and faction leaders also press the administration to pursue certain strategies. Presidents are compelled to consider these demands so as not to jeopardize the reelection of their party's congressional membership. In addition, cooperating with important members of Congress, as well as with influential interest groups, bureaucrats, and others, may encourage these actors to employ their own resources on behalf of the administration's program.

INSIDE STRATEGIES. The inside strategy is one of bargaining. Although often seen as underhanded, presidents must frequently employ bargaining tactics to accomplish legislative objectives. This is particularly true when presidents are faced with an effective, committed opposition within Congress. Knowing when, where, and how to make a deal with the members and factions of Congress requires information and skill on the part of presidents and their legislative advisors. Successful bargaining also accounts for formal rules of the game, the composition of the Congress, public opinion, and other resources.

The cost to the president of doing business with Congress depends on political context. When the president is popular, legislators are more likely to be happy to be associated with the president and his program and fewer legislators will require special attention to get their votes. When the president is unpopular, the cost of attracting members' votes – whether by making concessions on the substance of policy proposals or by offering other incentives – will be higher.

Presidents may use the stick as well as the carrot. In 2006, Representative Peter King (R-New York) was the target of retribution after refusing to support President George W. Bush's proposal to allow a Dubai company to assume operations at six major U.S. ports. King, who was chair of the House Homeland Security committee, threatened to block Bush's port deal. In a matter of days after King issued the threat, the Pentagon notified him that it would no longer provide an aircraft and military support for his upcoming trip to Iraq – a trip that had been cleared months earlier.

OUTSIDE STRATEGIES. Observers of presidential strategies have noticed that presidents have become more reliant on outside strategies in recent decades. Twentieth-century presidents as early as Theodore Roosevelt sought public support to strengthen their hand against Congress, but only recent presidents have routinely done so. Through such activities as televised prime-time addresses, press conferences, domestic and foreign travel, exclusive interviews, timely leaks, and now television talk shows and call-in programs, presidents are increasingly cultivating external allies to strengthen their position within Washington.

"Going public," as the outside strategy is labeled by the political scientist Samuel Kernell, is an attractive strategy for several reasons. First, technological advances, such as transcontinental jets and live satellite feeds, have increased the ease of reaching a wide audience. Second, campaign finance practices and diminishing presidential coattails have reduced legislators' dependence on support from the president and the parties. Third, the administration's advantage in information and expertise has weakened, as rank-and-file members have benefited from the diffusion of power and staff within Congress. Finally, budgetary constraints have reduced the president's supply of projects and other favors that he can use to trade with individual members.

Fundamentally, going public is about taking credit and issuing blame. With this strategy, the president seeks to increase the benefits to legislators of supporting him and to increase the electoral costs of opposing him. Every move, however, produces countermoves. Opposition leaders are encouraged to develop public relations strategies of their own, and, in doing so, they are motivated to propose alternatives to the president's program that the president and his supporters would be embarrassed to oppose. In this way, outside strategies encourage early public commitments by legislators, foster partisan maneuvering and grandstanding, and discourage bargaining and compromise that require a softening of positions and a sharing of credit and blame.

A high-profile appeal, such as a special televised address to the nation from the Oval Office, entails risks for a president. Members of Congress sometimes view this approach as an effort by the president to go over their heads. They may not appreciate a president who creates problems for them in their home constituencies. Because the president cannot make such appeals frequently, he must reserve this approach for only those issues of significant importance in which his appeal is likely to generate critical support. Failure to gain more public or congressional support may damage the president's reputation, reducing his effectiveness in future legislative battles and perhaps hurting his own reelection chances. Therefore, more cautious, less publicized, and more narrowly targeted approaches, such as speaking before certain groups and calling on small groups of newspaper editors, may be preferred at times.

President Barack Obama speaks in support of his health care plan at a live and online town hall meeting at the Annadale Campus of Northern Virginia Community College.

The Role of the Media in Going Public

The media play a central role in the president's ability to go public. Quite simply, the president needs a way to disseminate his message, which is where the mass media enters the story. But the media also reap benefits by covering the most visible American public official, and so the relationship between the two is generally viewed as being a symbiotic one. However, the media is not always amenable to providing the president with a platform to communicate with the public. Countervailing considerations, such as ratings, may prompt media outlets to deny the president access.

Such was the case with President Obama's immigration address in November 2014. The White House requested that it be able to address the public at 8:00 PM EST regarding Obama's planned executive action on immigration reform. However, the major networks, including ABC, NBC, CBS, and FOX, all rejected the request. Network insiders justified the decision on the grounds that the networks have an agreement among themselves not to air addresses that are overtly political. Some have questioned this justification on the grounds of the content of previous prime-time presidential addresses. Nonetheless, the networks are subject to considerable pressures during these time slots. November is a particularly important time of year for assessing ratings, and the major networks use the 8:00 PM EST slot for shows that attract large audiences.

In the end, cable news networks picked up the speech. Perhaps more importantly, considering the content of the policy message, so too did Univision and Telemundo. The address was also made available on the White House website.

President Barack Obama is adding a new direction to the outside strategy. His 2008 campaign organization developed a database of e-mail addresses for about 13 million supporters. This database was given to a group overseen by the Democratic National Committee, which employed it to request that people work in their communities and contact legislators in support of the president's budget proposals. The group, called Organizing for Action (originally, Organizing for America), played an important role in President Obama's 2012 reelection and remains active today, with the goal of furthering the president's legislative goals by activating the public.

The Veto Threat

The veto inserts the president into the legislative game. A threatened veto may lead congressional leaders to set aside certain legislation or to make concessions to the president before passing the legislation. Particularly when control of the Congress and presidency is divided between the parties, the veto gives the president a critical source of leverage with legislators. It has been argued that the increasing polarization of Congress has limited the president's ability to bargain directly with Congress and has therefore elevated the relative importance of the veto within the president's arsenal.

Veto threats are relatively infrequent events, but they tend to result in policy changes that are favorable to the president. Veto threats are most common when the legislation under consideration is important and the president is faced with a Congress dominated by the opposing party. One study estimates that presidents threaten to veto roughly 14 percent of important measures; under divided party control of the White House and Congress, the number is 23 percent.

Moreover, it appears that presidents are often quite successful in extracting policy concessions from Congress when veto threats are issued. In fact, by one approximation, roughly 90 percent of bills that encounter a veto threat are modified, to varying extents, to accommodate the preferences of the president. Given the success of veto threats, why do we not see presidents issuing them on *all* congressional proposals?

The answer to this question lies largely in the fact that successful veto threats require credibility. It would be neither feasible nor politically prudent for a president to veto all legislation, and therefore threatening to do so would result in the veto threat losing its credibility with members of Congress. A president who fails to follow through on threats is likely to gain a reputation for bluffing.

Members of Congress are certainly not passive bystanders in the veto game. Members frequently solicit a veto threat from the administration to solidify their bargaining position on Capitol Hill. Sometimes a congressional party will bait the president with a bill that it knows he will find unacceptable to force a veto of a popular bill. A well-documented example of this was the 1995–1996 legislative struggle over welfare reform in which a Republican-controlled Congress presented President Bill Clinton, a Democrat, with a bill it knew to be unacceptable to him, received the expected veto, approved another virtually identical bill, and received another veto. Congressional Republicans hoped to portray Clinton as an opponent of welfare reform as the 1996 elections approached.

The Veto Process

To veto a bill, the president signs a veto message that is sent to Congress (Figure 9.3). The message may contain the president's reasoning. The house of Congress that first passed the legislation acts first on the veto. That house may attempt an override, pass new legislation without an override attempt, or take no further action. The bill dies if a two-thirds majority is not acquired to override the veto. If the first house overrides the veto, the other house may also attempt an override, pass new legislation without an override attempt, or take no further action. The bill dies if a two-thirds majority is not also acquired in that house to override the veto. New legislation may reflect concessions to the president. It must be approved by both houses and sent to the president for signature or veto.

Statistically, attempts to override vetoes are associated with low presidential popularity, a strong opposition party in Congress, and bipartisan support for the legislation. Low presidential popularity and bipartisan support for the legislation also contribute to the success of override attempts. Generally, highly partisan legislation, as vetoed legislation tends to be, is not overridden because a two-thirds

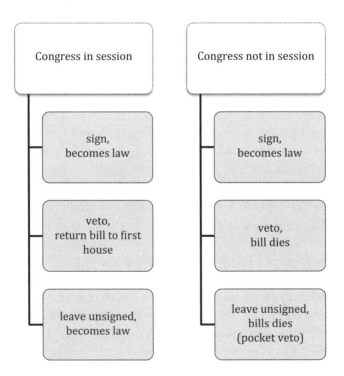

Figure 9.3 Presidential Veto Options Depend on Whether Congress Remains in Session.

majority is required. Parties seldom have close to the two-thirds of the seats in both chambers needed to override a veto.

Controlling the Executive Branch

Much of the competition between Congress and the president concerns control of the executive agencies whose responsibility it is to implement policy. Agencies become players in the legislative game once they are established and begin to perform functions that are valuable to others. They have resources of their own to bring to the legislative battle. Much of the information and expertise about federal programs resides in the agencies. That information and expertise can be shared selectively with Congress and the White House. Agencies also have friends within the interest group community and the general public to whom they can appeal for support.

An unfavorable agency policy is not always easy for Congress to change. The need for agreement among all three legislative institutions – House, Senate, and president – makes a formal legislative response difficult and perhaps impossible. Consequently, members of Congress, presidents, and the organized interests seek means other than the legislative process to control agencies.

For presidents, the most direct means of control is to appoint department and agency heads who support administration policies. Agency heads who share the president's policy goals tend to be more responsive to the directions and suggestions offered by the White House. There is variation across agencies in terms of the president's ability to appoint loyalists. In the Small Business Administration, for example, the president appoints the director, assistant directors, and regional administrators, none of whom need to be confirmed by the Senate. In cabinet departments, however, confirmation is required for most top administrators. Nonetheless, confirmation is required for approximately twelve hundred appointees, while several thousand more are "at will" appointees who serve at the president's discretion without the need for Senate confirmation.

The central organizational tool of the president for controlling the executive branch is the Office of Management and Budget (OMB). This agency, like its predecessor, the Bureau of the Budget, constructs the president's budget proposals for the federal government. Furthermore, central clearance – the job of coordinating and approving all executive branch proposals sent to Congress – is the responsibility of the OMB. OMB responsibilities also entail scrutinizing written proposals and preparing the congressional testimony of executive branch officials to ensure consistency with the president's policy goals. In addition, the OMB reviews enacted legislation to provide the president with a recommendation either to sign or to veto it.

In recent decades, the OMB has become more politicized and has expanded its bureaucratic control functions. By appointing aides to run the OMB who were ideologically aligned with his views, and by centralizing the rule-making process within the OMB, President Reagan turned the OMB into a major instrument in shaping national policy and managing relations between the administration and Congress. By executive order, Reagan authorized the OMB's Office of Information and Regulatory Affairs (OIRA) to review the proposed rules and regulations of executive agencies and to evaluate them by a strict cost-benefit analysis. In practice, granting this authority to OIRA provided a means for the president to make certain that agency activity was in step with his preferences or policy objectives. On numerous occasions during the Reagan administration, OIRA intervened in agency rule making and stopped agencies from issuing congressionally mandated regulations. This intervention was principally achieved through the use of return letters – a letter from the administration that returns a rule for further consideration. These requirements undercut the independence of agency and department heads, delayed action on many regulations, and ultimately led to killing or substantially changing some regulations.

Congressionally Speaking . . .

The Constitution requires that the president, as chief executive, "take care that the laws be faithfully executed." In recent years, the practice by the president of issuing a signing statement at the time that he signs legislation has raised questions about whether the president is fulfilling this constitutional obligation.

Signing statements are written declarations that the president issues to indicate to Congress how he intends to direct his administration in the implementation of the law and often to articulate constitutional limits on the implementation of certain provisions. In practice, the signing statement has become reminiscent of the line-item veto. Although proponents of signing statements say that they communicate valuable information to Congress, opponents contend that they are used by presidents to pick and choose the provisions they wish to either enforce or implement.

Some scholars credit President Ronald Reagan for developing the signing statement into a policy-making tool, but President George W. Bush issued signing statements with unprecedented frequency. During his presidency, Bush used signing statements to challenge approximately 1,200 provisions in more than 150 bills. The number of provisions challenged under Bush exceeded the number for all previous presidents combined. Some observers speculated that the signing statement supplanted the veto in Bush's arsenal. The advantage of the signing statement is that it is far less visible than the veto, allowing the president greater flexibility to shape policy out of the public eye and without creating a veto override showdown with Congress.

Early in his administration, President Barack Obama issued a memorandum requiring executive agencies to consult with the attorney general before enforcing provisions of his predecessors' signing statements. Obama said that he would use signing statements only to address "constitutional concerns." He soon thereafter issued a signing statement to list five objections to provisions of a large economic stimulus bill. For example, he observed that Congress lacks the authority to demand that executive officials reallocate certain money after gaining the approval only of congressional committees. In fact, one of Obama's most controversial decisions is a result of a signing statement. Law stipulates that the president must notify Congress at least thirty days prior to transferring any Guantanamo Bay detainees. Yet, when Obama secured the return of captured Army Sergeant Bowe Bergdahl by releasing five Taliban combatants, the president did not notify Congress until two days after the detainees had been released. It turns out that Obama had issued a signing statement questioning the constitutionality of the thirty-day requirement when it was passed by Congress as part of the 2014 National Defense Authorization Act. Although the quantity of signing statements has declined under President Obama, it is clear that signing statements remain an important means for presidents to assert objections to provisions of bills and ultimately influence policy outcomes.

Under the George H. W. Bush administration, the OMB's regulatory review functions were supplanted to some extent by the efforts of the Council on Competitiveness, also created by executive order. The council was officially located in the office of, and headed by, Vice President Dan Quayle. This organizational arrangement protected, under the umbrella of executive privilege, the council's inner workings from the public and congressional scrutiny to which the OMB is subject. As the administration intended, members of Congress, lobbyists, and the media found it difficult to anticipate or react to unfriendly White House efforts to interpret law and mold regulations required by law (executive privilege is discussed in Chapter 10).

President Bill Clinton did not reestablish the Council on Competitiveness; instead, he returned authority to the OMB. Early in his administration, Clinton issued an executive order supplanting the executive order issued by Reagan that had governed regulatory review up to that time. Clinton's executive order preserved the use of cost-benefit analysis in evaluating regulatory rules and their alternatives but also mandated "the primacy of Federal agencies in the regulatory decision-making process." Although OIRA under Clinton maintained its powers of bureaucratic oversight, it reviewed only the most salient regulatory matters. Furthermore, Clinton restructured OIRA to allow for preferred interest groups to gain greater access to the decision-making process.

Under President George W. Bush, OIRA's role in regulatory oversight returned to a state similar to that seen under the Reagan administration. Much like Reagan, George W. Bush used his broad appointment powers to place individuals with like ideologies in key positions. Bush's OIRA issued many more return letters than had Clinton's, reflecting the Bush administration's opposition to agency proposals. Moreover, the Bush OIRA created a new tool of control over the regulatory process known as a "prompt letter." Whereas return letters require agencies to reevaluate proposed regulations, prompt letters request that agencies reconsider an existing regulation. The addition of the prompt letter gives the president greater ability to curtail regulations according to his preferences. In 2007, President Bush signed an executive order that mandated that all agencies put into place a regulatory policy office to supervise the development of agency rules. The regulatory policy offices were run by appointees of the president. The addition of these offices, imbedded in the agencies, effectively gives the White House another gatekeeper to monitor agency activity and to block, if not preempt, rules that are unfavorable to the administration.

President Obama appointed the Harvard law professor Cass Sunstein as his "regulatory czar" in charge of OIRA. Before heading OIRA, Sunstein had co-authored a book called *Nudge* in which he advocated a concept known as "libertarian paternalism." This school of thought borrows heavily from behavioral economics in suggesting that rather than shape the behavior of actors through direct regulation, a government can indirectly shape outcomes by incentivizing certain behaviors or nudging people in the "proper" direction. An example of this kind of regulation by the Obama administration was a directive allowing and incentivizing employers to automatically enroll workers in 401K retirement plans unless the workers chose to opt out. Previously, employees had to opt in to such systems. Sunstein's research had demonstrated that allowing the automatic enrollment results in more workers saving for retirement. In June 2013, Sunstein was replaced by Howard Shelanski, who previously served as the director of the Bureau of Economics at the Federal Trade Commission (FTC). Since assuming his role as the regulatory czar, Shelanski has emphasized the importance of cost-benefit analysis in evaluating regulations.

Foreign and Defense Policy

The legislative politics of foreign and defense policy are typically different from the politics of domestic affairs. Political scientist Aaron Wildavsky argues that the presidential activities associated with these policy arenas differ substantially. Moreover, the degrees of success that presidents have in foreign and domestic affairs are sufficiently different that the American presidency can be thought of as two distinct presidencies. Although the "two presidencies" thesis is not always useful, it is true that the rules of the game often advantage the president in foreign policy. Under the Constitution, the president more clearly takes initiative and has greater autonomy over action related to foreign and defense matters than he does in domestic affairs. He appoints ambassadors (with the advice and consent of the Senate), makes treaties (subject to the approval of a two-thirds majority in the Senate), receives the ambassadors of other countries, serves as the commander in chief of the armed forces and of state militias when they are called into federal service, and commissions the officers of the United States. Although senators have become increasingly involved in monitoring treaty negotiations, the president largely retains control over U.S. diplomacy.

Congress is not helpless, of course. In fact, the Constitution gives Congress many resources. Because funding is required for much international activity, control of appropriations inserts Congress as a critical factor in foreign and defense policy. The Constitution also gives Congress the power to declare war, create and organize armed forces, regulate foreign commerce, and define offenses against the law of nations. In practice, however, substantial ambiguity exists about the proper role of the two branches. How much discretion is granted to the president in using troops, making minor agreements with other governments, or conducting secret negotiations is not clearly defined in the Constitution. For the most part, the courts have left it to Congress and presidents to work out their differences.

Presidents who claim broad implicit powers argue that they are free to ignore Congress on some matters of foreign and defense policy. This position has been strengthened by the increasing importance of world affairs during the twentieth and twenty-first centuries. Scientific and technological advances have integrated economies and yielded weapons of mass destruction, increasing the importance of the president's ability to coordinate U.S. policy, act with secrecy, and respond quickly. Presidents often argue that the dangers of the modern world and the prominent role of the United States in international affairs require that the president be free to conduct diplomacy, launch secret operations, and even deploy armed forces as he sees fit. Several Supreme Court cases have endorsed an unfettered right of presidents to conduct foreign policy. Chief among these rulings was *United States v. Curtiss-Wright Export Corp.*, a 1936 ruling asserting that even if extensive powers over foreign affairs were not spelled out for the president in the Constitution, the president is best suited to assume those responsibilities.

As international affairs gained importance to the United States, control of national security was increasingly centralized and institutionalized in the White House. The 1947 National Security Act consolidated control of the military in a single Defense Department and created the Central Intelligence Agency and National Security Council. All three organizations are headed by individuals who are directly accountable to the president – the secretary of defense, the director of central intelligence, and the national security advisor. In 2004, new legislation created the position of director of national intelligence, appointed by the president, to supervise intelligence activities of the government and serve as the principal intelligence advisor to the president. These developments have enhanced the president's ability to collect and digest information and to act promptly without substantial congressional participation.

Public expectations of presidential leadership also give the president an advantage in the area of foreign policy. Because the electorate supports centralized leadership on national security matters, particularly in times of international crisis, congressional opposition to an assertive president is unpopular with the electorate. The public is especially supportive of the president if the lives of Americans are at stake.

In the decades after World War II, the liberties given to the president to fight world communism led some observers to believe that Congress was acting as if it ought to defer to the president on matters of foreign affairs. By the early 1970s, as Congress was beginning to assert itself against presidential policies it opposed, views about congressional deference to the president began to change. The national consensus about Cold War policy, however, generated a basic agreement between Congress and presidents about international affairs that effectively returned Congress to a state of greater passivity. When that consensus began to disintegrate, members of Congress looked for ways to recapture their influence. In the immediate aftermath of the terrorist attacks of September 11, 2001, however, the president was once again poised to forge the way in foreign and defense policy. With growing discontent over the war in Iraq, and an administration embroiled in controversy, the current shifting balance in power is reminiscent of the early 1970s.

The reassertion of congressional power in the early 1970s represented the beginning of a tug-of-war between Congress and the president that is still evident today. Recent presidents rarely had uninterrupted periods of unified government. Therefore, partisanship confounded matters by reinforcing institutional conflict between the branches. In addition, legislative action became increasingly central to the making of foreign policy as international economic relations, human rights, environmental problems, and other issues gained a more prominent role in this sphere of policy making. This, in conjunction with the ideological gap between Congress and the president (see section titled "Ideological Outlook" later in this chapter) that prevailed for the better part of this period, made deference to the president particularly costly for Congress.

The Changing Congress: Evolving War Powers

The Constitution grants Congress the power to declare war (Article I, Section 8), but it also makes the president the commander in chief of the armed forces (Article II, Section 2). Congress has formally declared war only five times – the War of 1812, the Mexican War (1846–1848), the Spanish-American War (1898), World War I (1917–1918), and World War II (1941–1945).

Presidents have used their commander-in-chief power, various treaty obligations, resolutions of the United Nations, and their implicit duty to provide for national security as grounds for committing U.S. forces abroad without a declaration of war. By one count, the United States had been involved in 192 military actions without a declaration of war by 1972. At least ten more have occurred since then, including the response to the Iraqi invasion of Kuwait in 1990 (the Persian Gulf War), the use of troops in Somalia beginning in 1992, the military efforts in Afghanistan following the events of September 11, 2001, the conflict in Iraq beginning in 2003, the 2011 military intervention in Libya, and the 2014 airstrikes in Syria against the Islamic State of Iraq and the Levant (ISIL). Many of these commitments were very brief, and Congress had no time to respond. In other cases, such as the Vietnam War, Congress implicitly supported the president by approving the funding he requested for the effort.

The costly Vietnam War in the 1960s and early 1970s stimulated efforts in Congress to limit the war powers that presidents had assumed. In 1973, Congress enacted, over President Richard Nixon's veto, the War Powers Resolution. This law requires that the president notify Congress about any commitment of military forces within forty-eight hours and terminate the commitment within sixty days unless Congress approves an extension or is unable to meet. The commitment may be extended by the president for another thirty days. Congress may halt the action at any time by concurrent resolution (i.e., by a resolution that does not require the president's signature).

No one seems particularly satisfied with the 1973 law. Supporters of broad presidential discretion argue that the act infringes on the president's constitutional powers; supporters of a literal interpretation of the Constitution claim that the act gives away Congress's constitutional powers by allowing the president to initiate wars. Since 1973, presidents have observed the reporting requirement but have sought alternatives to formal congressional approval. In 1983, President Reagan and Speaker O'Neill negotiated a timetable for the involvement of U.S. Marines in Lebanon. In 1991, Congress approved a resolution that authorized President George H. W. Bush to use "all necessary means" to enforce the United Nations resolution calling for the removal of Iraqi forces from Kuwait. In 2002, Congress approved a resolution that authorized the use of force against Iraq to "defend the national security of the United States against the continuing threat posed by Iraq" and to "enforce all relevant United Nations Security Council resolutions regarding Iraq," which concerned weapons of mass destruction. In all three cases, the president avoided endorsing the constitutionality of the War Powers Resolution. In none of the cases did Congress actually declare war, but in the latter two instances Congress indicated that the terms of the War Powers Resolution requirement for congressional authorization were met.

There have been several efforts to revise the War Powers Resolution. In 2008, a private commission headed by two former secretaries of state, a Democrat and a Republican, recommended new war powers legislation that would (a) require the president to consult with Congress before any military operation that is expected to last more than a week, (b) require discontinuation of the operation if Congress has not approved it by concurrent resolution within thirty days, and (c) allow Congress to approve a joint resolution of disapproval to force discontinuation of the operation, by overriding a presidential veto, if necessary. More recently, Senators John McCain (R-Arizona) and Tim Kaine (D-Virginia) offered a proposal in 2014 that would have mandated closer consultation between the president and Congress for any conflict lasting more than seven days. Importantly, it would also have shortened the time requirement for congressional approval (by vote) to thirty days. To date, none of the proposals has been successful, which is not entirely surprising considering that they would require a presidential signature or a supermajority in both chambers to override a veto.

Policies governing the intelligence agencies have been a prime source of conflict between Congress and the president. The tension between the branches increased significantly after the revelations of the Iran-Contra affair. In 1985 and 1986, the Reagan administration secretly sold arms to the Iranians in an effort to negotiate the release of American hostages in the Middle East. Furthermore, the administration used the profits from the arms sales to fund the Contras, a rebel group in Nicaragua, which violated congressional restrictions on funding and covert assistance to the Contras.

PRESIDENTIAL RESOURCES

The strategies adopted by presidents and members of Congress to influence policy outcomes are affected by the quality and quantity of resources available to
each. The president possesses numerous resources that strengthen the role of the
presidency in legislative politics. Some of these resources, such as constitutional
powers and White House staff, information, and expertise, are relatively secure
and may even expand during a president's term of office.

The president has a sizable staff operation to assist him in managing relations
with Congress. The president controls the size of his White House staff, although
it is subject to congressional appropriations. In recent decades, the White House
staff has expanded, particularly in the offices for legislative affairs, communications, and domestic and foreign policy. In addition, presidents have enlarged
agencies within the larger Executive Office of the President, such as the Office
of Management and Budget and Council of Economic Advisors, to enhance their
policy-making capability. These staffs help the president to monitor developments on Capitol Hill and work with committees and leadership, and they give
him adequate representation on legislative matters.

Congress has moved to curtail the president's discretion in managing executive office staff. In the 1970s, after the OMB had gained great importance in the
development and implementation of policy, Congress required the president to
receive Senate confirmation for the director of the agency just as for cabinet
secretaries. In the 1980s, when President Ronald Reagan was proposing cuts in
domestic programs, congressional Democrats made sure that funding for White
House staff was constrained as well. In 1992, House Democrats moved to eliminate funding for Vice President Dan Quayle's Council on Competitiveness to
show their opposition to its role in disapproving regulations proposed by federal
agencies. In general, however, presidents have been able to organize their staffs
as they choose and have had adequate funding to do so.

Some resources, such as information and expertise, may increase during a presidency as experience is acquired. For example, a lack of Capitol Hill experience
was a serious shortcoming of President Jimmy Carter and his top aides when he
entered office in 1977. As time went on, the Carter team gained familiarity with
the people and ways of doing business in Congress. Carter also recognized the
limitations of his White House staff and moved to hire more experienced people.
An important element of the change was that it gave more responsibility to Vice
President (and former Senator) Walter Mondale in the planning of legislative
strategies.

In contrast, the president can suffer losses of other resources while in office.
One scholar called this the "cycle of decreasing influence." Party strength in
Congress and public support often diminish during a president's term. Recent

exceptions aside (see Chapter 3), the president's party typically loses congressional seats in midterm elections.

Public support for a president often declines during a presidential term, weakening support for the president in Congress. As President Johnson reportedly once told his staff:

> You've got to give it all you can that first year. Doesn't matter what kind of majority you come in with. You've got just one year when they treat you right and before they start worrying about themselves. The third year, you lose votes . . . The fourth year's all politics.[3]

This advice, which most presidents take to heart, encourages presidents to try to move quickly on their legislative programs early in their terms.

Presidents eventually run out of time. The two four-year terms that a president may serve under the Twenty-second Amendment are a long time, to be sure, but they are shorter than the legislative careers of many members of Congress and far shorter than the time horizons of many lobbyists and most bureaucrats. In fact, the president often seems to be in more of a hurry than others in Washington. Beyond the diminishing political capital that results from typical patterns of decreasing public and congressional support associated with the natural progression of the presidency, members of Congress, lobbyists, and even bureaucrats tend to limit their relations with the incumbent president nearing the end of his term.

CONGRESSIONAL RESOURCES AND STRATEGIES

The tendency to see legislative-executive relations as a zero-sum game is strong. Observers tend to think that if the president is gaining power, Congress must be losing power. That perspective is too simplistic. Both Congress and the president have gained power as the role of the federal government has expanded over the decades. Moreover, neither branch is monolithic. Within the executive branch, power has been distributed in a variety of ways between the White House, departments, and independent regulatory commissions. Within Congress, the somewhat different constitutional responsibilities of the House and Senate have meant that their power has not always shifted in the same direction. Moreover, developments that seem to affect the power of Congress may adversely enhance the power of certain members, factions, or parties within the institution. Because members of Congress and the president represent different audiences with different interests,

3 Henry B. Hogue, "Recess Appointments: Frequently Asked Questions," CRS Report, Congressional Research Services, September 10, 2002; Henry B. Hogue, "Recess Appointments: Frequently Asked Questions," CRS Report, Congressional Research Services, January 16, 2007.

it also may be the case that the changes in the legislative-executive relationship benefit both branches even if one side appears to be gaining an advantage.

Thus, it is wise to keep in mind that Congress does not really use its resources – individual members, groups of members, and legislative parties use the institution's resources as they pursue their political goals. The exercise of congressional power is usually the by-product of the competition among members within the institution. In other words, congressional output is the result of (sometimes intense) competition between members with different preferences. Given the degree to which preferences in Congress diverge, seldom do all members consider themselves to be winners on important matters.

Legislative Resources of Presidents

Partisan base in Congress. The size of the House and Senate caucuses of the president's party can boost presidential success in enacting the president's priorities. When a president's partisans in Congress are cohesive and ideologically in step with him, the advantages offered to the president increase.

Formal powers. Presidents gain leverage with legislators by using, or threatening to use, their formal powers. The most obvious power is the power to veto legislation. In addition, the president may issue executive orders that interpret laws or regulate the behavior and decisions of executive branch agencies.

Visibility and public approval. The national media concentrate on the president. Unlike Congress, which finds speaking with one voice difficult, the president can dominate the news and manipulate the types of information Americans receive about his activities. If the president mobilizes public support for his initiatives, members of Congress must carefully weigh the costs of opposing him.

Expertise and information. Broad policy expertise is available to the president from the agencies of the executive branch.

White House staff. The president has a large personal staff in the White House that allows him to monitor and communicate with Congress, lobbyists, the media, and others.

Patronage and projects. Presidents and top cabinet officials use personnel appointments to assert control of the bureaucracy and to do favors for members of Congress. Modern presidents make more than seven thousand executive and judicial branch appointments. Presidents and top administration officials can influence decisions about who wins federal contracts and the location of federal installations and buildings.

National party organizations. The president effectively controls the resources of his party's national committees, which can be used to do favors for members of Congress.

Campaign resources. The president may exploit his campaign apparatus to generate support for his program. President Obama did this in using the large e-mail list he developed as a candidate.

Congress's most fundamental resources are the formal powers granted to it by the Constitution. The ability to exercise those powers effectively depends on the human and technological resources of the institution. The motivations of the membership, committee and party structures, parliamentary procedure, staffing arrangements, electronic information systems, relations with outside experts and information sources, and other factors affect Congress's performance. Congress has periodically attempted to better equip itself to compete with the expanding capabilities of the president. The Legislative Reorganization Acts of 1946 and 1970, among many other less-extensive efforts, enlarged staff, reorganized committees, and changed procedures. In sum, Congress has developed a battery of resources to support a growing repertoire of strategies for responding to challenges from the executive branch.

Multiple Uses of Sunset Provisions

Although the concept of a sunset provision – a provision in law that requires periodic reauthorization of a program – dates back to the writings of Thomas Jefferson, its use as a legislative tool is a recent phenomenon. Sunset provisions grew in popularity among reformers in the late 1960s and 1970s who argued that programs must be reexamined by Congress from time to time. When the Republicans, who opposed many federal programs, took control of Congress in 1995, they made widespread use of limits on the lifespan of programs.

A prominent example of the recent use of sunset provisions is the Patriot Act, first enacted in 2001. At the time, the Republican leadership added sunset provisions as a concession to Democrats and members within their party who were skeptical about the intelligence-gathering authority granted to law enforcement and national security agencies. Senator Dianne Feinstein (D-California) declared that the sunset provisions were an "important element of the continued vigorous oversight necessary to ensure this law is carried out in an appropriate manner." Major provisions of the Patriot Act were subsequently reauthorized in 2006, 2009, and again in 2011, with these reauthorizations containing sunset provisions of their own. Many of the provisions most recently reauthorized are set to expire in mid-2015.

Republican majorities have used sunset provisions on tax cut bills for a different purpose. By making specific provisions to the tax cuts temporary, they were able to minimize projected costs and present a more favorable long-term estimated budget. Such was the case with the tax cuts pass under George W. Bush in 2001. Congress and President Obama faced the expiration of these cuts in late 2010 and were forced to either extend them or see taxes increase across the board. In late December 2010, the cuts were extended for two more years so as not to effectively raise taxes during a recession. Today, many of those tax cuts have been made permanent because of the American Taxpayer Relief Act of 2012.

Periodic Authorizations

Historically, most agencies and programs have continued indefinitely once they were created. Although they must receive annual appropriations from Congress, most of the basic laws establishing and empowering the agencies have been permanent. Delegating authority to an executive branch agency in such a manner increases the difficulty of retracting or altering the authority later. After all, a new law requires the agreement of the House, Senate, and president, or, in the case of a presidential veto, a two-thirds majority in both houses of Congress.

In recent decades, Congress has moved away from permanent authorizations. When Congress enacts legislation creating a program or establishing a new policy, it may limit the length of the authorization. A sunset provision sets an end date for a program, and thus new authorizing legislation is needed to continue a program or policy past that date. This approach requires administration officials to return to Congress to justify the continuation of the program, and it ensures that Congress will periodically review the law underlying the program. An important example is the authorization for defense programs, which must be passed each year. Before the 1960s, defense programs were authorized for an indefinite period. During the 1960s and 1970s Congress added more defense programs – military personnel, weapons systems, research and development, and so on – to the annual defense authorization bill. The immediate effect was to give members of the armed services committees greater influence over the activities of the Department of Defense. The long-term effect was to give all members of Congress a regular opportunity to influence the direction of defense policy.

Designing Agencies

In practice, much of the conflict over legislation is about the design of the agencies charged with implementing policy. The line of authority, decision-making and appeals procedures, decision-making criteria, rule-making deadlines, reporting requirements, job definitions, personnel appointment processes and restrictions, and salaries all may affect the ability of Congress, the president, the courts, and outside interests to gain favorable action by agencies. Legislators, responding to political pressures from organized interests and others, generally seek to insulate agencies from unfriendly influences, including future Congresses and presidents, and to guarantee that agencies are guided by their policy preferences. Presidents, on the other hand, generally seek to place new programs in the hierarchy of executive departments to which they can appoint politically loyal individuals to important administrative positions. Thus, congressional and presidential views about the organization and control of agencies are often in conflict.

The effort to elevate the Environmental Protection Agency (EPA) to department-level status – making the head of the EPA a member of the president's cabinet – is a good example of structural politics. Democrats in Congress sought to modify the EPA's status in 1990 to give environmental programs more priority and authority within the executive branch. The bill, passed by the House on a vote of 371 to 55, also called for the creation of a Bureau of Environmental Statistics, which was to be independent of the new department. In addition, the bill would have established a separate Commission on Improving Environmental Protection, with the purpose of coordinating the regulations of the new department and other federal agencies with environmental jurisdiction.

The independent department was designed to be insulated from political manipulation. In fact, the bill required the department to report its findings directly to Congress, without review by the OMB or the new secretary of the environment. Furthermore, the multimember commission would have added a policy-making unit outside of the president-department line of authority. The White House, which wanted a bill that would reinforce President George H. W. Bush's claim to be the "environment president," opposed the bureau and commission on the grounds that they undermined the president's line of authority over agency activities. The bill stalled in the Senate because of credible threats of a filibuster by Republicans after the administration threatened a veto.

In the next Congress, the bill passed the Senate on a voice vote after its Senate sponsors met the Bush administration's demands by folding the statistics bureau into the new department and restricting the policy-making authority of the commission. House Democrats refused to act on the Senate bill. The bill died in the House Committee on Government Operations because House Democrats wanted to deny President Bush an opportunity to claim credit for pro-environmental legislation in an election year.

The EPA bill is typical of the conflict between Congress and the president over the structure of agencies. Agreement about the general policy was not enough to guarantee enactment because the conflict over presidential control of the agency proved to be too divisive. Conflict over the control of information and personnel in this case was at least as controversial as the policy. Specifically, the point of contention was whether the executive branch official controlling the information going to Congress would be responsible to the president or to an independent bureau chief. The president's veto power ultimately forced concessions from Senate Democrats, but House Democrats were more concerned about the political sacrifices than about raising the EPA to cabinet status.

Structural politics is not limited to original authorizations and reauthorizations. The fight is continuous, as the issue of personnel ceilings demonstrates. In recent decades, Congress has become more specific in dictating the design of executive agencies. On occasion, administrations have undermined congressional efforts to bolster agency resources by refusing to hire or replace important personnel. The appropriations committees have responded in committee reports by specifying a minimum number of personnel for agencies, requiring reports on deviations, and insisting on a formal presidential request when an agency seeks to reduce spending with a personnel ceiling. Increasingly, Congress has imposed statutory restrictions on personnel ceilings, thereby limiting the administration's control over agencies' personnel resources.

The structure of many executive agencies is the result of compromise. The give-and-take process can produce a variety of outcomes, ranging from agencies that are distant from the president and responsive to Congress to agencies that are firmly under the control of the executive administration. The decision of political actors to make concessions on some aspects of structural policy and not on others is principally a function of the impact that the given agency has on preferred constituents. Members of Congress and the president are reluctant to relinquish power over an agency when the agency under consideration has a significant direct effect – either positive or negative – on constituents of interest.

The Power of the Purse

A major congressional strategy for controlling policy and its implementation involves Congress's "power of the purse" – the constitutional provision that "no money shall be drawn from the treasury, but in consequence of appropriations made by law." Because laws must originate in Congress, the legislative body can refuse to appropriate funds for certain purposes or condition the use of funds on certain stipulations. Therefore, the authority over appropriations gives Congress the ability to shape the actions of the executive branch in a manner consistent with congressional preferences. Certainly, conditioning appropriations on specific activity explicitly mandates behavior consistent with the will of Congress. Even the threat that appropriations for an agency or program will be reduced or eliminated may achieve the same end.

In the field of foreign and military affairs, the power of the purse is often the only effective tool for Congress to influence policy. Congress's ability to restrict the uses of appropriated funds is well supported by court decisions, giving Congress a clear avenue of response to a president who asserts broad constitutional powers. By forbidding the executive branch from spending federal monies for certain purposes, Congress can prevent the president from pursuing a policy it opposes.

Committee Reports

Committees often make clear their expectations about the implementation of programs in the reports that are required by House and Senate rules to accompany legislation when it is sent to the floor. Reports usually indicate the objectives of the legislation and sometimes interpret the language used, both of which may guide rule-making decisions by agencies. At times, committee reports indicate that the committee "clearly intends," "expects," or even "anticipates" that an executive branch official or agency will or will not do something. Earmarks for specific projects are sometimes listed in committee reports. Although they are not legally binding, committee reports often guide courts when they seek to interpret ambiguous statutory language. More important, reports make explicit the expectations of important members of Congress who will influence future legislation affecting an agency.

Packaging Strategies

The Constitution requires that the president have an opportunity to sign or veto legislation passed by Congress, but it does not indicate the size or format of the legislation that Congress presents to the president. For example, a variety of items are often included in one bill to facilitate bargains among members of Congress, the president, and other interested parties. By using their ability to package legislation, members of Congress may encourage or discourage a presidential veto.

Congress exercises considerable influence over policy outcomes from its ability to package multiple measures and present the president with a single take-it-or-leave-it offer. When several bills or aspects of bills are combined into one package that includes legislation both favored and opposed by the president, Congress reduces the president's capacity to control national policy. Because the president does not have the formal authority to strike from a bill those provisions that he finds unfavorable, he is forced to make a difficult decision. Issuing a veto means losing, at least temporarily, those provisions of the legislation that he finds satisfactory. Of course, a packaged proposal that encounters a veto may result in Congress losing valued provisions as well.

The advantages and disadvantages of packaging can be seen in the use of omnibus continuing resolutions (CRs), which combine two or more regular appropriations bills for the coming fiscal year into one giant package. CRs are required when Congress and the president fail to appropriate bills enacted before the beginning of a new fiscal year. If the president vetoes the bill that contains the funding for some executive agencies and no new bill is enacted, those agencies must shut down. Hence, the president needs to weigh carefully how effective a veto would be. Congress also risks losing measures packed into a CR that provoke the president's opposition. For example, Representative John Dingell's (D-Michigan) attempt in 1987 to codify in the CR the "fairness doctrine" governing broadcasters (a bill previously vetoed by President Reagan) was dropped from the bill after Reagan drew attention to its inclusion in the CR. The bundling strategy on these bills and other "must pass" legislation – such as bills to raise the federal government's debt ceiling – thus have the potential to help Congress reassert influence over the legislative game.

Recent presidents have promoted the line-item veto as a means to combat Congress's packaging strategies in appropriations bills. Adopting the line-item veto, an authority held by forty-four state governors, would allow the president to strike out individual provisions nestled in individual or omnibus spending bills. However, creating a line-item veto may require a constitutional amendment. The Supreme Court ruled the line-item veto as passed by Congress in 1996 unconstitutional, although efforts to pass a constitutionally viable version of the line-item veto have resurfaced under the Obama administration (see Chapter 10 for further discussion). Presidential signing statements have been used to register a president's objections to provisions in larger bills, particularly to provisions considered to be unconstitutional, even when the president chooses to sign the bill (see earlier discussion).

Presidential Nominations

The Senate is given a special opportunity to influence the administration every time the president nominates someone for a top executive branch post. Beyond judges, ambassadors, and "other public ministers and consuls," the Constitution allows Congress to determine by law who must stand for confirmation by the Senate. Each Congress, the Senate considers approximately two thousand civilian executive branch nominations. Judicial nominations and confirmations are considered in Chapter 10. In addition, the promotions of all military officers are submitted to the Senate.

The Senate tends to defer to the president on executive branch appointments, particularly on positions below the cabinet level. This is not to say, however, that the president's appointments go unchecked. In fact, in 1989 President George H. W. Bush's first nominee for secretary of defense, former Senator John Tower, was rejected by the Senate largely because of concerns about the senator's private behavior. The president swiftly moved to nominate House Republican Dick Cheney, a choice calculated to be far more acceptable to the Senate. In 1993, President Bill Clinton's first nomination for attorney general was withdrawn when it was discovered that the nominee, Zoe Baird, had hired undocumented immigrants as household help. In 2009, President Obama's choices for secretary of health and human services and for chief performance officer, a new position within the Office of Management and Budget, were withdrawn after irregularities in their past tax payments were made public. Others, including Treasury nominee Timothy Geithner, were also subject to intense scrutiny because of tax irregularities. In 2013, President Obama's nominee for secretary of defense, former Senator Chuck Hagel, was given close scrutiny because of views he had expressed in the past about gay rights and U.S. policy toward Israel.

Occasionally, Congress acts to require that certain executive officials be subject to Senate confirmation. In 1973, Congress required the president to receive Senate confirmation on appointments to director of the OMB. In 1986, Congress extended their authority by requiring that the president also receive Senate confirmation on appointments to head OIRA. When Congress approved legislation to create the Department of Homeland Security in 2002, the new secretary of the department automatically became subject to Senate confirmation.

Moreover, Congress may, and does, get involved in executive branch personnel matters beyond Senate action on presidential nominations. Congress is able to specify in law the qualifications required of presidential appointees, and it may even grant department heads, rather than the president, the authority to appoint certain officials. Congress also may limit the ability of the president or agency heads to dismiss employees. In these ways, Congress may seek to insulate certain executive branch officials from White House pressure.

In recent years, growing polarization between the parties in the Senate has made it increasingly difficult for presidential nominees to receive a confirmation vote (affirmative *or* negative). This is due to the ability of Senate minorities to block the consideration of an executive nominee by filibuster. Senate majorities have long argued that the Constitution requires that presidential nominees receive an up or down vote, given the Senate's constitutional responsibility to advise and consent to presidential nominations. Republicans and Democrats alike – while in the majority – have further argued that a supermajority should not be necessary to arrive at this up or down vote. On the other hand, Senate minorities maintain their right to block nominees they oppose. This matter came to a head during the Obama administration when Senate Republicans blocked a record number of nominees from coming to a vote. Of the 168 times that cloture motions were filed on presidential nominees prior to November 2013, representing efforts by majorities to overcome instances of minority obstruction of nominees, 82 occurred during Obama's presidency. Outraged by this, Senate Democrats, under the leadership of then-Senate Majority Leader Harry Reid (R-Nevada), carried out the nuclear option to set a precedent for a simple majority vote on all executive nominees except those to the Supreme Court (see Chapter 7 for further discussion).

Oversight

A member of Congress dissatisfied with agency performance or with presidential directives to an agency can choose from several oversight strategies to try to bring the bureaucracy into line. Oversight strategies centered on formal hearings include committee or subcommittee hearings, which regularly bring agency heads in front of legislators; special hearings designed to draw attention to a disputed policy or agency action; and more dramatic investigations, such as the Watergate hearings in 1973 and 1974 and the 1987 Iran-Contra hearings, usually conducted by special committees.

Less formal methods of monitoring and influencing agency behavior include written and telephone communications with agency officials, discussions with agency heads and other interested parties during informal office visits, public relations campaigns, and threats to pursue new legislation. Such approaches can be useful in congressional efforts to increase agency responsiveness to the interests of Congress. Although a considerable amount of bureaucratic oversight occurs within the committee forum, there are oversight mechanisms available to members that are independent of committees. Members seeking to influence agency actions in their districts also have recourse to informal visits and more formal inquiries conducted by staff. Often, members acting on behalf of communities in their district will pressure agency officials to respond to local concerns. For example, individual members frequently push the Environmental Protection Agency to investigate hazardous waste sites or to initiate cleanups in their districts.

Congressionally Speaking . . .

The Constitution and many statutes require that the president submit the names of certain appointees to the Senate for confirmation. The Constitution also allows the president to make a *recess appointment* when the Senate is not in session. A recess appointment is good until the end of the next session of Congress, which could be more than a year in duration. Presidents have used recess appointments to avoid the regular confirmation process, but they usually announce their intention to forward a regular nomination to the Senate at the time the appointment is made. Because recess appointments are a way for the president to circumvent, at least for a short while, the authority of the Senate, this practice can and does create animosity.

President George W. Bush employed the recess appointment with greater frequency than his two predecessors, although he lagged slightly behind President Ronald Reagan, and was eventually thwarted by a parliamentary maneuver. Over the course of his two-term presidency, George W. Bush made 171 recess appointments, whereas President Bill Clinton made 139 over two terms, and President George H. W. Bush made 77 in his single term. Reagan made 240 recess appointments during his eight years in office. Senate Democrats blocked recess appointments in the last year of the George W. Bush administration by avoiding long recesses. Rather than taking a recess, the Senate could remain officially in session by holding a pro forma session every three days. Why three days? The Constitution does not define a recess. A 1993 Justice Department opinion argued that the president may make a recess appointment during a recess of more than three days (i.e., more than a long weekend).

In a pro forma session (an informal name), the Senate session opens, no business is conducted, and the session is immediately gaveled closed by the only senator in attendance.

In 2012, President Barack Obama challenged this Senate strategy by making recess appointments during the period between the first and second sessions of the 112th Congress (2011–2012). He relied on a Justice Department opinion that the Senate is unavailable to receive nominations when it is holding pro forma sessions, and therefore the president may exercise his recess appointment power. In a unanimous decision, the Supreme Court later found that Obama had exceeded his constitutional authority in doing so. Justice Stephen Breyer, writing for the majority, argued that, "The Senate is in session when it says it is, provided that, under its own rules, it retains the capacity to transact Senate business." The decision invalidated three recess appointments that President Obama had made to the National Labor Relations Board during the intersession period. However, the Court maintained that the president has the ability to make recess appointments during more substantial breaks, of ten days or more.

At other times, members will compel the administration not to act in their district when agencies have the potential to adversely affect preferred constituents.

Some observers have distinguished between "police-patrol" and "fire-alarm" oversight. Under police-patrol oversight, Congress pursues routine, systematic surveillance of executive branch agencies on its own initiative. In contrast, fire-alarm oversight is more decentralized. Instead of initiating and maintaining patrols, Congress develops a system that lets others "pull the alarms." Citizens, interest groups, or the media bring agency decisions to the attention of legislators and motivate them to act. Members may prefer fire-alarm oversight because it is more cost efficient and because it allows them to claim credit for acting when the alarm bells ring.

Yet police-patrol oversight appears to have become more common since the early 1970s. Fiscal constraints may have led members to turn away from legislation for new programs and instead to focus on overseeing the implementation of established programs. Expanded committee staffs and the independence of subcommittees, some devoted exclusively to oversight activities, have also facilitated more conventional oversight. Furthermore, the centralization of the executive branch's regulatory process in the OMB and the Council on Competitiveness motivated members to pursue formal oversight hearings more aggressively. Partisan rivalries when there is divided party control of Congress and the White House have encouraged legislators to be more aggressive in their oversight activities.

Congress has increasingly turned to the Government Accountability Office (GAO) to assist with oversight. The GAO is an agency of Congress and is authorized to examine any federal agency. It gives members of Congress the option of having its expert, nonpartisan staff conduct an investigation of executive branch performance without a large commitment of time on the part of members or their staff. The duties of the GAO were expanded under the Legislative Reorganization Act of 1970, and since then the GAO has significantly increased the range and number of its audits and analyses of program effectiveness.

In recent decades, Congress has more frequently required the president and executive agencies to provide written reports on their actions and performance. In some cases, the requirement is designed to ensure the timely receipt of information – for example, just before Congress must reauthorize a program. In other situations, Congress demands that an agency conduct a special study of a problem and report the results. Executive branch officials often complain that they spend too much time writing reports that few members, if any, read. From Congress's perspective, however, the exercise is another aspect of police-patrol oversight that shifts the burden to the agencies themselves.

Beginning in 1978, police-patrol oversight was extended by the creation of offices of inspectors general within major departments and agencies. Inspectors general are given substantial independence from political appointees and agency heads, are authorized to conduct wide-ranging audits and investigations, and are required to submit their reports directly to Congress. With few exceptions, Congress has looked favorably on having a full-time, on-site bureaucratic oversight mechanism.

Police-patrol oversight also is reflected in Congress's intensified scrutiny of "reprogramming" by agencies. Congress usually appropriates funds for executive branch activities in large lump-sum categories, with the understanding that the funds will be spent in accordance with the more detailed budget justifications that agencies submit each year. Frequently, variation from the budget justifications – reprogramming – is deemed prudent or even necessary because of changing conditions, poor estimates, or new congressional requirements. Agencies and the White House, however, have occasionally taken advantage of reprogramming discretion to spend money for purposes not anticipated by Congress – or even opposed by it. Congress has responded by establishing more and more requirements, such as demanding that it receive advanced notification of reprogramming actions and even insisting on prior approval by the appropriate committees.

The Iran-Contra Affair

A Lebanese newspaper reported in early November 1986 that the Reagan administration had been engaged in trading arms to Iran for the release of hostages held by Islamic extremists in Lebanon. When Attorney General Edwin Meese later that month uncovered a memo outlining the diversion of profits from the arms sales to the Nicaraguan Contras, a series of executive and congressional investigations ensued. Together, these events sparked the biggest scandal of President Reagan's two terms in office and helped precipitate Reagan's marked decline in popularity and influence.

An investigation by special House and Senate panels into the Iran-Contra affair uncovered a remarkable series of events in which officials of the Reagan administration lied to Congress and helped subvert normal democratic decision-making processes. The Reagan administration essentially pursued secret policies that were in direct conflict with public policy objectives. On one hand, the administration's public policies were to ban arms shipments to Iran and to make no concessions for the release of hostages. On the other hand, the administration pursued secret policies of selling sophisticated missiles to Iran and trading weapons to get the hostages back. Although Reagan originally told a special investigatory commission that he approved the shipments, he later reversed this statement. In the end, he testified that he could not remember whether or not he had approved the shipments.

Reagan's advisors admitted to directing the covert arms transactions and the subsequent attempts to divert the profits to the Contras. They confessed to concealing these activities and, at times, outwardly lying about them to Congress. The arms sales violated laws requiring that such transactions be reported to Congress. Even though laws prohibited military or paramilitary assistance to the Contras, the National Security Council (NSC) staff sought illicit funding from foreign countries and private citizens, and turned over much of the operation to private arms merchants. The private enterprise accumulated approximately $10.6 million in carrying out covert U.S. policies in a way that was entirely unaccountable to Congress.

Eventually, several senior administration officials were convicted of lying to Congress.

National security is an area in which Congress's ability to oversee the executive branch and publicize what it learns is somewhat limited. Several committees, including those concerned with appropriations, national security, and intelligence, receive classified information from executive agencies and hold hearings on classified matters in executive sessions. Committee reports from hearings or investigations are cleared with executive agencies and frequently must exclude materials that the agencies determine should remain classified. In 2004, as a part of a large intelligence reform package, Congress assigned the Public Interest Declassification Board (PIDB), comprised of members appointed by both Congress and the president, to resolve disputes between Congress and executive agencies about classified material that Congress wishes to publish.

Legislative Veto

A congressional strategy of disputed constitutionality is the use of the legislative veto. A legislative veto is a provision written into a law that delegates authority for certain actions to the president or agencies, subject to the approval or disapproval of one or both houses of Congress, certain committees, or even designated committee leaders. The legislative veto gives Congress a way to check executive branch action without having to pass new legislation that would require presidential approval. Congress can, then, avoid writing detailed laws by delegating rule-making power to the executive branch, and still retain the final say over executive decisions. Legislative vetoes may, at first glance, appear to be a strategy used exclusively by congressional players against the president. The origins of the legislative veto, however, convey a different story. In 1932, Congress and President Herbert Hoover reached an agreement on executive branch reorganization that included the first legislative veto. The compact delegated reorganization powers to the president, provided that Congress did not disapprove his plan within sixty days. The agreement effectively gave the president wide latitude in exercising powers delegated to him, but it also gave Congress a chance to control those actions without having to enact another law. The provision seemingly benefited both Congress and the president by expanding the powers of the president but giving Congress an opportunity to nullify those decisions.

The Supreme Court eventually saw it differently and declared legislative vetoes unconstitutional in 1983 in *Immigration and Naturalization Service v. Chadha*. The majority of the Court noted that some legislative vetoes circumvent constitutional requirements that legislative actions be passed by both chambers. Perhaps more important, the Court said, legislative vetoes violate the constitutional requirement that all measures subject to congressional votes be presented to the president for signature or veto. The Court's position was evident: If Congress wants to limit executive branch use of delegated authority, it must pass new legislation by the traditional route.

Congress has devised no consistent strategy to replace the legislative veto. At times, Congress has written more detailed legislation or committee reports, added new procedural requirements for agencies, or turned to sunset provisions. At other times, it has turned toward informal agency-committee spending agreements, which require agencies to notify certain committees before they act. Although advance notification requirements have been upheld by the courts, committees actually retain an implicit form of veto under these arrangements. Specifically, agencies encountering opposition from the committees that fund them are not likely to proceed with their original plans out of fear of reprisal when their authorizing and appropriations legislation is next before Congress.

Despite the Court's 1983 ruling, Congress has continued to add legislative vetoes to new laws. In just over a year after the *Chadha* decision, an additional fifty-three legislative vetoes were enacted into law. By the completion of the 105th Congress (1997–1998), more than four hundred new legislative vetoes had been enacted. New forms of legislative vetoes are still being attempted and, in some cases, enacted. These efforts reflect the desire of Congress, the president, and the executive agencies to find mutually acceptable ways to balance the delegation of power with checks on the use of that power. The president and agency officials know that courts would rule in their favor if they chose to challenge legislative vetoes, but they often agree to comply with them because legislative vetoes are a necessary condition for the latitude that accompanies them.

A convenient inference is that the Supreme Court's 1983 decision had little practical effect on interbranch relations. Such an inference is premature and probably incorrect. A scholarly review of interbranch relations in the foreign policy arena indicates that the 1983 decision eliminated an important means for resolving conflict. Where Congress and the executive branch are in serious disagreement, the executive branch appears unwilling to accept even symbolic legislative veto provisions, and Congress seems unwilling to delegate power that the executive branch seeks. Changing the rules of the game seems to have affected the ability of the branches to identify cooperative strategies.

IDEOLOGICAL OUTLOOK

Figure 9.4 demonstrates the effect of elections on the changing ideological position of the House, the Senate, and the presidency in recent decades. High scores indicate a conservative outlook, and low scores indicate a liberal outlook. Not surprisingly, the line for the presidency varies widely as it moves back and forth between Democratic and Republican control. Democratic presidents take a more liberal position than the typical member of the House or Senate, and Republican presidents take a more conservative position. In contrast, the ideological positions of the House and Senate are more stable, which reflects the tendency of single elections to produce only a small change in the overall membership of Congress.

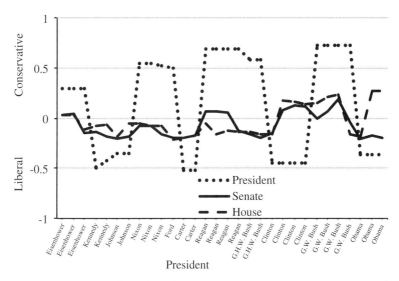

Figure 9.4 House, Senate, and Presidential Conservatism, 1955–2014. Source: Data provided by Keith Poole and Howard Rosenthal, http://www.pooleandrosenthal.com.

The patterns revealed in Figure 9.4 are consistent with what might be expected. During most of the period since the 1950s, all presidents have faced challenges in gaining cooperation from the two chambers of Congress. As we might expect, Republican presidents Nixon (after his first two years), Ford, Reagan, and George H. W. Bush differed from the Democratic houses of Congress by a larger margin than did Democratic presidents Kennedy, Johnson, and Carter. Republican President Eisenhower, however, did not differ a great deal from the Democratic Congresses that he faced in the late 1950s.

Moreover, the 1980 and 1986 elections, both of which produced a change in party control of the Senate during Reagan's presidency, are associated with changes in the ideological placement of the Senate relative to the House and the presidency. The Senate became more like the Republican White House after the 1980 elections, although it was still not as conservative as the administration. After the 1986 elections, the Senate reverted to its usual place, close to the House, with Presidents Reagan and George H. W. Bush taking far more conservative positions. The divergence between the House and Senate again appeared in the aftermath of the 2010 midterm election during the Obama administration, which ushered in a Republican House majority. Therefore, in the 112th and 113th Congresses (2011–2014), the Senate was far closer to Obama's policy positions than the House. This divergence between the chambers will likely evaporate under the unified Republican control of the 114th Congress (2015–2016).

The patterns in Figure 9.4 are important because they show that elections change the ideological alignment of the three institutional players. They indicate that the House and Senate are usually not too distant from each other and that the president is often the outlier. If left to their own devices, presidents probably would produce more radical shifts in policy than they are allowed to do in the three-player game. Nevertheless, important shifts do occur within Congress as well. For example, Congress moved considerably farther away from President Clinton following the 1994 election, leading to a conflict-ridden six years of divided government, but the 107th through 109th Congresses (2001–2006) were very sympathetic to President George W. Bush's legislative agenda.

The extended period of divided party control of government under Presidents Reagan, George H. W. Bush, Clinton, George W. Bush, and Obama have rekindled a debate about the policy consequences of divided control of government. Many observers have characterized the period as one of political deadlock: Conservative presidents have checked the initiatives of a liberal Congress, and the liberal Congress has blocked the proposals of conservative presidents (and, under Clinton and Obama, vice versa).

Partisan competition exacerbates the already difficult task of gaining agreement among the House, the Senate, and the president. This depiction of the state of American national government has led many critics to recommend radical reforms, so we must know whether it is accurate. Does divided party control of government make any difference?

THE DIVIDED-GOVERNMENT DEBATE

THE MAYHEW THESIS. Political scientist David Mayhew investigated the question of divided control in his book *Divided We Govern*. He examined the frequency of major congressional investigations of the executive branch and the enactment of major legislation for the period between 1947 and 1990. During that period, one party controlled both houses of Congress and the presidency for eighteen years and neither party controlled both houses and the presidency for twenty-six years (including 1981 to 1986, when Republicans controlled the Senate and White House but not the House). He found that "unified as opposed to divided control has not made an important difference in recent times" with respect to either the undertaking of high-profile investigations or the rate at which important laws are enacted. Mayhew concluded that "it does not seem to make all that much difference whether party control of the American government happens to be unified or divided."

Mayhew's somewhat surprising findings call attention to the forces in American politics that lead to cooperation between the House, the Senate, and the president. All three institutions must respond to the same national problems, and they share many constituents. Furthermore, members of Congress and presidents both have strong electoral incentives to establish a positive record of accomplishment.

TABLE 9.1. Presidential success on roll call votes: The effect of divided government, 1953–2013

	House (%)	Senate (%)
Unified government	83.0	82.0
	(24)	(31)
Divided government	48.6	66.1
	(37)	(30)

Note: Percentages reflect average success rates of presidents on roll calls on which they took positions. Data collected by the authors from *Congressional Quarterly Weekly Report*. Number of years indicated in parentheses.

Even if public opinion varies greatly among different congressional constituencies, shifts in public mood, which are produced by changing conditions and events, tend to propel all elected officials in the same direction.

OTHER EVIDENCE. Nevertheless, evidence seems to show that divided party control does make some difference. To make sense of patterns in the direction of public policy over time, we must take into account the ideological distance between the House, the Senate, and the president at specific points in time. After all, divided control may not always cause a large gap between the policy positions of the president and the two chambers of Congress, nor is it true that unified control ensures ideological alignment between the president and Congress. We have seen that ideological distance between the House, the Senate, and the president is related to party control. In addition, we can examine direct measures of policy agreement and disagreement among the three institutions. In fact, three such measures – the rate of success for presidential proposals, presidential success on congressional roll call votes (see Table 9.1), and presidential vetoes – show the expected differences between unified and divided control. The president's recommendations are adopted less frequently under divided party control, the president's position on roll call votes wins less frequently, and the president resorts to the veto more frequently under divided control than under unified control. In his first year in the White House, President Obama was successful on an astounding 94 percent of House votes that he took a position on. In 2013, he was successful on a mere 21 percent, as Obama and House Republicans repeatedly butted heads over public policy.

The partisan divide we currently see in Washington is exacerbated by changes in the racial and ethnic makeup of the United States and the correlation between ethnic background and voting behavior. In 2012, President Obama won reelection by winning big margins among nonwhite voters. According to exit polls, he won 93 percent of the African American vote and more than 70 percent of the Latino and Asian vote but gained only 41 percent of the white

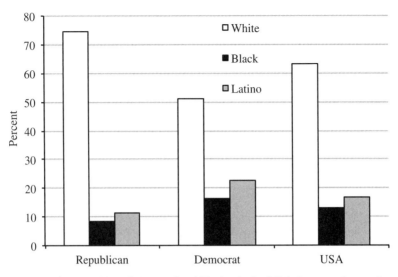

Figure 9.5 Racial Composition of Congressional Districts in the 113th Congress. Source: Census data compiled by David Wasserman.

vote. Obama now faces a Republican-controlled House in part because of redistricting and the "sorting" of voters into politically similar neighborhoods. As Figure 9.5 reveals, the average congressional districts represented by Democrats and Republicans are strikingly different from one another in terms of racial makeup and neither is particularly representative of the U.S. population as a whole. Therefore, much of the frequent policy disagreement we see between the president and congressional Republicans can be attributed to the different constituencies that they represent.

A fair conclusion is that the party balance in Congress, a direct product of elections, is an important force among the many different forces that shape relations between the House, the Senate, and the president. Because party control is related, albeit imperfectly, to ideological distance, it affects the degree to which the president's policies are accepted by Congress and vice versa. Other forces are at work as well, and many of them push the House, the Senate, and the president in the same direction even when partisanship divides the three institutional players.

CONCLUSION

This review of congressional and presidential strategies suggests how dynamic and complex the relationship between the legislative and executive branches has become. As political conditions have evolved, senators, representatives, presidents, and bureaucrats have devised new and sometimes ingenious strategies to influence policy outcomes. Dissatisfaction with the likely or realized outcomes of the game has often yielded institutional innovations, such as expanding the responsibilities of the OMB, creating the line-item veto, expanding the use of executive orders, and creating legislative vetoes. Incrementally, the web of statutes, court rulings, and informal understandings produced by this process of innovation has made interbranch relations more complex. On the whole, the separation of powers between Congress and the president has become less clearly defined with the expansion of the president's legislative powers and Congress's administrative capabilities. What keeps the system operating is a minimal level of agreement among the House, Senate, and president, or at least an understanding that compromise is essential to prevent complete gridlock.

The three-institution legislative game of the House, Senate, and presidency generates cooperation and conflict as the policy preferences and political interests of officeholders vary across issues and over time. However, the requirement that the three institutional players agree before new law can be made, in the absence of sufficient congressional support to override a veto, leads to exploitation of extrastatutory tactics and often necessitates informal accommodation. Accommodation is frustrating to players set on gaining outright victories, and it often is possible only after a long struggle. Furthermore, accommodation produces unstable results. New Congresses and presidents seeking new strategies to meet their own political needs frequently alter the state of the institutions. Consequently, relations between the branches seldom remain in equilibrium for long.

SUGGESTED READINGS

A. The following reading provides a useful case study of presidential bargaining with Congress.

Woodward, Bob. *The Price of Politics.* New York: Simon and Shuster, 2012.

B. The following readings describe systematic studies of presidential influence in Congress, including the importance of divided party control of Congress and the presidency.

Binder, Sarah. *Stalemate: Causes and Consequences of Legislative Gridlock.* Washington, DC: Brookings Institution Press, 2003.

Edwards, George C. *The Strategic President: Persuasion and Opportunity in Presidential Leadership.* Princeton, NJ: Princeton University Press, 2009.

Kernell, Samuel. *Going Public: New Strategies of Presidential Leadership.* Washington, DC: Congressional Quarterly Press, 1986.

Mayhew, David. *Divided We Govern: Party Control, Lawmaking, and Investigating, 1946–1990.* New Haven, CT: Yale University Press, 1992.

C. The following readings describe constitutional issues in congressional-presidential relations.

Fisher, Louis. *The Politics of Shared Power: Congress and the Executive.* College Station: Texas A&M Press, 1998.

Krutz, Glen S., and Jeffrey S. Peake. *Treaty Politics and the Rise of Executive Agreements: International Commitments in a System of Shared Powers.* Ann Arbor: University of Michigan Press, 2009.

Mayer, Kenneth R. *With the Stroke of a Pen: Executive Orders and Presidential Power.* Princeton, NJ: Princeton University Press, 2001.

DISCUSSION QUESTIONS

1 What is the formal constitutional role of the president in the legislative process?

2 What resources does the president have to influence the actions of Congress?

3 How can the president make public policy without the involvement of Congress?

4 What resources does the Congress have to check the power of the president?

10 Congress and the Courts

The Supreme Court as viewed from the dome of the U.S. Capitol.

The battle over judicial nominees has raged in the past two decades at least in part because the House, Senate, and president are not the only institutional players in the policy-making game. Federal judges serve, to use Chief Justice Roberts's terminology, as "umpires" in encounters between players in the legislative and executive arenas and help determine the boundaries of each institution's powers. In separation-of-powers cases, for example, judges often draw lines between the two branches and specify the constitutional powers on each side. Judges also consider the scope of legislative powers generally, including the congressional power to investigate the executive branch and where the line between federal and state jurisdictions should be drawn. They rule on many controversial issues, including voting rights, gun control, and health care reform.

Solicitor General and Supreme Court nominee Elena Kagan meets with Senate Minority Leader
Mitch McConnell (R-KY) during a round of meetings on Capitol Hill

As both political and legal institutions, the courts are more than umpires in the
legislative game. In the past generation, judges have increasingly contributed to
making policy – not merely interpreting statutes already enacted. The growth of
judicial activism since the 1970s and the reactions to judicial activism are an important part of the story of relations between Congress and the courts. In fact, in
recent years the topic of judicial activism has dominated confirmation hearings
for the nation's highest court. Senators, reluctant to cede policy-making authority to the Supreme Court, have spent hours grilling nominees over their interpretation of the Court's limits. Nominees, perhaps in an effort to achieve confirmation, have attempted to reassure legislators that they respect these boundaries.
During her 2010 confirmation hearings for a seat on the Court, for instance,
Elena Kagan asserted: "The Supreme Court is a wondrous institution. But the
time I spent in the other branches of government remind me that it must also be
a modest one – properly deferential to the decisions of the American people and
their elected representatives."

Congress is not a quiet bystander to the decisions of the courts. Most important
areas of law are the product of interaction between the legislative institutions
(Congress and the president) and the courts. The legislative institutions have a
number of ways to influence, at least indirectly, the decisions the courts make,
as Congress and the president determine the courts' composition. The president
nominates the judges, and the Senate must confirm the nominees. Moreover, the
size of the Supreme Court and lower courts, the organization and funding for the

federal court system, and the Supreme Court's jurisdiction wit'
from lower courts are determined by law, making them subj
process controlled by the House, Senate, and president. Mc
and the president anticipate and react to court rulings. Th
with, ignore, or even reverse judicial decisions. Moreover, they ...
or even exclude court consideration of certain matters in the way they write ...
This chapter takes up each of these subjects – the courts as umpires, the courts
as policy makers, and congressional resources and strategies.

COURTS AS UMPIRES

The Constitution does not explicitly grant to the Supreme Court the power to
declare actions of state and federal legislatures and executives unconstitutional.
The Court, however, has inserted itself into the dynamics of the legislative game
for more than two centuries. In *Marbury v. Madison* (1803), the Court first asserted that it had the power of *judicial review* or the ability to declare laws unconstitutional and has continued to use that power from time to time.

Most cases come to the courts when a private party, sometimes an interest
group, challenges the constitutionality of an act of Congress after an executive
agency seeks to implement or enforce the act. Occasionally, members of Congress file suit against the executive branch for its failure to implement laws in a
manner consistent with the members' expectations. In fact, members have been
plaintiffs in suits filed against the executive branch in more cases during the past
two decades than in all previous decades. Issues of great importance are appealed
from lower courts to the Supreme Court, although this process might take years
after the original enactment of the legislation.

As Figure 10.1 shows, the Supreme Court has overturned federal and state
provisions at an uneven pace over its history. Before 1865, few provisions were
overturned. In fact, for much of its history, the Supreme Court has exercised its
review powers only intermittently. Intense legislative-judicial conflict is relatively
infrequent, occurring in the decades around the New Deal and in more recent
decades. Even then, historically the majority of laws and provisions overturned
by the Court are actually minor or relatively unimportant. This has changed in recent years as the Court has taken on high-profile, high-impact legislation such as
the Voting Rights Act, the Violence Against Women Act, the Religious Freedom
and Restoration Act, the Bipartisan Campaign Reform Act, and the Affordable
Care Act.

In this section, two types of cases involving the interpretation of the Constitution are discussed: cases involving the separation of powers between Congress and
the executive branch and cases concerning the scope of congressional powers. The

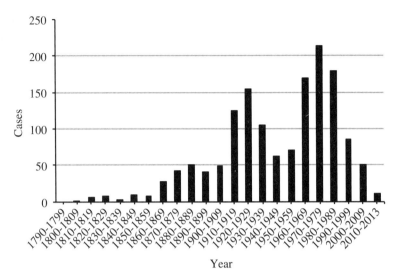

Figure 10.1 Number of Cases Where Provisions Were Ruled Unconstitutional by the Supreme Court. Sources: Lawrence Baum, *The Supreme Court,* 11th ed. (Washington, DC: Congressional Quarterly Press, 2013), and the United States Supreme Court Database.

section concludes with a discussion of the role of courts as umpires in disputes about the meaning of statutes.

Separation-of-Powers Cases

In the decades before the 1970s, court involvement in separation-of-powers cases was uncommon. Because Congress was relatively deferential to the executive branch, few encounters were likely to provoke conflict over the powers of each branch. That situation changed dramatically during the Nixon administration (1969–1974) and in the following years when Congress moved to reassert itself.

President Richard Nixon asserted broad presidential powers in his conflict with a Congress controlled by the Democrats. The most conspicuous conflict was Nixon's battle with Congress over federal spending. Nixon claimed a right to withhold funds from executive agencies – a process called impoundment – even after the appropriations legislation was enacted into law. For example, Nixon impounded funds appropriated for sewage treatment plants administered by the Environmental Protection Agency. The impoundments were frequently challenged in the courts and Nixon usually lost. In 1973 and 1974 alone, only six of more than fifty cases upheld the president's position on impoundments in any way. Most of the decisions were made at the U.S. district court level and were not appealed by the administration to higher courts. In the sewage-treatment case, the Supreme Court ruled that the president was obligated to follow the law and allocate the funds.

In the 1980s, partisan dissension between the Republican White House and the Democratic Congress continued to drive each branch to the courts for redress against the perceived excesses of the other branch. For most of the Reagan and George H. W. Bush presidencies, the Supreme Court followed a "doctrinal notion of separated powers" – the view that a sharp line can be drawn between executive and legislative powers. Two particularly revealing decisions in which the Court decided against Congress during this period were *Immigration and Naturalization Service v. Chadha* (1983) and *Bowsher v. Synar* (1986). These decisions merit attention in light of the ways in which the Court refereed contentious encounters between the branches. A later case, *Clinton v. City of New York* (1998), further demonstrates the Court's willingness to draw sharp distinction even in the absence of interbranch contention.

In the *Chadha* decision, the Supreme Court ruled seven to two that the legislative veto (see Chapter 9) was unconstitutional. According to the Court, Congress was to present bills to the president, who had the sole power to veto them. Arguments that the legislative veto was a workable means of extending authority to the executive short of formal enactment of a law were rejected. Congress, however, has largely ignored the ban on legislative vetoes, and hundreds have been enacted post-*Chadha* – often with the agreement of the executive branch. Although the *Chadha* decision has forced Congress to be more creative in crafting provisions that give the legislature a potential veto, the response to the decision shows the weakness of the Court as an umpire when Congress and presidents agree on mutually beneficial ways to distribute power between themselves.

Building on *Chadha*, the *Bowsher* decision advanced a stricter concept of separation of powers. *Bowsher* struck down a provision of the 1985 Gramm-Rudman-Hollings Act that required the president to implement spending reductions determined by the Comptroller General when the budget deficit exceeded a prescribed maximum. A majority of the Court concluded that such budget cuts were a power belonging to the Executive. Furthermore, the Court asserted that the Comptroller General, who can be removed from office by a joint resolution of Congress, was essentially an officer of the legislative branch. Therefore, this provision was deemed an unconstitutional infringement by the legislative branch on the powers of the Executive. Although the *Bowsher* decision focused on a relatively narrow legal question, it ultimately forwarded a model of legislative-executive relations in which the legislative branch has a limited role in supervising the implementation of the laws it enacts. The Court wrote, "[O]nce Congress makes its choice in enacting legislation, its participation ends. Congress can thereafter control the execution of its enactment only indirectly – by passing new legislation." As discussed in Chapter 9, the strict model forwarded by the Court in *Bowsher* has clearly not been practiced by the branches.

The Supreme Court's decision in *Clinton v. City of New York* (1998), striking down the line-item veto, demonstrated the Court's willingness to enforce the separation of powers between Congress and the president even when the two branches are not in conflict. In 1996, Congress passed and President Clinton signed the line-item veto, which gave the president the power to remove or veto specific tax breaks or spending from bills while signing the underlying bill, with the law taking effect after the presidential election of 1996. Presidents had long sought this power to control federal spending, but many in Congress were eager to let the president help control it and take the blame for cutting popular programs. In striking down the line-item veto, the Court ruled that allowing the modification of a bill before signing it violated the constitutionally prescribed legislative process, specifically the "presentment" clause of Article I. During the presidency of George W. Bush, he and many members of Congress expressed their desire to reenact a version of the line-item veto, but the Court's ruling has made it clear that the Court will guard the constitutionally prescribed separation of powers. The topic of the line-item veto has resurfaced during the Obama presidency. In 2011, a bipartisan group, led by Senators John McCain (R-Arizona) and Tom Carper (D-Delaware), introduced legislation presenting a new version of the line-item veto in an effort to curtail nonmandatory spending. This variant would give the president forty-five days from signing to rescind funding contained in the legislation. Congress would then have the authority to reject the cuts within ten days of receiving notice of the president's decision. It is unclear whether, if challenged, the Court will view this version as more constitutionally viable than previous iterations.

Several actions of the George W. Bush administration, many related to the War on Terror, exposed tensions regarding the limits of legislative oversight of the executive branch. Of particular interest in legislative-executive relations have been questions relating to executive privilege. President Bush's broad claims of executive privilege on sensitive matters marked some of the most expansive use of the privilege in history, which enraged many in Congress. Perhaps the most controversial use of executive privilege came when Bush instructed former White House Counsel Harriet Miers and White House Chief of Staff Joshua Bolten to ignore congressional subpoenas related to the investigation of the firing of nine U.S. attorneys that was thought by many in Congress to have been politically motivated. After a lengthy struggle between the branches, a deal was struck that required Miers (and former Deputy Chief of Staff Karl Rove) to be interviewed under oath by the House Judiciary Committee in closed depositions. This agreement averted an almost certain path to the Supreme Court.

More recently, the Supreme Court did step in to arbitrate a dispute between President Obama and Congress regarding the president's recess appointment powers. The Constitution clearly grants the president the power to fill vacant positions during congressional recesses, but it does not clearly define what constitutes a recess. President Obama had appointed three members to the National Labor Relations Board during a congressional recess lasting three days. This recess occurred during a much longer de facto recess that had been occasionally interrupted by pro forma Senate sessions in which no business was conducted. The Obama administration insisted that the pro forma sessions should not be counted as valid sessions, while Senate Republicans argued that they should be counted and thus the appointments were invalid. In a unanimous opinion, the Supreme Court ruled in *NLRB v. Noel Canning* (2014) that the executive had to rely on the Senate definition of a recess. In doing so, the Court bolstered the power of Congress to prevent recess appointments from occurring.

Congressional Powers

The courts also referee the legislative game by their involvement in questions of congressional powers. Although Article I of the Constitution specifies in some detail the powers of Congress, the Supreme Court has often ruled on whether certain acts of Congress are permissible. In contrast, the Supreme Court has heard relatively few cases on Congress's authority over its internal affairs. On questions of membership qualifications, Congress's ability to punish its members, and speech privileges of members, the Court has generally given Congress a good deal of leeway. A few examples show how difficult the issues can be and how much the role of the courts as umpire can change in particular areas of the law.

THE COMMERCE CLAUSE. The most frequent way that the courts have refereed legislative politics is by interpreting the limits of congressional power under the Constitution. Perhaps the best examples are Supreme Court rulings that interpret the commerce clause of the Constitution (Article I, Section 8). The commerce clause allows Congress to enact legislation that regulates interstate commerce, and it has been used by Congress to regulate many aspects of American life that are related, however indirectly, to interstate commerce. Over the years, the Supreme Court has decided many cases that affect the limits of what activities are related to interstate commerce. As the national economy became more integrated and as Congress sought to establish more uniform policies for the nation in the late 1800s and early 1900s, congressional powers under the commerce clause became a controversial issue.

In the late 1800s and early 1900s, the Supreme Court took a narrow view of interstate commerce. If an activity concerned production or manufacturing, concerned only intrastate exchange, and did not directly affect interstate commerce, the Court tended to protect it from federal regulation. This interpretation greatly limited the ability of Congress and the president to respond to the rapidly changing national economy. In fact, the Court's narrow view of the commerce clause led it to strike down Franklin Roosevelt's New Deal legislation in the early 1930s, which was enacted in response to the Great Depression. After Roosevelt requested, but failed to get, congressional approval to enlarge the Court so that he could change the balance of opinion on the Court, two justices changed their views on the commerce clause, and the Court reversed itself on several major decisions.

Since the 1930s, step-by-step, the Court has allowed Congress to determine what activities are related to interstate commerce. In *Wickard v. Filburn* (1942), the Supreme Court ruled that a law limiting the amount of wheat a farmer could grow on his own land for his own use was permissible under Congress's commerce clause powers. In the 1960s, the Court affirmed the right of Congress to forbid owners of public accommodations with an interstate commerce connection (e.g., hotels, restaurants, etc.) from denying access on the basis of race or color. In the 1980s and early 1990s, the Court upheld laws that set minimum wages for employees of state and local governments, prohibit age discrimination by agencies of state government, and ban threats and extortion to collect on loans. Until the mid-1990s, Court action appeared to erase the line between intrastate and interstate commerce and leave very broad powers for Congress under the commerce clause.

In 1995, led by conservative justices, the Supreme Court changed the direction of seventy years of rulings in favor of congressional discretion to determine the breadth of the commerce clause. In *United States v. Lopez*, the Court struck down a 1990 law that prohibited anyone from knowingly carrying a firearm in a school zone. The government argued that Congress had implicit authority, from its ability to interpret the commerce clause, to regulate firearms for such a public purpose. The Court ruled that nothing in the commerce clause or other constitutional provisions authorizes Congress to regulate such behavior, absent compelling evidence that the presence of firearms in school zones had an adverse effect on interstate commerce.

The Court continued its efforts to set limits on Congress's ability to stretch the commerce clause by striking down parts of the Violence Against Women Act in *U.S. v. Morrison* (2000). The 5–4 ruling invalidated a portion of the statute allowing women who were victims of sexual assault to sue their attackers in federal court. Congress had granted women this power citing numerous studies indicating that fear of violence had a chilling effect on the mobility of female students and employees. The majority opinion in *U.S. v. Morrison* held that Congress's attempt to regulate crimes against women in this manner could "obliterate the Constitution's distinction between national and local authority," whereas the dissent held that Congress had adequately demonstrated the link between violence against women and interstate commerce.

The conservative majority that had seemed intent on limiting the power of Congress under the commerce clause splintered in *Gonzales v. Raich* (2005). The case dealt with whether or not the federal government could prohibit states from enacting laws sanctioning the use of medicinal marijuana. The government argued that the Controlled Substances Act – a law regulating the use of drugs such as marijuana – did not allow the use of the drug for medicinal purposes. The defendants argued that the Controlled Substances Act was unconstitutional because the drug was homegrown, did not cross state lines, and was not sold – and therefore did not involve interstate commerce. A 6–3 majority of the Supreme Court disagreed, finding that Congress did have the power to regulate medicinal

Supreme Court chief justice nominee John Roberts gives testimony before the Senate Judiciary Committee on the second day of his confirmation hearing.

marijuana under the commerce clause, signaling a reversal in the Court's tightening of Congress's powers under the commerce clause.

The Affordable Care Act and Judicial Legitimacy

The Supreme Court's ruling in *National Federation of Independent Business v. Sebelius* (2012) was a major victory for President Obama and proponents of universal health care. It was also one of the most anticipated and analyzed Court decisions in recent years. Many Court watchers wondered if the conservative majority on the Court would be willing to strike down the signature domestic policy achievement of President Obama and a Democratic congressional majority. Some observers argue that the Court runs the risk of losing the confidence and trust of the public if it regularly overturns the decisions of the democratically elected branches of government. In recent terms, the Court has issued a number of bitterly divided 5–4 rulings on major issues such as campaign finance reform and the 2000 presidential election between George W. Bush and Al Gore. Public approval of the Court has declined in the past decade in the wake of these decisions.

Did fears of declining confidence in the Supreme Court motivate the justices in the Affordable Care Act case? We may never know for sure, but there is some evidence to suggest that Chief Justice Roberts switched his vote at the last minute to uphold the law. The tortured logic used in the majority opinion, along with a number of passages in the dissenting opinion that refer to the majority opinion as the dissent, suggests to some that the coalitions that supported and opposed the law were unstable in the days leading up the decision. It is certainly plausible that the Chief Justice was willing to compromise his position in this particular case to preserve the legitimacy of the Court in future cases and controversies.

The most noteworthy commerce clause case to arise in recent years dealt with President Obama's signature domestic policy achievement – the Affordable Care Act. In question was the requirement that Americans maintain a minimum level of health insurance or a pay a fine. Proponents of the legislation argued that the commerce clause gave Congress the authority to impose such a requirement. The argument is that in the absence of this requirement, along with the mandate that insurance companies cover all individuals regardless of preexisting conditions, there is an incentive for individuals to buy insurance only when it is needed. Such a scenario, proponents contend, would dramatically affect insurance premiums and therefore substantially affect interstate commerce.

In June of 2012, the Court ruled in *National Federation of Independent Business v. Sebelius* that the individual mandate was impermissible under Congress's power to regulate interstate commerce. However, the Court also ruled that the mandate was permissible under the taxing authority granted to Congress. With President Obama's reelection in 2012, it is likely that the Affordable Care Act will remain in place for the foreseeable future (see box "The Affordable Care Act and Judicial Legitimacy").

POWER TO INVESTIGATE. One area in which the courts have been more active in interpreting congressional powers has been Congress's power to investigate. Although the power to investigate is not mentioned explicitly in the Constitution, investigatory authority has traditionally been considered an implied power of Congress. In general, the authority to acquire information is usually seen as necessary for the proper functioning of a legislature. For example, the investigative and contempt powers of the English Parliament are exempt from judicial review. Although most investigations by the U.S. Congress are carried out without ending up in court, the Supreme Court has on occasion reached some rather controversial decisions about the scope of congressional investigatory authority. In particular, the Court has refereed cases contesting the subjects that Congress can investigate and the rights that congressional witnesses retain. The Court originally took a narrow view of congressional investigative and contempt authority in *Kilbourn v. Thompson*, decided in 1881. In overturning the arrest of Hallet Kilbourn, who refused to provide information to the House about certain real estate deals, the Supreme Court limited Congress's ability to investigate private matters. The Court also delineated several principles concerning the proper scope of congressional powers to investigate. Specifically, the Court limited the extent of congressional authority to matters on which Congress could legitimately legislate and on which the chamber conducting the investigation had indicated its intent to legislate.

Those standards stood for nearly fifty years, until the Supreme Court broadened congressional authority in *McGrain v. Daugherty* in 1927. The Court ruled that Congress had no general power to investigate private matters, but the Court extended the scope of congressional authority to any subject of *potential* legislation. The Court also affirmed Congress's power to compel private individuals to testify; but the Court reserved for individuals the right to refuse to answer certain questions if they were not pertinent to the general investigation. Reserving a right for individuals to refuse to testify was to become central to Senator Joseph McCarthy's (R-Wisconsin) investigations of subversive activities in the 1950s.

In the 1950s and 1960s, the Court under Chief Justice Earl Warren moved to protect the right of private individuals to refuse to answer questions based on their Fifth Amendment privilege against self-incrimination (*Watkins v. United States*, 1957; *Bernblatt v. United States*, 1959). *Watkins* concerned the rights of persons convicted of contempt of Congress for failing to answer questions about their association with the Communist Party that were posed by the House Un-American Activities Committee. In this case, the Court ruled that the committee did not have a sufficiently well-defined legislative purpose to justify requiring an individual to respond to questions. Chief Justice Warren, writing for the Court, noted that "there is no congressional power to expose for the sake of exposure."

REGULATING CAMPAIGN SPENDING. In overturning parts of campaign finance legislation passed in 1974, the Supreme Court ruled in *Buckley v. Valeo* (1976) that Congress cannot limit individual or group expenditures in a political campaign when those expenditures are made independently of a particular candidate or party. The Court said that the First Amendment of the Constitution, which guarantees freedom of speech, prevents the government from regulating political speech – in this case, speech funded by an individual on her own behalf.

The Court said that limitations on campaign expenditures, as for any restraint on political speech, are constitutional only if some compelling government interest exists. The determination of what constitutes a compelling interest requires the courts to exercise discretion and judgment. In this case, the Supreme Court decided that the goal of limiting the electoral influence of wealthy individuals or groups was insufficient and ran directly counter to the intent of the First Amendment.

The Court reached a different conclusion in a case regarding the constitutionality of the 1974 law restricting the amount of money that political parties could spend directly on behalf of candidates. In reversing a previous decision by a circuit court, the Supreme Court held in *FEC v. Colorado Republican Federal Campaign Committee* (1996) that coordinated spending by political parties was not protected by the First Amendment and thus could be constitutionally regulated. Further, a majority of the Court found that there was a compelling government interest in regulating the spending activities of political parties. The Supreme Court upheld Congress's most recent attempt to regulate campaign finance, the 2002 Bipartisan Campaign Reform Act (BCRA), in *McConnell v. FEC* (2003). The Court allowed Congress to ban soft money and set restrictions on issue advocacy ads placed on television. However, the BCRA came under additional fire in subsequent years. In 2007, the Court ruled against the BCRA's ban on issue advocacy ads in the sixty days preceding general elections (*FEC v. Wisconsin*

Right to Life). More recently, in *Citizens United v. FEC* (2010), the Court struck down the BCRA's ban on corporate funding of independent political broadcasts in candidate elections, a decision that unleashed a flood of independent spending in American elections (see Chapter 3 for more details on spending in congressional elections).

The Politics of Statutory Interpretation

When courts act as umpires in the legislative game, they often make judgments about the meaning of statutes. The imprecision of language, inconsistencies among various laws adopted at different times, and evolving circumstances to which a statute must be applied guarantee that the courts will face difficult decisions about the interpretation of laws. Compounding matters is that the legislators and presidents responsible for drafting legislation may have disagreed about the legislation's meaning or even deliberately left certain provisions vague to smooth over differences among themselves that would have been obstacles to enactment. Judges, when asked to resolve disputes about the interpretation of statutes, may affect the direction of public policy and sometimes alter the strategies of legislators, presidents, and others who care about policy.

Judges and legal scholars have developed several approaches to interpreting statutes, each reflecting a different view about how Congress functions, how legislative outcomes are reached, and how capable judges are of understanding congressional intent. The most traditional approach to interpreting statutes relies on the "canons of statutory construction." The canons outline for judges how to interpret the language of laws and are often stated in Latin. For example, one canon – *inclusio unius est exclusio alterius* – means that the inclusion of one thing indicates the exclusion of another. Other canons apply to specific subjects. For example, the "rule of lenity" stipulates that statutes that make certain conduct unlawful and impose penalties must be construed to apply narrowly to the conduct specified.

Unfortunately, canons often conflict and there is no canon to help judges choose the appropriate canon. One school of legal scholars advocates that judges determine the objective or purpose of the statute and then deduce the outcome most consistent with the law's purpose. Another school insists that judges should determine how legislators, motivated by the special interests influencing them, would decide a question if asked to do so. Others, however, contend that judges should be free to interpret and reinterpret statutes as the societal or legal context changes. Not surprisingly, some scholars argue that judges should refuse to resolve ambiguities and insist that they be resolved in the legislative process.

Perhaps the most important issue in statutory interpretation is being waged over the relevance and content of legislative histories. A few purists argue for strict construction of statutes. Rather than turning to committee reports and floor debates to interpret legislative intent, supporters of this approach urge courts to restrict themselves to the "plain meaning," or intrinsic meaning, of a statute's text. This view seems to be gaining support in the federal judiciary. Its most prominent proponent is Supreme Court Justice Antonin Scalia.

In practice, most judges still gladly accept guidance from committee reports, the record of floor debate, statements of bill or amendment sponsors, presidential messages, and other documented evidence of the intent of a bill's authors. Because legislative histories often encapsulate conflicting views, however, they are not straightforward guides to statutory interpretation for judges. Further, members of Congress can try to add things to the legislative history to influence the decisions of judges. Most judges seem willing to exercise some judgment about which views should be considered most authoritative. Some effort has been made in recent years to improve communication between the federal judiciary and Congress so that problems of statutory interpretation can be minimized.

In recent years, a majority of justices on the Supreme Court have begun to look more carefully at legislative histories in the context of federalism cases. In striking down major provisions of the Americans with Disabilities Act, the Violence Against Women Act, and the Religious Freedom and Restoration Act, and upholding provisions of the Family and Medical Leave Act, the Court has cited legislative histories extensively in their opinions. The Court in these cases has used the content of legislative histories to determine whether Congress has generated a record of mistreatment of individuals by the states. The Court has reasoned that a substantial legislative record is necessary for Congress to abridge states' Eleventh Amendment protection against lawsuits in order to enforce the equal protection clause of the Fourteenth Amendment.

The most recent example of the Court evaluating the quality of the legislative process was decided in the landmark case of *Shelby County v. Holder* (2013). The question in this case was whether certain sections of the Voting Rights Act, which was originally enacted in 1965 and reauthorized in 2006, were constitutionally permissible. Section 5 of the Voting Rights Act required states and municipalities that had a history of racial discrimination in voting rights law to receive "preclearance" from the Justice Department before any change in election policy could be enacted. The states and municipalities that were required to seek preclearance were listed in Section 4 of the law. Shelby County, Alabama, challenged its coverage status and asked the courts to invalidate Sections 4 and 5 of the law. Both the federal district court and the Court of Appeals for the D.C. Circuit upheld the law, in part based on the language of the Fifteenth Amendment to the Constitution, which reads:

> Section 1: The right of citizens of the United States to vote shall not be denied or abridged by the United States or by any state on account of race, color, or previous condition of servitude.

Section 2: The Congress shall have power to enforce this article by appropriate legislation.

The Supreme Court reversed both lower court decisions by a contentious 5–4 vote. The majority opinion – authored by Chief Justice John Roberts – argued that Congress had overstepped its authority in reauthorizing the law in part because of Congress's use of data that was more than four decades old in some instances. The majority opinion struck down Section 4 of the act and made Section 5 unworkable without a valid list of covered jurisdictions. In the wake of this decision, many formerly covered jurisdictions have enacted new election laws policies that in many cases have made it more difficult for racial minorities and citizens of lower socioeconomic status to register and vote.

This new scrutiny of the lawmaking process by the Court has altered the balance of power between Congress and the states. New questions have been raised about the quality and content of legislative deliberation, such as what standards of evidence Congress should be held to in demonstrating the need for new laws.

Members, lobbyists, and administrations often anticipate that legislative history may be important when issues are taken to the courts. Sometimes, the language of committee reports is the subject of as intense a fight as the bill language itself. For example, after the House Energy and Commerce Committee voted to approve a major overhaul of clean air laws in 1990, it took nearly a month for committee staff to hammer out report language that was acceptable to all sides. On most matters, carefully prepared statements by committee chairs and bill sponsors are made on the floors of the two chambers to give weight to a particular interpretation of the major provisions of legislation and to set a record that judges cannot easily ignore.

JUDGES AS POLICY MAKERS

Although the courts' primary role is to serve as an umpire for disputes about legislative authority and procedure, the relationship between the courts and the legislative institutions is more complex than that. In recent decades, federal judges have been seen as policy makers – players and not just umpires. At times, judges have even moved aggressively to place themselves at the center of political disputes. In many areas, however, Congress and the president have encouraged courts' policy-making activities in the legislation they have enacted. The assertiveness of the Warren Court in the 1950s in addressing racial desegregation marked a considerably more active and aggressive involvement of the courts in national policy making. Although the Burger Court (1969–1986) impeded somewhat the extent of judicial involvement in policy making, the Rehnquist Court (1986–2005) was one the most "activist" ever (see Figure 10.1). Moreover, it

TABLE 10.1. Supreme Court voting agreement scores in the 2013–2014 term

	Ginsburg	Sotomayor	Kagan	Breyer	Kennedy	Roberts	Alito	Thomas
Ginsburg								
Sotomayor	71							
Kagan	83	74						
Breyer	68	67	71					
Kennedy	40	38	58	56				
Roberts	32	38	50	56	76			
Alito	25	22	35	33	63	62		
Thomas	28	25	38	36	48	67	88	
Scalia	44	33	46	36	56	57	71	84

Source: Data taken from SCOTUSblog statpack.

seems quite clear that justices are *not* impartial automatons in this process. In fact, there is striking consistency in voting coalitions on the Court, which suggests that judicial decisions are to some extent made through the lenses of personal ideology (see Table 10.1). Justices are more likely to vote with colleagues who are situated near them along the left-right continuum. There is no reason to suspect that these coalitions emerge based on pure legal interpretation.

Congressionally Speaking . . .

Members frequently attempt to establish a clear record about how certain provisions of a bill should be interpreted. One way of doing this is to discuss the provisions in the *committee report* that accompanies the bill. Committee reports provide the background and justification for the bill and its provisions and often provide detailed sections on the meaning of key words or phrases. They are drafted by committee staffs and approved by committees, sometimes after long debate. Members also engage in *colloquies* – scripted exchanges on the floor among two or more members to clarify the interpretation of a bill or an amendment. Colloquies, of course, are transcribed in the *Congressional Record*, where judges, executive branch officials, and others can find floor statements.

   In recent years, presidents have used *signing statements*, issued at the time they sign legislation, to offer their interpretation of controversial provisions. These statements send a message to administrative agencies about the interpretation of the law. Courts have not yet placed much weight on signing statements in their reading of legislative histories. They have tended to place greater weight on *veto statements* when the veto is not overridden by Congress and the legislation is modified in the direction suggested by the president.

Judicial activism may be prompted by legislative activism on the part of Congress and the president. The wave of legislation between the mid-1960s and mid-1970s created new civil rights, broadened eligibility for welfare and health benefits, established new consumer rights, and set new public health, safety, and environmental standards. Much of the legislation required administrative agencies to design new regulations. Other legislation required agencies to account formally for additional factors in making their decisions. In addition, some new laws were enacted that assigned the executive branch the duty to achieve certain policy goals. At the same time, new and often complex procedures were imposed on agencies by new legislation – the Freedom of Information Act, the Privacy Act, the Government in the Sunshine Act, and other laws. These procedural requirements were designed to open agency decision making to public scrutiny, protect individual rights, and ensure that agency officials heard all interests and views. New laws and regulations create opportunities for the federal judiciary to settle conflicts brought to the courts by interests affected negatively by the policies.

Although the role of the courts in the administrative process is, in part, the result of judges' assertiveness, it is much more than that. The creation of new substantive and procedural rights is often the direct product of interest group politics and congressional decisions. Groups and friendly legislators who lack confidence in decisions by regulatory agencies often view litigation as an alternative route for securing favorable policy outcomes. The type of agency decisions that are reviewable by courts, the actions courts may take, the parties who have standing to sue, and other issues are subject to the give-and-take of legislative politics.

The result is that courts are often left to enforce new rights and procedures, determine whether certain factors were given adequate weight in decisions, and evaluate the effectiveness of agency strategies for achieving specified goals. On the procedural side, judicial review sometimes encourages or even requires agencies to elaborate decision-making processes in ways unanticipated by Congress. Political scientist William Gormley observes that

> by stressing the need for due process and by defining due process very broadly indeed, many federal courts have encouraged administrative agencies to adopt cumbersome procedures when handling individual cases, such as welfare or social security cases. A similar development in rule-making review has stimulated the growth of "hybrid ruling-making" procedures, including opportunities to cross-examine witnesses and other procedural guarantees. In practice, hybrid rule-making often benefits special interest groups, who need little additional protection. That is because such groups can afford the legal representation that hybrid rule-making requires.[1]

The courts have often taken the step from procedural matters to the substance of agency decisions. In some cases, the law provides explicitly for the appeal of agency decisions to the courts. For example, the law requiring public schools to provide education for children with disabilities provides for appeals to give local groups a chance to challenge federal, state, and local decisions affecting

---

1 William T. Gormley, Jr., "The Bureaucracy and Its Masters: The New Madisonian System in the U.S." *Governance* (January 1991): 10–11.

education in their communities. In such cases, courts are called on to judge what constitutes adequate education. In doing so, the courts are asked to direct public policy, even to influence the spending priorities of government.

In other cases, lawsuits pursued by affected parties or interest groups unhappy with agency decisions have led courts to make policy judgments. Gormley explains:

> Citing the "hard look doctrine" popularized by the late Judge Harold Leventhal, [courts] have insisted that agencies take a hard look at the available evidence, engage in reasoned decision-making, and give careful consideration to alternatives. All of this sounds rather innocuous. In practice, however, the hard-look doctrine enables judges to substitute their judgment for that of administrative officials who possess far greater technical expertise.[2]

Thus, by applying judicially derived doctrine for situations in which agencies have been delegated substantial policy-making discretion, the courts sometimes have become policy makers themselves.

The question of why Congress has tended to devolve quasi-legislative powers to agencies and the courts remains. Plainly, institutional politics has become quite complex. Some commentators argue that legislators delegate power to executive agencies and the courts to avoid difficult choices and political blame. According to this view, legislators often are unable or unwilling to resolve their differences, so they give up and leave legislation ambiguous or include contradictory provisions, a practice that sometimes leaves interested parties no option but to take the matter to court. Other observers note that Congress and the courts have largely been willing allies in the expansion of the federal bench into the legislative arena. Unwilling to trust agency regulators under Republican administrations, Democratic majorities in Congress repeatedly turned to the courts to help put teeth into increasingly complex and detailed legislation in the 1970s and 1980s. Other analysts, however, emphasize the influence of interest groups to whom Congress and the president are responding when they approve legislation.

Each of these interpretations seems to fit at least some major legislation. Members of Congress have certainly tried to use the courts when they have lacked the political support to secure policy goals through legislation. Failed efforts by legislators to enforce the War Powers Resolution in the courts show the limits of enticing the courts to resolve political controversies, but Congress's tendency to draw the courts into the policy arena also reflects the cumbersome nature of legislating under divided government. Unable to procure favorable outcomes from regulators, members of Congress and organized groups have deliberately sought the assistance of the courts in battling administrators.

2 Ibid.

CONGRESSIONAL RESOURCES AND STRATEGIES

Congress has formidable tools for dealing with an unfriendly federal judiciary. The framers of the Constitution left several tools for Congress and the president to use to check the actions of the courts. Lifetime tenure of federal judges is intended to provide some autonomy to the courts, as is the prohibition against reducing the compensation of judges. Neither Congress nor the president, however, has been willing to give a free hand to the federal judiciary. Congress has used its constitutional authority to impeach federal judges, change the number of judges and courts, set the courts' budgets, and alter the appellate jurisdiction of the Supreme Court. Perhaps most familiar to even casual observers of American politics, the president and Congress frequently struggle over appointments to the federal bench.

In addition, Congress has responded legislatively to court decisions. Congress often enacts new legislation that is adapted to court rulings. For example, in 1993 Congress enacted the Religious Freedom and Restoration Act – a direct refutation of the Court's decision in *Oregon v. Smith* (1990), which dealt with religious practice and federal unemployment benefits. When Congress objects to a court's interpretation of a law, Congress sometimes passes a new bill that clarifies its intentions. In some cases, Congress adjusts the new legislation to take into account a court's ruling about the constitutionality of certain kinds of provisions. In recent years, several bills have been introduced in Congress to remove federal court jurisdiction from certain policy areas. Of course, Congress may propose a constitutional amendment to overrule the courts' interpretation of an existing provision.

Congress and the Structure of the Federal Judiciary

The Constitution vests judicial power in the Supreme Court but grants to Congress the authority to establish inferior courts when it chooses. The size, budget, and appellate jurisdiction of the Supreme Court, as well as the structure, size, budget, and jurisdiction of lower courts, are determined by law and are therefore subject to the normal legislative process. In addition, Congress is authorized by the Constitution to create what are known as Article I courts, or legislative courts – the military courts, tax court, customs courts, and bankruptcy courts. These courts are located in either the executive or judicial branches, the judges are appointed by the president with Senate confirmation, and the judges serve fixed, limited terms.

Partisan politics has been an ever-present condition in Congress's handling of the judiciary. The first major effort to structure the courts for political purposes occurred in 1801, when the defeated president John Adams and his Federalist supporters in Congress created new circuit court judgeships to be filled with Federalists.

The effort to influence the character of the federal bench failed, however, when the new Republican Congress repealed the act and abolished the judgeships. Even though Congress postponed the next meeting of the Supreme Court to prevent it from hearing a challenge to its repeal, the Court upheld Congress's power to repeal the Federalists' Judiciary Act of 1801 a year later.

Congress has only once limited the jurisdiction of the Supreme Court. In 1868, after having struck down parts of Reconstruction legislation in 1866, the Court was scheduled to hear another case on Reconstruction law – the Habeas Corpus Act, which concerned the rights of individuals held in detention. Anticipating that the Court would use the occasion to find all Reconstruction laws unconstitutional, Congress enacted a law to prevent the Court from hearing cases related to the Habeas Corpus Act. The Supreme Court, incidentally, backed down from any confrontation with Congress when it upheld the constitutionality of the repeal of its jurisdiction a year later.

With the exception of the Reconstruction-era episode, efforts to curb the Supreme Court's jurisdiction have failed. This result is not too surprising. After all, the House, Senate, and president, or two-thirds of both houses of Congress, must agree to legislation curbing Court jurisdiction before it is enacted. Nevertheless, members of Congress continue to introduce bills that would restrict the jurisdiction of the Supreme Court or of all federal courts. Between 1975 and 2002, according to one count, 132 bills were introduced to limit the federal judiciary's jurisdiction in some way. Although none of these efforts were successful, and none have been since then, many members see them as an opportunity to demonstrate to judges that Congress can limit jurisdiction, and these efforts are often popular with constituents.

Congress also has had a mixed record in efforts to control the Supreme Court by changing its size. Several times in the nineteenth century, Congress used its power over the size of the Court to exert pressure on the Court and to help change its ideological shape. Although Presidents James Madison, James Monroe, and John Quincy Adams each claimed that a growing nation needed a larger Supreme Court (which started with just six members), Congress did not change the Court's size until 1837. Even then, it postponed the change to nine members until the last day of President Andrew Jackson's term that year. Later, by increasing the size of the Court to ten justices, Congress gave President Abraham Lincoln an opportunity to solidify a pro-Union majority on the Court. Soon thereafter, Congress reduced the number of justices from ten to eight to prevent President Andrew Johnson from filling any vacancies. When Johnson's successor, Ulysses S. Grant, took office, Congress changed the number of justices to nine, where it has remained.

The best-known attempt to influence Supreme Court decisions by altering its size was the "court-packing" plan of President Franklin Roosevelt. Roosevelt, disturbed by rulings that struck down important parts of his New Deal legislation, proposed in 1937 that the Supreme Court be expanded from nine to fifteen justices so that he could appoint new justices and change the balance of opinion. Congressional resistance, as well as a series of Supreme Court decisions more favorable to Roosevelt's New Deal legislation, led Roosevelt to drop his plan. The uproar over the Roosevelt plan has had a chilling effect on other presidents and Congresses that might have pushed legislation to alter the size of the Court for political purposes.

The Senate and Judicial Nominations

The shared power of appointment remains the primary means by which senators and presidents influence federal courts. Needless to say, the president and the Senate do not always agree on what course federal courts ought to take. Historically, this battle was largely fought over presidential nominations to the Supreme Court, with the nominations of Judge Robert H. Bork in 1987 and Judge Clarence Thomas in 1991 standing out as particularly controversial. As we explore in the following section, recent years have seen the controversies extend to appointments to the lower courts.

LOWER COURT NOMINATIONS. Senators of a president's party typically have had a great deal of influence over the president's appointments to federal district courts and the courts of appeal. These senators usually play an active role in the nominating process by suggesting acceptable candidates to the administration. Only a few senators usually have an active role in Senate deliberations considering judicial appointments at the district level. Unlike nominations to the Supreme Court, and more recently circuit courts, which elicit much broader interest, district court seats generally draw fairly localized interest from the Senate body. In most instances, the Senate's Judiciary Committee staff studies lower-court nominees, receives reports from the American Bar Association and the Federal Bureau of Investigation (FBI), and routinely recommends approval to the full Senate, which confirms the nominees with little or no discussion.

The record of judicial appointments during the Reagan and George H. W. Bush presidencies continued the pattern of routine approval for most nominees, but with the addition of a few very controversial cases. During the Reagan and George H. W. Bush presidencies, more than 460 appointments were made to appeals and district courts, meaning that by the end of the George H. W. Bush administration, more than 70 percent of sitting federal judges had been appointed during these two administrations. These appointments have produced a much more conservative federal bench. Although the Democrats controlled the Senate for more than half the period, they largely acquiesced to presidential preferences for more conservative, younger, white federal judges. Not until the few months before the 1992 presidential election did the Judiciary Committee, under then chair Senator Joseph Biden (D-Delaware), take a more aggressive stance against the administration's nominees, apparently emboldened by the possibility that the Democrat Bill Clinton would win the presidency. After suggesting that he would be more selective about which Bush nominees would receive hearings before the election, Biden and the

Judiciary Committee slowed the pace of confirmation hearings for appellate court appointments.

When Bill Clinton assumed the presidency in 1995, he had ninety-nine seats on the federal bench to fill – seats that observers expected would be filled by a greater proportion of minorities and women than were filled by Bush and Reagan. With a Democratic majority in the Senate during his first two years in office, Clinton was successful in getting rapid confirmations. After the Republicans took majority control of the Senate in 1995, however, the speed of Senate confirmations declined markedly. In 1998, Chief Justice William Rehnquist complained about the slow pace, noting that 101 judicial nominees had been confirmed in 1994 but only 17 were confirmed in 1996 and 36 in 1997. Many vacancies had gone unfilled for more than eighteen months, with some going up to four years between nomination and confirmation. Senate Judiciary Committee Chairman Orrin Hatch (R-Utah) insisted that the Republican Senate had been just as responsive as the Democrats had been for President George H. W. Bush.

The battle over judicial confirmations continued into the administration of President George W. Bush. Bush had inherited a sizable number of judicial vacancies, but he faced a deeply polarized Congress when his administration began in 2001. Although Bush quickly submitted nominations to fill these vacancies, the partisan divisions in the Senate brought their consideration to a grinding halt. The administration experienced the longest average duration between nomination and confirmation of federal judges in recent history, as Democrats made frequent and visible use of the filibuster to hold up confirmation. In fact, the debate over confirmations had become so heated during the George W. Bush presidency that Republican senators threatened to execute a "nuclear option" to bypass Democratic filibusters of judicial nominees. Concerned about the precedent that would be set by such an action, a group of fourteen senators (seven from each party) negotiated a plan for the consideration of less objectionable nominees and thus averted a procedural circumvention of the filibuster.

President Barack Obama, like Bush, inherited many judicial vacancies, and progress toward filling those vacancies was slow during his first Congress as president (2009–2010). Republicans made extensive use of filibusters and secret holds to stall the confirmation of nominees thought to be liberal activists. That alone, however, does not explain the lengthy durations to confirmation. By one count, Obama was on average more than one hundred days slower in submitting his nominations to the Senate than was his predecessor. In part, this appears to be the product of Obama's more deliberative vetting of potential nominees. As a consequence of these factors, nineteen of Obama's judicial nominations expired at the conclusion of the Congress, and more than ninety vacant seats were left unfilled. Several of these were deemed "judicial emergencies" as the sitting judges were unable to handle the caseload. Justice Roberts even made a plea in his 2010

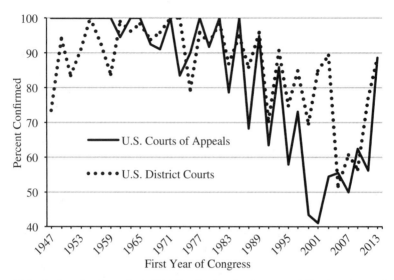

Figure 10.2 Confirmation Rates for Judicial Nominations by Congress, 1947–2014. Source: Forrest Maltzman and Sarah A. Binder, *Advice and Dissent: The Struggle to Shape the Federal Judiciary* (Washington, DC: Brookings Institution Press, 2009). Additional data collected by the authors from the American Bar Association.

year-end report for more expeditious confirmation considerations, imploring the political branches "to find a long-term solution to [the] recurring problem" surrounding the filling of judicial vacancies. It remains to be seen whether the parties can reach a compromise to address this growing concern.

Although there has been some variation in the confirmation rate for district court nominees, there has been a more appreciable decline in court of appeals confirmations (see Figure 10.2). The confirmation rates for district court nominees have exceeded 80 percent in recent presidencies, with George H. W. Bush having the lowest rate of approximately 79 percent. In contrast, there has been a precipitous drop in the circuit court confirmation rates over this period. The Carter administration enjoyed an approximately 92 percent confirmation rate for circuit court nominees, which fell to 73 and 71 percent for the Clinton and George W. Bush administrations, respectively. In his first two Congresses as president (2009–2012), Obama's confirmation rates remained below 65 percent for circuit nominees, with mixed results for district court nominees.

Senate Democrats and President Obama were increasingly frustrated by Republican obstruction of judicial nominees during the 113th Congress (2013–2014). After repeated attempts to bring up three nominations for the U.S. Court of Appeals for the D.C. Circuit, then majority leader Harry Reid (D-Nevada) invoked the so-called nuclear option (see Chapter 7) to lower the threshold for cloture on executive calendar nominations from sixty to a simple majority. As Figure 10.3 reveals, the effects were dramatic. The number of confirmations by

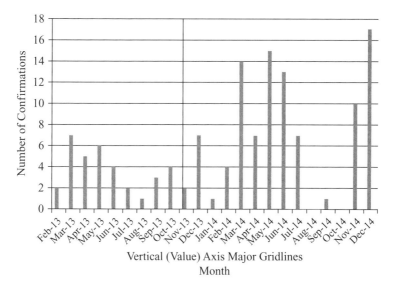

Vertical (Value) Axis Major Gridlines
Month

Figure 10.3 Senate Confirmation of Lower Court Judges, 2013–2014. Data collected by the authors.

month increased sharply after the rules were altered in November 2013. By the end of the 113th Congress, the Senate had confirmed more than 88 percent of President Obama's nominees to U.S. district courts and U.S. courts of appeals. This marked the highest rate of confirmation since the 101st Congress (1989–1990) during the presidency of George H. W. Bush.

Congressionally Speaking . . .

Senatorial courtesy is the practice of conferring with senators of the president's party whenever a vacancy in a position subject to presidential appointment is located within the senators' state. The practice applies to vacancies in federal district courts. For many years, senators could exercise a virtual veto over appointments affecting their states. The practice rests on the willingness of the Senate and its Judiciary Committee to refuse to act on nominees opposed by those senators. It gives senators a form of patronage with which to reward political friends.

Senatorial courtesy is institutionalized through the use of *blue slips* – blue sheets of paper sent out by the Judiciary Committee asking senators from a nominee's home state his or her opinion of the nominee. A home state senator who objects to a nominee will often write on the blue slip that the nominee is "personally offensive." This practice has existed since the early 1910s, with negative blue slips usually meaning that the Judiciary Committee will not act on a nominee. Although not always the case today, a negative blue slip usually makes confirmation of the nominee extremely difficult.

The influence of partisanship in appointments to the lower courts is clear. More than 90 percent of nominees to the lower courts are affiliated with the party of the president nominating them. Moreover, lower-court nominees in the fourth year of a four-year presidential term are much less likely to be confirmed than are nominees sent to the Senate in other years, and the confirmation process typically takes much longer when the Senate and presidency are controlled by different parties. At the end of a president's term, senators of the opposition party often prefer to leave judgeships vacant until they see which party wins the presidency. If their party wins the presidency, the new president can submit new names – presumably more to their liking.

SUPREME COURT NOMINATIONS. Supreme Court nominations are not routine. Unlike the appointment process for district court seats, presidential nominations to the Supreme Court garner a much broader spectrum of interest across the Senate. In fact, lower court nominees are often screened more carefully if they are thought to be potential Supreme Court nominees. After a president makes a nomination, the Senate Judiciary Committee has the nominee complete a lengthy questionnaire, orders its staff to conduct an extensive background investigation on the nominee, receives an evaluation from the American Bar Association, and then holds several days of hearings. Recently, interest groups have actively lobbied senators and generated publicity for the groups' views. The administration, which sometimes discusses a list of possible nominees with senators in advance of the nomination, coaches the nominee in preparation for the hearings.

The outcomes of Supreme Court confirmation efforts hinge on numerous factors. First, the partisan makeup of the Senate matters. When the president's party has been in the majority, close to 90 percent of nominees have been confirmed. In contrast, during times of divided government, only 59 percent of nominees have been approved by the Senate. Second, the timing of the nomination also has implications. Not only does partisanship in Congress tend to increase in election years, but the president's influence in the legislative arena usually declines during the course of his term in office. Presidents also appear to be more successful when they make public statements on behalf of their nominees. Overall weakness of a president clearly affects his ability to get a nominee approved by the Senate. Reagan nominated Robert Bork in 1987 after the revelations of the Iran-Contra scandal had significantly weakened the president's standing in Congress and his public approval. Bork was turned down by the Senate.

Timing is important from other perspectives as well. Many argue that senators up for reelection give greater weight to public opinion than do senators who do not face reelection in the near future. Most senators appear to take into account the qualifications and ideological outlook of nominees. The greater the distance the nominee's positions are from the senator's, and the less qualified the nominee is, the lower the probability that the senator will vote in favor of the president's choice. The appearance of one or more of these factors – partisan balance, presidential popularity, proximity to the end of the presidential term, ideological placement, or nominee qualifications – increases the likelihood of conflict in the Senate during the confirmation process. On many confirmation votes, individual senators are also likely to be influenced by constituency concerns. With the nominations of Thurgood Marshall and Clarence Thomas to the Court, state racial composition had a determinative effect on the votes of senators who represented states with large African American populations.

The Senate has failed to confirm only twenty-six of presidents' nominations to the Supreme Court, by means of postponement, rejection, or forced withdrawal of the nominee. Twentieth-century presidents have had better luck than their predecessors, but even recent presidents have stumbled. President Lyndon Johnson was forced to withdraw two nominations, two nominees of President Richard Nixon were rejected, President Reagan withdrew one nomination and one nominee was rejected, and both presidents George H. W. and George W. Bush withdrew one name. Two nominations deserve special mention: President Reagan's nomination of Robert Bork, which was rejected by the Senate, and President George H. W. Bush's nomination of Clarence Thomas, which was approved by a narrow margin.

In 1987, President Reagan faced a Democratic Senate when he nominated Judge Bork, then a judge on the U.S. Court of Appeals for the District of Columbia and a former solicitor general and law school professor. Bork's long-standing and well-published opposition to affirmative action and the established ruling on abortion, along with his judicial activism, stimulated an extraordinary and influential effort by civil rights groups and others to prevent his confirmation by the Senate. Interest in his nomination stimulated unprecedented scrutiny by the media – the media even reported Bork's videotape rentals. The Senate voted fifty-eight to forty-two against his confirmation.

Four years later, President Bush nominated Clarence Thomas, also a sitting judge on the U.S. Court of Appeals for the District of Columbia, and a former chair of the Equal Employment Opportunity Commission (EEOC). Thomas had relatively little judicial experience. He had been on the appeals court for only eighteen months and had never argued a case before a court. The American Bar Association's review committee rated him "qualified" on their three-point scale (highly qualified, qualified, and not qualified), with two members of the committee voting "not qualified," making Thomas the only Supreme Court nominee rated by the Bar Association to receive such a weak evaluation. Thomas had a record of commitment to conservative views on many issues, leading liberal groups to mobilize against him and drawing tough questions from the liberal Democrats on the Judiciary Committee.

Nevertheless, Thomas's confirmation seemed likely until the eve of the scheduled vote by the full Senate. National Public Radio reported that a complaint of sexual misconduct against Thomas had been disclosed to Judiciary Committee staff and noted in an FBI report, although it had not been mentioned in the initial committee hearings. The committee reopened the hearings to listen to the testimony of Anita Hill, a University of Oklahoma law professor who had worked for Thomas at the EEOC. At the hearings, she repeated her charges against Thomas.

He responded, and the committee heard character witnesses for both Thomas and Hill, all before a very large national television audience.

After Thomas was confirmed by the full Senate by a vote of 52–48, the committee and the Senate were criticized for the manner in which they had conducted the hearings. Senator Arlen Specter (R-Pennsylvania) ran into difficulty in his 1992 reelection bid because of the way he had grilled Professor Hill. In response to the criticism, Senator Biden announced changes in Judiciary Committee practice. These changes would guarantee that all information received by a committee and its staff would be placed in the nominee's FBI file, ensure all senators access to FBI reports, and provide for closed briefings for all senators so that if there were any charges against nominees, they could be reviewed. Additionally, in a conspicuous move to make sure that any sexism on the committee would be held in check, two women – Senators Dianne Feinstein (D-California) and Carol Moseley-Braun (D-Illinois) – were appointed to the committee in 1993.

Congress and the Impeachment of Judges

Under the Constitution, judges "shall hold their offices during good behaviour," but the House is empowered to bring and vote on impeachment charges against judges. If a judge is impeached by the House, the Senate conducts a trial on the charges. A two-thirds vote of the senators present is required to convict and remove a judge – the same number required for removing a president from office. Removal of a judge by House impeachment and Senate conviction is rare. Over the course of the history of the federal bench, no Supreme Court justice has been removed from office by Congress. In 1804, Republicans tried to impeach Justice Samuel Chase on several charges, but they failed to get a two-thirds vote to convict. Fourteen lower federal judges have been impeached by the House, eight have been convicted by the Senate, and three others resigned from office.

Congress's impeachment power has not proven to be a source of leverage over the courts. Even the threat of impeachment has only once been credited with inducing a change in Supreme Court membership: Justice Abe Fortas resigned in 1969 after revelations of questionable financial practices. Impeachment trials do pose certain challenges for a Senate already having trouble managing its time and discharging its duties. Any trial procedure involving the full Senate inevitably distracts the Senate from its legislative agenda. To address this problem, the Senate moved in 1986 to form a special twelve-member committee to gather and review evidence regarding impeachment on behalf of the full Senate.

Legislative Responses to the Courts

Interaction between Congress and the courts does not necessarily end with judicial action. Congress can, of course, use its traditional legislative powers to respond to court decisions. For example, after the Supreme Court decided in 1988 that burning the U.S. flag in protest of government policy should be afforded First Amendment protection as a form of political speech, Congress eventually enacted a statute designed to strip flag burning of its constitutional protection. In another case, Congress overrode a presidential veto to reverse a Supreme Court decision concerning sex discrimination in colleges and universities.

But successful reversals of unpopular Supreme Court decisions are not automatic. On some occasions, efforts to reverse decisions pass one chamber and get stalled in the other. Other efforts often get stymied at the committee level, after hearings are held on possible legislation to reverse the decision.

Studies show that Congress responds to about one-third of these Supreme Court moves to nullify a federal law. Why only a third? The three-institution legislative game makes a response to the Court difficult. All three institutions must agree, or at least two-thirds of both chambers must agree, to any legislative response. If the committees with jurisdiction over the affected legislation recognize that gaining the approval of the House, Senate, and president is impossible, they may choose to take no action. Nevertheless, Congress sometimes does respond to court decisions (see box "Legislative Response to a Court Decision"). Several factors appear to motivate congressional efforts to respond to court decisions. One study emphasizes the important role of public opinion in motivating Congress to act. If the majority of public opinion is in favor of action by Congress, the probability of a congressional response increases dramatically. Salience of the issue to organized interest groups, sometimes indicated by the participation of groups in the case before the Supreme Court, also appears to influence congressional decisions to respond. In many instances, however, members seem to have been motivated to take preliminary steps to respond to demands, but they did not push the legislation to the point of passage.

Legislative Response to a Court Decision

In a 2010 decision (*United States v. Stevens*), the Supreme Court struck down a 1999 law banning the creation, sale, or possession of videos depicting graphic violence to animals. The Court ruled the law unconstitutional under the First Amendment on the grounds of being "substantially overbroad." The Court reasoned that there were a number of legitimate depictions adversely affected by the law, such as hunting videos.

The Court's decision offered guidelines for a narrower definition of unacceptable depictions, and Congress responded almost immediately. Less than eight months after the decision, President Obama signed the new legislation into law. The new law restricted the ban to clearly defined acts of cruelty against animals, such as crushing, burning, or drowning. Moreover, the legislation extended exceptions to areas of visual depiction that the Court had intended to protect in its decision.

Not surprisingly, Congress also is more likely to respond to Supreme Court decisions when invited to do so by judges on the bench. On occasion, the Court rules that although particular provisions are unconstitutional, Congress could remedy the problem by rewriting the provision. In effect, the Supreme Court outlines the boundaries of what changes would be considered constitutional. Such guidance by the courts markedly increases the chances that Congress will undertake efforts to respond to or reverse the nullifying decision. Judicial invitations to review give a different cast to relations between Congress and the courts. Far from the conflict that many normally assume exists when the Court overturns a federal law, these invitations to reverse reflect a more cooperative relationship between the branches.

Amending the Constitution

A frequent response of members to court decisions is to propose a constitutional amendment. Since the Supreme Court's decision in *Roe v. Wade*(1973), for example, many members have supported a constitutional amendment that would reserve to the states the power to regulate abortions. The constitutional requirement that an amendment receive the support of two-thirds of both chambers before it is sent to the states for ratification sets a high threshold that has seldom been met. Only four amendments to the Constitution were adopted in direct response to Supreme Court decisions: the Eleventh Amendment, on the ability of citizens of one state to bring suit against another state; the Fourteenth Amendment, on the application of the first ten amendments to the states; the Sixteenth Amendment, on the federal income tax; and the Twenty-sixth Amendment, on the right of eighteen-year-olds to vote.

CONCLUSION

The courts occupy a critical place in forming national policy. The roles played by the courts vary widely – from separation-of-powers umpire to congressional overseer and partner in policy making.

Relationships between the branches clearly depend on the rules of the game. Those rules, as we have seen, are themselves often the product of political battles. The rules of the policy-making process can be ambiguous, and this ambiguity gives the courts an opening into the legislative game. As a result, members of Congress have an incentive to watch over the actions of courts carefully and, on occasion, to enlist judges in their campaigns against a recalcitrant executive branch.

Judges, however, are not always willing to take the bait. Sometimes, the courts smell a political contest and send the dispute back to congressional players to resolve themselves. Other times, judges simply define respective powers of each contending actor and set boundaries for future interactions between the players.

Although Congress and the president can shape the membership of the bench, other congressional tools rarely give members enough leverage over the courts to limit judicial independence and discretion. When the courts have chosen to enter the policy process, however, major changes in policy making have often occurred. Whether expanding procedural rights of individuals or forcing executive agencies to work more assiduously to follow congressional intent, federal courts in recent decades have made inroads into the legislative arena. Attention to the interactions of judges, legislators, and executives thus markedly affects our understanding of how separate branches are indeed sharing power to shape national policy.

SUGGESTED READINGS

A.   These books focus on the politics of judicial nominations.

Binder, Sarah, and Forrest Maltzman. *Advice and Dissent: The Struggle to Shape the Federal Judiciary.* Washington, DC: Brooking Institution Press, 2009.
Epstein, Lee, and Jeffrey A. Segal.*Advice and Consent: The Politics of Judicial Appointments.* New York: Oxford University Press, 2005.
Wittes, Benjamin. *Confirmation Wars: Preserving Independent Courts in Angry Times.* Lanham, MD: Rowman & Littlefield, 2006.
Yalof, David. *Pursuit of Justices: Presidential Politics and the Selection of Supreme Court Nominees.* Chicago: University of Chicago Press, 1999.

B.   These books focus on interactions between Congress and the Court.

Barnes, Jeb. *Overruled?: Legislative Overrides, Pluralism, and Contemporary Court-Congress Relations.* Stanford, CA: Stanford University Press, 2004.
Epstein, Lee, William M. Landes, and Richard Posner. *The Behavior of Federal Judges: A Theoretical Study of Rational Choice.* Cambridge, MA: Harvard University Press, 2013.
Fisher, Louis, *The Supreme Court and Congress: Rival Interpretation.* Washington, DC: CQ Press, 2008.
Geyh, Charles Gardner. *When Courts and Congress Collide: The Struggle for Control of America's Judicial System.* Ann Arbor: University of Michigan Press, 2006.

DISCUSSION QUESTIONS

1   What explains the Supreme Court's evolving views of the commerce clause of the Constitution?

2   Judges insist that their political preferences play no role in their decision making, how might a judge explain the data in Table 10.1?

3   Why have lower federal court confirmation rates declined?

4   Why does Congress so rarely overturn court decisions?

11 Congress, Lobbyists, and Interest Groups

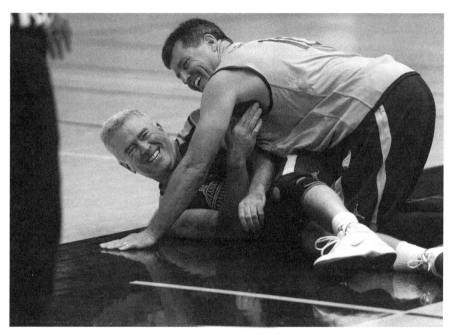

Representative Brad Wenstrup (R-Ohio), *left*, is covered by lobbyist Danny Leonard during the Hoops for Youth 16th annual charity basketball game, which was held at George Washington University's Smith Center, September 8, 2014. The members of Congress team beat the lobbyist team 46–40.

The First Amendment to the Constitution provides that Congress may make no law abridging the right of the people to petition the government for a redress of grievances. Court rulings interpret the amendment broadly to include organized and paid representatives of the people, therefore limiting Congress's ability to regulate lobbying. In practice, interest groups and their lobbyists are a very important means by which the public conveys their expectations and demands to Congress. Nevertheless, Americans believe that members of Congress are beholden to special interests and lobbyists. A 2009 survey conducted by the Center on Congress at Indiana University found that 60 percent of Americans believe that Congress neither listens to nor cares about what ordinary citizens think; more than 73 percent of those surveyed gave Congress a D or an F on its ability to control the influence of special interests. In fact, when asked what they thought was the main influence on members of Congress, respondents were approximately three times more likely to answer special interests than they were to answer constituents.[1] A 2010 CBS/New York Times survey found that 80 percent of Americans agreed that most members of Congress are more interested in serving special interest groups than in serving the people they represent.[2]

These contrasting views – that lobbyists are essential to democracy and yet reviled by the public – give interest groups and lobbyists an uneasy place in congressional politics. Representation of organized interests is a rapidly growing industry in Washington. In this chapter, we review the evidence on lobbying, discuss the evolving strategies of interest groups, and review the limited efforts of Congress to regulate lobbying. Congress, in accordance with the Constitution, has been able to put in place only minimal rules on lobbying. As an alternative, Congress has placed more severe restrictions on legislators, as it is allowed to do, with respect to their relations with organized interests. Restrictions on campaign contributions from organized interests were detailed in Chapter 3, but there are a variety of rules the each house has imposed on its members with respect to receiving gifts from lobbyists. In this chapter, we concentrate on developments in the legislative strategies of groups and lobbyists.

THE EXPANDING COMMUNITY OF LOBBYISTS AND INTEREST GROUPS

Lobbyists have been present since the first Congresses. The wide reach of federal policy and Congress's central role in shaping it motivates many citizens, organized groups, and lobbyists to converge on Washington (see box "Congressionally Speaking . . . "). Congress's internal decision-making processes are largely responsible for this. Reliance on committees and subcommittees for writing the details of most legislation gives outsiders many points of contact with legislators and staff. Even congressional parties are quite permeable. Many legislators influence party strategies through their participation in party caucuses, committees, and task forces. If legislators can be influenced so too can party

---

1 Survey conducted by the Center on Congress at Indiana University in October 2009. Available at www.center-oncongress.org/october-2009-public-opinion-survey.
2 CBS News/New York Times, February 5-10, 2010.

strategies. The vast institutional partitioning of Congress (i.e., bicameralism, parties, committees, subcommittees, etc.) gives lobbyists more opportunities for influence than they find in most other national legislatures. The more complex the legislative process and the more places that interests can be protected, the more valuable the experienced lobbyist is to the average citizen.

Generalizing about lobbyists is difficult. Some lobbyists are officials of organized interest groups such as the U.S. Chamber of Commerce, the Sierra Club, and the National Cable Television Association. Other lobbyists are lawyers, former members or staff of Congress, or public relations specialists who have their own lobbying firms that are hired by interest groups, corporations, or other organizations to represent their interests, sometimes on a specific bill or issue. Many lobbyists are called "federal relations" directors and work for universities and colleges or for state and local governments. Even foreign governments hire lobbyists who seek to influence federal policy. Frequently, lobbyists are citizens who have traveled to Washington to make their case in person. As discussed later in this chapter, important legal distinctions are made between those hired to lobby for a person or organization and citizens who lobby on their own behalf.

Congressionally Speaking…

Lobbyist is a term that referred originally to reporters waiting in the lobby of the British House of Commons to speak to members of Parliament. In the mid-nineteenth century, the term came to be used for people seeking to influence legislators and it soon gained quite negative connotations because of the money and other resources with which lobbyists plied legislators.

Today, a lobbyist has a more technical meaning in federal law – someone who is paid to communicate with Congress on behalf of others. And lobbyists now see themselves as specialized professionals. They even have their own professional association, the American League of Lobbyists.

Most interest groups represent occupational or organizational communities. Occupational groups include organizations representing doctors, teachers, accountants, and even association executives. Government employees have many specialized interest groups – the American Association of State Highway and Transportation Officials, for example. Many, perhaps most, interest groups are associations made up of organizations. Most trade associations, such as the American Petroleum Institute, the Association of American Railroads, and the National Association of Wholesaler-Distributors, represent corporations in a particular sector of the economy. But associations representing member unions, universities, local governments, and other organizations are important as well. The Association of American Universities and the National League of Cities are prominent examples.

Citizens' groups compose about 20 percent of the interest group community. Citizens' groups include Citizens for Tax Justice, Common Cause, the National Association for the Advancement of Colored People, the National Organization for Women, and Ralph Nader's Public Citizen. Their members generally are individuals rather than representatives of organizations or institutions. The political scientist Jack Walker observed that these groups usually arise in the wake of broad social movements concerned with such problems as the level of environmental pollution, threats to civil rights, or changes in the status of women. Citizens' groups often are created by political entrepreneurs operating with the support of wealthy individuals, private foundations, or elected political leaders who act as their protectors, financial supporters, and patrons. It is common to see a few individuals bearing much of the cost of group formation. Such an arrangement is often essential to overcoming the numerous obstacles associated with collective action.

The greatest dilemma that interest groups encounter in the formation process is that of free riders – individuals who consume the benefits of a public good without paying a fair share of the costs of its production. All groups seek to attract members by appealing to a sense of obligation to support a cause, but often that is not enough to attract and retain members. Some groups overcome this problem by offering selective benefits restricted to those who contribute. For example, members of the AARP (formerly, the American Association of Retired Persons but now using just the initials) receive a variety of benefits, including discounts on airfare, car rentals, hotels, and cruises, as well as reasonably priced legal services and health care. Others offer special events, club memberships, or other social benefits to attract members.

The number of lobbyists and groups is somewhat difficult to measure, but the numbers are large. The most rapid documented growth in interest groups occurred between the 1960s and 1980s, during which many federal programs were created and expanded. A 1982 survey of twenty-eight hundred organizations that had lobbying offices in Washington found that 40 percent had been created since 1960 and an additional 25 percent since 1970 (CBS News/*New York Times* Poll, February 5–10, 2010). One analyst found that the number of Washington offices for trade associations – the National Association of Manufacturers and the National Association of Broadcasters, for example – nearly tripled, from about twelve hundred in 1960 to thirty-five hundred in 1986. Even greater proportionate growth in the number of corporations with offices in Washington occurred in the same period.[3]

In recent years, the Center for Responsive Politics reports, the number of lobbyists registered with the secretary of the Senate, as required by the Lobbying Disclosure Act, has been around twelve thousand, often with multiple lobbyists

---

3 Jeffrey M. Berry, *The Interest Group Society*, 2nd ed. (Glenview, IL: Scott, Foresman, 1989), 20–21.

TABLE 11.1. Bills most frequently mentioned as targets of lobbying and number of lobbyists' clients in Senate reports, 2014

Bill	Number of lobbyist clients
HR 83, Consolidated Appropriations for Fiscal 2015	852
HR 3547, Consolidated Appropriations for Fiscal 2014	475
S 2260, EXPIRE Act of 2014	390
HR 4870, Department of Defense Appropriations	379
HR 4435, National Defense Authorization Act	359
HR 5771, Tax Increase Prevention Act of 2014	358
HR 4923, Energy and Water Development Appropriations	336
HR 3080, Water Resources Reform and Development Act of 2014	335
HR 4660, Commerce, Justice, Science, and Related Agencies Appropriations	314
S 601, Water Resources Development Act of 2013	289

Source: https://www.opensecrets.org/lobby/top.php?indexType=b&showYear=2014.

representing one trade association or corporation. Those lobbying registration reports indicate that nearly $3.5 billion is spent on lobbying per year, up from $1.57 billion in 2000. In 2009, the privately published directory *Washington Representatives* listed more than eighteen thousand "persons working to influence government policies and actions" – a number that more than quadrupled since the early 1970s. Today, nearly five thousand organizations have some kind of representation in Washington.

Many factors have contributed to the proliferation of the interest group community and lobbying activity. Most important is that the expanding role of federal programs and regulation motivated individuals, firms, and local governments to organize and lobby. This is reflected in the legislative interests mentioned in the lobbying registration reports. Table 11.1 indicates the bills most frequently mentioned in lobbying reports in 2014. Most concern federal spending on programs and projects in a variety of appropriations bills, along with the bill that authorizes defense projects and a major tax bill.

Most lobbyists act and most lobbying is conducted in behalf of business interests. Table 11.2 lists the major categories of lobbyists in order of lobbying expenditures. The top six categories reflect trade associations, corporations, and other business interests. For example, the energy and natural resources category is dominated by oil and gas associations and companies, electric utilities, and mining companies. By one estimate, 70 percent of organized interests in Washington are business groups. The "other" category, listed as seventh largest, includes education associations and nonprofit institutions. Labor unions collectively are ranked twelfth, with public employee unions leading the way.

TABLE 11.2. Major categories of lobbying spending in Senate reports, 2014

Lobbying client category	Lobbying spending
Miscellaneous business	$552,487,810
Finance, insurance, real estate	$495,759,815
Health	$484,114,392
Computing, telecom, electronics, TV/movies/music	$381,272,131
Energy, natural resources	$345,182,074
Transportation	$217,192,170
Other (education, nonprofit)	$209,828,954
Ideology, issue groups	$132,436,043
Agribusiness	$126,408,021
Defense	$125,756,939
Construction	$51,160,867
Labor unions	$44,886,822

Source: https://www.opensecrets.org/lobby/top.php?indexType=c&showYear=2014.

A series of social movements, such as civil rights, women's rights, environmental protection, and consumer rights, swept the country, redefined the nation's policy agenda, and spawned lasting interest groups. And organization spurred counterorganization. For example, Planned Parenthood was challenged by the National Right to Life Committee, and gun control advocates were countered by the National Rifle Association and other groups. The consequence of organization and counterorganization was the proliferation of strongly issue-oriented citizens' groups and greater diversity in the kinds of groups found in Washington. In total, their spending on lobbying is large but far below what business interests spend in Washington (Table 11.2).

The enlargement of the middle class and the use of technological advances also contributed to the growth of the Washington interest group community. The middle class has become an important base of support for occupational and citizens' groups that depend on membership dues and other contributions for financial support. Technological advances in communications and computer-generated mailings have facilitated the growth of groups that require support from the general public. Also, advances in communication and transportation have made it more convenient and affordable for groups to headquarter in Washington, far from concentrations of their members.

Finally, the federal government is responsible for directly stimulating the creation of some groups and underwriting their costs of operations. Much of the domestic legislation of the 1960s and 1970s required some kind of citizen participation in executive agency rule making or provided for the creation of community-based groups. Many interest groups representing citizens, environmental

David Schnittger poses at Squire Patton Boggs in early 2015. In December 2014, the law and lobbying firm issued this press release: "Squire Patton Boggs is pleased to announce that David Schnittger, Deputy Chief of Staff to U.S. House Speaker John Boehner (R-OH), will join the firm's Washington, D.C. office in January as Senior Policy Advisor for Squire Patton Boggs' Public Policy practice.'Dave Schnittger is one of the most capable and respected staff members on Capitol Hill. We are delighted that he is joining us at Squire Patton Boggs,' said former Senate Majority Leader and co-chair of Squire Patton Boggs' Public Policy practice, Trent Lott."

action groups, and legal and health care organizations for the poor were stimulated by these public policies. Indeed, the activists running many of the new social programs vigorously promoted the creation of new organizations to represent their clients' interests. In other situations, federal agencies encouraged the formation of groups to facilitate communication between the agencies and the sectors they served and to build a base of support for their own programs and budgets. Additionally, as federal domestic programs expanded, many more citizens' groups received grants or contracts from the federal government to conduct studies or to perform services for executive agencies.

The enlarged community of lobbyists and interest groups has altered the political environment of members of Congress in important ways. The most obvious effect is that the expanded lobbying community has increased the diversity and intensity of demands placed on members of Congress. Issues of even modest importance are more likely to generate conflict among groups, and no one group is as likely to dominate policy making as was often the case at mid-twentieth century. There is now greater uncertainty about the mix of organized interests that will seek to influence congressional action and hold members accountable for their individual actions.

DEVELOPMENTS IN INTEREST GROUP STRATEGIES

Influencing Congress involves much more than gaining the votes of individual members. Lobbyists work hard to find legislators who are willing to champion their causes. Lobbyists need members to introduce their proposals as legislation, to offer amendments in committee and on the floor, and to help them get issues on, or keep issues off, the agendas of committees and subcommittees.

Moreover, lobbyists spend more time gathering, digesting, and reporting information to their clients than they do trying to influence Congress. They help their clients anticipate and track legislative developments that are difficult for people not experienced in congressional politics to follow. Because congressional politics and federal policy are so much more complex and important than they were a few decades ago, corporations and other organizations need the assistance of experienced insiders to observe and interpret congressional activity that might affect their interests. A good lobbyist seeks to develop access to well-placed members and staff on Capitol Hill to meet the demands of his or her clients for information.

Corner on the Lobbying Market

Lobbying is subject to market forces. Lobbyists who specialize in the hot issues of the day are in high demand. Many lobbying firms have experts in numerous policy areas to serve a wide variety of clients' needs, and firms are responsive to the ebb and flow of issues on the national agenda. When new issues emerge, competition among lobbyists ensues. For example, more than $1 billion was spent on health care lobbying between 2009 and 2010, causing lobbying firms to dramatically increase the number of health care experts on staff and giving rise to new, specialized – "boutique" – firms. The number of lobbyists working on health care increased from fourteen hundred to thirty-seven hundred over the course of 2009 alone. And health care lobbyists have remained in demand as individuals and organizations seek to modify the law.

Source: Shawn Zeller, "Boomtown for Lobbyists," *CQ Weekly*, April 12, 2010; Joe Eaton and M. B. Pell, "Lobbyists Swarm Capitol to Influence Health Reform," *The Center for Public Integrity*, February 24, 2010.

Lobbyists employ a wide range of techniques, which have evolved as lobbyists have adapted to changes in technology, society, and Congress. The empowerment of House subcommittees in the 1970s, the greater individualism in the membership, and expansion of congressional staffs since the mid-twentieth century have forced lobbyists to develop relationships with more members and staff and follow the activity of more committees and subcommittees. At the same time, developments in electronic communications and computers have enabled lobbyists and interest groups to reach people throughout the country with ease.

These developments have stimulated important changes in the way lobbyists do their work. Many observers of Washington politics have noted the change

from inside lobbying, or face-to-face efforts to influence a few important legislators, to outside strategies, or public relations efforts to generate public support for special interest causes. Perhaps more accurately, outside strategies have
supplemented the old-style inside strategies that once dominated Washington
lobbying.

INSIDE LOBBYING

The more traditional form of lobbying – inside lobbying – involves personal
contact between a lobbyist and members of Congress. Successful lobbyists use
access to important decision makers, a network of contacts, mastery of the process, policy expertise, Washington experience, and money to develop strong ties
to legislators and their staffs. Their success often depends on their being able
to phone a prominent member of Congress, get the call returned promptly, and
gather critical intelligence about when an issue will be raised or which member
is wavering on an important provision. An aide to a former House Speaker characterized the work of the inside lobbyist this way:

> They know members of Congress are here three nights a week, alone, without their fami-
> lies. So they say, "Let's have dinner. Let's go see a ballgame." Shmooze with them. Make
> friends. And they don't lean on it all the time. Every once in a while, they call up –
> maybe once or twice a year – ask a few questions. Call you up and say, "Say, what's
> Danny [Rostenkowski, chair of the House Ways and Means Committee] going to do on
> this tax-reform bill?" Anne Wexler [a former official in the Carter White House, and now
> a lobbyist] will call up and spend half an hour talking about left-wing politics, and sud-
> denly she'll pop a question, pick up something. They want that little bit of access. That's
> what does it. You can hear it. It clicks home. They'll call their chief executive officer, and
> they've delivered. That's how it works. It's not illegal. They work on a personal basis.[4]

Career Washingtonians – former members, former executive branch officials, and
even some family members of prominent public officials who have developed personal friendships with members and their staffs – are greatly advantaged in direct
lobbying. Former members are particularly advantaged because they retain special
privileges of access on Capitol Hill, and many have long-standing relationships
with legislators. They also benefit from the political and policy expertise gained
from service in Congress, a certain visibility in Washington and in the country, and
their established contacts with people and organizations with money. In 2015, the
Center for Responsive Politics reported that, of the ninety-seven members leaving
Congress at the end of 2012, eighteen became employed by lobbying firms and seventeen were hired by organizations that hired lobbyists. The Center identified more
than three hundred former members of Congress working as lobbyists.

4 Hedrick Smith, *The Power Game* (New York: Ballantine Books, 1988), 232.

The Largest Lobbying Firms

Finding lobbyists with genuine expertise in both tax policy and congressional politics is no simple task. Those who have both are able to command steadily rising fees for their services. Capital Tax Partners, a firm co-founded by a former assistant secretary of the treasury for tax policy and a tax counsel to a senior member of the Senate Finance Committee. In 2013, the firm was hired by Amazon to lobby on the tax rate for foreign income that the company brings back to the United States and on sales taxes for online sales. The firm's website boasts about employing more than a half dozen former staff members of the House Ways and Means and the Senate Finance Committees.

Capital Tax Partners ranked only 14th in lobbying spending among lobbying firms in 2014. The two largest lobbying operations are Akin Gump and Squire Patton Boggs, both of which are law and lobbying firms that reported more than $30 million in lobbying spending that year for dozens of clients. The most expensive lobbying efforts reported for Akin Gump were for Samsung, for a Native American casino interest, and for a patent reform coalition comprising some of the largest corporations in the United States. For Squire Patton Boggs, the most expensive efforts were on behalf of CITGO Petroleum, the Wholesale Market Brokers' Association (over-the-counter securities brokers), and the Depository Trust & Clearing Corporation (services to the financial markets), with Amazon coming in fourth.

Akin Gump was founded in 1945 and includes more than eight hundred attorneys and other professionals in Washington and elsewhere. Squire Patton Boggs emerged from Patton Boggs, a firm that dated to 1962, and has about fifteen hundred attorneys. Both firms conduct nongovernment legal practices, but their lobbying and regulatory practices are very large. Both firms include dozens of former members, staff, and executive branch officials.

Former congressional staff aides and federal employees share many of the advantages and knowledge enjoyed by former members, so they also make ideal lobbyists. In 2008, for instance, more than one-third of the top congressional staffers who left their positions that year went on to work for lobbying firms or other groups seeking to influence the government.[5] Another study found that roughly half of the lobbyists hired by the financial sector since 2009 have been former federal employees (including seventy-three former members of Congress). Because staff aides and federal employees develop contacts and skills that make them attractive to law firms, corporations, and lobbying firms, many individuals enter jobs on the Hill with the intent of going from them to these other, more lucrative positions (see box "Limits on Lobbying after Leaving Capitol Hill").

Beyond personal relations, money and information are essential ingredients of successful inside strategies. Money, of course, can be used as an outright bribe, though it seldom is any longer. But money has been a vital asset to gaining access to legislators. In recent years, money allowed lobbyists to arrange for members to take trips to exclusive resorts to attend conferences or charity

5 Matt Kelley, "Third of Top Aides Become Lobbyists," *USA Today*, December 26, 2008.

functions that are also attended by lobbyists and corporate leaders; to host outings to golf courses, ball games, and concerts; and to sponsor lunches, dinners, and receptions in Washington. However, such behavior was severely curtailed after the House and Senate passed rules changes in 2007 in response to a series of high-profile scandals linking several members of Congress to former lobbyist Jack Abramoff. Both chambers placed heavy restrictions on the gifts that could be accepted from lobbyists and imposed more extensive oversight of member-lobbyist relations. Although gifts from lobbyists valued at less than $50 were permitted by the former rules, both chambers eliminated this exception to the gifts restriction. Moreover, the rules changes now require members to get prior approval from the appropriate ethics committee before accepting travel paid for by an outside, private source. It is important to note, though, that money allows lobbyists to do more than simply dole out goodies. With adequate financial means, lobbyists are also able to acquire other resources, such as the assistance of policy experts, which are often critical in dealing with legislators and their staffs.

The most obvious, and perhaps most important, use of money is for campaign contributions. Some lobbyists are able to make considerable contributions themselves. And many are in a position to maximize their influence with a few legislators by orchestrating contributions from numerous political action committees and wealthy individuals.

Limits on Lobbying after Leaving Capitol Hill

In Washington, the exchange of personnel between high-level public- and private-sector positions is commonly referred to as the *revolving door*. Upon leaving their positions within government, former members of Congress as well as congressional staffers and employees of the federal government frequently enter private-sector positions to serve as lobbyists. Furthermore, it is often the case that individuals in top positions within industries are called upon to fill key roles within the government, such as agency directors.

The heightened access that former members, congressional staffers, and federal employees have does not, however, go unchecked. As established by the Lobbying Disclosure Act of 1995 (LDA), exiting members of Congress are banned from lobbying in Congress for a duration of time, known as a "cooling-off" period. The cooling-off period for House members is currently one year, which is the duration originally set by the LDA. In 2007, the Senate changed its rules to extend the cooling-off period for senators to two years. Congressional staff whose salaries are at least 75 percent of members' salaries (or $130,500 in 2011) are also prohibited from lobbying in Congress immediately after leaving their positions. In the House, there is a one-year ban on senior staff lobbying the committee or member for whom they worked. The 2007 rules changes prohibit senior Senate staff from lobbying *any* senator or employee of the Senate for a period of one year. In addition, former members and senior staff are prohibited from lobbying the executive branch on behalf of another party for one year as well.

Just how much influence is exercised through campaign contributions is an open question. Most campaign contributions appear to flow to members who already support the positions of the contributors – the money follows the votes, the saying goes. But measuring the influence of campaign contributions is very difficult. Some contributions are intended to encourage members to remain inactive, or at least not to challenge policies favored by groups. Other contributions are designed to generate action at less visible stages of the legislative process – to offer an amendment in a subcommittee markup, to hold to a policy position in private negotiations in conference, and so on. Of course, members in key positions, such as party leaders or committee chairs, attract substantial contributions. In light of his likely ascendancy to the speakership, contributions to John Boehner (R-Ohio) in the 111th Congress (2009–2010) increased by more than $4.6 million compared to his previous two years of service ($5.16 million in 2007–2008, and $9.8 million in 2009–2010).

Despite the difficulties in gauging the influence of campaign contributions, few doubt that contributions are an important link between members and those lobbyists who can generate large sums for the members' campaigns. We can infer from interest group behavior that there are returns to making contributions (see box "An Unlikely Winner"). In recent years, members have increasingly called upon lobbyists to organize fund-raising activities on their behalf. Lobbyists often do not dare refuse, because they fear losing access that they have worked so hard to gain.

Information is a critical resource for the lobbyist engaged in inside lobbying. Legislators appear to have an insatiable desire for information about the policy and political consequences of their actions. The political scientists David Austen-Smith and John R. Wright contend that legislators are imperfectly informed about constituency preferences, and, therefore, lobbyists provide an important source of information. Furthermore, they argue that competition among interests induces truthful behavior from the interest groups. Lobbyists who develop a reputation for having reliable information at hand are called on more frequently by legislators and are more likely to gain the access necessary for exercising influence. Of course, the amount of technical information a professional lobbyist is likely to have is limited, so the lobbyist's success depends on having a network of contacts in research institutes, universities, executive agencies, corporations, or wherever expertise relevant to the lobbyist's interests is found. In fact, many lobbying firms and interest groups hire technical specialists such as lawyers and social and physical scientists so that they can provide timely information to decision makers and even conduct original research of their own.

Outside Lobbying

The most dramatic change in the lobbying business in recent decades has been the increase in outside, or grassroots, lobbying. Rather than relying solely on Washington

TABLE 11.3. Percentage of interest groups that reported using a lobbying technique

Testify at hearings	99
Contact government officials directly to present your point of view	98
Engage in informal contacts with officials – at conventions, over lunch, etc.	95
Present research results or technical information	92
Send letters to members of your organization to inform them about your activities	92
Enter into coalitions with other organizations	90
Attempt to shape the implementation of policies	89
Talk with people from the press and the media	86
Consult with government officials to plan legislative strategy	85
Help draft legislation	85
Inspire letter-writing or telegram campaigns	84
Mount grassroots lobbying efforts	80
Have influential constituents contact their congressperson's office	80
Make financial contributions to electoral campaigns	58
Publicize candidates' voting records	44
Run advertisements in the media about your position on issues	31

Source: TABLE (Adapted) – "Percent of Interest Groups That" from *Organized Interest and American Democracy* by Kay Lehman Schlozman and John T. Tierney, 150. Copyright ©1986 by Kay Lehman Schlozman and John T. Tierney. Reprinted by permission of HarperCollins Publishers, Inc.

lobbyists to make appeals on behalf of a cause, groups often attempt to mobilize their membership or the general public to generate outside pressure on members of Congress. Successful mobilization of members' constituents increases the stakes for members by increasing the likelihood that their actions will have electoral consequences. The survey of lobbying groups reported in Table 11.3 shows that more than 80 percent of groups inspired letter-writing or telegram campaigns, 80 percent mounted grassroots lobbying efforts and prodded influential constituents to contact their congressional representatives, and about one-third ran advertisements in the media about their positions on the issues. And evidence suggests that grassroots campaigns do influence legislators' decisions, which we might expect considering the widespread use of this technique.

Technology and money have driven innovations in outside lobbying. Throughout the history of Congress, groups of people from around the country have converged on Washington to demand action on their programs. Improved means of transportation have increased the frequency with which groups mobilize their members or the general public for marches, special lobbying days, and other events in Washington that are designed to heighten congressional interest and support for their causes. Mass marches have always been the necessary strategy of large groups without the money and experienced Washington lobbyists essential to execute effective inside strategies. But today, many groups, even well-established groups, bring large numbers of people from around the country on special occasions to pressure members of Congress.

An Unlikely Winner

The prospects of financial reform in the aftermath of the banking crisis brought out all of the heavy hitters. The financial reform bill attracted innumerable banking and financial organizations that aggressively petitioned members of Congress to limit regulation. Receipts for lobbying in the financial sector totaled more than $930 million in 2009 and 2010. Yet the public outcry against Wall Street resulted in Congress passing a relatively stringent bill clamping down on many of the practices that at one time made the barons of finance rich. Interestingly, one group did score a major success – automotive dealers.

The reform bill threatened to place the lending practices of auto dealers under the oversight of the Consumer Protection Financial Bureau, a new watchdog agency intended to protect borrowers from predatory lenders. By one estimate, auto dealers brokered 80 percent of the nearly $850 billion in the nation's auto loans and received fees and interest for doing so. Unfortunately, there was no shortage of accounts of questionable lending practices. One study found that over a one-year period, dealers made $20 billion by increasing the rates of loans above those charged by the lenders and keeping the difference. But auto dealers argued that they were not responsible for the financial crisis, as they were merely middlemen in the lending industry. In addition, they asserted that the regulation would have devastating consequences for auto sales because it would increase the difficulty of getting a car loan.

In the end, lawmakers gave auto dealers an exemption from oversight by the new agency. How did the auto dealers do it? Effective lobbying. Money was not the only key to their success, although the National Automotive Dealers Association spent nearly $6.3 million on lobbying in 2009 and 2010. Perhaps more important, they orchestrated massive grassroots campaigns. With roughly eighteen thousand auto dealerships nationwide that employ approximately one million people, they were well positioned to do so. And lobbyists were quite successful in depicting the automobile industry as "Main Street" as opposed to Wall Street, deflecting the stigma associated with the financial sector. Representative Barney Frank (D-Massachusetts) surmised that auto dealer lobbyists were "more powerful than the bankers."

Sources: James Surowiecki, "Masters of Main Street," *The New Yorker*, July 12, 2010; Steven Brill, "Government for Sale: How Lobbyists Shaped the Financial Reform Bill," *Time*, July 1, 2010.

By the 1970s, computer-generated mailings allowed groups to send "legislative alert" letters to group members or targeted groups in the general public to stimulate an avalanche of mail and waves of phone calls to congressional offices. Members of Congress soon learned to identify and discount orchestrated letter-writing campaigns. Nevertheless, as lobbyist Bill Murphy observes, "The congressman has to care that *somebody* out there in his district has enough power to get hundreds of people to sit down and write a postcard or a letter – because if the guy can get them to do *that*, he might be able to influence them in other ways. So, a member has no choice but to pay attention."[6] At a minimum, a member must worry that those same constituents could be motivated, by the same means used to stimulate their letter writing, to contribute their money to or cast their votes for a member's opponent.

Today's lobbyists take outside strategies several steps further. For example, Washington-based firms have adapted telemarketing strategies to congressional politics. Working from computer-generated lists of Americans likely to support a particular point of view, telephone operators dial homes, ask a few questions, and then transfer the call to the appropriate congressional offices so that constituents' views can be registered with their representatives and senators. Particular geographic constituencies can be targeted to maximize the pressure on a few members of Congress.

The Internet also serves as a valuable, low-cost resource for interest groups looking to engage the public. Large-scale e-mail campaigns have become a common grassroots strategy among organized interests. And considering the minimal cost of the approach, the returns tend to be sizable. In one instance, an e-mail campaign organized by the National Education Association (NEA) encouraged public education advocates to pressure members of Congress to back a class-size reduction and a 15 percent increase in education funding – an ambitious proposal. The effort prompted twenty thousand e-mails and resulted in a 12 percent increase in the education budget. Lobbying firms have even turned to social media websites, such as Twitter and Facebook, to promote grassroots activities.

Media advertising has become an increasingly integral part of lobbying strategies. Most advertising of this variety is intended to increase the visibility of an issue or cause and shape opinion in the general public. For the most part, the media ads are designed and produced by the same people who produce election campaign ads. One group, the U.S. Chamber of Commerce, produces its own television programs that are shown on local stations throughout the country. It uses its production and satellite facilities to link its Washington studios (which are just one block from the White House) with corporate sponsors.

A particular advantage of outside lobbying is that there are few registration and disclosure requirements. Under current law, organized interests and representatives of organized interests that engage exclusively in grassroots lobbying are not obligated to register as lobbyists or file any disclosure statements. Disclosure of grassroots lobbying is triggered only by participation in direct, or inside, lobbying. Groups that have limited lobbying ambitions may, therefore, adopt grassroots strategies to avoid reporting burdens. This loophole has, however, led to the emergence of massive grassroots lobbying organizations whose practices go largely unchecked. There have been a number of recent efforts by reformers to close this loophole by extending disclosure requirements to grassroots lobbyists.

---

6 Quoted in John T. Tierney and Kay Lehman Schlozman, "Congress and Organized Interests," in *Congressional Politics*, ed. Christopher J. Deering (Chicago: Dorsey Press, 1989), 212.

In fact, the Honest Leadership and Open Government Act of 2007 – the major lobbying and ethics reform legislation passed at the outset of the 110th Congress (2007–2008) – contained such a provision, but the legislation was later amended to remove all disclosure requirements for grassroots lobbyists. Recent ethically suspect grassroots efforts may well cause legislators to revisit this matter. In one instance, Bonner & Associates, a grassroots firm hired by the American Coalition for Clean Coal Electricity in 2009, circulated at least twelve forged letters to congressional offices claiming to be from the members of nonprofit organizations, including the NAACP.

The growing importance of outside strategies has led to the proliferation of "full-service" lobbying firms. These large firms combine traditional insider lobbyists with policy experts; specialists in public relations, graphic arts, and electronic media; speechwriters; fund-raisers; communications and computer technicians; and pollsters. Firms with the capacity to effectively employ both inside and outside strategies must determine the mix of strategies that will position them to best meet their goals. According to the political scientists Marie Hojnacki and David Kimball, organized interests are likely to use inside lobbying to target allies in committee, so as to influence the content of legislative proposals. Outside lobbying, on the other hand, has the broader goal of maintaining and expanding the base of legislative support, and, therefore, is used to influence members irrespective of their policy position. Outside lobbying, however, has less potential to affect meaningful policy change (also see box "The Choice of Strategies").

Coalitions

Whatever an interest group's mix of inside and outside strategies, it seldom stands alone in major legislative battles. Many coalitions are created for specific issues and then disappear once congressional action on certain legislation is complete. Other coalitions are more enduring. Some coalitions have formal names; others do not. Coalitions are a means for pooling the resources of lobbyists and groups. They also are a means for lobbyists and groups to demonstrate a broad base of support for their cause and to make their effort appear to be as public-spirited as possible. Some coalitions are the creation of lobbyists looking to manufacture a new client.

Grass Roots versus Astroturf

New technologies and strategies have greatly expanded efforts to influence members of Congress by generating an avalanche of phone calls and letters to Capitol Hill. A type of grassroots lobbying, astroturf lobbying refers to seemingly spontaneous citizen-based lobbying efforts that are in reality orchestrated by organized groups.

Sometimes these strategies are too obvious to succeed. For example, a group called the Health Care Coalition had operators call small business owners who were likely to be affected by an amendment pending in the House, tell them that the amendment would be bad for managed health care, and then offer to connect them to the office of the member from their district. Dozens of calls were targeted at critical members.

In another case, hundreds of telegrams were dumped onto the floor of the House Commerce Committee to show public opposition to a telecommunications bill. Perhaps thousands more were sent directly to members. Suspicious congressional aides discovered that many of the telegrams were sent without the signatories' permission by a group called the Seniors Coalition. The public relations firm in charge of the effort blamed shoddy work by a mass marketing subcontractor. Some of the signatories proved to be deceased.

Legislators are likely to discount communications that are so heavily coordinated, but they cannot ignore such communications altogether. It is possible that the citizens who acquiesced to the astroturf scheme could also be motivated to vote against the member in the future.

Source: Juliet Eilperin, "Dingell Takes on Bogus Mailgram," *Roll Call*, October 16, 1995, 1, 20. Reprinted by permission.

An impressive example of an interest group coalition was the Coalition for Derivatives End Users, which played a prominent role in shaping the 2010 financial reform bill. The coalition comprises more than 170 businesses and trade associations, including the National Association of Manufacturers, the U.S. Chamber of Commerce, and the Business Roundtable. At stake in the bill was the future of the derivatives industry. Derivatives are contracts that guarantee a payoff based on the value of some other source; they were identified by some analysts as being a prime culprit in the financial meltdown. The coalition seeks to limit derivatives regulation on end-users – nonfinancial entities that use derivatives to hedge against risk. The original Senate bill would have placed considerable constraints on the use of such derivatives, which prompted action from the coalition. The coalition waged a powerful lobbying campaign urging legislators to limit the extent of the regulation. The final version of the bill reflected substantially more lenient constraints on derivatives end-users, exempting them from many of the bill's derivative-related requirements.

The Choice of Strategies

In an effort to learn more about interest group strategies, the political scientist Jack Walker conducted a detailed survey of the top officers in 734 national interest groups. Walker found that

> most groups adopt a preferred style of political action early in their histories, and, when these early choices are made, group leaders naturally emulate the tactics being employed at that time by the most successful groups. Once either an inside or outside

(continued)

The Choice of Strategies (*continued*)

strategy becomes the association's dominant approach, it is very difficult to move in a new direction. Choices made early in the history of a group establish a strategic style that restricts innovation, largely because political strategies are so intertwined with other basic organizational decisions.

Not surprisingly, Walker discovered that groups facing organized opposition to their goals tend to more aggressively pursue both inside and outside strategies than do other groups. Outside strategies, however, are more frequently the choice of groups with many local chapters or subunits, citizens' groups, and groups from the nonprofit sector (local governments, universities, nonprofit professions, and so on). Inside strategies are more likely to be the choice of groups representing business and groups that have established large central office staffs, usually in Washington.

Source: Jack L. Walker, Jr., *Mobilizing Interest Groups in America: Patrons, Professions, and Social Movements* (Ann Arbor: University of Michigan Press, 1991), 103–121; quote from 119–120.

Much remains unanswered about interest group coalitions. There is, for instance, no clear-cut answer for why coalitions emerge when they do. There is a tremendous amount of variation across issues in terms of the number and size of coalitions that form. Scholars have suggested that the emergence of coalitions is systematically related to such factors as issue conflict and salience. There is, however, only tentative support for these hypotheses. Also it is somewhat unclear whether interest groups in coalitions are actually more successful than ones acting alone. Whereas the Coalition for Derivatives End Users appears to have been successful in 2010, not all coalitions are so fortunate. Moreover, there were organized interests that acted alone on the financial reform bill, such as the National Automotive Dealers Association (NADA), that also were successful in achieving their policy objectives. One study of coalition success found that a mere 58 percent of coalitions accomplished any of their goals.[7] This lackluster rate could reflect some of the disadvantages to coalition formation – namely, greater collective action problems to overcome – but it also may show that coalitions are formed to lobby in the most difficult legislative battles.

Legislators Influencing Organized Interests

The path of influence between lobbyists and members is a two-way street. Plainly, lobbyists seek to influence outcomes in the legislative process by persuading at least a few members to support or even champion their cause who would not have done so otherwise. But legislators often want something from lobbyists, too. And because lobbyists want to cultivate or maintain good relations with key

7 Christine Mahoney and Frank Baumgartner, "When To Go It Alone: The Determinants and Effects of Interest-Group Coalitions," *American Political Science Review* 89 (2004): 566–581.

legislators, they are often quite responsive to legislators' demands. Legislators frequently pressure interest groups to generate campaign contributions for them. They ask lobbyists for assistance in attracting support from other legislators, the public, or others on issues not directly of concern to the lobbyists. Legislators may enlist the support of lobbyists on matters before the executive branch or encourage lobbyists to take action in the courts. Lobbyists may resist these pressures. After all, the requests may not be compatible with other objectives that the lobbyists pursue. But lobbyists must assess how important the legislator is, or will be in the future, to their groups' or their personal interests. Ignoring senior party and committee leaders can come at a significant cost.

The Revolving Door

Under the Lobbying Disclosure Act, a lobbyist must register and report the identity of his or her client. In addition, the report must indicate whether the lobbyist has held a "covered" position – a member or staff position in Congress. The report that follows (Figure 11.1) is excerpted from one filed in early 2015 for Microsoft and indicates that a former top aide to Senator Mitch McConnell, who had become Senate majority leader that month, was working for Microsoft.

CLIENT *A Lobbying Firm is required to file a separate registration for each client. Organizations employing in-house lobbyists should check the box labeled "Self" and proceed to line 10.* ☐*Self*

7. Client name   Microsoft Corporation

Address   901 K Street, NW

City   Washington   State DC Zip 20001   Country USA

8. Principal place of business (if different than line 7)

City   Redmond   State WA Zip 98052-7329 Country USA

9. General description of client's business or activities
Technology company

LOBBYISTS

10. Name of each individual who has acted or is expected to act as a lobbyists for the client identified on line 7. If any person listed in this section has served as a "covered executive branch official" or "covered legislative branch official" within twenty years of first action as a lobbyist for the client, *state the executive and/or legislative position(s) in which the person served.*

First	Last	Suffix	Covered Official Position (if applicable)
Malloy	McDaniel		Policy Advisor, Senate Minority Leader Mitch McConnell
Malloy	McDaniel	cont.	Whip Liasion, Senate Majority Whip Mitch McConnell
Malloy	McDaniel	cont.	Floor Assistant, Senate Majority Leader Trebt Lott
Malloy	McDaniel	cont.	Cloakroom Assistant, Office of the Republican Secretary
Kristi	Remington	cont.	Deputy Assistant Attorney General, US Department of Justice
Kristi	Remington	cont.	Senior Counsel, House Government Reform Committee

Figure 11.1 Microsoft Lobbying Disclosure Filing. Source: soprweb.senate.gov

When congressional Republicans gained majority party status in 1995, GOP leaders launched a project to pressure Washington lobbying firms to hire Republicans for top positions. Called the K Street Project, Republican leaders tracked the party affiliation of Washington lobbyists and rewarded those lobbyists who were loyal. With like-minded individuals in key lobbying positions, congressional Republicans could limit the power of opposing interests. With unified control of Congress and the White House between 2000 and 2006, lobbying firms had to stay in the good graces of Republicans if they wished to exert influence over legislative outcomes. Whereas lobbying firms have historically hired lobbyists from both parties to accommodate changes in party control, there is reason to believe that the lobbying firms predicted lasting Republican dominance. This, along with the strict oversight of the K Street Project, led many lobbying firms to pass up Democrats for important lobbying positions. After the Democrats took majority control of the House and Senate in 2007, changes were made to chamber rules to address the practices of the K Street Project. No longer could members of Congress dictate the hiring practices of lobbying firms. The House and Senate now prohibit members from influencing "on the basis of partisan political affiliation, an employment decision or employment practice of any private entity."

Changes in the electoral climate since have generated corresponding changes in the partisan composition of lobbying firms. Demand for lobbyists with Republican connections faded following the 2006 elections, when the Democrats won majorities in the House and Senate. Demand for Republican lobbyists returned after the Republicans regained a majority in the 2010 House elections.

REGULATING LOBBYING

Modern lobbying is remarkably clean and ethical, at least when compared with lobbying during most of American history. In the nineteenth century, lobbyists ran gambling establishments to put legislators in their debt and openly paid members for representing their interests on Capitol Hill. With few (recent) exceptions, the retainers and bribes are gone. In fact, lobbyists now have their own professional code of ethics.

At various points throughout history, congressional, journalistic, and criminal investigations have exposed remarkably corrupt lobbying practices, but on only a few occasions did Congress or either house impose any restrictions on lobbying. In 1876, for example, Congress for the first time required that lobbyists register, but the rule was in effect for only one Congress. Congress did not pass its first comprehensive lobbying regulations until 1946 when the Federal Regulation of Lobbying Act was adopted as a part of the Legislative Reorganization Act.

The central feature of the 1946 law was the requirement that people who solicit or receive money for the purpose of influencing legislation must register with the clerk of the House or the secretary of the Senate. Lobbyists were required to file quarterly reports on the money they received for and spent on lobbying. The authors of the 1946 act hoped that disclosure of lobbyists' clients and legislative purposes would put members, reporters, and the public in a better position to evaluate lobbyists' influence.

The law proved to be unenforceable. In 1954, the Supreme Court ruled in *United States v. Harriss* that the registration and reporting requirements applied only to those persons who are paid by others to lobby, who contact members directly, and whose "principal purpose" is to influence legislation. The Court argued that the First Amendment to the Constitution, which prohibits Congress from making a law that abridges the right "to petition the Government for a redress of grievances," limits Congress's ability to regulate an individual's right to represent himself or herself before Congress and to organize others with the intent of influencing Congress. By confining the force of the 1946 act to those lobbyists whose principal purpose it was to influence legislation, the Court created a large loophole for anyone who wanted to claim that influencing legislation was not his or her principal purpose. A Government Accounting Office report found that only a small fraction of individuals who were actively involved in lobbying had registered as lobbyists, and the lack of an audit created considerable uncertainty surrounding the accuracy of information reported by lobbyists.

Interest in creating meaningful registration and reporting requirements was renewed in the early 1990s. Ross Perot gave great emphasis to the influence of "special interests" in his 1992 presidential campaign. Perot's theme was reinforced by television reports about members' all-expenses-paid trips to vacation resorts where they fraternized with lobbyists. In response to the heightened public scrutiny of the relationship between lobbyists and members of Congress, a large number of members elected for the first time in the 1990s had promised to reduce the influence of special interests in Washington. The result was the consideration of significant lobbying reforms.

In late 1995, Congress enacted new legislation designed to close some of the loopholes in the 1946 law. The new law, titled the Lobbying Disclosure Act of 1995 (LDA), extended the 1946 law that covered only people who lobbied members of Congress, to also include those who seek to influence congressional staff and top executive branch officials. The LDA formally defines a lobbyist as:

> Any individual who is employed or retained by a client for financial or other compensation for services that include more than one lobbying contact [Defined as any oral or written communication (including an electronic communication) to a covered executive branch official or a covered legislative branch official that is made on behalf of a client], other than an individual whose lobbying activities constitute less than 20 percent of the time engaged in the services provided by such individual to the client over a six month period.

Anyone who is hired to lobby a covered public official and spends 20 percent or more of his or her time in paid lobbying, must register with the clerk of the House and the secretary of the Senate within forty-five days of being hired or making the first contact, whichever is earlier. Under the LDA, individuals who received $5,000 or less in a six-month period and organizations that spent less than $20,000 in a six-month period are not required to register. This exception was included to allow average citizens to have their voices heard without needing to register. Lobbyists are required to file reports that disclose who their clients are, the general issue area they were hired to influence, and a good faith estimate of the total amount paid by their clients. The LDA originally called for these reports to be filed on a semiannual basis. Lobbyists for foreign governments or organizations must also register. The registration requirement excludes grassroots lobbying, such as efforts to persuade people to write to members of Congress.

Owing to the introduction of these registration requirements, the LDA had the effect of more than doubling the number of registered lobbyists. Among the newly registered were a variety of lobbying coalitions – organized groups of lobbyists, associations, and lobbying firms – that had not been registered under the old law. Even still, the law fell short of registering many individuals who acted as lobbyists.

Separately, the House and Senate also adopted rules limiting lobbyists' gifts to members and staff. The rules banned gifts valued at more than $50, including meals and entertainment. Gifts from any one source could not exceed $100 in value for a year, with gifts under $10 excluded from the calculation. Gifts from family members and gifts of token value (e.g., T-shirts, mugs) were also excluded. In addition, chamber rules permitted privately funded trips but banned travel paid for directly by a lobbyist.

In the months leading up to the 2006 elections, the public witnessed an inordinate number of lobbying scandals. In March 2006, former Representative Randall "Duke" Cunningham (R-California) was convicted of accepting $2.4 million in bribes primarily from defense contractors in return for securing contracts. In May 2006, the FBI raided the home of Representative William Jefferson (D-Louisiana) to find $90,000 in his freezer. The government claimed that Jefferson took in excess of $400,000 in bribes. He was later indicted on sixteen charges of corruption. In October 2006, former Representative Bob Ney (R-Ohio) pled guilty to accepting gifts in exchange for favorable action on behalf of convicted lobbyist Jack Abramoff's clients. The election outcomes were, at least in part, a reaction to the many scandals. In a CNN exit poll of voters in the 2006 congressional elections, corruption was more frequently cited by voters as "extremely important" than any other issue, including terrorism, the economy, and Iraq.[8]

After gaining majorities in the House and Senate in the 2006 elections, the Democrats set out to fulfill their promises about ethics and lobbying reform.

8 "Corruption Named as Key Issue by Voters in Exit Polls." Available at CNN.com, http://www.cnn.com/2006/ POLITICS/11/07/election.exitpolls/index.html.

House Democrats did so immediately by including reforms in their chamber rules. The Senate opted to pursue statutory reforms, and passed legislation containing rules changes similar to those the House passed days earlier. The result was the Honest Leadership and Open Government Act of 2007, agreed to by both chambers and signed into law by President George W. Bush. The newly passed act amended the LDA of 1995 in several important areas, including, but not limited to, disclosure requirements, revolving-door restrictions, and gift limitations.

The act requires quarterly instead of semiannual filing of lobbying disclosure reports, and it reduces the monetary thresholds by half to conform to the new quarterly periods. Reports must identify if a client is a state or local government, department, agency, or other instrumentality, and they must be filed electronically to facilitate transparency. For former senators, the act bans directly lobbying in Congress for two years after leaving office, rather than one year as under the LDA. The House, however, retained the one-year "cooling-off" period specified in the earlier legislation. The act also prohibits senior Senate staff from lobbying any senator or employee of the Senate for a one-year period. In addition, the act prohibits a member's staff from having lobbying contact with the member's spouse or immediate family member, should the relative be a registered lobbyist. The Senate makes an exception for spouses who were serving as registered lobbyists at least one year prior to the senator's election. Legislators are furthermore banned from negotiating private employment until after their successor is elected, unless they file a report disclosing the name(s) of the entity involved in the negotiations.

Considering the events leading up to the elections, perhaps the most pertinent reforms relate to restrictions on gifts from lobbyists to members and their staff. The act sharply limits gifts to legislators, striking the exception that previously permitted members and their staff to receive gifts under $50. According to the act, members and their staff are not permitted to accept privately financed travel from lobbyists or entities that employ lobbyists. Moreover, they are prohibited from traveling with lobbyists present on any segment of the trip. The rules do allow travel for one day and one night to locations where there is minimal lobbyist involvement. Some additional exceptions are made for travel to approved educational (House and Senate) or charitable (Senate) institutions. The act further requires members to receive advanced approval for all travel paid for by an outside, private source. To promote adherence to the lobbying laws, the act increases the maximum civil penalty for violations of the provisions, from $50,000 to $200,000, and provides for criminal penalties of imprisonment for deliberate noncompliance. Both Congress and the president have taken additional steps in recent years to reform the lobbying practices of executive officials as well.

MEMBERS' GROUPS AND LEGISLATIVE SERVICE ORGANIZATIONS

Groups of members frequently coalesce or even formally organize to pursue specific political interests. In fact, informal groups of members have been prominent features of Washington politics since the early Congresses. In the early nineteenth century, members tended to find lodging in boarding houses where they found like-minded colleagues. Informal but conspicuous intraparty factions, such as southern Democrats, have been quite important from time to time. And state delegations, particularly those of the larger states, have been the building blocks for coalitions throughout the history of Congress. Two developments of recent decades have altered the character of membership groups.

The first is that intraparty factions developed formal organizations with formal memberships, elected leaders, staff, offices, and even membership dues. The prototype, and still the largest such group, is the Democratic Study Group (DSG). The DSG was formed in 1959 by House Democratic liberals to counter the strength of the conservative coalition of Republicans and southern Democrats. The services of the DSG – especially issuing and scheduling reports – eventually became so highly valued that nearly all Democrats joined and contributed dues to take advantage of the group's work. Nevertheless, the DSG remains the organizational focal point for liberal activists in the House.

Since the 1970s there has been a remarkable increase in the number of single-issue caucuses (Figure 11.2). Today there are more than 250 such caucuses, and many

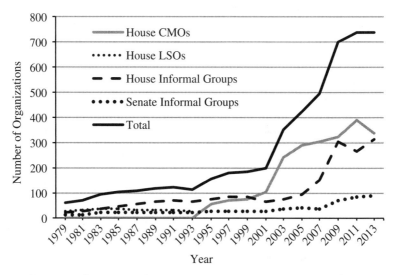

Figure 11.2 House and Senate Member Organizations, 1979–2014. Source: Matthew E. Glassman and Robert Jay Dilger, "Congressional Member Organizations: Their Purpose and Activities, History, and Formation." CRS Report, R40683, February 10, 2015.

have bipartisan memberships. The Congressional Arts Caucus and the Congressional Sportsmen's Caucus formed to promote certain public funding for the arts and to oppose many proposed regulations on firearms, respectively; regional interests are promoted by the Northeast-Midwest Congressional Coalition and the Congressional Western Caucus. Both constituency concerns and personal circumstances provide a foundation for the Congressional Black Caucus, the Congressional Hispanic Caucus, and the Congressional Caucus for Women's Issues. District economic interests are reflected in the Congressional Coastal Caucus, the Congressional Steel Caucus, and the Congressional Tourism and Travel Caucus. In the 111th Congress (2009–2010), caucuses ranged in size from 2 to 355 members, having an average size of 55.

Caucuses, now officially called congressional member organizations (CMOs) in the House, are a way for members to become involved in and demonstrate a commitment to a particular cause or issue that falls outside of the scope of their regular committee duties. This is particularly true in the House, where most members are limited to two committee assignments. In fact, about 90 percent of caucuses are found in the House. In most cases, a caucus is a basis for publicizing a cause or an issue and building policy coalitions within Congress. Outside interest groups seeking to cultivate congressional support for their interests have stimulated the creation of many congressional caucuses.

Until recently, many caucuses were formally recognized in the House as "legislative service organizations," or LSOs, and were subject to audits and a few regulations. LSOs were controversial because they received dues from members' office accounts and had office space in House office buildings. Critics charged that this practice allowed money from office accounts to be spent indirectly for purposes, such as dinners, for which office account funds cannot be spent directly. Moreover, many LSOs bridged the gap between interest groups and congressional caucuses by creating foundations and institutes with close ties to both external groups and internal caucuses. In the view of some critics, the ability of lobbyists and interest groups to contribute money to these new foundations was just another way for special interests to support travel and social events for members and congressional staff participating in the work of the foundations. These critiques of LSOs paved the way for the second significant development in membership groups in recent decades.

The newly elected Republican majority of 1995 fundamentally changed the character of membership groups by banning LSOs. Membership groups lost several special privileges – the ability to receive dues paid from official budgets and to occupy office space in House buildings. Slowly, the congressional member organizations replaced LSOs and were granted more limited privileges. Members of CMOs may jointly pay for staff and other functions, but they do not pay dues for separate staff and activities. Dozens of member organizations have been created and, among other activities, serve to advertise legislators' interest in subjects important to key groups in their districts and states.

THE INFLUENCE OF LOBBYISTS AND INTEREST GROUPS

Even experienced and insightful watchers of the lobbying and interest group community have mixed views about the influence of special interest lobbying. A popular view in the 1950s and 1960s was that policy making was dominated by "subgovernments" or "iron triangles" – tightly bound sets of interest groups, executive agencies, and committees. According to this view, cozy relationships among lobbyists, bureaucrats, and members prevented other interests from influencing policy choices and implementation. The subgovernments perspective was always recognized as an overly stylized view, but it captured an important feature of Washington politics: In many policy areas, only a few groups, agencies, and members took an interest in the issues, so they dominated the policy choices that were made.

The classic case of subgovernment policy making was mid-twentieth-century agriculture policy politics. Generally, only those agriculture groups directly affected by certain federal commodities programs, the Agriculture Department bureaus that ran the programs, and a few members sitting on the agriculture committees of Congress took an active interest in farm policy. Those groups, bureaucrats, and members interested in the various farm commodities assisted each other in gaining congressional approval of the periodic legislation that supported federal programs. Although federal taxpayers paid for these programs, the costs were not so high as to breed resistance. And the lack of conflict among agriculture-sector groups and decision makers helped keep others from paying attention.

Many political scientists responded to the subgovernments' perspective by noting the special conditions that allow a subgovernment to develop and dominate policy making. The most important feature is that there is little conflict. Conflict among the interested groups and members would encourage the contending forces to recruit supporters from a broader range of groups, legislators, executive branch officials, and even the general public. Expanding the scope of the conflict in this way usually alters the balance of forces and the policy outcome. The low level of conflict, in turn, is the product of the concentrated benefits and widely distributed costs of some programs. The beneficiaries are motivated to organize and lobby to protect their interests, and the fairly small burden on taxpayers stimulates little opposition. But the number of people affected by the policy choices, the distribution of costs and benefits, and the scope and intensity of conflict differ greatly across policy areas. The result is significant variation in the role of groups in shaping policy choices.

The political scientist Hugh Heclo has noticed that policy areas once dominated by subgovernments had lost their insular character by the 1970s. Heclo coined the term *issue networks* to capture the more diverse, mutually antagonistic, and fluid character of the lobbying and interest group community found in many policy areas. Many factors contributed to the change. In the 1960s and 1970s, new citizens' groups, many of which were by-products of broad-based social movements, challenged established groups. Groups representing economic interests proliferated, partly in response to new government policies and regulations, which led to a fragmentation of Washington representation in many policy areas that were once dominated by just one or two groups. In addition, congressional reforms made Congress more open, accessible, and democratic, which encouraged new groups to lobby and stimulated more members of Congress to champion the cause of once-neglected interests.

Analysts are divided over the political implications of the expansion of the interest group community and the breakdown of subgovernments. Tierney and Schlozman emphasize the continuing numerical advantage of business-oriented groups. They also observe that the explosion of interest group activity has

> introduced a potentially dysfunctional particularism into national politics. If policymakers in Congress are forced to find an appropriate balance between deference to the exigencies of the short run and the consideration of consequences for the long run, between acquiescence to the clearly expressed wishes of narrow groups that care intensely and respect for the frequently unexpressed needs of larger publics, the balance may have shifted too far in the direction of the near-term and the narrow.[9]

The Tierney-Schlozman thesis is reinforced by the analysis of the political scientists Martin Gilens and Benjamin Page, who examined the relationship between federal legislative outcomes on 1,779 issues and the preferences of economic elites, business groups, mass-based interest groups, and general public opinion. Their findings indicate that economic elites and business groups are positively correlated with policy outcomes, and that average citizens and mass-based groups have little influence. They emphasize that the distribution of economic resources and the strength of organized business groups matter for political choices.[10]

The political scientist Robert Salisbury disagrees. He insists that the large number of corporate lobbyists and the tremendous resources of business groups should not lead us to conclude

> that business interests or even self-serving groups invariably prevail. The total system of policy advocacy is far broader than the array, vast as it is, of organized interest groups. Every holder of public office – indeed, every candidate for public office – is or may be an advocate of some policy alternatives. Members of Congress do not wait passively for lobbyists to persuade them one way or the other; they too are advocates, as are the more prominent members of the administration, the editorialists and commentators in the mass media, the academic pundits and writers, and a host of other citizens who write letters, attend rallies, argue with each other, and generally make their views known on policy questions of the day.[11]

9 Tierney and Schlozman, "Congress and Organized Interests," 216.
10 Martin Gilens and Benjamin I. Page, "Testing Theories of American Politics: Elites, Interest Groups, and Average Citizens," *Perspectives on Politics* 12:3 (September 2014): 565–581.
11 Robert H. Salisbury, "Putting Interests Back into Interest Groups," in *Interest Group Politics*, 3rd ed., ed. Allan J. Cigler and Burdett A. Loomis (Washington, DC: Congressional Quarterly Press, 1991), 382–383.

Besides, Salisbury contends, most business group resources are devoted to monitoring government activity important to business decisions rather than to influencing policy choices.

It seems fair to say that the critical view advocated by Tierney and Schlozman, and reinforced by Gilens and Page, is more widely shared among sophisticated observers of congressional politics than is Salisbury's more forgiving perspective. Nevertheless, Salisbury's note of caution is important. Lobbyists and interest groups are not the only source of pressure on members, nor are they the only important source of change in the nature of congressional politics. Communications and transportation technologies, electoral campaigns, the structure of the legislative process, the distribution of power within Congress, and other factors affect the balance of forces influencing congressional policy choices as well.

CONCLUSION

Lobbyists and interest groups are among the most controversial and least well-understood features of the legislative game. They appear to be both an essential part of the representation of interests before Congress and a potential source of bias in the policy choices made by Congress. Generally, they direct members' attention to narrow and parochial issues that might otherwise not be addressed. Whatever its consequences, the relationship that lobbyists and interest groups have with members of Congress has changed markedly over the years. In particular, transformations in Congress have caused lobbyists and interest groups to evolve. They are now:

- a much larger and more diverse community than just a few decades ago,
- more professional, with increasingly developed infrastructures,
- a more entral player in congressional elections, both in terms of direct contributions and advocacy efforts, and
- better able to provide legislators with quick and accurate information.

These developments have sensitized the general public about the influence of special interests and produced new efforts to regulate lobbyists and lobbying.

SUGGESTED READINGS

A. The following books are classic treatments of influence and interest groups in America.

Schattschneider, E. E. *The Semisovereign People.* New York: Holt, Rinehart, and Winston, 1960.

Truman, David. *The Governmental Process.* 2nd ed. New York: Knopft, 1971.

Walker, Jack L. *Mobilizing Interest Groups in America.* Ann Arbor: University of Michigan Press, 1991.

B.   The following readings discuss the influence of organized interests on congressional policy making.

Gilens, Martin, and Benjamin I. Page, "Testing Theories of American Politics: Elites, Interest Groups, and Average Citizens." *Perspectives on Politics* 12:3 (September 2014): 565–581.

Hall, Richard L., and F. W. Wayman. "Buying Time: Moneyed Interests and the Mobilization of Bias in Congressional Committees." *American Political Science Review* 84 (1990): 797–820.

Hansen, John Mark. *Gaining Access: Congress and the Farm Lobby, 1919–1981.* Chicago: University of Chicago Press, 1991.

Schlozman, Kay Lehman, and John T. Tierney. *Organized Interests and American Democracy.* New York: Harper Collins, 1986.

C.   The following books provide more popular treatments of developments in lobbying and interest group activity in the last few decades.

Hacker, Jacob, and Paul Pierson. *Winner-Take-All Politics.* New York: Simon and Shuster, 2011.

Kaiser, Robert G. *So Damn Much Money: The Triumph of Lobbying and the Corrosion of American Government.* New York: Vintage, 2010.

Lessig, Lawrence. *Republic, Lost: How Money Corrupts Congress – and a Plan to Stop It.* New York: Twelve, 2012.

DISCUSSION QUESTIONS

1   Why does the First Amendment to the Constitution make it difficult for Congress to reform lobbying laws?

2   What evidence would be necessary to support the argument that lobbying has a significant effect on policy outcomes in Congress?

3   Are lobbyists a good or a bad feature of modern congressional policy making?

4   Why are business interests so strongly represented in the lobbying community?

Congress and Budget Politics

A Senate Budget Committee staff member unpacks copies of President Obama's budget in February 2015.

The federal budget is often the center of congressional politics. For fiscal year 2016, the federal government's spending will exceed $3.4 trillion, or more than $10,000 for every American.[1] Although many people are bored to tears when the details of spending and tax policy are discussed, the budget reflects fundamental choices about the role of government in American life, and action on the annual budget tends to generate the most heated fights in Washington. The budget – what money is spent on, where the money comes from, how large is the deficit – is at the center of the partisan divide. The twists and turns of budget politics have strongly

1 The most recent budget figures and estimates are available in the current budget projections section of the Congressional Budget Office's website, www.cbo.gov.

influenced winners and losers in elections, shaped the political careers of the most prominent politicians, reshaped congressional decision-making processes, and altered the distribution of power within Congress.

Federal budgeting since the 1970s has been a roller coaster ride. Beginning in the late 1970s and continuing for more than a decade, presidents and Congress struggled with annual deficits. In fiscal year 1992, the federal government spent about $290 billion more than it received from taxes and other revenues. To pay the interest on the debt that had accumulated over the years (nearly $4 trillion by that point), the federal government spent a little more than $200 billion – about 14 percent of its $1.5 trillion budget for fiscal year 1992. By 1998, the budget picture had improved markedly. Fiscal year 1998 ended with a small surplus, and annual surpluses were achieved in the three following years. Deficits returned by late 2001 during an economic recession. The fight against terrorism and the war in Iraq prompted increases in defense and homeland security spending, and tax cuts enacted in 2001 and 2003 cut into revenues. Deficits were looming again by 2002 and have continued through to the present, greatly deepened by the recession of 2007–2008 and the policies to deal with it. The annual deficit reached over $1.2 trillion in three successive years during the great recession. The annual deficit has fallen by less than $0.5 trillion since then, but the accumulated national debt in 2015 rose to over $18 trillion.

During the past four decades, political battles stimulated by budget deficits have produced a series of procedural innovations in the way that Congress drafts the budget. In the 1970s and early 1980s, the process was modified to force congressional committees to write legislation that would either reduce spending or raise more revenue. Since then, the emphasis has been on enforcing multiyear budget plans. Each new effort to enforce deficit and spending agreements has been a response to legislators, whose votes are often pivotal to passing budget legislation, to take credible action against deficits. In the second decade of the twenty-first century, fiscal discipline, the search for processes to enforce it, and the need to fund vital programs remain central issues for Congress.

This is an important story. Step-by-step, efforts to manage conflict over fiscal policy have reshaped the congressional decision-making process. Partisanship has been particularly intense on budget issues, and power has shifted from the standing committees to party leaders. The strengths and especially the weaknesses of Congress as a representative and lawmaking body have been exposed repeatedly.

Overview of the Federal Budget

Figure 12.1 shows the history of the federal deficit since the end of World War II. In the aftermath of the war, the federal government managed small annual budget surpluses about as often as it experienced small deficits. In the 1960s, small deficits were the

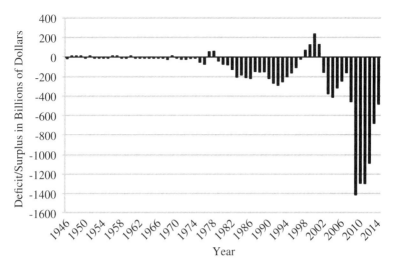

Figure 12.1 Annual Surplus (+) or Deficit (–) in Billions of Dollars, for Fiscal Years 1946–2014.
Source: Congressional Budget Office.

norm. Deficits crept upward during the 1970s and became a dominant issue in the 1980 presidential campaign, which ended with the election of the Republican candidate, Ronald Reagan, and a Republican majority in the Senate. During the 1980s and early 1990s, the deficit never approached the level experienced in 1980, Jimmy Carter's last year as president. The deficit contracted a little in the mid-1980s, but it returned to a pattern of continued growth thereafter. President Clinton confronted this situation when he entered office in 1993. Clinton left office after surpluses had returned, and his successor, George W. Bush, served while deficits expanded. With a deep recession and countercyclical spending, President Obama's first two years in office brought the largest deficits in history.

The federal deficit must be seen in the context of the overall size of the U.S. economy, which has grown a great deal in the last half century. Figure 12.2 shows the size of federal expenditures and revenues as percentages of the gross domestic product (GDP), an annual measure of all of the goods and services produced in the United States. The figure demonstrates that federal revenues as a percentage of GDP have been fairly stable since World War II, seldom reaching 20 percent of GDP. It also shows that the deficit since 2002 is the result of both higher spending and generally low revenues relative to GDP.

The increase in federal outlays that has put spending over more than 20 percent of GDP in most years since the early 1980s is the product of both defense and domestic spending. Higher defense spending accounted for about half of the overall increase in expenditures between 1979 and 1983 and again after 2001. Most of the rest of the increase – and nearly all of it since the mid-1980s – is due to the rising cost of entitlement programs.

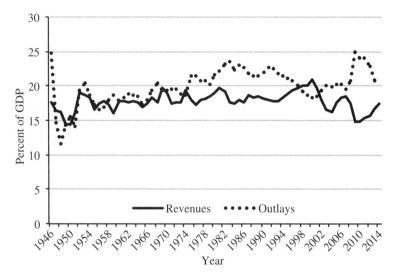

Figure 12.2 Federal Revenues and Outlays as a Percentage of Gross Domestic Product (GDP), Fiscal Years 1946–2014. Source: Congressional Budget Office.

Entitlements are provisions in laws that guarantee individuals certain benefits if they meet eligibility requirements. The spending is considered mandatory – unless Congress changes the law it must provide the required funding. In contrast, for discretionary programs year-to-year spending is not dictated by eligibility requirements but rather is determined annually by Congress. Social Security, Medicare (health care for the elderly), Medicaid (health care for

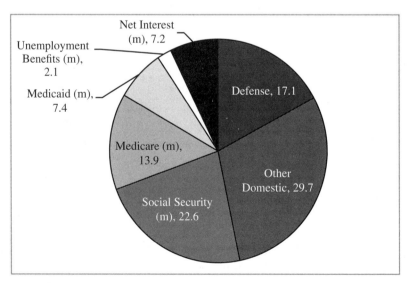

Figure 12.3 Major Categories of Federal Spending, Fiscal 2014. Mandatory programs designated with (*m*); others are discretionary. Source: Congressional Budget Office.

the poor), veterans' benefits, and other income-security programs such as pensions are the major entitlement programs with mandatory spending. Defense, education, environmental protection, medical research, and space programs are examples of discretionary spending programs. Entitlements have grown so much that they now account for more than 60 percent of federal expenditures.

CREATING A CONGRESSIONAL BUDGET PROCESS: 1974

In the early 1970s, interest in budget reform was spurred by chronic deficits and political tensions between the Democratic Congress and a Republican president. In retrospect, the deficits of that period seem small, but they were unprecedented for a time without a declared war. The shortfall was largely the result of new and expensive domestic initiatives (President Lyndon Johnson's Great Society program) and the Vietnam War. Promising to gain control of the budget, Republican Richard Nixon won the 1968 presidential election and then proceeded to engage in intense battles with the Democratic Congress over spending and taxes. These battles motivated Congress to strengthen its own budget-making capacities by adopting the Congressional Budget and Impoundment Control Act of 1974, usually called the Budget Act.[2]

Congressionally Speaking . . .

The *fiscal year* for the federal government begins on October 1 and runs through September of the following year. For example, fiscal year 2010 starts on October 1, 2010, and ends on September 30, 2011. Thus, Congress aims to have spending and tax bills for the next fiscal year enacted by October 1 of each year. The president proposes a budget in February, leaving Congress less than eight months to act on it. Failure to pass bills that approve spending for federal agencies, called *appropriations bills*, may force a shutdown of some government agencies. In most such cases, Congress passes *continuing resolutions*, which are joint resolutions of Congress that authorize temporary spending authority at the last year's level or at some percentage of that level.

The Budget Act created a process for coordinating the actions of the appropriations, authorizing, and tax committees. Each May, Congress would pass a preliminary budget resolution setting nonbinding targets for expenditures and revenues. During the summer, Congress would pass the individual bills authorizing and appropriating funds for federal programs, as well as any new tax legislation. Then, in September, Congress would adopt a second budget resolution,

2 On the developments leading up to the enactment of budget reform in 1974, see Allen Schick, *Congress and Money: Budgeting, Spending and Taxing* (Washington, DC: The Urban Institute, 1980), 17–81.

providing final spending ceilings. This resolution might require adjustments to some of the decisions made during the summer months. Those adjustments would be reflected in the second resolution, and additional legislation, written by the proper committees, would then be drafted to make the necessary changes. This process of adjustment was labeled "reconciliation," to reflect the need to reconcile the earlier decisions with the second budget resolution. The reconciliation legislation was to be enacted by October 1, the first day of the federal government's fiscal year.

The Budget Act provided for two new committees, the House and Senate Budget Committees. The budget committees write the budget resolutions and package reconciliation legislation from various committees ordered to adjust the programs under their jurisdiction. The Congressional Budget Office (CBO) was created by the act to provide Congress with nonpartisan, expert analyses of the economy and budget.

The Budget Act also modified Senate floor procedures in a critical way. The act barred nongermane amendments and set a limit of twenty hours on debate over budget resolutions and reconciliation legislation. These rules meant that budget measures could not be loaded with extraneous floor amendments or killed by a Senate filibuster. However, the rules did not restrict the kinds of provisions committees could write into budget measures. Consequently, the door was left open for committees to include provisions unrelated to spending and taxes in reconciliation bills. Including such provisions became a common practice once reconciliation bills became a central feature of the budget-making process in the 1980s.

REDUCING THE DISCRETION OF COMMITTEES: 1980 AND 1981

The new budget process worked smoothly during its first four years, primarily because congressional Democrats did not use budget resolutions to constrain or compel action from appropriations, authorizing, or tax committees. But in 1979 and 1980, the last two years of the Carter administration, escalating deficits spurred a search for new means to control spending. An effort in 1979 to include reconciliation instructions to committees in the second budget resolution ended in failure, in part because of resistance from some committees to reducing spending on programs under their jurisdiction. Confronting projections of a rapidly rising deficit, as well as a reelection campaign in 1980, President Carter and Democratic congressional leaders agreed to include reconciliation instructions in the first budget resolution, adopted in May. That is, at a point in the process before the usual authorization and appropriations legislation was considered later in the summer, they decided to order some committees to report legislation that would reduce spending to be incorporated in a reconciliation bill in June. This switch meant that the initiative would shift from the various authorizing committees to the budget and party leaders, who together with administration officials would negotiate the reconciliation instructions. The innovation worked. The 1980 reconciliation legislation reduced the deficit by $8.2 billion through a combination of spending cuts and tax increases. Since then, the term "reconciliation" has been used to describe any bill ordered by budget resolutions, although it no longer is limited to the originally intended process of reconciling the decisions of the summer months with the second budget resolution adopted just before October 1.

Impoundment

During the early 1970s, the Nixon administration began to cut off funds for programs opposed by the president. That is, the president unilaterally stopped spending for programs for which funds had been appropriated by law. The practice, known as *impoundment*, created a constitutional crisis. Many members of Congress charged the president with violating his constitutional responsibility to see that the laws are faithfully executed. The courts agreed, for the most part, although some programs had been irreparably harmed by the time a court had ruled on the issue.

Congress responded in its 1974 budget reforms by providing for two types of impoundments – rescissions and deferrals. To withhold funds permanently for a particular purpose (make a rescission), a president would have to gain prior approval from both houses of Congress. To temporarily delay spending (make a deferral), a president would only have to notify Congress. The president could defer spending unless either house specifically disapproved.

In 1983, the Supreme Court ruled that the legislative veto was unconstitutional because it allowed Congress to check an executive action without passing a regular bill. The ruling implied that the deferral process of the 1974 reforms was unconstitutional. Congress responded in 1987 by formally limiting the deferral authority to routine administrative matters.

Rescission authority continues to be used, but it has involved only a very small fraction of total federal spending. Between 1976 and 2005, presidents requested nearly $73 billion in rescissions but Congress approved only about $25 billion.

Republicans learned from the experience of the Carter years and used reconciliation instructions to force much deeper cuts in domestic programs once they took over the White House and the Senate after the 1980 elections. The Republicans managed to gain adoption of reconciliation instructions and pass a reconciliation bill that cut spending for fiscal year 1982 by about $37 billion.

Figure 12.4 illustrates how the inclusion of reconciliation instructions in the first budget resolution has altered the budget process. Reconciliation, authorization, and appropriations legislation now proceed simultaneously, so there is no need for a second budget resolution.

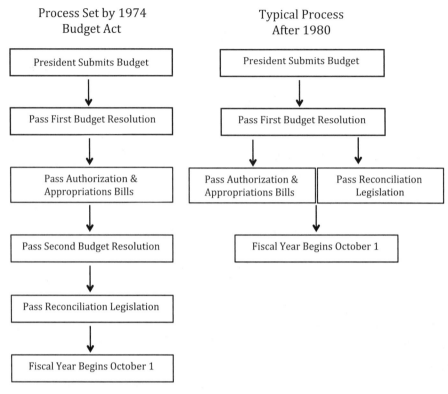

Figure 12.4 Steps in Budget Process.

Sequestration: 1985 and 1987

The savings achieved by the 1981 reconciliation bill were more than offset by a large tax cut enacted in separate legislation that year, continued increases in entitlement and defense spending, and the budget crisis, which intensified in the early 1980s. A tax increase in 1982 – initiated by Senate Republicans and quietly accepted by President Reagan – helped reduce the deficit a little, but it was not enough to change the deficit's long-term upward trajectory.

In 1985, a trio of senators – Phil Gramm (R-Texas), Warren Rudman (R-New Hampshire), and Ernest Hollings (D-South Carolina) – pushed a seemingly irresistible amendment to a debt-ceiling bill, establishing the amount of outstanding debt the federal government is permitted to carry. The Gramm-Rudman-Hollings proposal was adopted as the Balanced Budget and Emergency Deficit Control Act of 1985. It provided for reducing the deficit by $36 billion in each of the following five years, so that the deficit would drop from about $172 billion in fiscal year 1986 to zero in fiscal year 1991. If Congress failed to meet any year's deficit target by more than $10 billion, across-the-board cuts in spending would be ordered by an amount necessary to reduce the deficit to the specified level. This process of withholding a certain percentage of funding from programs was called "sequestration." Sequestration, it was argued, would be so distasteful to lawmakers that Congress and the president would be motivated to find a way to reduce the deficit without triggering the automatic cuts.

To reinforce this deficit-reduction scheme, the 1985 law barred floor amendments to budget resolutions and reconciliation measures that would raise the projected deficit beyond specified levels. A point of order could be made against any ineligible amendment. But the Senate had a history of overruling its presiding officer on points of order, and dozens of popular nongermane amendments were proposed to the reconciliation bill considered in the fall of 1985. Senator Robert Byrd (D-West Virginia) therefore proposed, and the Senate approved, a new rule that provided that the presiding officer's ruling on the germaneness of an amendment to a reconciliation bill could not be overturned unless a three-fifths majority agreed. The "Byrd rule" reinforced the 1974 Budget Act's restrictions on floor amendments and debate and made Senate rules governing the content of budget measures and amendments to them even more restrictive than those in the House.

On paper, Congress and the president met the deficit targets in the next three fiscal years. But, in each case, this goal was accomplished through a combination of creative accounting and absurdly optimistic estimates about the economy, future demands on federal programs, and the next year's revenues. "Blue smoke and mirrors" became the catch phrase used to describe federal budgeting. As a result of this budgetary legerdemain, the actual deficit in fiscal 1988 turned out to be $155 billion rather than the targeted $108 billion.

In late 1987, another debt-ceiling bill presented an opportunity to restart the Gramm-Rudman-Hollings process. Congress attached to the bill a new set of targets, this time moving the zero-deficit deadline back from 1991 to 1993. The measure also made it more difficult for the Senate to waive the deficit targets, by requiring a three-fifths rather than a simple majority vote. But many observers, including stock market investors, thought that merely restarting the Gramm-Rudman-Hollings process was woefully inadequate, a view that appeared to contribute to a crash in the stock market in October 1987.

The crisis of the stock market crash and the November 20 sequester deadline motivated Congress and President Reagan to reach a new agreement. The agreement was unique because it provided separate spending ceilings for defense and nondefense spending for a two-year period – fiscal 1987 and 1988. This compromise allowed the Reagan administration to end with a truce with Congress on the budget. Neither party was eager to continue the battle into the election year of 1988.

Congressionally Speaking . . .

Only a few congressional rules are known by the name of their original author. One of them is the Byrd rule, named after Senator Robert C. Byrd (D–West Virginia), the former majority leader and former Appropriations Committee chair.

The *Byrd rule* bars extraneous matter from reconciliation bills. A provision is considered to be extraneous if it does not change spending or revenues, concerns issues that lie outside of the jurisdiction of the committee reporting it, or leads to a net increase in spending or decrease in revenues for the years beyond those covered by the bill. In addition, strangely, any change in Social Security, Washington's political sacred cow, is considered a violation of the Byrd rule.

The rule is enforced by points of order raised by senators from the floor and upheld by a ruling of the chair, who depends on the advice of the Senate parliamentarian. The Senate may overturn the ruling of the chair as long as sixty senators agree. If a point of order is successful, either through a ruling of the presiding officer or by a vote, the entire bill falls. The rule gives a sizable minority the ability to force certain kinds of provisions from reconciliation bills. It is one of the few places in which Senate rules are more restrictive than House rules.

PAYGO: 1990

The partisan war over the budget resumed in 1989, the first year of the Republican George H. W. Bush administration. By late 1989, it was clear that the Gramm-Rudman-Hollings procedure had been a failure. Instead of a $100 billion deficit, as targeted in the 1987 Gramm-Rudman-Hollings Act, the deficit turned out to be a record $221 billion because of a slumping economy. The Gramm-Rudman-Hollings procedure was shown to have a major weakness: the absence of a means for forcing further reductions during a fiscal year for which the original deficit estimates had been too optimistic.[3]

The 1990 budget package set a new direction for enforcing agreements, as indicated by its title – the Budget Enforcement Act (BEA). The 1990 BEA focused on spending limits rather than on deficit reduction per se. For fiscal years 1991 to 1993, the BEA provided for three categories of nonentitlement spending (defense, international, and domestic) and established spending ceilings for each. These ceilings were to be adjusted for inflation each year so that economic conditions would not make them more or less onerous. If a category's ceiling was exceeded, sequestration would apply only to programs within that category – thus, this process is called categorical sequestration. "Firewalls" were established; that is, it became a violation of the rules to transfer funds among the three categories. In this way, Republicans would not fear a raid on defense funding to increase domestic spending, and Democrats did not have to worry about transfers in the opposite direction.

---

3 On the 1989 budget battle, see Lawrence J. Hass, *Running on Empty: Bush, Congress, and the Politics of a Bankrupt Government* (Homewood, IL: Business One-Irwin, 1990).

The 1990 BEA added teeth to the budget-making process by requiring that all tax and direct spending legislation be deficit neutral. That is, if a bill cut taxes or increased spending, it also would have to provide fully offsetting tax increases or spending cuts. This pay-as-you-go mechanism – known as PAYGO – was enforced by a provision allowing any member to raise a point of order against a bill on the grounds that it was not deficit neutral. If a bill that was not deficit neutral were to sneak through, a sequester on spending in the appropriate category would be applied.

The PAYGO focus on spending ceilings rather than deficit-reduction targets meant that Congress and the president had given up on the Gramm-Rudman-Hollings approach. Of course, if the economy slumped and revenues declined, the deficit would go up even if the spending ceilings were obeyed. But if the economy performed better than expected, spending would be controlled as expected, revenues would flow into the Treasury faster than expected, and the increased revenues would reduce the deficit.

The 1990 budget deal made it more difficult for authorizing and tax committees to propose new policy initiatives. Legislation that would create a new program that entailed spending would have to provide for spending cuts somewhere else. Tax-writing committees could not propose tax breaks to some groups or industries unless they increased taxes or cut spending for other programs under their jurisdiction. The net winners under the 1990 rules seemed to be the appropriations committees. Although they had to operate under the spending ceilings, the ceilings were viewed as reasonably generous, given the programs that had to be funded, and would be adjusted for inflation. The appropriators also had substantial flexibility on how to set priorities within the broad categories.

Deficits shot upward in 1991 and 1992, despite the fact that domestic discretionary spending was constrained. The economy did not perform well, which reduced revenues over those two years by nearly $90 billion from what had been predicted in 1990. The slow economy contributed to increased spending on entitlements – particularly Medicare, Medicaid, and farm price supports – that were outside the discretionary spending limits. Moreover, unanticipated expenditures for the Persian Gulf War and disaster aid to help Florida and Hawaii recover from hurricanes added to the deficit. The 1992 deficit of $290 billion was nearly $140 billion larger than the deficit in 1989.

DEFICIT-REDUCING TRUST FUND AND ENTITLEMENT REVIEW: 1993

Congress demonstrated remarkable creativity in devising new rules and processes for budgeting during the 1970s, 1980s, and early 1990s. But the impressive array of budgetary enforcement devices – reconciliation, sequestration, points

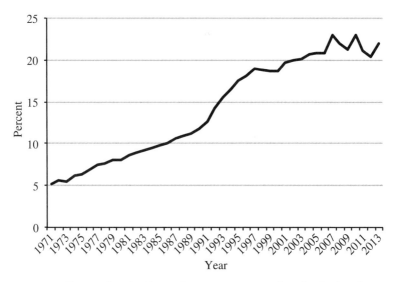

Figure 12.5 Medicare and Medicaid Spending as a Percentage of Total Federal Outlays, 1972–2013. Source: Congressional Budget Office.

of order, spending ceilings, PAYGO, and firewalls – left sizable budget deficits. Deficits were never put on a downward path during the Reagan and George H. W. Bush administrations, as the major deficit-reduction packages had promised. By the time Bill Clinton was sworn in as president in January 1993, the public was deeply cynical about federal budgetary politics, the annual deficit was at a record high, and the deficit was a major obstacle to the new president's other policy objectives.

Entitlement spending, particularly health care spending, spurred large annual increases in the budget. As Figure 12.5 demonstrates, the escalating costs of health care programs pose serious threats to deficit control. The major government health care programs, Medicare and Medicaid, are entitlement programs for the elderly and the poor. Cutting those programs entails either reducing the number of eligible people, which is an unpopular option, or cutting payments to hospitals, doctors, and state governments. Reducing payments, however, leads hospitals and doctors to shift their costs to people with private insurance, thereby increasing the cost of health care for everyone else. Domestic programs that do not involve entitlements – most education, law enforcement, transportation, housing, energy, research, construction, and space programs – have declined as a percentage of GDP since 1980.

In 1993, with a new president, Bill Clinton, seeking to reduce the deficit, Democrats moved budget measures at a more rapid pace and incorporated Clinton's proposed tax increases in the reconciliation bill. Placing the tax increases in the reconciliation bill had important advantages for the Democrats. Selling never-popular tax increases might be easier as a part of a larger deficit-reduction package. Furthermore, reconciliation instructions to committees set deadlines on reporting legislation. This change meant that the two tax-writing committees, House Ways and Means and Senate Finance, could not indefinitely delay decisions about taxes. And just as important, the reconciliation bill was subject to a twenty-hour limit on debate in the Senate, which protected it from a Republican filibuster. These special budget procedures meant that Republican opponents of the tax legislation could not delay Senate action.

To deal with the concerns of conservative Democrats, new procedural devices – a deficit-reduction trust fund and a mandatory review of entitlement spending – were invented. The trust fund plan provided that an amount equal to the projected deficit reduction from the bill be placed in a trust fund that could be used only to pay maturing public debt obligations, thereby reducing the national debt. Democratic leaders also agreed to address entitlement spending if such spending ultimately exceeded levels specified in the budget bill. In this way, the conservatives were assured that Congress would consider more serious entitlement reform if the budget plan proved too optimistic. Moreover, President Clinton acted unilaterally to add credibility to the promise that the new tax revenues would be used to reduce the deficit rather than to increase spending. By executive order, he created the deficit trust fund and established an entitlement review process to measure whether legislators were abiding by the budget plan's requirements.

The 1993 episode was notable for another reason. The vote on the budget conference report in the House eventually turned on the vote of a freshman member, Marjorie Margolies-Mezvinsky, a Democrat from a Republican-leaning district just outside Philadelphia. She had voted against the president's position on the budget resolution and on passage of the House bill, but reportedly she had promised the president her support if her vote turned out to be pivotal – no doubt hoping it would not be. Early in the fifteen-minute period for the vote, Margolies-Mezvinsky cast a no vote. But with no time left in the vote, the Democrats had only 216 votes – two votes short of a majority – so the Speaker held the vote open. Representative Ray Thorton (D-Arkansas), who had not yet voted, signed a red voting card to vote no. Only if both Margolies-Mezvinsky and Pat Williams (D-Montana) changed their votes to yes would the conference report pass. Williams was a fourteen-year veteran Democrat from Montana who had made the same promise as Margolies-Mezvinsky. Williams changed his vote first, and then all eyes fell on Margolies-Mezvinsky, who was being ushered to the front desk by a group of colleagues. The Republicans chanted, "Goodbye, Marjorie," referring to her reelection prospects if she voted against them. She signed a green card to vote yes, and the Speaker gaveled the vote closed.

Margolies-Mezvinsky spent the next few days explaining her vote. She appeared on local television and radio and immediately aired radio ads in her district to justify her vote. Her explanation was that she had extracted an important promise from the president. Minutes before the vote, she was called to the phone to talk to him. Asked what it would take to get her vote, she told the president that she wanted a high-level conference for a serious discussion of cutting entitlement spending. Clinton agreed and she voted yes. The next week, Secretary of Health and Human Services Donna Shalala traveled to Philadelphia to discuss plans for the conference. The full conference finally took place in December, with the president in attendance. Margolies-Mezvinsky lost her bid for reelection in 1994.

TAX BILL CERTIFICATION: 1995–1996 AND BUDGET BRINKSMANSHIP

Budget legislation became the central battleground for the new Republican majorities elected to the House and Senate in the 1994 midterm elections of President Clinton's first term. In designing their budget resolution and reconciliation bill in 1995, the congressional Republican majorities combined the goal of achieving a balanced budget by 2002 with a plan to cut taxes by $245 billion over seven years, which meant that federal spending had to be cut deeply. They sought to limit Medicaid spending and to give the states administrative responsibility for the program, stem the growth of Medicare, eliminate three executive departments (the Departments of Education, Commerce, and Energy), cut welfare spending, limit environmental regulations, and eliminate dozens of federal programs.

Procedural innovations were once again used to help bridge policy differences. Many senators were concerned that the deep tax cuts proposed would undermine the effort to balance the budget. To gain their support for the budget resolution, a provision was included that required the Finance Committee to wait to mark up tax cut provisions for the reconciliation bill until the Congressional Budget Office had officially certified that the bill would actually balance the federal budget by 2002. In this way, a nonpartisan staff arm of Congress, the CBO, had to approve estimates of the long-term effects of the budget package *before* a committee could act on the budget package.

By the time Congress approved the budget resolution, in the early summer of 1995, the House Republican leadership had devised a strategy that they hoped would gain President Clinton's signature for their reconciliation bill, which would incorporate their spending and tax legislation. The Republicans would refuse to pass two critical sets of legislation – appropriations bills and a debt-ceiling increase – until the president agreed to approve their reconciliation bill. Failure to enact appropriations bills would force many departments to shut down at the end of the fiscal year (at midnight on September 30). Failure to increase the debt limit when needed would force the government to stop borrowing and possibly default on its debt obligations. The ceiling would be reached sometime in the fall. The strategy was predicated on the assumption that the Republican budget plan would be popular with the public. The Republicans' view, articulated by Speaker Gingrich, was that the president would not dare to shut down federal services or allow the government to default on its loans and would feel compelled to sign their legislation.

As the October 1 deadline approached, talk of the "train wreck" that would occur if the appropriations bills were not enacted began to dominate Washington. As talks took place, Congress passed continuing resolution that extended spending authority to federal agencies for six weeks. By mid-November, Congress had failed to pass any appropriations bills or the reconciliation bill, but, despite the fact that public opinion was turning against them, Republicans remained eager to force a showdown with the president. They passed an extension of appropriations authority through December 15 and a temporary debt-ceiling increase measure extending the government's borrowing authority to December 12. The debt-ceiling bill included provisions that prevented the president from juggling accounts to cover government expenditures and would revert the debt limit to its previous level on December 12. The continuing resolution was designed to be unpalatable to the president – it reduced spending in the affected agencies to just 60 percent of the previous year's level and canceled a scheduled reduction in Medicare premiums.

To the Republicans' surprise, Clinton vetoed both bills. As the administration knew, the Republicans lacked the two-thirds majority in each house required to override a presidential veto. The result was a shutdown of the unfunded federal agencies, forcing about 800,000 "nonessential" federal workers to be furloughed. Additional accounting moves made the veto of the debt-ceiling bill inconsequential, but the shutdown caused by the veto of the continuing resolution proved politically costly – for the Republicans. Although the Republicans blamed the shutdown on Clinton's unwillingness to bargain, the public blamed the Republicans over Clinton by a 2-to-1 margin. The fact that Republicans had made their strategy so conspicuous but still did not have a reconciliation bill ready to pass hurt their cause. Worse yet for the Republicans, the president's willingness to take a stand enhanced his popularity with the public, giving the president a stronger bargaining position. The Republicans had misjudged Clinton's willingness to veto the bills and had badly miscalculated the general public's response.

Scrambling to determine what to do next, the Republicans adopted another continuing resolution – which ended a six-day shutdown – and soon approved a conference report on the reconciliation bill. It was expected that the reconciliation bill would be vetoed as well, so the issue was how to conduct negotiations to find a version acceptable to the president and to both houses of Congress. The second continuing resolution included a new feature: It stipulated that the president and Congress must agree to a plan to balance the federal budget within seven years – by 2002 – using economic estimates provided by the Congressional Budget Office. The Republicans viewed the commitment to a balanced budget as a large victory, but the details of a new budget plan were to be negotiated at a future date.

Partisan rhetoric sharpened. Differences between the parties over the reconciliation bill continued to concern the size of spending cuts in domestic programs and the size of tax cuts. A handful of regular appropriations bills passed and received presidential approval, but several others remained unfinished by December 15, again forcing a shutdown of many federal agencies, this time involving approximately 260,000 workers. House Speaker Gingrich and Senate Majority Leader Bob Dole appeared to be willing to pass another continuing resolution, but hard-line House Republicans made it plain that they would not support another resolution. Before they would agree to fund certain federal agencies, they wanted concessions from the president that the president seemed unwilling to grant. The result was that this shutdown lasted twenty-one days.

News stories of hardships suffered by government workers over the holidays worsened the standing of the congressional Republicans in the polls. By the first week of January, Clinton's poll ratings were heading up, and the Republicans were eager to pass continuing resolutions. In fact, they passed three measures – one narrow appropriations bill, to keep the most popular programs funded through September 1996; a second appropriations bill, to fund a couple of other programs through March 15; and a continuing resolution to keep the remaining programs and agencies open until January 26. Meanwhile, deep divisions among Republicans concerning the efficacy and political costs of their strategy began to emerge.

The debt limit loomed on the horizon yet again. The financial adjustments that had allowed the administration to avoid defaulting on the country's debt obligations were just about exhausted. To avoid being blamed for playing games with the debt limit, Republican leaders wrote President Clinton that they intended to increase the debt limit when required. No progress had been made on the reconciliation bill by late January, five months into the fiscal year, so another continuing resolution was enacted. The process for drafting a budget for the next fiscal year began on February 5, when the president submitted his budget proposals to Congress. Plainly, those proposals meant little in the absence of a budget for the current fiscal year.

Just before March 15, for the fifth time since September of the previous year, a continuing resolution was passed to avoid a shutdown of federal agencies, this time for only a week. This practice of passing short-term continuing resolutions went on for several more weeks. Eventually, late in the evening of April 24, nearly seven months late and after a total of fourteen limited spending bills and short-term continuing resolutions, the president and congressional Republican leaders agreed on a budget. The next day, Republican leaders rushed through to passage an appropriations bill to fund government agencies for the rest of the fiscal year. Compromise spending and tax cuts were quickly enacted.

The 1995–1996 confrontation between President Clinton and the Republican Congress, led by Speaker Newt Gingrich, was an experience that Washingtonians have not forgotten. The episode ended with President Clinton far more popular than he was a year earlier. Speaker Gingrich suffered badly in public opinion and, because his strategy to force the president to sign his budget bill failed, appeared to lose the confidence of many of his Republican colleagues. In response, the Speaker took a less visible role and eventually was threatened with a challenge from other leading Republicans. He retired from his position after the 1998 midterm elections when it seemed likely that his Republican colleagues would elect someone else as Speaker.

Major Developments in the Budget Process, 1974–2011

1974 Congressional Budget and Impoundment Control Act
Created the modern budgeting process, established the budget committees, and provided for congressional review of presidential rescissions and deferrals.
1980 Reconciliation Bill
Provided that (for the first time) reconciliation be used at the start of the budget process. Committees were required to forward legislation drafted specifically to reduce spending as required by the first budget resolution.
1985 and 1987 Gramm-Rudman-Hollings Rules
Set fixed annual targets for deficit reduction and established a sequestration process to bring spending down to levels required to meet targets.
1990 Budget Enforcement Act
Dropped the fixed deficit targets of the Gramm Rudman-Hollings approach and replaced them with caps on spending in domestic, defense, and international budgetary categories; pay-as-you-go rules for spending and revenues; and restrictions on loans and indirect spending.
1993 Omnibus Budget Reconciliation Act
Modified spending priorities and extended the enforcement provisions of the 1990 act through 1998.
1996 Balanced Budget Act
Modified spending priorities, extended the enforcement provisions of the 1993 act through 2002, and projected a balanced budget in fiscal year 2002.
2002
PAYGO enforcement provisions allowed to expire.
2007
PAYGO rule adopted; rules requiring sponsors of earmarks to be identified; House rule provides a "trigger" that establishes a point of order against tax-cut legislation that does not require that the OMB certify that the tax cuts cost less than $179.8 billion through fiscal 2012 or more than 80 percent of any surplus projected for 2012 at the time.

(continued)

Major Developments in the Budget Process, 1974–2011 (*continued*)

2009
PAYGO rule changed in the House to align it with the rule in the Senate so that both chambers use the same CBO baseline to assess compliance, to allow separate House-passed bills to be considered collectively deficit neutral provided that they are linked at engrossment, and to include an emergency exception to the PAYGO rule; rule providing a point of order against any earmark inserted in a general appropriations conference report.

2010
The National Commission on Fiscal Responsibility and Reform, a presidential commission, produced a nonbinding plan for discretionary and mandatory spending caps, budget process reforms to enforce the caps, and tax changes to reduce rates, broaden the tax base, and eliminate tax breaks.

2011
The House adopted the "CutGo" rule, which requires that new mandatory spending be offset with cuts to existing programs (exempts tax cuts and repeal of health care reform); placed funding cut from appropriations bills through floor amendments in a separate account so that it cannot be used for other purposes; eliminated the "Gephardt rule," which provided for automatic approval of a debt limit measure upon adoption of a budget resolution by both houses; and gave the Budget Committee chair the authority to set spending caps for the remainder of fiscal 2011. The Budget Control Act of 2011 reinstituted sequestration for a ten-year period, totalling $1.2 trillion in spending cuts equally divided between defense and domestic programs.

DROPPING, REINSTATING, AND MODIFYING PAYGO RULES: 1997–2011

With the 1996 budget plan in place, the Republicans did not challenge President Clinton on the budget again; instead, they turned to tactical fights on individual appropriations bills. They had no interest in repeating the political disaster of the 1995–1996 budget fight. Many Republican conservatives did not like Speaker Gingrich's willingness to compromise with Clinton, but, at least in the Speaker's view, there was little to be gained by laying down more ultimatums for the president. By the end of 1997, a strong economy, which yielded both reduced spending and increased tax revenues, had cut the deficit much faster than expected. In fact, a balanced budget was achieved in 1998, four years earlier than predicted in the 1996 budget. The large strategic moves of deficit politics were replaced with the less visible, tactical moves of surplus politics, with congressional Republicans and the Democratic president fighting over the details of appropriations bills.

Partisan differences caused four straight years of gamesmanship with appropriations bills. Sparring over spending details routinely led to delays in passing appropriations bills, which required that Congress pass numerous continuing resolutions. Moreover, when agreement was finally reached, compromises often extended over several appropriations bills and many extraneous measures that were packaged in large omnibus appropriations bills. In 1998, for example, eight of the thirteen regular appropriations bills and more than thirty nonappropriations measures were included in the omnibus appropriations bills for fiscal 1999. In 2000, twenty-one continuing resolutions were adopted before an omnibus appropriations bill was passed a few days before Christmas. That bill included the provisions of three regular appropriations bills, some new emergency spending, and nonappropriations legislation on Medicare, Medicaid, medical savings accounts and other tax provisions, immigration, and commodities regulation. This multidimensional bill represented many bargains and reflected members' realization that it was the last opportunity to address some issues before that Congress ended.

The political tables had turned in Washington after Republican President George W. Bush was elected in 2000. Bush was in office for less than a year when the 9/11 terrorist attack occurred. The subsequent airline and New York subsidies, homeland security, war on terrorism, and Afghan and Iraqi wars cost many hundreds of billions for the federal government, contributing to the creation of the first deficit after four years of surpluses. A prolonged recession and spending on national security contributed to the deficits, as did a tax cut enacted in 2001 when surpluses were still projected. Despite significant loss of revenue, the 2001 Bush tax cuts were passed without sequestration due to some shrewd maneuvering. Fearing that PAYGO might prevent the tax cuts from becoming permanent, congressional Republicans allowed it to expire in 2002. The Senate did, however, adopt its own PAYGO rule shortly after the statute expired, a rule that did not affect the House.

In February 2003, President Bush proposed a budget deficit of more than $300 billion for fiscal 2004. He proposed more tax cuts, some of which were opposed by at least a few Senate Republicans, and some spending increases. The administration argued that much of the tax proposal and some of the spending hikes were needed to boost the economy. The proposals, if adopted, would require Congress to adjust spending ceilings in the budget enforcement mechanisms.

The return of deficits was accompanied by failure to pass appropriations bills on time. From 2001 through 2004, most appropriations bills were not enacted until after the October 1 deadline and most were wrapped into large omnibus bills. For example, in 2002, when the appropriations bills for fiscal 2003 were considered, no appropriations bill was enacted by October 1 and eventually ten continuing resolutions were adopted. Democrats argued that Republicans deliberately delayed action on a few of the bills so that Republicans would not have to cast potentially embarrassing votes just before the 2002 election. Not until January 2003, more than four months after the bills were due to be passed and after a new Congress was in place, did the House and Senate pass an omnibus bill that incorporated eleven of the thirteen regular appropriations bills. Conference committee negotiations over the bill were not complete until February – six months late and halfway through the fiscal year. The Republican Congress passed all appropriations bills in 2005 and 2006 before adjourning. Although many were passed long after the October deadline, Republicans were confronted with difficult choices in the 2006 election year, leaving work on nine of eleven appropriations bills incomplete after they lost their House and Senate majorities.

The new House Democratic majority of 2007 reinstated the PAYGO rule, having scored political points against Republicans in the 2006 campaign for letting the deficit drift upward. House Democrats did not include a sequestration process, so the more recent adoption lacks the tough enforcement mechanism that was included in the 1990, 1993, and 1996 versions. Instead, they provided for only a point of order, which can be waived by approving a special rule, to be raised against a bill or amendment that increases the deficit. The Senate had implemented its own PAYGO rule in 2002, following the expiration of the statute, and extended the rule with some revisions in 2007. The Senate rule, which remains in place, enforced PAYGO requirements by point of order. In the Senate, points of order raised against a bill for PAYGO violations can be waived with sixty votes. Since PAYGO now exists only in the form of chamber rules, the houses have greater flexibility to set aside the rules when they prove to be an obstacle. For this reason, President Obama has advocated statutory PAYGO but has received some resistance from within Congress. As of the time of this writing, Congress has taken no such action.

In 2007, both houses also moved to put in place new rules governing earmarks, the term used to describe funding for specific projects. The rules did not ban earmarks but rather required the disclosure of the name of the legislator sponsoring each project, publication of a justification for the project, and certification that the project does not benefit the legislator or his or her spouse. In addition to spending on construction projects, the rule applied to tax and tariff provisions geared to individual firms or organizations.

The House passed some changes to its PAYGO rule in 2009. One change aligned the House rules with those of the Senate so that both chambers use the same Congressional Budget Office baselines when estimating the costs of bills. Another change allowed the House to pass one bill that offsets the spending in another bill, provided that both are linked at engrossment. Previous rules required all bills passed by the House to be independently deficit neutral over a one- and five-year period. Finally, the House inserted an exception that permits the House to waive the PAYGO rule for provisions designated as emergency spending. In addition to the PAYGO rules, the 2009 rules changes also prohibited conference committees from inserting earmarks into general appropriations bills that did not appear in either of the chamber bills.

The Battle over Earmarks

In early 2006, Republicans found themselves embarrassed by the volume of earmarks – totaling about $20 billion – included in a supplemental appropriations bill, which President George W. Bush threatened to veto. Earmarks are provisions to fund individual projects that are championed by individual members, often in collaboration with outside interests and lobbyists. Republican leaders passed the bill only after promising earmark reform. The promised reform included a requirement that the names of earmark sponsors be made public. Members of the appropriations committees believed that they were being singled out for earmarks when members of the tax-writing committees used legislation to write into law narrow provisions for tax breaks or tariff protection. As a consequence of the bad publicity for the bill and other developments, particularly a lobbying scandal, Republicans started but never completed work on an ethics reform bill that addressed earmarks.

House Democrats, after gaining a majority in the 2006 elections, incorporated earmark reform, including provisions that Republicans invented but did not adopt in the previous Congress. In response to the reform, House committees must keep a record of requests for earmarks. Critics of the reform approved of the provision requiring publication of sponsors' names but preferred that floor votes be guaranteed on individual earmarks. The Senate adopted similar rules included in the passage of the Honest Leadership and Open Government Act of 2007.

The House and Senate rules banning earmarks remain in place (House Rule XXI(9) and Senate Rule XLIV(9)). The reforms have limited the number of earmarks, but legislators and lobbyists have looked for ways to circumvent the new requirements. Lobbyists have increasingly turned their attention to persuading executive branch officials to include specific projects in the president's budget requests so that legislators do not have to file requests with committees. Executive officials are also lobbied to use their discretion to favor certain projects after receiving appropriations.

In late 2009, frustrated with Congress's inability to successfully address the spending and tax issues involved in moving to a balanced budget, legislators from both parties proposed, along with outside groups, the creation of a commission to produce a long-term budget plan. The idea was modeled on the military base closing process, started in 1988, in which a bipartisan commission recommended legislation that was subject to congressional action under special rules. The rules guaranteed implementation of the commission's recommendations in a limited period if Congress failed to act and prevented amendments to the commission recommendations. The 2009 proposal, like the earlier processes, reflected a judgment that legislators could not vote for a plan that would include unpopular spending cuts or tax hikes. The proposal was not adopted, but its promise led President Obama to name a commission that issued a nonbinding report in late 2010. The report received wide praise, but it received no endorsements from congressional party leaders who approached budget decisions in 2011 with little mention of the commission.

The ballooning federal deficit and spending were significant issues in the 2010 midterm elections that produced a Republican majority in the House. Falling revenues and spending on antirecessionary measures contributed to the large deficit during the deep recession of 2007–2009. House Republicans, continuing the pattern of previous Congresses, moved to change House rules as a means for addressing fiscal challenges. Most important, the House adopted the "CutGo" rule that requires that new mandatory spending be offset with cuts to existing programs. The new rule replaced the old PAYGO rule, which allowed spending initiatives to be offset with new revenues. The rule exempts tax cuts and repeal of health care reform, both important Republican policy priorities, so that increases in the deficit caused by such legislation would be allowed. The Republican-backed rules also provide that money saved through floor amendments to appropriations bills be placed in a separate account so that it cannot be used for other purposes. The House rules also eliminated the "Gephardt rule," which provided for automatic approval of a debt limit measure upon adoption of a budget resolution by both houses.

THE SUPER COMMITTEE, THE FISCAL CLIFF, AND THE RETURN TO SEQUESTRATION: 2011–2015

In mid-2011, the debt limit was again about to be reached and the Republican majority in the House decided to refuse to pass the legislation to extend it unless the Democratic Senate and Democratic President Obama agreed to a budget plan that called for deep spending cuts and a cap on future spending. The Republican proposal was rejected by the Senate and the president, and subsequent efforts to negotiate a "grand bargain" – a comprehensive, long-term plan for spending, taxes, and the deficit – failed. With partisan name-calling and blame-throwing reaching a fever pitch, the August deadline approached with a greater chance of federal default on its debts than ever before. In the middle of the process, Standard & Poor's, one of the major credit-rating agencies, reduced the federal government's rating, and another one of the big three credit-rating firms, Moody's, gave the government a negative outlook; both were a signal to investors to be more concerned about buying government bonds.

With little time to spare, a deal was negotiated that formed the Budget Control Act of 2011 (BCA). The BCA extended government borrowing authority and created a committee – known as the Super Committee – between the House and Senate that was charged with creating a package of spending cuts and tax hikes to achieve $917 billion of deficit reduction over ten years. To motivate the commission and the rest of Congress to adopt a plan, the deal included a requirement that even more, $1.2 trillion, be cut by sequestration over ten years, equally distributed between defense and domestic spending if the Super Committee process failed. The large sequestration, divided evenly between defense and domestic spending, was supposed to make sequestration so unacceptable to both Democrats and Republicans that the Super Committee process with its intended negotiated outcome on a smaller total deficit reduction was sure to work. It failed.

The result of the 2011 episode was that the first defense and domestic sequestration cuts were to take effect in January 2013. The timing was not good. At about the same time as sequestration was to be imposed, the Bush tax cuts, enacted ten years earlier, were about the expire. This created a crisis that was called the "fiscal cliff" because large tax cuts would expire (and taxes increase) and deep spending cuts would take place simultaneously. While this would have reduced the deficit, it also was projected to cause a mild recession and higher unemployment. A tax bill was passed on January 1, 2013, the day after the tax cuts expired, to provide new tax rates, although it required somewhat higher tax rates for high-income individuals to satisfy Democrats. Sequestration was delayed but not materially changed, and it governed spending policy through most of 2015.

Even with the fiscal cliff averted, 2013 did not go smoothly. House Republicans sought to delay and defund Obamacare, the health care program, just as the program was first opening, but the Democratic Senate refused to go along. The result was a sixteen-day shutdown of government agencies, which most of the public blamed on the Republicans, and an eventual agreement on a continuing resolution for the remainder of the calendar year. Having been beat up in the polls, Republicans allowed a continuing resolution for the remainder of the fiscal year to be passed in January 2014.

At the time of this writing in 2015, leaders of the Republican Congress are contemplating several moves. Under active consideration is the use of budget reconciliation procedures to repeal or undermine Obamacare and to pass tax legislation. By doing so, Republicans can avoid a Democratic filibuster that surely would make it difficult to address Obamacare and tax policy through regular legislation. Republicans also are eager to reduce the size of future defense spending cuts under the terms of the BCA's sequestration process, but changing the terms of the BCA for defense but not for domestic spending would likely produce strong Democratic opposition and possible opposition from the president.

Dynamic Scoring

At the start of the 114th Congress in 2015, House Republicans adopted a rule that requires the Congressional Budget Office (CBO) and Joint Tax Committee (JTC) staff to take into account the macroeconomic effects of a policy change when reporting on the fiscal effects of proposed legislation. (House Rule XIII(8)). This is called "dynamic scoring." The rule applies to all spending and tax proposals that affect 0.25 percent or more of gross domestic product or that is designated for dynamic scoring by the House Budget Committee or Joint Tax Committee chair. The idea is that a policy change may alter the behavior of economic actors (producers, consumers, taxpayers) and alter total output in

(continued)

Dynamic Scoring (*continued*)

the economy, thereby affecting the net fiscal effects of the policy change. At this writing in early 2015, Senate Republicans are planning to add a dynamic-scoring requirement in a budget resolution.

Republicans have argued that tax cuts enhance incentives for productive economic activity that generates tax revenues. If so, then the revenue losses from tax cuts are at least partly balanced by increased revenue from new economic activity. This is likely to reduce the estimates of revenue losses from tax cuts and make it easier to justify the cuts.

Democrats and many economists object to this argument by observing that economists do not have good theory about how economic behavior changes in response to policy changes and that dynamic scoring will introduce greater uncertainty into the quality of CBO and JTC estimates. Among other things, estimates will turn on policy changes other than the legislation that is being scored because any one piece of legislation is not all that will affect economic incentives in the future. The CBO has observed that "Doing macroeconomic analysis of all proposed legislation would not be feasible; nearly all legislation analyzed by CBO would have negligible macroeconomic effects (and thus negligible feedback to the federal budget); and estimates of macroeconomic effects are highly uncertain."

It is too early to know how CBO reports will change, but some observers expect the CBO to provide both traditional and dynamic estimates to meet the requirements of the new rule. Some observers fear that political argument will become even more confusing with the two parties citing different forms of CBO estimates.

CONCLUSION

The history of budgetary politics discussed in this chapter illustrates several important features of congressional politics that have been recurrent themes throughout this book:

1   Legislative outcomes in the United States are the product of a three-player legislative process in which the House, the Senate, and the president must negotiate and reach compromises. In the budget battles described in this chapter, differences in policy preferences among the three institutional players, combined with the necessity of gaining the consent of all three, produced compromised efforts to reduce the deficit and procedural innovations designed to force other players to act.

2   The president is a central player in congressional politics. When the president proposes a change in direction in budget policy, it usually changes Congress's agenda. The president's proposals may be set aside by the majority party in Congress, as they were initially in 1995. Doing so entails great political risks, however. For the party controlling the White House, the president, not the party's congressional leaders, tends to be the chief strategist for the party.

3   Rules matter. The constitutional requirement of a two-thirds majority in each house to override a presidential veto prevented the majority party in Congress from imposing its budget priorities in 1995 and 1996. Statutory limits on appropriations authority and the debt limit proved vital. The Senate rule that prevents extraneous amendments from being attached to budget bills (the Byrd rule) limited the options of House and Senate committees. Also, enforcement provisions included in previous budget agreements were essential to crafting compromises that the players could trust would be honored. Except for the basic rules outlined in the Constitution, all of these rules were subject to change and became a part of the debate over budget policy.

4   The Budget Act, and how the different players made use of it, altered the traditional relationship between the parent houses and their committees. Historically, committees had taken the initiative in setting the policy agenda and designing legislation within their jurisdictions. The new budget process, however, allowed top party and budget leaders to present comprehensive budget resolutions to the parent houses and required committees to produce legislation, after the fact, which they most certainly would not have drafted had they been left to their own discretion.

5   The rules of the legislative game are changed by the players. The players often turned to new procedural rules to guarantee that promises critical to achieving a compromise would be kept in the future. New enforcement mechanisms were invented on several occasions to convince key groups of legislators that uncertainties about the future would not work to their disadvantage.

6   Elections have clear and powerful effects on policy making. In the history described in this chapter, elections produced realignments in the preferences of key players – the president and members of Congress – concerning budgetary policy. Divided party control of the House, Senate, and White House was the direct product of elections and shaped the players' strategies in basic ways. Less significant, but clearly present, were the effects of election timing. On several occasions, approaching elections tended to dampen partisanship and encourage compromise on the part of the party with the greater public relations problem. In addition, public opinion polls, which are taken as a gauge of the potential electoral consequences of political events and policy positions, appeared to alter players' strategies on many occasions.

7   Parties are the primary building blocks for creating voting coalitions, but party discipline is far from perfect. Leaders of both the Democratic and the Republican parties, when in the majority in Congress, first attempted to satisfy enough fellow party members to create a majority before soliciting support from the other party. In the end, voting on the budget plans, which typically encapsulated the major policy priorities of the majority

406 Congress and Budget Politics

party, was very partisan. Those party members who voted against the position of their own party leaders were criticized but ultimately faced no formal punishment.

8 Party leaders are important players in Congress, but they are not all-powerful. In the budget negotiations described in this chapter, the distribution of power within Congress showed a fairly centralized pattern that was partly the result of the rules governing the budget process and partly a reflection of the need for high-level negotiations to work out differences of great importance to the parties and the two branches. The large differences in the two parties' budgetary policy preferences and each party's fairly great internal cohesiveness encouraged party leaders to be assertive strategists on behalf of their party. But party leaders, it appears, were more than mere agents of their parties. They focused agendas, made good and poor tactical decisions, and shaped their parties' images with the general public in ways that had consequences for the eventual legislative outcome. Some reliance on party leaders is inevitable, given the difficulty of producing collective action among the dozens of members in each of the four congressional parties. Still, as was most obvious in the 1995–1996 budget battle, even the most aggressive leader is constrained by what his or her party colleagues are willing to accept in terms of strategy and policy.

9 Committees play a central role in the legislative process, but their influence varies widely over time. Budgetary politics since the late 1970s has tended to push key decisions up to central budget and party leaders, and to reduce the independence of committees and their chairs. And yet, it is important to qualify this important consequence of budgetary politics by observing that committees were still responsible for writing the details of most of the legislative provisions of budget packages, even if they were highly constrained by agreements negotiated elsewhere. Even when the top party leaders and administration officials were hammering out the overall shape of the budget deals, most of the language of the budget packages was written by committees, and hundreds of specific policy provisions were negotiated by committee representatives.

The importance of parties, leaders, and committees in congressional policy making will continue to be shaped by the alignment of members' policy preferences, the nature of the issues, and the inherited rules of the game. Perceptions and preferences about budgetary issues are particularly important because of the pervasive effect of the budget on policy initiatives throughout the government. If budget issues begin to lose salience as the deficit fades from memory, then more policy initiatives originating from interest groups and creative members may rejuvenate the committees.

SUGGESTED READINGS

A.   The following online readings provide essential background on the congressional budget process.

Center on Budget and Policy Priorities. http://www.cbpp.org/cms/?fa=view&tid=155 (accessed March 2015).

Congressional Research Service reports at the Senate Committee on Rules and Administration. http://www.rules.senate.gov/public/index.cfm?p=BudgetProcess.

B.   The following books discuss the history and politics of the congressional budget process.

Farrier, Jasmine. *Passing the Buck: Congress, the Budget, and Deficits.* Lexington: University of Kentucky Press, 2004.

Joyce, Phillip. *Congressional Budget Office: Honest Numbers, Power, and Policymaking.* Washington, DC: Georgetown University Press, 2011.

Schick, Allen. *The Federal Budget: Politics, Policy, Process.* Washington, DC: Brookings, 2007.

DISCUSSION QUESTIONS

1   How did the adoption of the Congressional Budget and Impoundment Control Act of 1974 affect the power of existing congressional committees?

2   How has Congress used procedural and budget rules to control its own policy choices?

3   How has divided party control of Congress affected the rules governing the budget process?

APPENDIX:INTRODUCTION TO THE SPATIAL THEORY OF LEGISLATING

Much of congressional politics has geometric characteristics. When we speak of most Democrats as liberals, most Republicans as conservatives, and some legislators as moderates, we have in mind an ideological or policy spectrum – a line or dimension – along which we can place legislators. In recent Congresses, the parties have been sharply divided, with very little overlap between the parties. Figure A.1 illustrates this for the 109th Congress (2005–2006) for senators. Using a statistical technique, senators were scored on the basis of their overall voting record in the Congress. Democrats and Republicans were concentrated on opposite sides of the spectrum, creating one of the most polarized Senates in history.

Legislators' policy positions also can be represented in two or more dimensions, when appropriate. In Figure A.2, senators' policy positions are identified in two dimensions for a debate on an immigration reform bill in 2006. Their locations are identified with the help of a statistical analysis of their votes on about three dozen amendments and other motions that were considered on the Senate floor. The most significant issue during the debate concerned the standards for allowing illegal immigrants to gain legal entry to the United States. Senators who opposed special arrangements for reentry lined up on the far right, while senators who favored standards that would ease reentry for work or citizenship were located on the left (the horizontal dimension). Other issues, such as the ceiling on the number of legal immigrants allowed, were debated, too, and sometimes divided senators differently than the votes related to the treatment of current illegal immigrants (the vertical dimension). Democrats tended to favor both standards that facilitated reentry and larger quotas, while Republicans were split on reentry standards and tended to favor smaller quotas.[1]

---

1 Figure A.2 is drawn to show greater variance on the first dimension, which explains far more the variance in voting behavior than the second dimension.

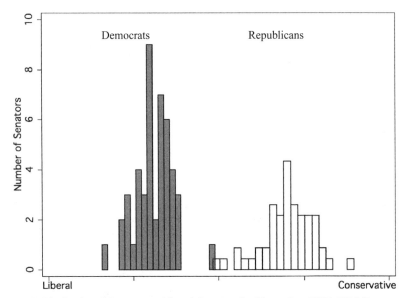

Figure A.1 Distribution of Senators on Liberal-Conservative Dimension, 2005–2006 (Democrats on left; Republicans on right). Source: Optimal Classification scores; www.voteview.com.

BASIC CONCEPTS FOR ANALYZING A LEGISLATIVE BODY

Political scientists have taken advantage of geometric representations to develop spatial theories of legislative politics. The theories provide a way to conceptualize the location of legislators, policy alternatives, and policy outcomes. Like all scientific theories, spatial theories are based on assumptions that allow us to draw inferences about expected behavior. With a few assumptions about legislators, the policy space, and the rules governing decisions, we can deduce remarkably useful and usually intuitive propositions about the location of legislative outcomes. Non-intuitive predictions are particularly useful because they

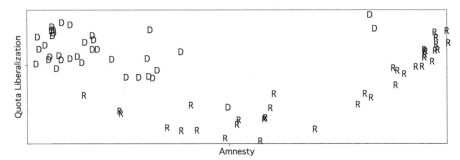

Figure A.2 Senators' Policy Positions on 2006 Immigration Bill in Two Dimensions (Democrats, D; Republicans, R). Source: Optimal Classification scores on Senate votes related to S2611, 109th Congress.

Figure A.3   Illustration of the Median Voter Theorem.

often yield insights that even the close observer of legislative politics might overlook.

PREFERENCES AND THE POLICY SPACE

Spatial theories assume the legislators, presidents, and other players have preferences about policy outcomes. Preferences may reflect personal beliefs or political influences. The preferences are assumed to be consistent. For example, if a legislator prefers policy A over policy B and also prefers B over C, then she favors A over C (transitive preferences, we say). When a legislator's preference is depicted geometrically, as in the figures, it is usually assumed that alternatives that are closer to the legislator's ideal point are preferred to more distant points (a Euclidean policy space, we say). Furthermore, it is assumed that each legislator chooses a strategy that she believes will yield the best possible outcome – that is, minimizes the distance between her ideal point and the outcome.

SIMPLE MAJORITY RULE AND THE MEDIAN VOTER THEOREM

Spatial theorists define "institutions" as a set of rules that govern decision making. Rules may concern who has the right to participate, the "weight" that each participant has in determining the outcome, the way in which policy proposals are constructed, the order in which policy proposals are considered, the standard for a final decision, and so on. Here, we assume that each legislator has the right to cast one vote and, to begin, that a simple majority of legislators is required for a proposal to be adopted.

In Figure A.3, a small legislature with five legislators is illustrated. With a simple majority decision rule, a winning majority will always include legislator C. As the median legislator, C can join two other legislators – to the left with A and B, to the right with D and E, or in the middle with B and D – to form a three-vote majority. Of course, larger majorities could form, but they will always include C. A spatial theorist would say that C is pivotal – C must be included in a majority and so can demand that the outcome be located at her ideal point. The *median voter theorem*, which we will not formally prove here, provides that if C's

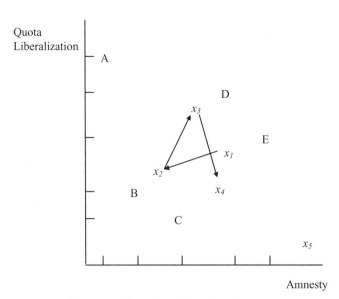

Figure A.4 Illustration of the Chaos Theorem.

position is adopted it cannot be defeated by another proposal. A corollary is that if two alternatives are presented, a majority will always prefer the alternative closer to the median legislator.

The median voter theorem means that when a median exists we can predict the outcome by knowing only the median legislator's ideal point. Spatial theorists refer to the stable prediction of the median outcome as an *equilibrium*. When a new legislature is elected, a new median location would lead us to predict a change in the outcome. That is, a new equilibrium is expected.

MULTIDIMENSIONAL SPACES AND THE CHAOS THEOREM

A multidimensional policy space, such as the one in Figure A.4, creates important complications for predicting legislative outcomes. No legislator is the median on both dimensions. C is the median on the amnesty dimension but E is the median on the quota liberalization dimension. What is the expected outcome? In fact, political scientists have demonstrated mathematically that in most cases there is no single predicted outcome, no equilibrium, as there is in the unidimensional case.

A thought experiment will demonstrate an important point. Let us assume that current policy is located at x_1. Legislator B might propose a policy at x_2 and would win the support of A and C, both of whom are closer to x_1 than to x_2 and so would join B to form a majority to vote for x_2 and defeat x_1. But then D might offer x_3 and win the support of A and E. This process can continue indefinitely with a new majority of three forming at each step. If the rules allow a continuous flow of new proposals, there is no single outcome that cannot be defeated by some other proposal. This illustrates the *chaos theorem*. The theorem provides that, as a general rule, we cannot expect a stable outcome from simple majority rule in two (or more) dimensions.

AGENDA SETTING, STRUCTURE-INDUCED EQUILIBRIA, AND POLITICAL POWER

The chaos result – or majority rule cycling – may seem surprising. Legislatures regularly make final decisions without endless cycling through proposals. Why that is the case is the subject of a vast literature in political science. We do not want to review the complexities here, but three important points about legislative politics need to be understood.

First, legislative rules may not allow multidimensional proposals or may limit the number of proposals that may be considered. Such rules would limit the range of possible outcomes and make those outcomes more predictable. If only unidimensional proposals may be considered, the median voter theorem applies and majority rule chaos is avoided. Theorists use the label *structure-induced equilibria* for constraints on outcomes that are imposed by the rules. Thus, even if legislators' preferences are multidimensional, the rules may generate median outcomes by either limiting the range of proposals that are allowed or imposing unidimensionality on the proposals that may be considered.

Second, special influence over the agenda, either granted under the rules or gained through informal means, may control the alternatives subject to a vote and further limit the possible outcomes. A Speaker or presiding officer may be able to limit who is recognized to offer a motion. A coalition of legislators, such as members of the majority party, may agree to support only those proposals that a majority of the coalition endorses, thus limiting the set of proposals that can win majority support.

Three, introducing a proposal that creates a new dimension can transform a situation that would produce a median outcome into one with no predictable outcome. A legislator who dislikes the median outcome might be motivated to offer a proposal on an issue that divides his colleagues in a new way in order to avoid the certain, but undesirable outcome. The original median legislator would be motivated to create an agenda that prevents the proposal on the new issue from being considered.

In practice, then, rules and legislative strategies can contract or expand the range of possible outcomes. Real politics is often played in this way. Political

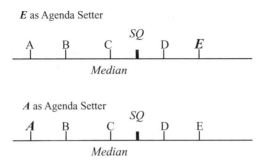

Figure A.5 Illustration of the Effect of the Status Quo and an Agenda Setter, the Unidimensional Case.

scientists have studied many of the consequences of a variety of rules and strategies, but continue to pursue research on the relationship between rules, strategies, and outcomes.

THE STATUS QUO AND AGENDA SETTING

A legislature often inherits policy from past legislatures. In most cases, the inherited policy, which we call the *status quo* (*SQ*), remains in place until a new policy is adopted. That is, the *SQ* is the default outcome if it is not defeated by a new proposal. The set of proposals that can defeat the *SQ* is called the *win set of SQ*. When there are no proposals that can defeat the *SQ*, we say that the win set is empty and predict that the outcome will remain at *SQ*.

The effect of the *SQ* on legislative strategies is important and intuitive. In Figure A.5, five legislators are arrayed on a single dimension. In the figure's top panel, let's assume that no proposal can be considered unless legislator E approves, but if a proposal is offered it can be amended. E, of course, wants the outcome at her own ideal point and might make a proposal there. However, A, B, or C might offer an amendment to move the outcome away from E and to the other side of *SQ*. Such an amendment would win a majority and E would be worse off than if he left the policy at *SQ*. Consequently, we would expect E to refuse to make an initial proposal. In this case, the agenda setter, E, protects the status quo. In contrast, in the lower panel in Figure A.5, legislator A is the agenda setter. Because A prefers the median's position over the *SQ*, A is willing to allow the legislature to consider a proposal and have it amended to C, the expected outcome.

Thus, the location of the status quo relative to the median determines the agenda setter's strategy. With the same agenda setter and median, different issues can generate different outcomes – the median or the *SQ*.

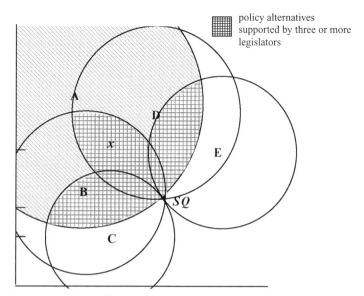

Figure A.6 Illustration of the Effect of the Status Quo and an Agenda Setter, the Multidimensional Case.

The same logic applies to the multidimensional case, as in Figure A.6. Legislators will support a proposal that improves on the status quo, *SQ*. In the figure, these *preferred-to* sets are denoted by the partial or full circles. For example, within the shaded circle centered on legislator A is the preferred-to set for A. The double shaded areas are the sets of locations preferred by at least three of the five legislators over *SQ*. Because points in the double shaded areas attract majority support for a proposal over the *SQ*, they define the win set of *SQ*. A large number of locations will not defeat *SQ* so majority rule narrowed the possible outcomes considerably. But, in this two-dimensional space, the win set includes a wide range of possibilities, many of which are less preferred to the *SQ* by one or two of the legislators. A, B, and D might agree to an outcome at *x*, which would make C and E worse off than leaving the policy at *SQ*.

BICAMERALISM, SEPARATION OF POWERS, AGENCY DECISIONS, AND LEGISLATIVE OUTCOMES

Bicameralism

In the previous section, we considered a single legislative body. Congress and many other legislatures are bicameral, and usually require that a majority of each chamber approve legislation before it is sent to the president or chief

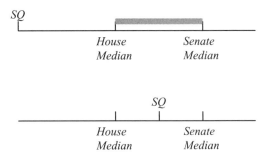

Figure A.7 Illustration of a Bicameral Outcome in One Dimension.

executive. Spatially, this means that we must consider the relationship between the outcomes in the two chambers.

In unidimensional space, shown in Figure A.7, the outcome would be negotiated between the House and Senate medians. If both medians favor some of the same proposals over *SQ*, as they do in the top panel, they will negotiate an outcome among the range of proposals that they both prefer to *SQ*. If *SQ* falls between the two medians so that each house median prefers *SQ* to anything the other house would prefer to *SQ*, as in the figure's lower panel, the houses will not agree to a new policy and the outcome will be *SQ*.

In multidimensional space, as depicted in Figure A.6, we would define the bicameral win set as the intersection of the win sets in the two houses. We do not show that situation here. The overlap in the win sets for the two houses can be very small or very large. Little overlap greatly narrows the range of possible outcomes. Large overlap creates the possibility that a conference committee charged with finding compromise legislation will be able to exercise great discretion in determining the location of the final bill and still be able to attract majority support in both houses for the final version.

THE PRESIDENT AND THE VETO

Under the Constitution, the president may veto legislation and a veto can be overridden only with the support of a two-thirds majority in each house of Congress. The threshold of a two-thirds majority in each house makes it necessary to appeal to more legislators than the requirement of a simple majority for initial approval of legislation. In our five-legislators illustrations, this means attracting the support of four of the five legislators (three of five would be less than the two-thirds required).

The president will veto any legislation that makes him worse off than *SQ*. In one dimension, several possibilities arise. In Figure A.8, the president's ideal point is P and the House and Senate medians are M_H and M_S, respectively. The

Figure A.8 Illustration of Upholding a Presidential Veto, in One Dimension.

two houses of Congress negotiate a bill at B somewhere between their medians. The president prefers SQ to B so he vetoes the bill. Both House and Senate medians would like to override the veto but they must gain the support of two-thirds of their colleagues. V_H and V_S are the *veto pivots*. That is, they are the legislators who are the leftmost members of the two-thirds majority that is required to override a veto. Without their support for the bill over the SQ, the veto cannot be overridden. In this case, V_H prefers SQ to B and so votes against the override. SQ is the outcome. Thus, the general rule is that a presidential veto will kill a bill whenever at least one of the veto pivots is on the same side of SQ as the president.

Other scenarios are easy to understand without illustration. Whenever the chamber medians are on the same side of SQ as the president, the president will sign the bill with a veto. Whenever V_H and V_S are on the same side of SQ opposite the president (not shown), the two houses of Congress can override the veto of the president.

As always, the multidimensional case is more complicated but it is still easy to visualize. In Figure A.9, there are two regions in which four of the five legislators of one house would favor the bill over the SQ. Consequently, a veto would be overridden any time the president vetoes a bill that is located in those regions. The bill also would have to be located in similar regions in the other house for both houses to override a president's veto. A bill that is located in the *veto win set of SQ* is one for which a veto can be overridden in both houses.

Plainly, the two-thirds majority requirement for a veto override shrinks the region of bill locations that can survive a veto to one that is smaller than the region of bill locations that can receive simple majority support in both houses. The implication is that the threat of a veto requires more careful negotiations within Congress and may have implications for legislators who win and lose. In Figure A.9, for example, the bill at x_2 survives a veto but a bill at x_1 does not, although both would receive simple majority support. But the outcome at x_2 is less favorable to legislators A and D and more favorable to B and C.

AGENCY DECISIONS

Political scientists often think of executive branch agencies as having policy preferences of their own. Staffed by people who have personal or professional

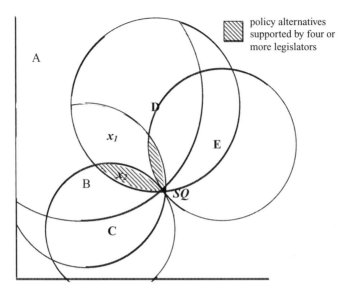

policy alternatives
supported by four or
more legislators

A

D

x_1

E

B

x_2

SQ

C

Figure A.9 Location of Veto Override Coalitions, the Multidimensional Case.

experience in a policy field, agencies are likely to devise rules and regulations that implement law in a manner that reflects their own preferences. Congress and presidents may seek to control the independence of agencies, but agency officials know that it may not be easy for Congress and the president to enact new legislation to place additional constraints on them. After all, new legislation requires the approval of the House, Senate, and president, or, in the case of a veto, a two-thirds majority in both houses. This is a high threshold. If a House majority, Senate majority, or president favors the direction an agency is taking, it can block legislation that would place new constraints in statute. (We have reported on other congressional strategies in Chapter 9.)

The strategic setting of agency decision making can be treated spatially, as we do in Figure A.10. To simplify, we characterize the House and Senate as having specific locations in multidimensional space just as the president does. If an agency took action to move a policy from a_1 (the current policy) to a_2, the Senate would like the move and block any effort by the House to enact legislation to require that the policy be returned to a_1. In this case, the agency, knowing that the Senate will protect its move, is free to shift policy without fear that the law will be changed. In contrast, if the agency sought to move policy as far as a_3, all three of the policy-making institutions would be better off by enacting legislation located on the line between S and P.

These scenarios demonstrate that the autonomy of an agency is limited to the range of policy moves that will not generate a new law. The farther apart the House, Senate, and president, the greater the discretion the agency enjoys. In fact, the triangle formed by the House, Senate, and president defines the limits of agency discretion. Any move that yields policy inside or to the edge of the

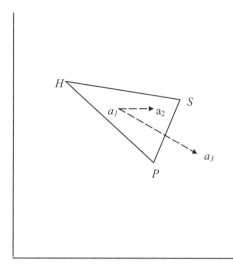

Figure A.10 Illustration of Agency Discretion, in Multidimensional Space.

triangle will be defended by at least one of the House, Senate, or president. Any move outside of the triangle will stimulate new legislation.

ADVANCED THEORY AND THE LIMITS OF SPATIAL THEORY

We have presented a rudimentary introduction to the spatial theory of legislative politics. Political scientists have extended the theory in many directions. They have developed additional theory on the conditions that limit the range of possible outcomes under majority rule, explored the effect of agenda control rules that advantage parties or committees, and considered the effects of different assumptions about legislators' preferences and decision rules. We encourage our readers to pursue these important subjects elsewhere.

Spatial theory is not the ultimate theory of legislative politics. The spatial theorist assumes that legislators' policy preferences are known and invariant and theorizes only about how they motivate strategies. The determinants of legislators' policy preferences are beyond the scope of spatial theory.

The effects of nonpolicy motivations, such as the desire for reelection or to serve in the majority party, also are beyond the scope of spatial theory. Such motivations may be the overriding consideration in some circumstances. A legislator whose bill is rejected by the House of Representatives might be seen as a loser by some observers, but she may benefit from favorable press coverage and an appreciative home constituency for putting up a good fight. A legislative majority that fails to override a presidential veto may use the issue in a campaign to get more fellow partisans elected in the next Congress. Winning and losing in politics is sometimes hard to judge, at least in the short term.

Nevertheless, spatial theory is a powerful tool for predicting behavior and legislative outcomes. It often establishes a baseline expectation for outcomes against which the effects of other considerations can be measured. We can better judge the effects of persuasion by party leaders or presidents once we have a prediction for the outcome expected on the basis of legislators' prior policy preferences. It also shows that policy preferences and parliamentary rules often do not yield very specific predictions and define sometimes large ranges of possible outcomes that can be influenced by other political forces at work. Most important, spatial theory yields important insights about the effects of institutions – the rules of the game – that are so transparent in legislative decision making.

Index